INSIDE OUT
A Collection of Autobiographies by Indian Anthropologists

About the Editors

P.C. Joshi superannuated from University of Delhi in 2021 as Vice-Chancellor I/C and Pro-Vice-Chancellor. Prior to that he was Professor of Social Anthropology and Head of the Department of Anthropology in DU. A widely travelled anthropologist, he had also served in Institute of Human Behaviour and Allied Sciences and H.N.B. Garhwal University. He had extensively written in areas such as Medical Anthropology, Himalayan Anthropology, Ecological Anthropology, Antibiotic Resistance and Disaster Risk Reduction. At present he is Ombudsman of Kumaun University and Chairman, Empowered Committee of Biodiversity Parks in Delhi besides holding advisory positions with IGNCA and IGRMS, Ministry of Culture, Government of India.

V.K. Srivastava conceptualized the idea of present volume with P. C. Joshi and passed away while the volume was under preparation. A gifted social anthropologist, he was heading the prestigious Anthropological Survey of India when he passed away. An alumnus of Department of Anthropology and Department of Sociology of University of Delhi besides Cambridge University, he taught in Hindu College and Department of Anthropology in DU. A fine litterateur and wordsmith, he was equally adept at eloquent lecturing. He wrote extensively on Research Methodology, Religion and Renunciation, Medical Anthropology, Ecological Anthropology and Anthropological Theories.

INSIDE OUT
A Collection of Autobiographies by Indian Anthropologists

Edited by
P.C. Joshi
V.K. Srivastava

CONCEPT PUBLISHING COMPANY PVT. LTD.
NEW DELHI - 110 059

ISBN: 978-93-6344-655-7

First Published 2024

Published and Printed by

Concept
Since 1974

Concept Publishing Company Pvt. Ltd.
A/15-16, Commercial Block, Mohan Garden
New Delhi - 110 059 (India)
T: +91-11-41101460
E: publishing@conceptpub.com, *W*: www.conceptpub.com

Cataloging in Publication--Courtesy: D.K. Agencies (P) Ltd. <docinfo@dkagencies.com>

Inside out : a collection of autobiographies by Indian anthropologists / edited by P.C. Joshi, V.K. Srivastava.
pages cm
Includes bibliographical references and index.
ISBN 9789363446557

1. Anthropologists--India--Biography. 2. Anthropology--India--History. I. Joshi, P. C., 1956- editor. II. Srivastava, Vinay K., editor.

LCC GN20.I57 2024 | DDC 301.092254 23

Preface

Indian anthropology completed its century of teaching in 2020 and to commemorate this watershed moment/massive milestone, several attempts have been made to compile information about the present and past anthropologists of India. Anthropology, in India, has been in existence as a research and teaching subject for quite some time. In fact, with the beginning of the Asiatic Society of Bengal, India with its varied cultures and customs was the subject matter of interest to colonial administrators and native intellectuals along with India's geography, fauna, flora, monuments and archaeology. Anthropologists, in India, have primarily been teaching in universities and colleges, serving the Anthropological Survey of India and myriad museums, tribal research institutes and various government and non-government organizations involved in the task of welfare and development. The first attempt in compilation of information about active anthropologists was made by the Anthropological Survey of India. The next such Directory of Professional Anthropologists was edited by Professor D.K. Bhattacharya on occasion of the Xth ICAES in 1978. Both these directories had listed the serving anthropologists, along with their educational qualifications, specialization, research works and publications. With the central and state competitive examinations asking about notable anthropologists some selected biographical notes have been made available in the last decade. In recent times, there have also been some books containing biographies of anthropologists. I have recently co-edited one such compendium on Indian anthropologists with Professor P.K. Nayak which contains a biographical account on nearly fifty anthropologists.

The present work is a sequel to this biographical volume. While the biographical work on notable Indian anthropologists was in progress, late Professor Vinay Kumar Srivastava suggested that a sequel to biographies should be initiated and existing anthropologists should be asked to pen down their own professional journey in first person account. We sent invitation of most of the existing Indian anthropologists and all of them had accepted our request. But the response was very slow and on our time line of six months, very few were able to accomplish the task and asked for more time. Both of us were worried about the slow response of many of the anthropologists who were taking more time than they had promised in completing writing about themselves. In a webinar, on multiculturism, organized by United Indian Anthropological Forum, Professor Srivastava publicly raised concern on the plodder authors. Within ten days unfortunately, he was in the grip of COVID-19 and we eventually lost him. His own autobiography is now untraceable and it is being now written by his wife Dr Kumkum Srivastava. He was my co-editor and will remain so while under his name, the entry will be biographical-autobiography.

P.C. Joshi
V.K. Srivastava

Introduction

In anthropology, there are plenty of autographical accounts available to us and one outstanding autobiography having immense literary value (it received Sahitya Akademi Award in 1965) was *The Tribal World of Verrier Elwin*, published by Oxford University Press in 1964. It is an outstanding work on the professional and personal journey of this extraordinary ethnographer. Another notable autobiography was of Margaret Mead titled *Blackberry Winter: My Earlier Years,* which eventually was nominated for National Book Award for Biography. This is another candid account of the life and journey of this outstanding champion of human rights. Her daughter, the most celebrated and photographed child Mary Catherine Bateson, has written her own memoirs in the book *With a Daughter's Eye*. Due to arrival of digital age, some outstanding autobiographical video documents are now available. For example, Clifford Geertz and Arthur Kleinman have recorded their personal journey as have so many others.

Autobiography (a narrative of one's journey life that reveals the seld as well) is a very special genre, challenging because one has to give an honest and truthful account of one's life journey and at the same time, there must be a storyline in the narrative. It therefore has the combination of an author, a narrator and above all a protagonist. A "truthful" description of one's own life journey in a prose format, where one has to make sure that the narrations also make some sense to the reader, entail straightening and editing of the plot in this genre. Raghuram Rajan, the former Governor of Reserve Bank of India has beautifully stated this paradox in his book, *I Do What I Do*,

> "Autobiographies are always written as if the author had it all mapped out with perfect foresight, ignoring the risks and uncertainty at that time. This misleads, as much as these beautiful photographs of the past holiday abstract from the heat, the mosquitoes, and the lack of connectivity."

It is but natural that self-critical appraisal would be absent in any normal self-memoirs but at the same time one can get the glimpse of the life journey against the backdrop of which we can understand and assess the personality of an author. An exception to all autobiographies perhaps would be Mahatma Gandhi's autobiography in which he candidly states, "I am not going to either conceal or understate any ugly things that must be told. I hope to acquaint the readers fully with all my faults and errors" (Gandhi, p.19). He liked to call his autobiography as *The Story of My Experiments with Truth*, for presenting the bare account of truth about his life and nothing but truth. In the process, Mahatma Gandhi presented to the world a unique genre as far as the autobiography can take one to. He clarified his stand by stating,

> "I simply want to tell the story of my numerous experiments with truth, and as my life consists of nothing but those experiments, it is true that the story will take the shape of an autobiography. For me [my experiments in political field], have not much value .... But I should certainly like to narrate my experiments in the spiritual field which are known only to myself, and from which I have derived such power as I possess for working in the political field." (Gandhi, pp. 16-17)

Autobiographies are like ethnographies and autoethnographies, where one attempt to "other" the self. Yet, autobiography is not always everything about the self-description. In the present volume, the autobiographies are oriented towards the journey of authors in becoming anthropologists and resultant professional life and activities. The accounts given in the volume would inform what it means to be an anthropologist and what are the inspirations, motivations, convictions and commitments that make and sustain someone as an anthropologist.

The present autographical compilation is unique in the sense that it is not one full-length portrayal of one anthropologist, but, a succinct and terse life sketch formatted around a framework by large number of active anthropologists of contemporary times right from the senior-most anthropologist R.K. Mutatkar to Somnath Bhattacharjee. As a result, what is presented in the book, is a unique compendium of narratives by Indian anthropologists.

The autobiographies presented in this volume are narratives on the circumstances and situation making people pursuing anthropology as a career choice amidst a galaxy of popularly known and socially reputable subjects. Leaving aside a miniscule exception, anthropology as a subject is quite risky for its unknown job prospects. First, as a subject, anthropology is not much known barring aspirants about their future and second, the liminality of the subject proper—between art and science; medicine and mythology; ethology and ethnology makes it not fitting into any sensible classification, thus making it "a thing out of order" according to Mary Douglas. This liminality in turn is also the strength of the subject as it provides an anthropologist quirky angle to examine, investigate and comprehend human being within the social and societal, cultural, biogenetic and historical perspective in one go. Furthermore, as anthropology deals with the imponderabilia of everyday life, the knowledge generation, comprehension and dissemination in anthropology entails peeping into insights of human society and culture.

In one sense, anthropologists are quite familiar with writing of biographies; their training in life history method acquaints them with biographical genre and in a way the ethnographic method can be termed as cultural biography. The training of anthropologists in looking at life in a multi-faceted and multi-dimensional framework is an additional advantage in writing of autobiography. Besides, the autobiographical account by anthropologists would be quite distinctive from the rests, in view of the fact that they have travelled through the academic path of reflexivity and self-bias involved in writing of other cultures.

The present book is quite unique in the sense that, for the first time perhaps, in the history of anthropology, the Indian anthropologists are writing about themselves, their struggles and achievements, their successes and failures, their likes and dislikes amidst the canvas of social, cultural, academic and professional milieu.

REFERENCES

Gandhi, M.K. *An Autography or the Story of My Experiments with Truth*. https://www.mkgandhi.org/ebks/An-Autobiography.pdf. (Accessed on 16 April, 2023).

Rajan, Raghuram (2017). *I Do What I Do*. Harper Collins, India. https://www.goodreads.com/quotes/8836756-autobiographies-are-always-written-as-if-the-author-had-it. (Accessed on 12 January, 2024).

Contents

List of Contributors

A.K. Sinha superannuated as Professor of Social Anthropology from Panjab University, Chandigarh. Prior to this, he served as lecturer in Guru Ghasi Das University, Bilaspur, Chhattisgarh. At present, he is a Senior Fellow of the Indian Council of Social Science Research.
Email: aksinha58@gmail.com

Abhijit Guha joined Vidyasagar University as Lecturer in 1985 and retired as Professor of Anthropology in 2016. He was a Senior Fellow of the Indian Council of Social Science Research during 2018-20 at the Institute of Development Studies Kolkata. He has been a reviewer of research proposals for the Wenner-Grenn Foundation, US and acted as an expert in a Standing Committee of the Indian parliament on the amendment of Land Acquisition Law.
Email: abhijitguhavuanthro@rediffmail.com

Abhik Ghosh is currently Professor of Social Anthropology at the Department of Anthropology, Panjab University, Chandigarh.
Email: abhikg@rediffmail.com

Amitabh Sarkar superannuated from Anthropological Survey of India in 2012 as Superintending Anthropologist (Cultural) where he served for nearly thirty-five years. A prolific writer, he was the Managing Editor of the *Journal of Anthropological Survey of India* and Officer-in-Charge of Publications between 2003-12. He was educated at the University of Calcutta.
Email: bhabbinimay@yahoo.com

Arbind Sinha is the former Associate Director and Acting Director of Mudra Institute of Communications (MICA), Ahmedabad, who presently serves as an Adjunct Professor at MICA. He also assumed the role of Director-General at Shanti Business School, Ahmedabad, for two years. He played a crucial role in coordinating several studies, including the Satellite Instructional Television Experiment (SITE) Communication Project, addressing the science-society-technology interface. Additionally, his work extended to rural and health communication, as well as disaster communication. Dr Sinha's international exposure includes lectures at universities in Sweden, Canada, USA, Thailand, and Singapore.

Email: arbind21@gmail.com

Barun Mukhopadhyay is a retired professor who was attached to the Biological Anthropology Unit, Indian Statistical institute, Kolkata till October 2019. He was awarded a Ph.D. degree in Anthropology from the University of Calcutta. He remained engaged in research on demographic aspects and sociocultural determinants of health and health care of the tribal populations of Sikkim-Darjeeling Himalaya since 1980s. His major areas of research interest are: biocultural dimensions of ageing, ethno-biology, and heat stress on livelihood and health as well as bioethics and research ethics. At present he is serving as one of the editorial advisors of the *Journal of the Indian Anthropological Society* and he also served as one of the consulting editors of the journal, *Collegium Antropologicum*. Currently, he is the Research Director of The Indian Anthropological Society.

Email: mukhopadhyay.barun@gmail.com

Bela Kothari is a social anthropologist who has worked in the area of health, technology and religion. She has worked as a consultant with the High-Powered Committee for Gujjars demand for reservation set up by the Government of Rajasthan. She was also associated with "Banking on Heritage", a project on heritage properties in Jaipur. She is currently Professor at University of Rajasthan, Jaipur.

Email: belaalok@yahoo.com

Deepak Kumar Behera is the present Vice-Chancellor of the Kalinga Institute of Social Sciences deemed to be University (KISS-DU). He is also the President of the United Indian Anthropology Forum. He has occupied the prestigious Vice-Chancellorship of Sambalpur University, Behrampur University and Rajendra University, Balangir. He was also the founding Chairman of the IUAES International Commission on Anthropology of Children, Youth and Childhood.
Email: behera.dk@gmail.com

Farhad Mollick is a Professor of Anthropology at Mahatma Gandhi Antarrashtriya Hindi Vishwavidyalaya (A Central University), Wardha, Maharashtra. He started his career as a Lecturer at Guru Ghasidas Vishwavidyalaya, Bilaspur, Chhattisgarh. In 2011, he became the Head of the Department at Wardha and remained so, till 2020. He again took charge as Head of the Department in August, 2023. He has been offered the academic position of Dean at the School of Humanities and Social Sciences and School of Management. His area of specialization is socio-cultural Anthropology, and his area of interest includes tribal studies.
Email: farhad.mollick@gmail.com

Geetika Ranjan is Professor and former Head of the Department of Anthropology at the North-Eastern Hill University, Shillong, Meghalaya. She is a recipient of prestigious awards like the Young Scientist Award given by the Indian Science Congress and, Research Award awarded by the University Grants Commission. Her areas of interest range from tribal and rural development, Anthropology of children, to diaspora, and migration. She carries the honor of being nominated by the Ministry of Environment and Forests, Government of India as a Member of a committee constituted for monitoring the village relocation from the tiger reserves in India in 2012.
Email: geetikaranjan19@gmail.com

K.R. Rama Mohan is a Professor at Department of Anthropology, Sikkim University, Gangtok. Before joining Sikkim University, he taught at various universities in India and abroad. His research publications primarily focus on developmental issues and relational well-being of ethnic communities.
Email: krrmohan@cus.ac.in

Kamal K. Misra was formerly the Vice-Chancellor of Utkal University of Culture, Bhubaneswar. He was a Professor of Anthropology and Dean, of the School of Social Sciences at the Central University of Hyderabad. He received the prestigious Fulbright Scholar-in-Residence Award in the USA and the Commonwealth Academic Staff Fellowship in the UK. He was honored with the Utkal University Gold Medal and Sarat Chandra Roy Memorial Medal by the Asiatic Society, Kolkata for contributing to Anthropology in Asia. Professor Misra was the Director of the National Museum of Mankind, Bhopal, and the Director of the Anthropological Survey of India, Kolkata. He taught at Utkal University, the University of Hyderabad in India, and Austin College in Texas, USA.
Email: kkmssin@gmail.com

Kh. Narendra Singh is currently the Professor and Head of Anthropology Department, Assam University (Diphu Campus), Assam (India). His research interests are in the field of Medical Anthropology, Applied Anthropology and Health Communication Besides anthropological research studies, Professor Singh has vast experience of conducting numerous national level surveys on health and demography.
Email: kh.singh@rediffmail.com

Kishor K. Basa is the current Chairperson of the Monument Authority of India. He taught and superannuated as Professor from the Department of Anthropology, Utkal University, Bhubaneswar. He was appointed as the Director of Indira Gandhi Rastriya Manav Sangrahalaya, (IGRMS), Bhopal from 2004 to 2008, and Director of Indian Museum, Kolkata from December 2008 to December 2010, and then the Director of Anthropological Survey of India for a year in 2010. He was the President of the Anthropological and Behavioural Sciences Section, Indian Science Congress in 2007 and a Senior Tribal Domain Expert in the Special Development Council, Odisha from April 2018 to April 2019. He was the Member Secretary and later the President of the Indian National Confederation and Academy of Anthropologists (INCAA). He also became the Vice-Chancellor of Maharaja Sriram Chandra Bhanja Deo University (formerly North Odisha University).
Email: kishorkbasa58@gmail.com

Kumkum Srivastava superannuated from Janaki Devi Mahavidhyalaya where she taught History. After her masters in history, she did M.Phil. and Ph.D. in Anthropology from University of Delhi.
Email: vks1@ymail.com

Lucy T.V. Zehol is a Professor of Anthropology at the North-Eastern Hill University, Shillong, Meghalaya. She has been the Warden of PG and Research Scholar hostels and Head, Department of Anthropology as well. She is the current Dean of School of Human and Environmental Sciences at North-Eastern Hill University, the first female to occupy this important position.
Email: lzehol@yahoo.com

M.C. Arunkumar is teaching social and cultural anthropology at Manipur University as a professor. Besides his academic works and engagement, he also writes critical plays on social and historical issues in Manipuri for which he receives critical appraisals. He is also news analysts at All India Radio, Imphal and other local cable channels. He is known for his critical evaluation of conventional wisdom in both academic and creative works.
Email: mcarun60@yahoo.com

Mayanglambam Mani Babu is a well-known prehistorian from the state of Manipur in north-east India. He superannuated as professor from the Department of Anthropology, Manipur University where he worked as Head of the Department.
Email: mmanibabu@manipuruniv.ac.in

Mini Bhattacharyya Thakur is a Professor of Social Anthropology at Gauhati University. She completed her BA in Anthropology from Cotton College, Guwahati in 1983 where she was the topper and "Best Graduate" in Bachelor of Arts under Gauhati University after which she received her MA in Anthropology from University of Delhi. She obtained her Ph.D. in Anthropology from Gauhati University in 1998 under the guidance of Dr A.C. Bhagabati. Her research interests include food studies, health and tribal development in north-east India.
Email: mbthakuranth@gauhati.ac.in

Mithun Sikdar is working as Superintending Anthropologist (Physical) under Anthropological Survey of India. He is the recipient of Young Scientist Award from Indian Science Congress

Association in 2010 and Professor B.M. Das Memorial Award from Sanskriti, Guwahati in 2015 for his contribution in the field of Anthropology. His main academic contribution includes the development of socio-economic scale on the basis of per capita monthly income for carrying out various biomedical researches. He has also identified three novel genotypes among an Indian population.

Email: msikdar@hotmail.com

Nabakumar Duary is devoted to research and visual documentation in the domain of human science and has been working for the Anthropological Survey of India since 1992. He received "Training in Visual Anthropology" in Satyajit Ray Film and Television Institute (SRFTI), Kolkata (2007) and has been a former member of Community Radio of SRFTI, Kolkata. He has also done significant research in the domains of tribal education, folklore, tribal culture, religious syncretism, folk painting, traditional knowledge, village study, caste occupation and so on. Dr Duary is an Assistant Research Director of the Indian Anthropological Society in Kolkata and has been the former Joint Secretary of the Society.

Email: nabakumarduary@gmail.com

Nadeem Hasnain is a former Professor & Head, Department of Anthropology, Lucknow University, Pro-Vice-Chancellor, Mahatma Gandhi Antarrashtriya Hindi Vishwavidyalaya, Wardha. He is a recipieen of Fulbright "Scholar in Residence" award, he also taught at the St. Lawrence University, New York. He has been a, Senior Fellow at the Indian Council of Social Science Research. Currently he is the, editor of *The Eastern Anthropologist and Manav*. His area of specialization is Tribal Studies and Anthropology of Islam.

Email: nadeemhasnain@gmail.com

Naresh Vaid runs Vaids ICS, a coaching centre for the civil service aspirants. He received his anthropology training from Panjab University, Chandigarh and University of Delhi.

Email: vaidsics@gmail.com

Nilakantha Panigrahi is presently working as the Professor of Anthropology in the Department of Anthropology and Tribal

Development at Guru Ghasidas Vishwavidyalaya (A Central University), Bilaspur, Chhattisgarh. Prior to this, he was working with the ICSSR-Government of Odisha Social Science Research Centre (NCDS) at Bhubaneswar for seventeen years.
Email: nilakantha.panigrahi@gmail.com

P. Venkatarao superannuated as Senior Professor from the Department of Anthropology, Central University of Hyderabad where he also served as Head of the Department and Dean, Social Sciences. He is also the editor of *The Eastern Anthropologist*.
Email: pvrao2000@gmail.com

Prasanna K. Nayak is a former professor of anthropology at Utkal University, Bhubaneswar, Odisha. He served as Director of the Scheduled Castes and Scheduled Tribes Research and Training Institute (SCSTRTI) and established the Museum of Tribal Arts and Crafts. He was also the Chairman of the Nabakrushna Choudhury Centre of Development Studies (NCDS), Bhubaneswar. He was an Alexander von Humboldt Fellow at the Free University of Berlin and Baden Wuertemberg Fellow at the University of Heidelberg, and also an ICCR Fellow at University of Vienna.
Email: prasannanayak51@gmail.com

R.R. Prasad was associated with the National Institute of Rural Development & Panchayati Raj (NIRDPR), Hyderabad for over three decades, and contributed immensely to the field of rural research, training and development for disadvantaged sections of the society. His areas of specialization include community mobilization, participatory development, social auditing, rural artisans, pastoral nomadism, human rights and development, etc. Besides his Master's Degree and Ph.D. in Anthropology, he also holds MA Degree in Economics and Management of Rural Development from Manchester University, UK.
Email: rrprasad21@gmail.com

Rajat Kanti Das retired as Professor of Anthropology from Vidyasagar University, Midnapore, West Bengal. After completion of regular service with full extension. he rejoined the Department following the award of UGC Emeritus Fellowship for two years. He was a Member of the National Advisory Council of the Anthropological Survey of India. He was the Editor-in-Chief of the *Vidyasagar University Journal of Biological Sciences* for two terms. At present,

he is the editor of the *Journal of the Indian Anthropological Society* (*JIAS*) and holds the Office of the President of the Indian Anthropological Society.
Email: rajat_p_das@yahoo.com

Rajesh Kumar Gautam is a Professor and Former Head of the Department of Anthropology at Dr Harisingh Gour Vishwavidyalaya (A Central University), Sagar, MP. In 2016 he was awarded the prestigious Raman Fellowship for pursuing Post-Dectoral studies from Montclair State University, NJ, USA. He is the only faculty from his department who is recognized by "AD Scientific Index 2021" as one of the World Scientist.
Email: goutamraj2006@gmail.com

Ramchandra Mutatkar was a student of Professor S.C. and Dr Leela Dube at Dr Hari Singh Gour Vishwavidyalaya, Sagar in 1959. He worked with Professor Irawati Karve as Faculty, at the Deccan College Postgraduate and Research Institute, Pune and then became the First Head of the Department of Anthropology, and the First Director of the Interdisciplinary School of Health Sciences, Savitribai Phule Pune University, Pune. He has been the Chairman of Indian National Confederation and Academy of Anthropologists (INCAA). Patron of United Indian Anthropology Forum and Society for Indian Medical Anthropology and Founder of the "The Maharashtra Association of Anthropological Sciences". He is a recipient of "International Gandhi Award for Leprosy" awarded to him by the Vice-President of India and "Adiwasi Sevak Puraskar" awarded to him by the Governor of Maharashtra.
Email: rkmutatkar@gmail.com

Ranjana Ray superannuated as Professor from the Department of Anthropology, University of Calcutta, Kolkata as a leading prehistorian. She is a member of the Executive Committee as well as member of Heritage Commission of The International Union for Prehistoric and Protohistoric Science (UISPP). She also became a life member of the Asiatic Society in 1968 and was elected as the Anthropological Secretary of the Society.
Email: ranjanaray@gmail.com

Ravinder Singh works as Associate Professor & Head, Department of Medical Anthropology, Institute of Human Behaviour and

Allied Sciences (IHBAS) Hospital, Delhi. He has been Assistant Director (Child Care) in Government of India prior to joining the current position. He teaches medical anthropology now to MD (Psychiatry), DM (Neurology) and M.Phil. Clinical Psychology students. He has organized several workshops on CRC, Social Policy and Legislation and Institutional and Non-Institutional Care of Children, Adoption, and its policies. Besides he has organized state level seminars in several states of the country.
Email: medicalanthropology.ihbas@gmail.com

S.B. Chakraborty is continuing as General Secretary of the Asiatic Society, Kolkata since 2016. He superannuated from the Anthropological Survey of India as Deputy Director.
Email: sbchakrabarti@gmail.com

Seetha Kakkoth is a Social Anthropologist who currently works as an Assistant Professor at the Department of Rural and Tribal Sociology at Kannur University, Mananthavady Campus, Wayanad, Kerala. She has gained recognition through various fellowships, such as the Sir Ratan Tata Post-Doctoral Fellowship at LSE, England; ICSSR General Fellowship; Child Rights and You (CRY) Fellowship, and Doctoral Research Fellowship from the Ministry of Tribal Affairs, New Delhi. Her research areas of interest include Hunter-Gatherer societies, Tribal Education and Ageing.
Email: skakkoth@gmail.com

Sekh Rahim Mondal is a former C.C. Sanyal Chair Professor of Anthropology and Director Centre for Himalayan Studies. He is the Founder Head of the Department of Anthropology and the Founder Director of Centre for Studies of Local Languages and Cultures of North Bengal, University of North Bengal. His interests include researchs on tribes, peasants, urban social groups, minorities, area studies, gender studies, refugees, highland societies and studies on globalization and critical anthropology that are well recognized. At present he is the Guest Professor at the Departments of Sociology, Women's Studies and Area & Strategic Studies at the University of North Bengal.
Email: rahimanthnbu@yahoo.co.in

Somenath Bhattacharjee is the Professor and Head, Department of Anthropology, Nagaland University. His specialization is in

sociocultural anthropology and his area of research interest include tribal ethnography, material cultural studies and anthropology of human rights. He has been doing his research on different ethnic groups like Karbi, Dimasa, Bodo, Reang, Mishing and Hajong in the states of Assam, Nagaland, Tripura and Meghalaya. Recently, he got the award of Promising Young Anthropologist, during the World Anthropology Congress-2023, held at KISS Bhubaneswar.
Email: somenath.anthro@gmail.com

Subhadra Channa retired as Professor, Department of Anthropology, University of Delhi in 2016. She was the Senior Vice-President of IUAES (International Union of Anthropological and Ethnological Sciences), from 2018-23 and former Chair of the Commission on Marginalization and Global Apartheid (IUAES 2013-21) and Chair of the Commission on Anthropology of Women (IUAES 2009-13). She received S.C. Roy Gold Medal from the Asiatic Society of Calcutta for Lifetime Achievement in Cultural Anthropology (2011) and Best Serving Teacher Award from Delhi University (2016). At present, she is the chief co-editor of *Reviews in Anthropology* (Taylor and Francis).
Email: channa.subhadra@gmail.com

Subho Roy is serving as Professor at the Department of Anthropology, University of Calcutta. Previously, he served at the University of Allahabad for four and a half years. His research is mostly focused on understanding health of a population from its biocultural perspective; precisely how social and cultural factors shape the health status of a population. He is the managing editor of *Journal of the Indian Anthropological Society* and Member Secretary of the Indian National Confederation and Academy of Anthropologists. He is also the Chairman of Institutional Human Ethics Committee of Anthropological Survey of India and a government nominated member of the Rashtriya Manav Sanghralaya Samiti (2020-25), Ministry of Culture, Government of India. He was elected as the Sectional President of the Anthropology and Behavioural Science Section, of the 104th session of the Indian Science Congress Association.
Email: srayanth@gmail.com

Tanka B. Subba retired as a Professor of Anthropology, North-Eastern Hill University (NEHU), Shillong, India in April 2022. Earlier, from 2012 to 2017, he served as the second Vice-Chancellor of Sikkim University. He received awards like the Homi Bhabha Fellowship (Mumbai), Dr Panchanan Mitra Lectureship and R.P. Chanda Centenary Medal for 2015 (Asiatic Society, Kolkata), DAAD Guest professorship at the Free University of Berlin, and Baden-Wuerttemberg Fellowship at the South Asian Institute, Heidelberg University. He is the sectional editor for Northeast India and Bangladesh, *Brill's Encyclopedia of the Religions of the Indigenous People of South Asia* (Brill, 2021 Gen. Editor Marine Carrin) and co-editor, *The Routledge Companion to Northeast India* (Routledge, 2022, Lead Editor Jelle J.P. Wouters). He is also a Visiting Professor at the University of North Bengal, Siliguri and an Adjunct Professor at Taylor's University, Kuala Lumpur.
Email: tbsubba.shg@gmail.com

Vineetha Menon superannuated as Professor from the Department of Anthropology, Kannur University, Thalassery.
Email: menon.vineetha@gmail.com

1

In Memory

Vinay Kumar Srivastava

Kumkum Srivastava

Vinay Srivastava was born on 3 December 1952 in a middle class Kayastha family of Purani Dilli. He was the first born, warmly welcomed by his maternal grandparents, as his mother was an only child. Very soon, they learnt that he was different. He neither wailed nor threw tantrums, neither demanded nor complained. His father, a government servant, was worried as a pundit had predicted that he would either take the spiritual path or become a "mad" genius—a wizard. Vinay was a bit of both—a mystic as well as a wise soul—combining the intellect of Plato, the serenity of an enlightened soul of Buddha and in his extravagant literary style and usage of the English language, he was no less than a great litterateur.

No challenge was daunting, no obstacle large enough to put him off track, to deter him. No task that he undertook was left incomplete; be it as a student—topping all his examinations, be it as a teacher, in which he excelled; whether as an administrator—as Principal of Hindu College, University of Delhi, or Professor and Head, Department of Anthropology (DU) or as the Director, Anthropological Survey of India. He completed all the projects he undertook, met all editorial or publishing deadlines. He was punctual to a fault be it his classes, lectures online or offline, presentations, meetings or his office. He arrived first and was the last one to leave the venue.

His simplicity attracted everyone, his smile which reached his eyes was mesmerizing, and his soft intonations attracted his audience. That he was an ardent, eloquent and excellent speaker is well documented but that he spent hours working on every document, reading and re-reading writing for a journal, or his books or preparing for his courses, to perfect the contents, to ensure that all the references were in order. He would scribble on whichever piece of paper he could lay his hands on. He was meticulous to a fault; his generosity knew no bounds—be it his time, his books, his other material possessions or the contents of his wallet. His house doors were open to all, his table always laid out and his heart always warm and welcoming.

His three loves were: love of learning, love of learners and loved bringing the two together.

Love/Ishq was his greatest strength. Loving others was what he did best. He loved his subject—anthropology, loved his profession—teaching, and shared both these loves with his colleagues, his students and with the general audience. His love for his family is well known. He was loyal, honest, steadfast, encouraging and supportive. He loved and he was loved abundantly in return. Once in a lifetime one comes across such a man. He influenced a whole generation of students, anthropologists, sociologists, law students, research scholars of every discipline and aspirants for the civil services.

He was a storyteller par excellence. He would use his personal details, experiences, anecdotes to make his lectures delectable and interesting. He did everything differently; he gambled on young people not on age or experience. He never bent to pressure. He was on the side of angels; Gandhiji had a great impact on him—his frugality, his simplicity in food, clothing, material things, his humility and his forgiving nature. He was a theorist, a philosopher a spiritualist, not a very religious person but followed and performed all necessary rituals and ceremonies.

For Professor Srivastava teaching was like a performing art and he was a star performer.

> "As if I was on stage, I moved around, I used the black or the white board, I moved my hands, I got excited, I laughed and got them to laugh with me, involved every student, they were listening, tuned in and enjoying my impromptu lecture, my little bit of theatrics took them where I wanted to take them."

His last words which he wrote in his diary were also related to this. "In a cinema hall or theatre, he who sits near the door, EXITS FIRST."

He exhorted everyone to discover their own strengths; to develop a vision they wanted to achieve, consider their own values and beliefs, pursue experiences that bring them joy, learn new things and always, even in dire circumstances maintain an optimistic outlook. "If you wish to learn, realise that you know nothing." Vinay was a magician, he cast a spell on everyone. Everyone spending time with him felt they had invested it not wasted it.

Vinay discovered Sufism when he married Kumkum, who was involved academically and philosophically with this spiritual belief and practise. He often quoted Hafiz Rumi and Amir Khusrau, sang Sufi poetry and enjoyed *qawwali*s at the shrine of Nizamuddin Auliya at Delhi.

Essentially, a reserved and dignified private person, he shone in the public sphere. When he entered a room, one always noticed Professor Srivastava welled himself to be an anthropologist. He knew nothing about the subject when he perforce joined the course, when he opted out of a premedical course at Deshbandhu College (DU) in August 1969. A chance advertisement in the newspaper caught his cousin's eye, and Vinay believed it was fate. He never stopped learning. Having joined late he was initially, all at sea. Professor D.K. Bhattacharya's lectures on prehistoric archaeology seemed mere garble. He worked diligently, spending long hours in the library, when others were sitting with friends in the canteen or café. He graduated in BSc Anthropology with a 1st class first, then his first masters in Physical Anthropology in 1974 and second one in Sociology in 1976 from the Delhi School of Economics brought his gold medals total to three. Subsequently, he obtained an M.Phil. in Chinese studies in 1983 from the University of Delhi. He began his career in teaching on 15 September 1976 as an Assistant Professor (Lecturer) in Sociology at Hindu College against the vacancy of Dr Mohini Anjum. His senior colleagues in the Department were P.D. Khera (whose obituary he was to write later) and Amrit Srinivasan. He taught papers in Introduction to Sociology, Tribes and Peasants, Social Stratification and Urban Sociology. In addition to theory, Professor Srivastava also taught ethnographic works, R.P. Dere's, *City Life in Japan* (1958) Gugler and Flanagan's *Urbanisation and social change in W. Africa* (1978). From this batch of 3rd year students emerged two eminent sociologists, Professor Sabyasachi, Vishwajit Pandya, a lawyer, Deepak Thakur, and an eminent journalist Brahma Chellaney. Professor M.S.A. Rao asked him to prepare a bibliography on Urban Sociology for M.A. Courses. Vinay's readings were not confined to just syllabus listing but also geography, architecture and planning ecology, demography and economics. He never hesitated to ask for advice and guidance from other scholars, Professor Ashish Bose, Andre Beteille, Professor T.N. Madan. Vinay, throughout his career, carried on his research and ploughed it back to teaching. He motivated his students to read the writings of A.M. Shah and M.N. Srinivas enriched his lectures. He borrowed from Professor Beteille the use of the blackboard while teaching quantitative methods and kinship. Like Professor J.D. Mehra, Vinay never carried notes, nor sat while teaching nor used transparencies or made power point presentations. One of his inaugural addresses was titled "The Magic of the Blackboard".

He also developed insights from his own fieldwork, but also those he carried out with his students, contrasting the book view with the field view "what men say and what they do"; advising his students to read one ethnography a month. For him the classroom was a laboratory "full of surprise". He was inspired by Professor

Madan, who himself held D.N. Majumdar as his model. Professor J.S. Bhandari shared his paper on tribes and peasants with him in 1985 and urban anthropology in 1986, when he joined the Department of Anthropology as a Reader. Often Professor Srivastava would write down each of his lectures which later were used for his books. His fieldwork notes whether from Bikaner, or Bhuj were extremely valuable in teaching the classification of cities—especially between orthogenetic and heterogenetic cities using Redfield (1954) and Singer (1979) Aidan Southall (1973), Richard Fox (1977) and Cohen's (1996) works. Ruth Benedict (1946), Leo Howe (1990) were also was read profitably.

Vinay's reputations as an "excellent teacher" grew, his theory classes were inordinately long; practically classes were often held past lunch. He engaged his students in "out of the box" projects-parks and gardens; morning walkers, Sufi shrines; zoological garden; study of the community of horse tenders—*saee*s who had *tonga*s; Kayasthas of *gali*, Kayasthan of Chandni Chowk. Another experiment he made was group teaching after he returned from Cambridge. He had done a course in medical anthropology and P.C. Joshi's doctoral dissertation impacted him strongly. After returning from Cambridge (Cantab) UK where he had gone on a Commonwealth scholarship to study for his Ph.D. in Social Anthropology (1988-92).

Vinay taught medical anthropology from 1993-2003, and urban anthropology from July 1993 continuing till 2010, when he joined as Principal, Hindu College where besides administrative duties he also taught sociological theory and methods. From July 2012, back at the Department of Anthropology he shared the paper, "Urban Anthropology" with Chakravarty Mahajan and Kennedy Singh. Urban Anthropology showed the value of methodology in studying urban settlements, Professor Srivastava's last class in 2017 was on the rise of communalism in urban India; the idea of composite culture Benedict Anderson (1983), the role of print media, sociology of biases, prejudices, hatred racial conflicts, discrimination and exclusion of communities.

His Writings

Professor Srivastava's doctoral thesis was published by Oxford as *Religious Renunciation of a Pastoral People* (1997). He proposed the Raika model of renunciation as an alternative to the demonian nation grounded in Sanskritic texts; based on the lived experiences of non-materialistic values. While at Cambridge, a volume, co-authored with Declan Quigley—*The Hidden Tribes of India* was published by Chene Paris in French, later translated into English by "Local Colours" Hongkong (2001). It had an introduction by Dominique Lapierre, "very well written, a jewel to display on my bookshelf". Vinay also wrote on occultism, witchcraft published in *Cambridge Anthropology* (1988) "Should Anthropologists Pay Their Respondents" (1992) in *Anthropology Today*.

A retrospective view of his writings show that they revolved around the following themes:

(a) Renunciation and other-worldly phenomenon
(b) Anthropological theory and methods; pedagogy
(c) Tribes, peasants, marginal communities—notified and denotified
(d) Issues of development
(e) Comparative religion
(f) Caste system
(g) Family dynamics
(h) Medical systems.

However, Vinay's engagement with theory fieldwork and methodology was central to his interests having edited two volumes on *Methodology and Fieldwork* (2004, Oxford) and *Contributions to Sociological Theory* (Sage, 2014) which he dedicated to his two teachers Professor I.S Marwah and J.S. Bhandari. He also wrote on people on the margins, tribes, elderly, peasants, children, racial inclusion and exclusion. In his critique of the Draft National Policy on Tribes he argued that the document emphasized the ideal situation, ignoring the real operational issues on the ground. As the Director, Anthropological Survey of India he had launched an innovative project to document and map the trajectories of the life of tribal communities of India to provide information to the Niti Aayog. Professor Srivastava also worked on mental health and illness (2002). It was ironic that he wrote a full-length essay on COVID-19 which was published by *Social Change* (2020). His earlier papers were a review article, with his wife, Kumkum, of "Death in Benares" by Jonathan Parry. Another macabre situation was that he became well known as the "writer of obituaries and deliverer of memorial lectures". He wrote *Religion & Mysticism*—in honour of J.D. Mehra (2016). *Teaching of Anthropology: A Tribute to Abhimanyu Sharma*, another for Professor I.P. Singh and P.D. Khera. He also honoured Ishwar Modi besides others. His last work as editor was *India's Tribes Unfolding Realities* (Sage, 2020) which was published while he was in hospital. His essay in the *Social Scientist* is an analytical journal and biographical exploration of teaching sociological theory to undergraduates reflected on the heterogeneity of sociology and social anthropology in social forces and negotiations, edited by Achla Tandon, Gopi Devdutt Tripathy and Rashi Bhargava (2021).

Fieldwork

In 1971, Vinay's first fieldwork was with Dr Kumbhnani and Dr P.K. Datta with Oraon and Munda community—Vinay used the term fieldwork always hesitantly for the physical work that anthropologists engaged in (2000). His other concern was whether anthropologists should pay their respondents. His second fieldwork was in Dharamsala with M.K. Bhasin and B.R. Ghosh among the Gaddis. Later, in his book he gave a detailed account of the character of social research ethnography, survey as well as ethical and ideological issues involved, importance of classification—relevance of comparison— restudying one's own field area. He worked with the Baigas in Nagaland, Raikar Rabaris, and Sentinelese in Jabalpur, Jains in Chhattisgarh, Bishnois of Rajasthan as well.

Administration

Professor Srivastava was as able an administrator as he was a teacher. In his two years tenure as Principal, Hindu College, he conducted the college through Commonwealth Games, cleared the backlog of appointments of teaching and non-teaching staff. As Professor and Head, Department of Anthropology, he guided the department and the subjects to achieve the highest pinnacles of glory. At time of his death, he held the position of the Director, Anthropological Survey of India (2017-20). From 2017-18, he was Director MAKAAIS, as well as Raja Rammohun Roy Library Foundation (RRMRLF), carrying out research in anthropology, tribal studies. This position was previously held by stalwarts and illuminati like B.S. Guha, Nirmal Kumar Bose, Surajit Sinha and K.S. Singh.

During his tenure at AnSI, on the 1 December 2017, Foundation Day, Professor D.K. Bhattacharya (DU) delivered the key note address. In March 2018, a seminar was held on Interconnection between Development and Sustainability and a panel discussion on "Concept of Happiness", chaired by Dr Shravan Kumar, Joint Secretary, Ministry of Culture (GoI). Professor Srivastava brought into the spotlight the well-stocked, amazing library of the AnSI. A new complex of the eastern region was built, state of the art auditorium, offices and lecture rooms. He led an empirical study of sixteen villages to examine the impact of development and planned changes on the lives of people and their coping up strategies (July 2019 to September 2018). Between (October-December 2018) a series of seminars related to Gandhi and Anthropology were organized at Mysuru, Udaipur and Shillong. One of the national projects of the AnSI is an ethnographic documentation of the denotified, nomadic and semi-nomadic communities—(borrowed from the Idate's report in 2018). Field studies began in 2018-19 and reports were submitted at NERC (Shillong), WRC (Udaipur), CRC (Nagpur) and ERC (Kolkata). He not only guided but attended the presentations of the researchers. Two-day seminars were organized in March 2019, at Jagdalpur highlighting the denotified communities and Scheduled

Tribes. Lecture were delivered by D. Idate and Dr Renke.

His most notable achievement as Director was that the *Journal of the Anthropological Survey of India* was henceforth published by Sage Publications (2019).

Professor Srivastava had written extensively and spoken on relevance of museums believing that they were an inextricable part of every anthropology department. He made sure that the central museum of AnSI as well as zonal anthropological museums were well stocked, up to date with information video and audio recordings, photographs, etc. The relation between the Department of Anthropology, University of Calcutta and AnSI was inextricable and the synergism rose under Vinay. Professor Srivastava was firmly dedicated to the marginal groups. So AnSI took up the project to study these 150 million people—803 communities—which would add to the volume of *People of India*.

Between April 2020 and 1 December 2020, Professor Srivastava spoke at many webinars on COVID-19—mental health, quarantine, stigma, social distancing, how to do fieldwork during pandemic, death during these times, tribals and the corona virus—the "walking class" migrants.

1 December 2020

On the day Professor Srivastava was hospitalized, he had participated in the AnSI Foundation Day. He was conducting his work, meeting deadlines, guiding even from his hospital bed. A workaholic to the core, a *karmayogi* and a people's person, he loved company but died alone; lonely, solitary unaccompanied, in a bleak, depressing environment. He could not even see the faces of his doctors or nursing attendants as they were in the protective gear. Thus, a great anthropologist, a superb teacher, a guide, a counsellor, facilitator, coach, mentor, supervisor, editor, confidante, dutiful son, big brother to his siblings, a loving husband, a caring father, a doting grandfather, a wonderful friend and an excellent employer, left the world a bleaker place, bereft of his wholesome, spiritual presence. He whose words filled his audience with awe and wonder, left them speechless, wondering what happened, why it happened.... He, who filled his students with optimism and purpose, kept them engaged, motivated, inspired and challenged, was never banal or mundane, never repeated his lectures, who never sat in class, was always moving around, constantly varying his speaking tone; a performer for whom the classroom was a stage; Professor Srivastava had performed his last act and taken the final bow; leaving his audience spellbound and in shock.

Books Published

1990: *Essays in Social Anthropology*. Calcutta: Institute of Social Research and Applied Anthropology

1993: *L'Inde des Tribus Oubliees*. Paris: Societe Nouvelle des Editions du Chene (with Declan Quigley). Preface written by Dominique Lapierre.

1994: [In Hindi] *Samajik Manav Vigyan: Ek Parichay* (*Social Anthropology: An Introduction*). Delhi: Palaka Prakashan.

1997: *Religious Renunciation of a Pastoral People*. Delhi: Oxford University Press.

2001: Edited {co-editor} *Human Ecology in the New Millennium*. Delhi: Kamla-Raj Enterprises.

2004: Edited the volume titled *Methodology and Fieldwork,* Under the Series Oxford in India Readings in Sociology and Social Anthropology.

2004: Jointly edited (with M.K. Singh) the volume titled *Issues and Themes in Anthropology: A Festschrift in Honour of Professor D.K. Bhattacharya*. Delhi: Palaka Prakashan.

2005: Paperback Edition of *Methodology and Fieldwork*. Delhi: Oxford University Press.

2006: Edited *Scheduled Tribes and Development*. New Delhi: Serials Publication (co-editors: H.S. Saksena and Sukant K. Chaudhury).

2006: English translation of *L'Inde des Tribus Oubliees* (1993) under the title *Tribes of India*. Bookwise (India) Pvt. Ltd.

2008: *I Raika, Allevatori di Cammelli del Rajasthan* (*The Raika, the Camel-breeders of Rajasthan*). Roma: Edizioni Progetto Cultura. [In Italian, with Umberto Mondini.]

2009: Edited *Social Anthropology in Eastern India*. (With Sachchidananda). New Delhi: Serials Publications.

2009: *Adivasi, Le Minoranze Etniche dell'India*. [In Italian, with Umberto Mondini.] Roma: Edizioni Progetto Cultura.

2010: Edited *Anthropology in India* (with H.S. Saksena, Nadeem Hasnain, Sukant K. Chaudhury, and Sameera Maiti). New Delhi: Serials Publications.

2010: Edited *Issues in Contemporary Society* (*A Festschrift in Honour of Professor B.N. Borthakur*) (with Joyanta Borbora). Guwahati: DVS Publishers.

2013: Edited *Tribes in India: Concepts, Institutions and Practices*. New Delhi: Serials Publications.

2

Practicing Anthropology as a Vocation

R.K. Mutatkar

Teaching of Anthropology in India was introduced at University of Calcutta in 1920. Following the Western model of Malinowski, Radcliffe Brown and some American Anthropologists, monographs of tribal communities in India were published by European and Indian anthropologists. Later the conceptual model of studying pre-literate tribal communities was applied to study the village communities, mainly influenced by Robert Redfield's interest in peasant communities which evolved to analyse Indian civilization, proposing the concepts of Great and Little tradition and their interaction. Massive community development programme for rural and tribal transformation introduced in 1952 with "Destination Man" as the motto, invited the services of American and Indian anthropologists to promote extension approach. The emphasis in Indian anthropology shifted from the study of "other people" by the Western pioneer anthropologists, to "our own people", whose aspirations for development had to be facilitated by empowering them through democratic decentralization, as delineated in the Constitution of India. This process has been branded as applied anthropology with synonyms such as practicing anthropology and action anthropology.

However Indian anthropology has yet to step out of the university system to develop as a vocation.

I have been fortunate to receive opportunities, as a faculty in the university, to apply anthropological concepts and research methods for analysing the policy and implementation issues, even to experiment developing intervention models.

Upbringing and Education

I was born in British India, at Gwalior, Madhya Pradesh, in February 1936, with childhood memories of Quit India movement, with anti-British processions near our primary school in 1942. We heard on the radio, 14 August 1947 midnight speech of Jawaharlal Nehru, heralding Independence, when the Tricolour National Flag went up to replace Union Jack. My family originally belonged to a village, Mutat, in Sindhudurg district in Kokan region of Maharashtra. They migrated to Sagar in Bundelkhand, Madhya Pradesh, as kin of the warrior-cook of Bajirao Peshwa, who was appointed administrator (*subhedar*) of Sagar region, in the year 1729. Sagar-Jhansi region was gifted to Bajirao by Maharaja Chhatrasal, in gratitude for helping regain his kingdom from the invaders, besides marrying his daughter, Mastani, from a Muslim concubine, to the Brahmin Bajirao Peshwa. Our small *zamindari* at Gwalior with authority to collect land revenue for the state in some villages, established contact with the peasantry since childhood.

The Maharaja of Gwalior, continuing to be known as "Scindhia" (British pronunciation of the surname, Shinde) established Marathi schools, importing teachers from Maharashtra, and promoted Marathi literature, theatre and Ganesh festival, with Pune as a reference city. Victoria College (now Maharani Laxmibai College, after the Queen of Jhansi) used to have a British Principal in the colonial period. One of the first Birla textile mill located at a suburb, gave rise to trade union activity led by the Communist Party. The legendary classical singer from Akbar's court, Tansen, belonged to Gwalior providing music identity to the city. Being close to Delhi, all national leaders, except Gandhiji, used to visit Gwalior and address public meetings. Culturally, Gwalior continued to be a pre-industrial city, the term used by Robert Redfield. As Maharashtrians living in Hindi belt, we had cross-cultural and bi-lingual living, inculcating objective attitude about diversity and plurality.

After graduation in social sciences in 1957, I was recommended to Dr B.N. Ganguly, Director, Delhi School of Economics for admission. Dr Leela Dube (nee Ambardekar), sister of my aunt, Dr Sumati Mutatkar, Director of Music, All India Radio, Delhi, invited me to join Anthropology at Sagar University as Professor S.C. Dube had joined University as the first Professor of Anthropology. Dr Ganguly strongly endorsed joining Sagar, commending Professor Dube as a good anthropologist.

At Sagar, it was impressive to see Professor Dube and other senior teachers in the university travelling widely, including to lecture at the civil services and rural development training institutes. The newly designed anthropology curriculum included courses in applied anthropology and research methods, not common in other Indian universities, and were taught personally by Professor Dube. He was a good teacher and available at his residence on the campus to the students all the time. We witnessed him writing the book, *India's Changing Villages*, the first such publication on community development. He wrote the research protocol for my Master's field dissertation in a village near Gwalior on "Changing Dimensions of Caste", which has been published as a book (1978). Professor Dube initiated the students to the All India Sociological Conferences at the Institute of Social Sciences, Agra; Indian Statistical Institute, Kolkata, and Department of Anthropology, Lucknow University, during 1958-60, and encouraged us to present research papers based on our field dissertation.

University Faculty

I was appointed as Research Assistant in a project, "Communication, Leadership and Decision Making" to test the democratic functioning of Statutory Panchayats, in the villages in Sagar district, immediately after the master's examination. I was selected as JRF of the first UGC batch in 1959, interviewed by a committee chaired by Sir C.P. Ramaswamy Aiyer. Since, I was appointed lecturer at Sagar due to emergent faculty vacancy, I declined the JRF.

Recommendations by Professor S.C. Dube and Professor Irawati Karve resulted in my appointment as lecturer in cultural/ social anthropology in July 1960, at the Department of Sociology and Anthropology at University of Poona, located at the Deccan College Postgraduate Research Institute. There was a significant difference between social anthropology oriented to applications at Sagar and ethnological perspective of anthropology of Irawati Karve, at the Deccan College, which nurtured classical scholarship through close interactions of ancient Indian history, archaeology, and linguistics as sub-disciplines of anthropology.

At the University of Poona, in the combined Department of Sociology and Anthropology, we two faculty members in anthropology felt threatened. Our request to Irawati Karve to start a distinct Masters course in Anthropology met with success in 1963. Irawati Karve expected me and my colleague in biological anthropology, as university employees, to develop teaching at the university. She gave us total freedom to design the common M.A./M.Sc. level anthropology curriculum, which was a mix of biological aspects from Delhi and social anthropology from Sagar, including applied anthropology and research methods, without any specialization. Fieldwork training of the students in interior tribal areas across Maharashtra as also in Odisha and Bastar, following the methodology of "going native" enriched the understanding of the empirical reality of tribal culture and society, and development issues. This experience and familiarity with all tribal regions in Maharashtra helped subsequently, in objectively adjudicating the issues of pseudo-tribalism, as an expert member of government committees.

Due to sudden passing away of Irawati Karve we shifted to university campus from Deccan College in July 1973. Continuing to be a part of the combined department, anthropology section could not seek research funding on its own. Western Regional

Centre, ICSSR, Mumbai funded anthropology section to organize Research Methodology Workshops in 1975 for social science faculty across Maharashtra and in 1976 in the tribal area, for the same participants. Responding to the wishes of the participants, an academic NGO with the broad title, "Maharashtra Association of Anthropological Sciences (MAAS)" was established with the full support of the vice-chancellor, with open door to all social sciences, government functionaries from tribal and forest departments and tribal activists. As per the UGC recommendation, anthropology was constituted as an independent department in 1977, under my headship. Several academic programmes could be organized jointly by the department and MAAS, including INCAA Congresses in 2007 and 2019.

Maharashtra was formed as a linguistic state on 1 May 1960, with Mumbai as its capital. Directorates of different departments of state government located at Pune sought assistance from anthropology, about social and tribal issues, about identity and development, for affirmative action. Irawati Karve's apathy to applications, as George Foster said, "the teachers like Herskovitz, Kroebar, Lowie consciously kept the students away from applications", led her to refer the issues to me as a cultural anthropologist, reminding my duty to respond to the government as a university employee. Thus, I responded to opportunities for practicing applied anthropology.

Medical Anthropology

Irawati Karve's recommendation to engage classes in 1963, at the postgraduate Preventive Medicine Department at the Armed Forces Medical College, Pune for Army Medical Core officers, followed by teaching at the B.J. Medical College, through formal Defence Ministry and state government notifications, both institutions being affiliated to University of Poona, led to development of medical anthropology at Pune in 1974. Ayurved College did not lag behind in interacting with anthropology at University of Poona. Post-Congess International Symposium on Medical

Anthropology at Pune in December 1978, after the International Anthropology Congress held at Delhi, with a special publication of *Social Science and Medicine* (1980) about Poona Symposium, bestowed international accreditation to Pune as a centre of medical anthropology in India. Subsequently, Professor P.C. Joshi and Professor H.K. Bhat established "Society for Indian Medical Anthropology (SIMA)", having attended the Poona Symposium, honoring me as the Patron. The great Indologist, Professor A.L. Basham's presence at Poona Symposium, as also of the medical anthropologists, Professor Charles Leslie and Professor Arthur Kleinman and the doyen of Ayurved, Pandit Shiv Sharma, led to International Congress on Traditional Asian Medicine (ICTAM) at Australian National University, Canberra in September 1979, culminating in the establishment of International Association for the Study of Traditional Asian Medicine (IASTAM). The Indian Chapter with me as the General Secretary and Pandit Shiv Sharma as the President was establishes at Mumbai, with inaugural meeting at the University of Poona. Later, after Dr K.N. Udupa's demise, who succeeded Late Pandit Shiv Sharma, I became the President of IASTAM-India. The international events of this organization including in India, facilitated the composition of a working group on AYUSH in Public Health under my Chairmanship, to be a component of Eleventh Five-Year Plan. Subsequently, the field research projects in four states, Himachal Pradesh, Madhya Pradesh, Chhattisgarh and Maharashtra funded by AYUSH Ministry led to publication of a book, *AYUSH in Public Health* in two volumes (2016).

Leprosy

Leprosy, the great disease (*maharog*), as one of the most ancient diseases, discussed in *Susrut Samhita*, afflicting only humans, defied treatment for cure till early 1940s. Cure was claimed with DDS and more surely in mid-1980s with MDT; science continuing to unravel the transmission process, despite identifying the causative lepra bacilli, since 1850s. This led to despondency, with total faith in divine intervention, with examples of miraculous cure by Hindu god Ram, Jesus, Mother Teresa, or compassion by Gandhi. There has been a tiff as to whether leprosy was primarily a social problem, with the risk of social death, due to social stigma for the afflicted, or a medical problem; shuttling the ball between Social Welfare and Health Ministries. Leprosy control programmers needed social science intervention to address social stigma by advising the community to seek medical advice, since leprosy was treatable, and deformities preventable. Leprosy programmers identified leprosy public health problem as that of "case finding and case holding". I was roped in to undertake research, evaluation and training by "Gandhi Memorial Leprosy Foundation (GMLF), Wardha", and international Christian organizations such as "The Leprosy Mission", and Danish and German organizations, including the WHO. With the first ever commissioned working paper by WHO on "Social and Economic aspects of Leprosy" (1981) from me, and a book, *Society and Leprosy* (1979), WHO and other international organizations extended their objectives of leprosy control, and definition of the "case of leprosy" to include preventing deformities and rehabilitation, as the essential component of control programme, instead of stopping at diagnosis and treatment with chemotherapy. WHO established "Centre for Social Science Research on Leprosy" at GMLF, Wardha, under my leadership, bringing me on deputation from University of Poona. I got an opportunity to interact with Tamil village communities, as a member of Leprosy Vaccine Trial committee, at the National Institute of Epidemiology (ICMR), Chennai. I was called upon to be a team member for Rajasthan and Maharashtra, and later as team leader for Assam, for WHO sponsored evaluations of National Leprosy Elimination Programme (NLEP). Following the keynote address at the plenary session of International Leprosy Congress at Delhi in 1984, meeting at the Pontifical Academy of Sciences, Vatican of invited twelve scientists ended with discussion with Pope John Paul II, for an hour, with a Vatican publication (1984), incorporating "Social Aspects of Leprosy". There has been formal recognition of contribution by bestowing International Gandhi Award for Leprosy to me on 30 January 2016, by the Vice-President of India in his capacity as Chairman of International Jury.

HIV-AIDS and Sexuality

Another stigmatized and difficult to cure affliction has been HIV, with a high risk of developing into fatal AIDS. Sexual behaviour was not a public health issue, until it was identified as a risk of HIV-AIDS becoming pandemic. Ford Foundation offered a capacity development programme to me, by way of small research grants to young scholars including Ph.D. fellowships. A book compiling the research papers has been published (2019). As Chairman of the Research Ethics Committee of "National AIDS Research Institute (NARI-ICMR)", anthropological research got a fillip with anthropologists occupying senior research positions. Representing India at the International Research Ethics Conference at Boston and presentation at Vatican in an interreligious dialogue about palliative care regarding infectious diseases (meant HIV-AIDS, but not made explicit due to reservations of Catholic Church about contraception) widened the research agenda about the use of microbicides by women in traditional societies.

Indian Council of Medical Research (ICMR)

These applications of Medical Anthropology led to establishment of "Social-Behavioural Research Unit (SBR)", later upgraded to "Division" at the Indian Council of Medical Research, recruiting several anthropologists in their regional and disease specific national institutes. I have had the honour of chairing the first Scientific Advisory Group of the SBR Division. There has been a joint ICSSR-ICMR panel on Health, whereby research grants and fellowships are offered in social-behavioural aspects of health.

School of Health Sciences

At University of Poona, "Inter-disciplinary School of Health Sciences" was established by the UGC, offering master's degree in Health Sciences, and Masters in Public Health, even to non-medicos. I was shifted from Anthropology in Social Science Faculty to be the first Professor-Director at this School in Science Faculty. The fieldwork training to Health Science students in tribal and rural areas changed their perspective of health, making it people-centric, addressing the concerns of "Bharat" than that of India, as acknowledged publicly, by succeeding directors of the school.

Tribal Issues

In common knowledge, anthropology is considered an exclusive academic discipline studying tribal communities. Tribal Research and Training Institute (TRTI) of the state government was established at Pune in 1962 with close networking with the university. Our academic assistance has been greatly valued by inviting to be a member/chairman of different committees in tribal development and social justice ministries, mainly addressing the reservation issues. In this capacity, besides meeting the delegations of communities and studying their memoranda, field investigations focusing more on qualitative study, such as visits to local pilgrimage centres, observing the houses, including kitchens, and informal discussions with lay women, proved decisive. The recommendations were upheld by the bureaucracy and judiciary. The Ministers of Tribal Development in successive state governments personally consulted us on important issues, with realization dawned on us, that the lone tribal minister was himself marginalized in the Cabinet, and had embarrassments if the non-tribals' claim for ST status was supported by powerful members of the cabinet in view of vote-bank politics. They confessed that the pseudo-tribalism was a political issue and relied on the anthropological objectivity of our recommendation. I, as Chairman of the Backward Classes Committee (1993) under the Social Welfare Ministry, Maharashtra, adjudicated the claims of 147 communities to get SC, OBC, VJ and NT status. I was member of all the committees to look into the claims for ST status, prominent being Halba-HalbaKoshti, Govari-Gond Govari, Koli-Mahadeo Koli, etc. There have been rare cases like land mafia grabbing tribal lands in Vasai region of Mumbai, managing certificates that the landowners were non-tribals. Genealogies of such families with their tribal kin living in neighboring villages with tribal certificates, settled cases in the law-court in favour of the tribal landowners. There have been issues about risk of displacement of tribal people and destruction of Sal forest due to hydro-electric dam project in Bastar, the beneficiaries of which were not meant to be the local tribal people. I was invited to study the tribal perspectives by a committee of foresters, which was done by visiting tribal villages on foot, following our methodology to find out emic perspectives. The dam project was abandoned.

Voluntary Organisations (NGOs)

Anthropologists are also invited by voluntary organizations/ NGOs who are under obligation by funding agencies to evaluate their programmes. This has to be done in the absence of benchmark data, in the "after only" evaluation mode. NGOs working in tribal and rural areas, in health and education, have been funded by governments and foreign agencies. Several senior doctors like Dr R.S. Arole, Dr N.H. Antia and Dr Banoo Coyaji, with social consciousness, started voluntary work in western Maharashtra villages with curative services, mainly for the poor, extending to preventive aspects and further addressing the general development agenda. Their NGOs, and a large NGOs like Bhartiya Agro-Industries Foundation (BAIF) working in several states, involved us in evaluation, and training about community research and documentation, more specifically in tribal and rural areas. Intimate interactions with eminent persons like Dr C.G. Pandit, first Director, ICMR; Professor P.V. Sukhatme, Director, Agricultural Statistics, FAO; Dr Manibhai Desai, founder of BAIF, Sri Davendrabhai, Member-Secretary, Gandhi Smarak Nidhi, Dr N.S. Deodhar, Epidemiologist, Dr Arole and many others from different walks of life extended the horizons of my anthropological understanding and its applications in the issues related to health, disease and development.

Young motivated educated activists working in tribal areas with their small NGOs, tribal litterateurs and tribal leaders, as also, bureaucrats from Forest and Tribal Development Departments of the state government shared MAAS platform, mainly due to association with the university. They said, "they recharged their conceptual batteries" in our seminars. This vision of networking the academics with the ground realities, provided more credible opportunities to get international funding and partnerships, such as with the London School of Hygiene and Tropical Medicine for a decade on TB and HIV as public health issues. MAAS was offered tribal intervention project due to *suo motu* injunction in Bombay High Court about tribal malnutrition by Maharashtra government, with an exclamation, "Let us be partners in development". The intervention, action project to address tribal malnutrition was designed as per the holistic and functional approach in anthropology, implemented by 500 male and female tribal volunteers in equal numbers, in 250 villages across Maharashtra in tribal areas, jointly with "Comprehensive Rural Health Project, Jamkhed" of Dr R.S. Arole. Confidence building and capacity building strategies were used in addressing various aspects of culture, impacting health and malnutrition. Some aspects of the intervention programme such as nutrition during pregnancy and lactation have been translated by the government in designing the schemes (2018).

While medical anthropology provided opportunities to interact with institutions and scholars in the field of health, interaction with mainstream anthropology remained limited to participation in seminars and conferences. However, as Chairman of Anthropology Panel at the UGC, and nodal person to prepare UGC Model Curriculum: Anthropology (2001) facilitated to play active role in the formation of Indian National Confederation and Academy of Anthropologists (INCAA), and grace the chairmanship. As recipient of Tagore National Scholarship from the Ministry of Culture with affiliation to Anthropological Survey of India (2012-

14), I had the opportunity to participate in the activities of the Survey, across the country. The book, *Anthropological Paradigm for Policy and Practice* (2020) summarises the lifetime work in practising anthropology. Recently, a new vibrant academic body, "United Indian Anthropology Forum" has been formed, honouring me as a patron of the organization.

Anthropology as a holistic discipline studying "other cultures" since colonial days, has now to address the concerns of the citizens of India, located within the post-colonial democratic governance. Anthropologists are generally invited to usher in the principle of equity and affirmative action, assured by the constitution in policy planning, administration and policy implementation, always championing the "whole" for stakeholders. Ethical issues become more predominant which are negotiated as per universal values and human rights, accepted internationally. Scientific objectivity does not preclude action for the good of the people.

Practising anthropology, the term used by Malinowski, relates to use of anthropological concepts, based on empirical realities in all situations, for poverty alleviation, rehabilitation due to disasters, and issues focusing on human development. Anthropologists are equipped to ask and answer the question, "why" about every static and dynamic human phenomenon. Politicians have to solicit and address people's demands, to retain power; bureaucrats deal with people as beneficiaries, but anthropologists have to be the advocates of people-centric policies and micro-level implementation, with people's involvement in thought and action. Post-colonial Indian Anthropology can be developed as a vocation with its strength of holistic approach, commonly expressed as cliché, "Think globally, act locally".

My Books

1978: *Caste Dimensions in a Village*. Poona: Shubhada Saraswat.

1979: *Society and Leprosy*. Wardha: Gandhi Memorial Leprosy Foundation.

2010: Mutatkar, R.K., *et al.* (eds). *Studies on Bio-Medical Anthropology*. New Delhi: INCAA, Aryan Books International.

2016: *AYUSH in Public Health*, vol. I & II. New Delhi: Concept Publishing Company (Pvt.) Ltd.

2018: *Tribal Health and Malnutrition*, New Delhi: Concept Publishing Company (Pvt.) Ltd.

2019: Mutatkar, R.K. & Nagarkar, Aarti (eds.). *Sexuality, Sexual Behaviour and Reproductive Health*. New Delhi: Concept Publishing Company (Pvt.) Ltd.

2020: *Anthropological Paradigm for Policy and Practice*. New Delhi: Concept Publishing Company (Pvt.) Ltd.

2023: *Ramayan: Soul of Indian Civilisation*. New Delhi: Concept Publishing Company (Pvt.) Ltd.

3

My Almost Lifelong Association with Anthropology

A Late Realization about Anthropology's Range of Influence

Rajat Kanti Das

My Initiation into Anthropology

I begin with a frank confession that my initiation into anthropology could find some fulfilment or a meaningful proposition only after I had completed my initial training in anthropology at the university level. I took anthropology as a subject at the B.Sc. level in Cotton College, Gauhati after I was denied admission in the Dibrugarh Medical College on the ground that I was underage. Harsh though it may sound, I had a feeling that anthropology was rather thrust upon me. I was then unaware of a subject like anthropology and what it was all about. Now, after associating myself with anthropology for about six decades, I could at least realize its importance and the questions it is capable of asking that are of crucial importance in the context of varied human existence which is becoming more and more problematic day by day. Now, it is also possible for me to go back to my childhood days when, as I see it today, the seeds of some anthropological queries, which have engaged my attention later, lay hidden. I could relate with them without much of a difficulty and find continuity between what were childhood curiosities or mere images with old age realization. That old age represents the second childhood has become meaningful to me, though in a different sense.

Relating Childhood Impressions to the Realm of Anthropology

A substantial part of my childhood was spent in two tea gardens in Assam, where my father was the doctor in-charge. My childhood memories of the tea garden in the Darang district of Assam were more like snapshots taken long time back but vivid enough to create an impression. A tea garden of that time could structurally be differentiated into three components: managers, *babu*s and workers forming the labour force, who, in common parlance, used to be called as "Coolie", a derogatory form of expression. Managers were the supremely privileged persons and were entitled services and demanded a type of loyalty from the subordinates by virtue of the posts held by them; *babu*s maintained a working relation with managers, but there was practically no social interaction between the two. They, however, interacted with the labour force to get the works done, met them occasionally on socio-religious events without sharing the same social platform as equal partners. In social functions, community-based activities, open air theatrical performances like *yatra,* they would maintain a safe distance from the working class or were allotted a special place and given special treatment by the latter.

I could still remember the night long *yatra* organized by the workers, where separate arrangement was made for us, those representing the *babu* group, with stools and chairs for sitting, while the rest representing the workers' group would sit on the ground. We were also quite used to such an arrangement and took it as a matter of our right. My father, though a doctor, was in the *babu* class and as members of that class we could freely interact with others of the same category. I was, however, intrigued by the poor living condition of the workers, alcoholic wife-bashing husbands among them, their quarrels and display of strong family level ties in the midst of all adversaries. As the doctor in-charge of the whole tea garden and its satellite wing, my father had to interact with the workers and their family members more frequently. They not only had access to the garden's hospital, but were also entitled health services at home in case of emergency.

When I think of it today, I cannot but appreciate our previous colonial masters because providing health services was one area which was in their priority list. A number of tea garden-based hospitals could attract patients from far and wide, where well trained, foreign doctors would make themselves available to provide medical aid to all categories of patients at a nominal cost. Father used to enjoy a special place of importance among the workers and even his harsh words were taken in good spirit. The untrained support staff came mainly from the workers' group, whom my father had carefully groomed to assist him in his work. Though they were close to our family, they themselves would keep a safe distance from us in order not to encroach on our higher social position. It was never a calculated stand on their part to remain lower down in the scale of hierarchic order, but they had no choice or more correct it is to say that they were not in a position to exercise their choice. These observations were, of course, made when I had already completed my schooling. Still, it was possible for me to seek the origin of such thoughts to my experiences as a child, which I now consider to be my first exposure to a situation where social differences manifest and become explicit. As long as I was a child, it did not occur to me nor was it possible for me to seek the reasons behind such differences, which were taken to be just like any other natural thing of the world. Changes in the interacting situation involving the three components gradually unfolded before my eyes as the time progressed.

Entering into the Domain of Anthropology

Amongst the early childhood memories, one that has a lingering effect on me relates to the picture of two fair-skinned young boys of the English Manager approaching me with extended hands just to pat me and I, a boy of hardly four to five years, hiding behind my father, desperately trying to cover my face. When I try to think about my behaviour at that time, I could vaguely establish a mental conditioning effect on me caused by physical differences, in this case, the colour of skin. Much later, I could find some sort of a relation between it and my first experience of teaching "race" at the undergraduate level. The full implications of A.C. Haddon's comments that a race type mainly exists in our mind could be understood by me when I try to project my childhood image in the light of known biases nurtured by us in the name of race. Probably my understanding could further be strengthened by another parallel picture, the context being the same. Here the focus is on a number of workers' children pushing a trolley from behind and I, sitting on it, mixed freely with them sharing the joy of a pleasure ride. Even then, a difference was maintained between "doctor *babu*'s" son and sons of the garden workers. Here I was the pleasure seeker and they were the providers. During that time any reversal of such roles was an impossible proposition, nor was it possible immediately after Independence. Adoption of a language of protest or defiance by the workers became noticeable only when they came under the influence of political unions and education made some headway among them.

We may have some reservations about the Leftist political groups, but it has to be admitted that initially the political slogans of protest provided by them earned some popularity and acceptance among the workers. I can still visualize a small bare bodied, rickety boy of a worker trying to raise his fisted arm in response to a political slogan in a rally of little consequence. Only recently, long after we had left the tea garden, I could come to know about some cases indicating a break in the rigid social structure. In the second tea garden, where my father served for an extended period of time, there were at least two cases of workers' sons joining the *babu* rank after equipping themselves with higher education. They also shifted to *babu* quarters, which was a landmark event from the perspective of social change. Incidentally, once I thought of doing my Ph.D. on the "Social Life of the Tea Garden Labourers of Assam". I prepared the proposal and sent it to Professor B.K. Roy Burman, who was then Professor at Viswa-Bharati University. He liked the proposal and asked me to join Viswa-Bharati University by taking at least one year's leave. I could not manage leave because I was in a government college, which did not accept my prayer for leave. The project was dropped, but to me the merit of the problem remained. That I did not pursue the problem further was because I became totally engrossed with the situation in Manipur where I continued to remain for a prolonged period of time. A couple of research papers, a Research Project on the Maring tribe further strengthened my interest. My initial interest in Manipur was partly because of the encouragement I received from Professor M.S.A. Rao, who happened to be the Subject Expert in the UPSC's interview for the post of a Lecturer in Anthropology in the Government D.M. College and for which I was a candidate.

Ultimately, after a seemingly longer period of uncertainty I did my Ph.D. from the University of Calcutta, when I was finally granted leave on UGC's F.I.P. Programme. My Ph.D. problem was on the Maring Social Structure, which was later published in 1988 in the form of a book with the title, *Tribal Social Structure: A Study of the Maring Society of Manipur*. Before that, in 1985, my first book bearing the title *Manipur Tribal Scene* came out as a collection of research papers based on studies undertaken by me in different periods of time. My association with Manipur, which has later been extended to some other areas of north-east India, is still continuing in some form even after I had left Manipur to take up an assignment in the Department of Anthropology of Vidyasagar University in 1987. Interest in north-east India has touched upon issues like tribes and their transformation, ethnicity and ethnic identity, culture and communication, pluralism and inter-community relations, politics and populism. In the books *North-east India in Perspective* (jointly edited with Debashis Basu in 2005) and *Tribalism and Beyond* (2004) I have made an attempt to examine some of these issues on the basis of my initial understanding. Later, I have tried to deal with these issues in one form or the other in some of my contributions to different edited volumes.

My tenure in Vidyasagar University is no less fruitful, may not be to the extent north-east India has brought me closer to the domain of anthropology. But then there may not be any fixed domain of anthropology which remains true for all situations one could think of. Studies undertaken by me in West Bengal, though on a limited scale, are at least a confirmation to this. These clearly suggest that anthropologist's mental orientation in a situation he or she is placed in at a particular period of time plays a key role in the process of selection of interest areas and his or her subsequent involvement with those. As far as I am concerned, probably I could not develop enough interest or mental courage to take up certain problem areas deep down from their genesis and trajectories they followed with the progress of time. Seen from a larger socio-political perspective or fast changing human interface, they could provide an ideal ground for anthropologists to delve into diverse manifestations of human possibilities, fallibilities and failures, many of which were self-imposed or self-created and politically dictated. My present assignment as the editor of the *Journal of Indian Anthropological Society* has given me the opportunity to acquaint myself with such questions of contemporary significance.

The Meaning of Anthropology

The initial impression one gets about anthropology is that it works with fixed stereotypic notions—race type, tribe, ethnic group, culture, small-scale society and the like. I had also carried the same impression and thought that anthropological methods were not particularly suitable for studying change. How wrong I was! True, at the beginning no particular method was separately developed to study the change phenomenon because change was considered ingrained in the society. With time, ideas changed, new concepts developed and along with these, anthropology's orientation also took new directions. New methods were called for as anthropology's own problems or problems challenging the stereotypic notions nurtured by it so long started emerging during the later half of the twentieth century. Of late, the process has gathered momentum and there have been developments in the field of anthropology that are more innovative than accidental. Now, there has been a noticeable shift from "individual self as a sociocultural construction" to "individual creating a sociocultural space" to be shared with others more as a purposive course of action or programme.

Apart from theoretical innovations and reorientations, special emphasis is now given on developing concepts for applied and developmental anthropology, cultural change and reinterpretation and, above all, for the uses of anthropology to other disciplines and areas which used to be considered lying outside the purview of anthropology. In a fluid and flexible situation which marks the contemporary world, tracking group relations or social relations from the level of community to that of the nation demands change in perspectives as well. Political variables now operate with greater effect, making it imperative for anthropologists to turn their attention on these for the sake of gaining contemporary relevance. In such a situation, any attempt to combine the basic holistic and integrative perspective of anthropology with a political economic perspective may appear to be a challenging task. Eric Wolf's (1999) exploration of the modes of power including "tactical" and "structural" power was a step in that direction. His lifelong search for explanations of asymmetrical power functional in the social field represented by tribes, peasants in the context of expanding global forces of power has encouraged many others to concentrate on this area of study. The operation of political variables and the way they interfere with the functioning of culture and enter into conflicting relations with the latter have also drawn me to this field of inquiry. Some of my papers have tried to examine this question at the specific contextual level. Wolf's expectations from contemporary anthropologists were, however, not limited to studies of individual societies and cultures. On the basis of my limited exposure, I cannot reach the stage when I shall be able to commit myself to the writing, in Wolf's language, of:

> "a critical and comprehensive history of the modern world which we spell out the processes of power which created the present-day cultural systems and the linkages between them. ..."

But I can at least draw the attention of anthropologists of today to this vast and exciting field of study—a "task" which demands all seriousness of purpose and a spirit of teamwork. As Wolf believed, a study of this magnitude would provide anthropologists "the intellectual grid needed to order the massive data" produced by them so far on individual societies and cultures. On the other side, though such a study is long overdue, the feasibility of undertaking a project of such a magnitude in the present situation may be questioned on the ground that it will involve a multidisciplinary, multidimensional approach that is hard to formulate at this stage.

For obvious reasons north-east India has occupied an important place in my understanding of communities in the form of tribe and tribe like formations. How do I look at them?

> "Basically, communities in north-east India are territorially organized and that's why, a territorial approach is thought to be appropriate to analyse them in the changing context. Territory denotes a physical space delimited by borders and often governed by a sub-national territorial authority. From another consideration, every territory these days has its stakes in a globalized system. It can no longer function as a self-contained system. Consequently, a community's representation is not confined to the atomistic social structure, which displays a type of "traditionalism" rooted to the site of one's birth. Actually, the social nature of such a community creates a feeling of

> liberalism strictly confined within the members of a territorially bounded community, if not in letters but in spirit."

It does not require intensive probe to say that communities are no longer self-regulated and the feeling of liberalism transcends the limits of a community's physical boundary. Increasing inter-community communication cutting across territorially grounded communities has placed them in a relational framework and day by day this framework is getting enlarged creating a plural situation marked by cooperation and conflict. Community orientation is also considerably influenced by local elitist moves and directions provided by them. One difference between elites and the common people lies in the fact that the elites could move much faster than others from one domain to the other, easily transcending the limits posed by unitary tribal form of existence and entering into a multi-ethnic context. In the process they find acceptance at the national level, which gets strengthened by their increasing global link. Yet, they are the ones fighting for ethnic unity, who provide leadership or mobilise people in that direction.

There may be differences of opinion about what exactly constitutes a multi-ethnic context, but at least on one point we may all agree that it involves pluralism in the sense that different groups in a specific context, separated on the basis of their sociocultural institutions, have been trying hard to come to terms with the type of political incorporation they have now been subjected to. One criticism against community is that it tends to silence the voices of most marginalised groups (Weil 2005). The question of domination and control linked with power is involved with it. Apparently, the instigation in this case comes from outside, from the state and other agencies of power. Anthropological knowledge, though radically particularistic, is full of ethnographic insights into social relations gaining intimate access to political arena with the aid of cultural support system. Focus is not only on the power processes controlled by the state but also on the community-linked cultural activities working behind the political representation of various social formations from time to time. At the applied level, when community spirit and organizational strength are used to enhance community development, the results are found to be quite encourageing. In Malaysia and some other Southeast Asian countries experiments with communities functioning like cooperatives and service providers have produced positive results. This is the impression I could get from Datuk Dr Denison Jayasoorja, who was connected with University Kesangsaan Malaysia and Binary University of Kuala Lumpur, with whom I had the opportunity to associate myself to get first-hand knowledge about some of the programmes in practise. Of course, from policy perspective there has been a shift from community-based public policy towards a national focus enabling government to actively participate in and contribute to the success of community-based action programmes. My experience of working with a few NGOs in West Bengal has given me the opportunity to derive some insight into the mode of functioning of community based development initiatives undertaken by the respective NGOs. The impression I could get is we are yet to reach the stage when state, corporate houses and NGOs representing the community or communities work together in unison for a common purpose and in a spirit of partnership. May be we are too diverse to work out a strategy for a common goal.

I was inclined to believe that anthropology's scientific credential to a large extent depended on physical or biological anthropology. This could be attributed to the fact that I had physical anthropology specialization at the M.Sc. level and was fortunate to have Dr S.S. Sarkar as my teacher who was largely responsible for giving a new dimension to the application of biology in anthropology. Much later when I had the opportunity to function as the editor-in-chief of the *Vidyasagar University Journal of Biological Sciences* for a couple of years, I could understand that there was scope for inter-disciplinary studies on problems of common concern where different biological sciences could come together and where anthropology could also be an important partner. At present the bio-cultural approach has been given prominence in anthropology, which is more in conformity with the known anthropological tradition of maintaining an integrated character of the discipline. I have tried to make some stray attempts to examine its use in health, demography, ecology and food. Health is one of the strongest areas of bio-cultural anthropology and cultural representation of the human body, time, life, death, illness, sickness and disease in the context of physical and mental health is now an accepted course of action. Recently, my "Commentary" on Shalina Mehta's article "Contested Domain of Biological Similarities and Sociocultural Diversity" published in the special issue of *Journal of Biosciences,* volume 44, July 2019, Indian Academy of Sciences, Bengaluru, has evoked enthusiastic responses from a number of important Bio-Scientific Institutes of the USA. and leading international journals devoted to bio-scientific research. This in no way means that I could qualify myself as a bio-scientist, but the overwhelming response speaks volume about the relevance of anthropological viewpoint. My publication was recently indexed in the Web of Science Core Collection (as informed by the Web of Science Group). I have reasons to believe that any innovative research conducted by anthropologists will get due recognition. There is no substitute to serious innovative research and it is also my conviction that there is no dearth of anthropologists in India who are capable of making their mark in their respective fields. Till now, there are glimpses of it.

My Books

1984: *Manipur Tribal Scene*. New Delhi: Inter-India Publications.

1987: *Tribal Social Structure: A Study of the Maring Society of Manipur*. New Delhi: Inter-India Publications.

Rajat Kanti Das & Abhijit Guha (eds.). *Discourses on Development: Anthropological Dimension*. Medinipur: Vidyasagar University.

2004: *Tribalism and Beyond*. Kolkata: Punthi Pustak.

2005: *Development From Tribal Perspective*. Kolkata: Classique Books.

2005: Rajat Kanti Das & Debashis Basu (eds.). *North-east India in Perspective*. New Delhi: Akansha Publishing House.
Rajat Kanti Das, Arabinda Basu and Abhijit Guha (eds.). *Perspectives of Rural Development: Problems and Prospects*. Indian Anthropological Society, Kolkata and Vidyasagar University, Midnapore.

2007: Rajat Kanti Das and Ajit K. Danda (eds.). *Anthropology of Management*. Jhargram: INCAA.

2012: Rajat Kanti Das and Dipak K. Midya (eds.). *Many Faces of Development*. Jhargram: INCAA.
Ajit K. Danda and Rajat K. Das (eds.). *Alternative Voices of Anthropology: Golden Jubilee Symposium*. Kolkata: Indian Anthropological Society.

2017: Bidhan Kanti Das and Rajat Kanti Das (eds.). *Rethinking Tribe in Indian Context*. Jaipur: Rawat Publications.

2023: Subir Biswas, Barun Mukhopadhyay and Rajat Kanti Das (eds.). *Writings on Indian Anthropology and Anthropologists*. New Delhi: Concept Publishing Company (Pvt.) Ltd.

2023: *A Profile of Social-Cultural Anthropology*. New Delhi: Kalpaz Publications.

4

My Autobiography

S.B. Chakraborty

A 5 year old boy had no knowledge of a historical turning point of a subjugated nation reeling under 200 years British Colonial Rule. The event was the Independence of India along with the painful Partition of the country in August 1947. Looking back at the age of 80 now, I can realize what a permanent impact it has made in the life of the people belonging to both the countries i.e., India and Pakistan. When we migrated to Calcutta (now Kolkata) in India from Dhaka in the then East Pakistan (now Bangladesh) sometimes in the year 1950, we had no shelter of our own. After initial stay over with the relatives here and there we got temporarily settled in a rented house in a mofussil town called Naihati in the district of 24-Parganas (now the North 24-Parganas in West Bengal).

Since I had no primary schooling due to these disturbances, my father who was a retired headmaster in Dhaka took me to a mofussil town school located in the vicinity of a traditional Sanskrit pundits, known as Bhatpara i.e., Bhattacharya neighbourhood. After some question-answers, the headmaster of that school decided to admit me in class VI, but my father somehow felt that I should begin from class V. It was 1953. As a result, I had lost two years in the beginning. In the next year i.e., in 1954, we got a permanent shelter in another neighbourhood of the same district, Habra-Asoknagar, where the Government of West Bengal arranged for some built houses constructed under the Refugee Rehabilitation Scheme with small two room accommodation for the migrant refugee families. I obtained my Higher Secondary Degree (this was the first batch of a newly introduced class-11 course) in 1960. I completed my graduation in three years degree course (first introduced at the college level) without any facility of honours classes. I had in my combination Botany, Zoology and Anthropology. After obtaining B.Sc. degree in 1963, unfortunately, I did not get a seat in postgraduate class immediately. I had to wait for another year for my admission in M.Sc. course in University of Calcutta. This means I had altogether lost three years in my academic life. Of course, I was appointed as a teacher in a reputed Higher Secondary School during that time. I obtained M.Sc. degree in Anthropology, with specialization in cultural anthropology in 1966.

Having completed my postgraduation, I got a Research Fellowship in Anthropological Survey of India, Government of India, in 1967. I started my research work under Professor Surajit Chandra Sinha, who was then the Deputy Director of the Survey and was already known in the world as an eminent anthropologist. I started my research work on Indigenous Social Stratification in Rural and Urban India, which was generally known as 'Bhadralok', 'Chotolok' and 'Madhyabitta'. It cannot perhaps be exactly translated into English, but the nearest equivalent of them would be gentry, peasantry of the lowest rung and the middle class. Due to some reasons, I left that fellowship after about a year and a half and chose to serve in a village Higher Secondary School in the same district of 24-Parganas, far away from the city of Kolkata. The school was very unique in a rural milieu, established in a village which was already well connected by road to the nearest urban centers, having the facility of electricity and primarily inhabited by a dominant social group i.e., Kayastha. This multi-caste village was also encircled by some Muslim dominated villages. I worked there for nearly two years against a temporary vacancy of a biology teacher. Interestingly, I was allowed to take classes in English in the higher classes. It could happen due to the intervention of the head Clerk of that school who was virtually all in all in the decision-making process from disbursement of salaries to the selection of the teachers. He himself was matriculate of the olden days and was very proficient in English. This particular phase opened before me a distinct fact of life. We were taught English in our High School by our headmaster who was an ordinary graduate in those days. He was not even having a Teachers' Training Degree.

My study in a school for refugees had exposed me to a group of teachers including my headmaster who taught us the respective subjects in such a way that it got permanently imprinted in my memory. I realized its benefit while passing through all the other phases in my academic life. I had returned to the Anthropological Survey of India again in 1971 after two years in a permanent post which was the Senior Technical Assistant in the division of Cultural Anthropology of the Survey.

This time I started with a fresh project for my Ph.D. degree under Professor S.C. Sinha. The project was Social and Cultural Context of Agriculture in a village of West Bengal. After initial preparation I went for a reconnoitre tour for selecting an area with a village which would be a multi caste village with primary emphasis on agriculture with the exposure of development programmes in agriculture.

Finally, I settled in a village under the district of Burdwan in West Bengal. The area had already undergone the phase of improved cultivation under the Intensive Agricultural District Programme (IADP), initiated by the Government of West Bengal since 1960s. I did my fieldwork by living in that particular village for nearly one year, collecting data on various aspects related to agricultural production, covering the major seasons of summer and winter cultivation. The major fieldwork was complete by the end of 1972 followed by further occasional visits. I had submitted my Ph.D. dissertation much later i.e., 1980 under Professor Ajit K. Danda, Director, Anthropological Survey of India. The Ph.D. degree was awarded to me in 1981 by the University of Calcutta.

I had developed an interest in Economic Anthropology in general and agrarian situation in the country in particular, both in peasant and tribal context, in a traditional sense of the terms. My particular focus of attention had been to study the "culture of agriculture" in the main. Apart from my in-depth study in a village of West Bengal, I had also done some fieldwork in certain areas of south India, north-east India and Andaman Islands. In addition to my engagement broadly with village studies, I got also involved with the studies on urban anthropology in a small way.

I worked in Anthropological Survey of India for about 33 years and retired from there as Deputy Director in January 2003. Apart from Head Office in Kolkata, I also served in the Regional Centres of the Survey, such as in Southern Regional Centre, Mysore; North-East Regional Centre, Shillong; Eastern Regional Centre, Kolkata and Andaman and Nicobar Regional Centre, Port Blair. I also attended academic programmes in other regional centres of the survey, such as North-Western Regional Centre, Dehra Dun; Western Regional Centre, Udaipur and Central Regional Centre, Nagpur. In addition to my normal assignments as a researcher, I also performed my administrative duties as Head at Head Office, Eastern Regional Centre, Kolkata and Andaman and Nicobar Regional Centre, in Port Blair. I looked after the publications of the survey for some years and was the joint managing editor of its home journal *Human Science*. I was also engaged for a brief spell with a few visiting faculty-positions in Arunachal University (2003), Vidyasagar University, West Bengal (2004) and Lal Bahadur Shastri National Institute of Administration, Mussoorie, Dehra Dun (1994). At present I am associated with the Asiatic Society, Kolkata (an institution of national importance by an Act of parliament which was founded by Sir William Jones in 1784). After Dr B.S. Guha (who was general secretary during 1939-42) I am the second anthropologist to be elected as the general secretary for the last three terms since 2016 and is continuing till now for the fourth term of two years. I have to discharge primarily the academic and administrative duties in the Society. This apart, I also hold the position of President, Kolkata Society for Asian Studies, Kolkata and an actively involved in the Council/Editorial Board at the Institute of North-East India Studies, Shillong, Indian Science News Association, Kolkata and a few others.

This academic sketch of mine perhaps will remain incomplete if I do not relate my personal inclination while pursuing my academic researches throughout. Before I entered into the discipline of anthropology at the graduate level, I got fascinated in the political ideology of dialectical materialism which seeks explanation of every social formation and transformation in a historical context. My formal training in anthropology, especially in its fieldwork tradition, added one direct link of coming close and knowing the people *in situ* based on structure-functional approach. This helped me a lot in understanding the human interactions and their intricate networks. At the end of the day, it is my firm conviction that anthropology as academic discipline stands out, comparatively speaking, as the most dependable of all so far the data base of a micro situation is concerned. This ultimately helps one, by and large, to generalize a macro situation.

My Books

1986: *Around the Plough*, Calcutta: Anthropological Survey of India.

1984: S.B. Chakraborty, B.R. Ghosh and Ajit K. Danda. *Agrarian Situation in India*, vol. I. Calcutta: Anthropological Survey of India.

1985: *Agrarian Situation in India*, vol. II. Calcutta: Anthropological Survey of India.

2002: S.B. Chakraborty, A.K. Singh, S.R. Das, G. Bera, P.K. Guha. *A Town in the Rural Millieu*, Kolkata, Anthropological Survey of India.

2002: *Tribal India: Agrarian Systems and Agrarian Laws*, Kolkata: Anthropological Survey of India.

5

From Dalei-sahi, Dongran-Kuan to Deutschland

The Personal Account of the Journey of an Anthropologist

Prasanna Kumar Nayak

Born in 1951 in Barihapur, a village in the district of Dhenkanal (a former feudatory state) in Odisha, and brought up in a large joint family, memories of my early childhood, my schooling, and of how I moved away from my village to acquire higher education come crowding into my head. It has been a long journey. And for all this the credit goes to my Dalei family, to my teachers who imparted quality education to me, to my field research visits to the Dongran-Kuan or Dongaria Kondh, one of the so-called PVTG tribes of Odisha, and finally to Germany, which also became my "fatherland". Of all the personal experiences acquired throughout my passage through life, what I valued the most was the "human love" that has immeasurably enriched my life and career.

My village was known as the largest in the sub-region, with close to 10,000 inhabitants divided into as many as twenty-four *jatis* or endogamous sociocultural groups bearing names based on their different traditional occupations, which they had carried on for generations. Fifteen of them had their dwellings contiguously in four core village *sahi*s (wards) alongside three main streets, while the other nine were distributed in four directions in six village *sahi*s on the outskirts of the village, each keeping its spatial and social distance from the others. In their day-to-day interactions, the social distance between them was minimal. Of all the *jati*s, the *chasa*s or farmers were a majority; this was the community my family belonged to. Interestingly, there was not a single Brahman family in the village. The *nahak*s or astrologers played important roles at birth, puberty, marriage and death rituals. The *barika* or barbers and the *dhoba* or washermen rendered significant services on all these ritual occasions. By occupation, the *mali* was the real priest, who performed worship at all the village shrines and temples.

Ritual kinship among different *jati*s was very lively. People, irrespective of their *jati* identity, used kinship terms to address and refer to one another. Adopting someone as a ritual brother or sister was part of social practice. For example, my mother once adopted a Pana as her brother, and ties of ritual kinship between the two families were strong. I used to address him as *mamu*, mother's brother, and he used to address me as *bhanaja*, sister's son. Among all kinship relationships, that between *mamu* and *bhanaja* was highly valued. The term *sahi-bhai* referred to brotherly cordiality between families dwelling in a *sahi* or village ward. Each *sahi* had a specific place for the *sahi* council or *chaupadi*, where the heads of the families sat together under the leadership of the *sahi-mukhia* to discuss and decide on day-to-day social, cultural and ritual matters and resolve family disputes.

My parental family was treated with respect. People in the sub-region knew it as a Dalei family. The title Dalei was bestowed on my grandfather's grandfather by the King of Dhenkanal in recognition of his role in getting a dam called Magarmuhana constructed, which saved vast tracts of low-lying paddy fields from flooding and provided irrigation facilities during drought. People remember him for the sacrifices he cheerfully underwent for getting the dam built.

I am grateful that I was brought up in such a family, and growing up in such a family has shaped my life and world view.

Two of my grandfathers and their children and grandchildren belonging to three generations lived together (thirty-six of them until 1968) at the eastern end of the village. The homestead land of 7 ha consisted of residential dwellings, large courtyards, a massive separate storehouse, gardens, a private family pond, a well, an open space for storing harvested paddy and thrashing unhusked grains, a long barrack house for the visiting Mahima monks and a cowshed for more than fifty cows on its easternmost boundary. The family also owned large fertile paddy fields and a big pond, the Dalei Bandha, which the villagers also used. Half a kilometre beyond our house, stood mango groves and palm trees, in addition to native varieties of fruit-bearing trees and beyond that stretched the village forest.

In keeping with the family's status and tradition, over the last several generations my family used to have marriage ties only with village headmen's families in the sub-region. After the death of my father's great grandfather, my father dropped out of high school and returned to the village to look after the landed property. The family harvested a lot of grain but was short on hard cash. Although my mother did not study in a school, she was privately taught by the family priest in her parental house. She was instrumental in many ways in financing the higher education of all her children by putting pressure on my father to sell huge quantities of paddy every month. In the entire village, my elder brother was the first person to acquire a graduate degree, and I myself was the first postgraduate. Following the ideals of the Dalei family and observing my mother's desire for education, other well-to-do families of the village were motivated to send their children to schools.

Seven children, five brothers and two sisters, were born to our parents; I was the fifth child. A few weeks before I was born, the third child, the second son of my parents, who was only four years old, died of smallpox. People thought that somebody's evil eye had fallen on him. Subsequently, when I was born, everyone thought that I resembled my deceased brother, so my mother was advised not to expose me to any outsider. Thus, I was never taken off the family premises. I was allowed to attend pre-primary school (one-year *shisu,* pre-primary class) only when I was four and half years old.

My grandfather was a devoted follower of Mahima Dharma and decided to live a little away from the family house, built a *tungi* and started spending all his time there like a monk. Very close to his *tungi* he built a barrack to put up Mahima monks when they visited our house. Of all the grandchildren, my grandfather selected me to sleep with him on the cot till I was seven and half years' old.

I completed my third year in the school and was sent to a residential school to spend the nights there. Here I did my homework and assisted teachers with cooking by cutting vegetables, lighting the *chulha* and washing utensils and cleaning the rooms. My friends and I massaged the limbs of our teachers.

After completing my studies at my village school in 1962, I had to move out of my village to pursue Middle English school in a nearby small town and was put up there in the students' hostel. After two years I came out first in the final examination.

In 1964, I went to a distant town, Kamakhyanagar, and continued my high-school education there, and lived in a hostel. As communication facilities were not good, my father took me there in a bullock cart along forest roads frequented by bears and tigers. I saw a bus for the first time in my life in 1967. I loved all my teachers, and they loved me too. To appear at the final-year high-school examination, all 96 students of my batch travelled to Dhenkanal, the district headquarters, by crossing river Brahmani by boat. The evening after the examinations were over, for the first time in my life, I went to a cinema hall having a thatched roof to watch a Hindi movie with some of my classmates.

As I was interested in studying sciences, my eldest brother wanted to get me admitted to the famous Ravenshaw College, Cuttack. I saw a train for the first time when I travelled to Cuttack. But, to avoid delay, my brother decided to enrol me at Angul College.

I attended lectures on physics, chemistry, mathematics, zoology and botany. All the teachers were good. After passing intermediate science I went to Puri and enrolled myself in the SCS college, where I did B.Sc. In the final examination I passed with distinction. Then I went to Utkal University to apply for admission in the M.Sc. in Botany course. While taking dinner, the brother of my classmate suggested that we do M.A. in Anthropology. This was the first time I heard the term "anthropology". He told us that it was a subject which studies both the biological and sociocultural aspects of humans. I felt keen to study the subject. The next day, I applied for anthropology, came first in the interview and was admitted to anthropology.

I attended classes regularly. After two months, I approached the Head of the Department and requested her to let me spend evenings in the department reading books. She allowed me to borrow 150 selected books from the department library. I spent many nights there reading and writing.

Four months before the results of the M.A. exams were declared, I joined the then Tribal Research Bureau (TRB), Bhubaneswar, as a research scholar in November 1974, thanks to a special recommendation from Professor L.K. Mahapatra, the then Head of the Department of Anthropology. I was assigned the task of undertaking fieldwork among the Bonda and the Dongaria Kondh, two hill tribes of Odisha, and to prepare ethnographic reports by conducting socio-economic surveys. The first draft of the monograph on the Dongaria Kondh prepared by me was later published by TRB. In August 1975, I joined the Department of Anthropology, Utkal University, as a research assistant and began taking regular classes besides assisting the Head of the Department in official matters. After a year, I was appointed a Lecturer in Social Anthropology at Utkal University.

Before reaching the Niamgiri hills, the Dongaria land, in February 1975, I witnessed a Dongaria Kondh congregation for the first time in Chatikona, a rural town in the foothills. The Shivaratri festival was being celebrated there. On the festival ground I saw the

Dongaria merrymaking, singing and dancing in separate groups. To my utter astonishment, all of a sudden, I saw a group fight break out among them, and the festival ground turned into a battlefield. All the celebrations came to an abrupt end. I wanted to investigate the incident, and the very next day I climbed the hills and reached Khambesi, a Dongaria Kondh village where I stayed for five months. Gradually I came to know about the clan feuds among the Dongaria Kondh. This prompted me to focus on clan feuds for my doctoral research. R.K. Merton labels this a "serendipity pattern of research".

In December 1981, I was awarded a UGC fellowship to undertake doctoral research under the guidance of Professor L.K. Mahapatra, an eminent anthropologist. With the permission of the village headman, I had my own house constructed at the end of one row of Dongaria houses and put up there. I learnt their language (Kui) and carried out intensive fieldwork for one and a half years. In subsequent years, I utilized vacations and holidays to make field visits to as many as eighteen Dongaria Kondh villages. I received my doctoral degree for my thesis, entitled *Structure and Function of Clan Feud among the Dongaria Kondh*, in 1985. In the same year, I became a Reader in Social Anthropology at Utkal University.

In 1987, I won Alexander von Humboldt (AvH) Fellowship to carry out post-doctoral research in the Free University of Berlin for two years. In 1990, I became a Professor of Anthropology at Utkal University at the young age of 38. Between 1976 and 2011, I received many awards and held key administrative positions. I retired in 2011.

I admire all the teachers who taught me. As a student I was a favourite of all my teachers. Everybody knew how close I was to L.K. Mahapatra, N.K. Behura and B.K. Behera, my revered mentors. My personal interaction with Professor F.G. Bailey inspired me to concentrate on case studies of feuds and make institutional analysis of them. Professor Mario D. Zamora, University of Virginia, was the external examiner for my Ph.D. thesis. He wrote the foreword to my book *Blood, Women and Territory* and invited me to contribute an article to his edited volume *The Anthropology of Peace* in honour of E. Adamson Hoebel.

I was passionate and sincere in teaching, preparing class notes and distributing copies to students to come prepared for the next classes. Despite being a social anthropologist, I believed in the integration of the discipline and so promoted specialization in biological anthropology. Soon after assuming the headship of the department, taking a risk, I convinced my colleagues on the Post-Graduate Council and persuaded the university authorities to reserve eight seats for students of biological sciences in the department to specialize in biological anthropology. I always wanted students of biological anthropology to accompany students of social anthropology during fieldwork, which was not the regular practice in the department previously. Realizing the importance of ethnographic fieldwork, I very often say, "fieldwork is the backbone of anthropology, and field settings are the laboratories for anthropologists". I was instrumental in organizing a celebration of the birth centenary of JBS Haldane and inviting Biju Patnaik, former chief minister of Odisha, to inaugurate the function. It was with Patnaik's blessings and support that the Haldane Chair was founded in the anthropology department. In order to enthuse my colleagues and students, I wrote an article, "Biocultural Anthropology: Limitations of Physico-chemical Research", which was published as an Occasional Paper under the Special Assistance Programme of the Department in 2007.

In order to enhance academic and research collaboration with international scholars, I invited Dr Nick Allen and Dr Robert Parkin from Oxford University, U.K., Professor Burkhard Schnepel from Heidelberg University and Professor Frank Heideman from Munich University, Germany, to the department of Anthropology, Utkal University, as visiting fellows and visiting professors for three months each to deliver lectures. I became a partner in the second phase of the German Odisha project and organized an international seminar in 1998 in which many German and European anthropologists, Indologists and historians participated.

I have published as many as five books and a number of journal articles and have prepared sixteen project reports. In addition,

I have participated in nearly eighteen national and twenty-two international seminars and presented papers there. As a research supervisor, I have guided thirty-seven M.Phil. students and fifteen Ph.D. scholars.

I have intensively studied the Dongaria Kondh, the Gadaba, the Bondo Highlanders, the Koya, the Kolha, the Kutia Kondh, the Ho, the Saors and the Pauri Bhuiyan. I have focused on the study of tribes, their social structure and culture and examined them in historical perspectives, exploring their connections and interactions with the ruling kings and vassal kings in the past. I consider the tribes to be kingly people. I share Evan-Pritchard's view that "they are different but not primitive". I lay my emphasis on emic conceptualizations in social anthropological studies. My research interests included kinship and conflict, the socio-political structure of tribes, the ethnography of tribes, tribal rites, rituals and arts, tribal and rural development, involuntary resettlement and development, and theories and methodology in social anthropology.

I have contributed to the understanding of Indian society, particularly tribal societies and cultures and the anthropology of development, through research articles published in national and international journals, and edited volumes. Most of my early writings, which date back to 1974, focused primarily on tribal economy. For instance, some of my research papers were on gift exchange among the Gadaba. These include "Transformation of Barter to Peasant Economy among the Gadaba of Jeypore", "Market and Money in Contemporary Tribal Economy of Orissa" and "Shifting Cultivation among the Koya Tribes". Later, I wrote extensively on problems of planned tribal development, issues of displacement and rehabilitation, ecology and development, tribal education, tribal art, craft and aesthetics, the role of anthropology in natural calamities, tribal forest economy, and gender and development under the broad theme of the anthropology of development. Some of my papers on this theme that deserve mention are: "Tradition and Development in Tribal Orissa", "Tribal Development: From Sport to Sonata to Science", "Revisiting Tribes and Reconsidering Tribal Development", "New Paradigm of Tribal Development", "Reconsidering Tribal Development in India", "The Rise and Fall of "Tribal" Development in Orissa" and "What Tribal Development is Not!".

I also applied anthropological thought and theories to the social problems and realities of Indian society. In this regard, it is worth mentioning that I wrote some seminal research papers such as "Levi-Strauss's Anthropology: An Appraisal", "Beginning of Anthropological Theory", "Elementary Structure of Beauty and Love", "Appraising Development Anthropology", "Appraising Methodology in Development Anthropology" and "New Role of Home-Country Anthropologists of the Developing World". Besides, some of my scholarly writings, such as "They are Different, but not Primitive", "Inheritance of Kingly Citizenship: Tribals at Cross-Roads in Modern State of Orissa, India", "Kingly Rites in Tribal Religions: Some Reflections from Middle India", and "Owning the King: Ethno-Cultural Politics in Bhuiyan Pirha", help one to understand the dynamics of tribal social institutions and their ramifications.

As the Coordinator of the UGC-sponsored Department of Special Assistance (DSA) programme in anthropology, I was instrumental in bringing out a volume entitled *Human Encounter with Drought*. While this was one of the most important anthropological publications on a development-related theme, it was the first of its kind on urgent anthropological issues. Being the editor of the volume, in my introductory article, "Anthropology and Natural Calamities", I spelt out anthropological perspectives and approaches to the study of calamities and stressed the need for a holistic understanding of the problems of the affected communities. Examining the situation of drought in Kalahandi, I suggested that disasters like drought could be overcome by analysing the sociocultural and institutional matrices of the people and putting them in practise while keeping the peoples" agenda in view.

My acclaimed book, *Blood, Women and Territory* (1989), offers an insight into clan feuds among the Dongaria Kondh of Odisha. It looks carefully at various definitions, approaches and explanations of feud delineates inter-clan and intra-clan feuds using extended case studies, and compares these two types of feud. I analysed feud as a culturally derived form of societal conflict in relation to the economic, political, kinship and magico-religious domains. I discussed the trends of transformation in this feuding society. The book is of immense interest to anthropologists, ethnologists, political scientists, social philosophers, development sociologists and social workers. Besides, I edited a book on *Tribes of Orissa* (1995) and presented brief sketches of all the sixty-two tribes of Odisha. My ILO-INDISCO study was published by the ILO and Ministry of Tribal Affairs under the title *From Bondage to Rural Enterprise: A Situational Analysis and Participatory Strategies with the Bondo Highlanders* (2005).

I was awarded the AvH Fellowship to pursue post-doctoral research. I also had an opportunity under the Europe Fellowship programme of the AvH-Stiftung to do research on the anthropology of development at the Institute of Social and Cultural Anthropology, Oxford University, the London School of Economics and the School of Oriental and African Studies, University of London, and the Institute of Development Studies, University of Sussex. In 1997 I received the Baden-Wuertemberg Fellowship, Germany, to participate in the teaching and research programme of the South Asia Institute at the University of Heidelberg. There, as visiting professor, I taught a full semester course on "Tribes and Castes in India today". In 2012, I was awarded the Indian Council of Cultural Relations (ICCR) Visiting Professorship to visit the Institute of South Asian-Tibetan and Buddhist Studies, University of Vienna, Austria, where I delivered lectures on "Scheduled Tribes in India: Changing Perspectives" and led semester seminars on "Marginalization, Maoism and the State in Central India".

I had the privilege of becoming expert member (Steering Committee, Consultative Committee, Working Group and Sub-Group committees on ST & SC Development, Revamping TRIs), Ministry of Tribal Affairs and Planning Commission (NITI Aayog),

Government of India, New Delhi (from 2000 to 2008 and from 2011-18); subject expert member, UPSC Selection Committees, Government of India since 2009; UGC subject expert to review the progress of work of Research Scientists, UGC Special Assistance Programs (SAP) since 1990; Member, Court, Central University Ranchi, Jharkhand (2010-15); Chairman of all Academic and Research Committees (Anthropology), Utkal University (from 1995 to 2009); expert member, cultural policy, Government of Orissa, 2003; Member, Advisory Committee, DSA/DRS, Department of Anthropology, Andhra University (2007-10) and Department of Anthropology, Central University of Hyderabad (2018-continuing).

I have visited many European institutes and delivered lectures on core anthropological topics. I worked on "Kinship and Clanship in Tribal Orissa : An Empirico-Theoretical Analysis" at the Institute of Ethnologie, Free University of Berlin. Prior to this, I attended a four-month German Language Course at the Goethe Institute, Berlin, which was sponsored by the AvH-Stiftung, Germany. As a visiting fellow of Wolfson College, Oxford, I attended the seminar lectures and guest lectures at the Institute of Social Anthropology and participated in the discussions held at the Centre for Asian and African Development Studies, Queen Elizabeth House, Oxford. I attended a three-week orientation course on "Rapid Rural Development Strategies and Methods" at the Institute of Development Studies (IDS), University of Sussex, commissioned by Professor Dr Robert Chambers. Under the Revisit Programme of the Alexander von Humboldt Foundation I was invited to the Institute of Ethnologie, Free University of Berlin, for five months in 1994, taught a semester course jointly with Professor G. Pfeffer, and conducted higher level researches on "Comparative Kinship". I was invited to the Department of Ethnology, South Asia Institute, University of Heidelberg, Germany in 1994 as a visiting fellow. I visited the Institute of Social Anthropology, University of Oslo, Norway, and Institute of Social Anthropology, University of Toulouse, France, in the same year. I was a visiting fellow at the

Department of Ethnology, South Asia Institute, Heidelberg, in 1998 and worked jointly with Professor Dr Burkard Schnepel. I was invited to the Department of Indology, University of Potenza, Italy, as Visiting Professor in October 1998 and delivered eighteen special lectures in collaboration with Professor Fabio Scialpi on the theme, "Indian society, economy, culture and politics: Challenges of the 21st Century". I was invited to the famous Institute of African and Oriental Studies, University of Rome, and delivered a guest lecture on "Women in Modern India" on 15 October 1998. I lectured at the Institute of Historical Anthropology, University of Frankfurt, in 2000 for six weeks. I spent another six weeks there in 2001. I was visiting professor at the Institute of South Asian and African Anthropology, University of Halle, Germany in 2003 for six weeks, 2005 for four weeks and in 2008 for four weeks. As Visiting Professor, I visited the South Asia Institute, Heidelberg (August-September 2009) and (September-October 2011). As visiting professor with an award from the ICCR I visited the Institute of South Asian-Tibetan and Buddhist Studies, University of Vienna, for a period of one Semester (September 2012-February 2013):

(i) delivered lectures on "Culture History: STs in India: Changing Perspectives" to twenty-eight graduate and postgraduate students,
(ii) organized and conducted seminars on "Regional History: Marginalization, Maoism and State in Central India" in which nine students participated regularly and evaluated their semester examination papers,
(iii) delivered two public lectures and
(iv) attended three guest lectures, a one-day workshop on Tibetan studies and a cultural programme organized by students of the Institute.

From 7 December 2012, as guest lecturer, I visited the Institute of Religion, Culture and Modernity, University of Lausanne, and Frobenius Institute of Ethnologie, University of Frankfurt, during the second week of December 2012 to deliver special lectures. In 2017, I taught a semester course on "Indian Anthropological Studies" at the Froebenius Institute, Goethe University, Frankfurt.

My administrative acumen impressed the state government, and in 2000 I was appointed the Director of the Scheduled Caste and Scheduled Tribe Research and Training Institute (SCSTRTI), Bhubaneswar. My notable achievements as its Director include the establishment of an ethnographic tribal museum, the first of its kind. I initiated the construction of a new library building and the conference hall. The innovative research and training activities of SCSTRTI, Bhubaneswar, were warmly appreciated by the Government of India and created avenues for regular flows of funds for its further development. Accordingly, it emerged as one of the most highly reputed and attractive tribal research institutes in India.

In addition, I also served as Head of the Department of Anthropology for two terms, Coordinator of the UGC-sponsored Assistance for Infrastructural Development of Humanities and Social Sciences (AIHSS) Programme in Anthropology, Coordinator of the UGC-sponsored Centre for Advanced Study (CAS) Programme in Anthropology, Syndicate Member of Utkal University and Dean of Faculty of Sciences. I deserve credit for my efforts to make the Anthropology Department of Utkal University a Centre for Advanced Study, the only Department in India to be accorded this status by the UGC.

My research collaborations with foreign universities such as Berlin, Frankfurt, Heidelberg, Halle, Munich, Bonn, Oslo, Paris, Rome, Oxford, London, Manchester, Leiden, Seoul and Lausanne have strengthened my credentials as an anthropologist. I was Member, Steering Committee and Field Director of the German-Orissa Research Project Orissa Revisited, which was sponsored by German Research Council (DFG) from 1999 to 2006. I was also Member, Steering Committee of the Excellence Cluster Project on Citizenship as a conceptual flow carried out by the South Asia Institute, University of Heidelberg, from 2007 to 2010. I also served as Member, Task Force on Resettlement and Development, Washington DC between 1992 and 1995.

After retirement, I assumed the office of the Chairman of the Nabakrushna Chaudhury Centre for Development Studies (NCDS), Bhubaneswar, and the ICSSR institute from 2012 to 2015. Currently, I am heading a registered trust, the Lavanya Institute of Indian Studies (LIIS), founded by me in the name of my mother Lavanya, and based in my residential premises. As Chairman of the Trust, I focus on organizing lectures on various topics of anthropological and Indological interest by inviting distinguished scholars from India and abroad. I find pleasure in inviting my intimate friends, scholars and students to participate in such academic deliberations. Under my tutelage, in 2022 LISS in association with Sikshasandhan has brought out two books, *When Humans Study Humans: Classic Themes in Social and Cultural Anthropology* and *Conceptualizing India's Tribes: Papers on Identity, Kinship and General Ethnography* written by Robert Parkin, my dear friend and colleague of many years standing.

To conclude, my life encompasses a humble beginning, support of my family, educational pursuits, passion for anthropological exploration and administrative responsibilities. My academic achievements have of course given me pride; but, more importantly, they reflect my commitment to foster knowledge and understanding among the young, who shape the future.

My Books

1989: *Blood, Women and Territory*. New Delhi: Reliance Publishers.

1991: P. K. Nayak & Anil Mahajan (eds). *Human Encounter with Drought*. New Delhi: Reliance Publishers.

1995: P.K. Nayak *et al.* (eds.). *Population Profile of Orissa*. Orissa Association PD, Bhubaneswar.

2003: *Tribes of Orissa* (edited self), 2nd edition, SCSTRTI, Government of Orissa.

2003: *From Bondage to Rural Enterprise: A Situational Analysis and Participatory Strategies with the Bondo Highlanders*. New Delhi: ILO Publications.

6

My Journey
Anthropology and Beyond

Barun Mukhopadhyay

I

I was born in October 1954 to a middle-class family in northern part of Howrah (now spelt as Haora) town, a place called "Salkia". Howrah town is located on the western side of the Ganges, on the other side of the city of Calcutta (now Kolkata). My grandfather was a freedom fighter and the Chairman of the then Howrah municipality. After his demise, my uncle (my father's elder brother) took to political profession and became vice-chairman of the said municipality. He died as a seating Congress MLA from North Howrah constituency in 1972. My father, however, was a lawyer, and didn't favour politics as a profession. He was, nevertheless, an ardent follower of Pandit Nehru. My mother was an affectionate housewife. I was socialized during my childhood and early adolescence in a political family and many people used to visit our household to meet my uncle for various reasons, and I had the opportunity to interact with many of them. I from then on could feel the problems of common men and women that need attention by the people's representatives. The whole culture of politics was different, then as I can perceive now. As a younger member of our joint family, I used to receive affection from seniors, in the midst of learning of disciplined behaviour following the cultural values, that the family cherished.

In 1968, owing to some unavoidable reasons, my father's family shifted to Kolkata, and therefore, I had to change my school (of vernacular medium) in Salkia to one in Kolkata. I got admitted in class X. I passed Higher Secondary (school leaving) examination in 1971. This is the time when anyone who wanted to continue education would try getting into a subject, preferably of one's own choice, for graduation. At this juncture of my life, one of my acquaintances elder to me, suggested to try honours course in anthropology which deals with study of human beings. Like many others, with a vague idea, what anthropology is all about, I applied for this honours course in anthropology in University of Calcutta (CU), having two more pass subjects, viz. botany and zoology, since I came from science stream. Following the norm, I got admission to Ashutosh College in South Calcutta, named after Sir Ashutosh Mukherjee, a great educationist and a brilliant mathematician, popularly known as the "Tiger of Bengal" for my pass courses. Sir Ashutosh Mukherjee became Vice-Chancellor of University of Calcutta in 1906 and became instrumental in the establishment of the postgraduate department of anthropology in CU. And I joined the honours course in anthropology, classes of which were held in the Anthropology Department of CU, located in 35, Ballygunge Circular Road, in South Calcutta, known popularly as Ballygunge Science College.

The student life in Ballygunge Science College began in 1971 and ended in 1979 with the publication of results of M.Sc. (with specialization in physical anthropology) examination. Although, normally results of our batch was supposed to be out in 1976, but because of delay in holding M.Sc. examinations for socio-political happenings in the then decade in Calcutta, three precious years were lost. However, students in those years had the opportunity to stay back for a longer period in the university ambience with undoubtedly accumulating experiences, both academic and personal, that I consider enriching for me, as well. One of the greatest opportunities in my student life owing to this delay of passing out was to be able to participate in the 10th International Congress of Anthropological and Ethnological Sciences held in Vigyan Bhavan, New Delhi in 1978 as a final year student. I could see a glimpse of world anthropology at work by participating in the 10th ICAES. A great academic exposure indeed! And of course, there are many sweet and sour memories of our student life. Attending few classes of anthropology made me relaxed and I became confident that the subject suits me and I can enjoy being a student of this eclectic science of man. The journey took many different turns, thereafter. And I am happy till date of being a student of anthropology.

II

Having been passed M.Sc. In 1979, it was my natural choice to continue with an academic career in anthropology. And the priority was to get a fellowship for doing doctoral research. I remain indebted to all my teachers of the Anthropology Department, whose inspiration, affection and skills to make anthropology lively have been my resources for retaining my academic interest. In November 1979 I came across an advertisement from the Anthropometry & Human Genetics Unit (AHGU) of the Indian Statistical Institute, Kolkata for the position of a "Project Assistant" for working in a research project conducted in the then Midnapore district of West Bengal on the Portuguese descendants of Mirpur village. Fortunately, I got selected and joined ISI. The project was undertaken by Professor Amitabha Basu, a very renowned biocultural anthropologist of this country. Certainly, this was a great opportunity for me and I aspired to learn anthropology at ISI with Professor Basu's tutelage. I vividly remember the first day of my work at ISI. I was told by Professor Basu to help Sanat-babu (Mr. Sanat Bhattacharjee) of the Biochemistry Unit in preparation of faeces samples necessary for examining intestinal parasites. This work was of another project of Professor Basu in collaboration with Biochemistry Unit. Thus, I began with work which was not at all in our anthropology training. And I got to know that anthropology is much more than what we have learnt in our M.Sc. curriculum. After passing the postgraduate course, my maiden venture out to a field site was for the collection of demographic data from Mirpur. This is the time when I learnt how to conduct a demographic survey in a community. Professor Basu was too thorough to make his students aware of the necessities of rigor, accuracy and mental involvement in collection of data. And this was a great experience with a very friendly community. After a year and few months, I got an opportunity to join another project of Professor Basu on the Lepchas, an indigenous tribal population of Sikkim-Darjeeling Himalaya as a research scholar (Junior Research Fellow). This project enabled me to begin my doctoral work under the supervision of Professor Basu among the Lepchas of Kalimpong. The project was specifically aimed at examining the effects of sociocultural factors on demographic, dietary and health aspects of the Lepchas, a project under the Human Adaptability Programme (HAP) of the Unit, initiated by Professor Basu. The title of my doctoral thesis was "Bioanthropology and its sociocultural correlates among the Lepchas of Kalimpong subdivision, Darjeeling district, West Bengal". The study intended to examine possible relationships between (a) religion, (b) rural-urban habitat, and (c) socio-economic developmental status, on one hand and dietary, demographic and some health related traits, on the other, in a small-scale situation in a tribal community. A single ethnic group, the Lepchas, believed to be the indigenous to the Sikkim-Darjeeling hills were little known bio-anthropologically then. The fieldwork associated with this doctoral work which continued for three long years (1981-84) in several instalments in several villages of Kalimpong subdivision ranging from the ones very near Kalimpong town to others very remote, far away from the town covering in all 628 households. The field training to begin with and conducting the fieldwork for collection of some type of data all by myself as well as with the help of others for some other types became the necessary steps in becoming a field anthropologist. My fieldwork which gave me opportunity to interact with the community very closely and with much interest to know their cultural and biological/health aspects was a very successful learning. I enjoyed every bit of their association and was successful too to learn their language, a bit. This rigorous field experience was the real test of my love with my discipline in one hand and my love and affection for the community I studied, on the other. I have been keeping contact with some of my Lepcha friends of Kalimpong, till date. After the submission of my Ph.D. thesis in University of Calcutta in 1987, I didn't have to wait much for a job. I got a position in AHGU of ISI as technical personnel. And I continued doing biological anthropological research involving myself in other ongoing projects under HAP. Collection of newer types of data, analyses of the same and writing papers were the usual jobs accomplished, as expected. Thus, my career in academic anthropology took a shape in an institute of repute.

III

I got a faculty position in the same Unit in 1991. I started exploring possibilities of undertaking new projects. In early 1992, I started working among the Lepchas of Sikkim. This project titled Human Biology among the Himalayan Populations, began among the Lepchas, the community I had prior experience of working with, and that also was on sociocultural determinants of health. This project provided the opportunity to examine a comparative health profile of Darjeeling and Sikkim Lepchas. At this juncture, Susmita Mukhopadhyay, my wife and colleague attached to the AHGU, ISI joined me as a collaborator. Till 2008, we worked together with our research scholars in various projects on different communities of Sikkim. Health profile of the Sikkimese Lepchas was evidenced by high prevalence of hypertension. However, on a check for their reporting of this problem in a remote health care sub-centre revealed very low reporting implying failure to identify this public health problem as an important one and thus becomes a public health ethics issue.

After the completion of the project on the Lepchas, I started a project on the effects of lifestyles on the cardiovascular risk factors among the Bhutias of Sikkim. This project was evidence of an epidemiological work of considerable worth in the state where no such data existed before. The results clearly demonstrated the significant effects of lifestyle factors, such as psycho-social stress, among others, on the cardiovascular risk factors, viz. hypertension among the Bhutias. It was also observed that metabolic syndrome was an important health issue in the midst of modernizing socio-economic milieu among this tribal population. I collaborated with Susmita in a study that examined effects of ethnicity on health by comparing two ethnic groups, viz. Bhutia and Rai, having dissimilar genetic ancestry and living in the same locale as well as one that investigated into the biocultural dimensions of reproductive health among the adolescent girls of Sikkim. Our research endeavours in Sikkim of eighteen years gave us enough opportunity to educate ourselves in many dimensions of bio-anthropological research and the experiences gathered could enrich us enormously. In this period, I could engage myself in many different collaborative projects with a multi-disciplinary focus, as well. The major ones are: Effect of *Alu* insertion/deletion, polymorphism at the DCP1 locus on blood pressures and lipid levels among individuals belonging to defined haplogroups drawn from two tribal populations of India; dynamics of primary health care; ethical dimensions of health research; medico-ethnobotanical survey of Sikkim, with special reference to the Dzongu area, North Sikkim; peoples' perception and conservation; people's use of forest resources vis-à-vis impact of forest depletion on livelihood issues of local people in the Sikkim Himalaya, and sociocultural aspects of fermented food consumption. I was fortunate to have my collaboration with the Care Laboratories, Sikkim Government College, G.B. Pant Institute of Himalayan Environment and Development, Department of Health, Government of Sikkim, and the Voluntary

Health Association of Sikkim. And as result of my research in Sikkim, many invited talks on the research findings were given, and many publications occurred.

Since mid-2008, till my retirement in October 2019, I engaged myself in ageing research. Unfortunately, we lost Professor Basu in 2009; he passed away after a brief illness. We miss him till today. I began with a study on the urban living, lifestyle and health among the middle class educated elderly of Kolkata city. The other one investigated the mental health aspects of the urban and rural elderly in Kolkata and Purba Medinipur district of West Bengal, respectively. The outcome was to have two doctoral theses and a few research publications. Furthermore, two other doctoral research studies were done. One on biocultural correlates of frailty among the rural elderly in Howrah district, West Bengal and the other on the health status, health related quality of life and health care practices among the rural elderly of 24-Praganas (North) district, West Bengal. These two projects are based on the UGC research fellowships given to the scholars who are working for these two projects. Overall, if one asks about my specific areas of research involvement and contributions, I would mention the fields of biomedical anthropology, biocultural dimensions of ageing, ethical issues of anthropological research and beyond as well as people and plants relationship.

Fact remains, that I although didn't have the chance to teach postgraduate anthropology students throughout my working life, I did have opportunities for teaching anthropology both at the under-graduate and postgraduate levels in many occasions. At ISI, teaching of basics in anthropology to B.Stat. students was a regular assignment in several years. Apart from that I served as guest teacher in the Departments of Anthropology of Vidyasagar University, and West Bengal State University in some of the past years. Needless to say, attending conferences, workshops, seminars, symposia is generally a regular activity for academic anthropologists. And I was not an exception. I regularly attended national and international conferences. List is too long, and cannot be provided here.

Notable anthropological ones were ICAES meetings in Vancouver, Williamsburg, and Kunming in addition to one in Delhi. Each of these meetings became sources for academic enrichment and sources of further motivation. Attending Annual Conferences of the Indian Anthropological Society and Indian Anthropological Congresses organized by INCAA in one hand and the conferences organized by the several university departments gave me an opportunity to take stock of the extant horizon of academic anthropology in India. Review work for international and national journals was one of my regular jobs, as well. And of course, adjudicating Ph.D. thesis in anthropology has been an enjoyable academic activity, too.

IV

Certainly, getting an opportunity to build an academic institution and to be able to do so is a big thing. And I didn't get that opportunity. However, I tried my best to remain as a disciplined and dedicated worker of ISI and contributed to the best of my ability in the realm of academics and administration. I participated in academic administration of ISI in various capacities. I served as the Professor-in-Charge of the Biological Sciences Division of ISI during a two-year term (18 September 2006-17 September 2008). I had the opportunity also to serve for a duration of six months (October 2017-March 2018) as the Chief Executive (Administration and Finance) of ISI. Furthermore, I served as either the chairman or a member of many administrative and review committees of ISI throughout my serving career.

My efforts have also been quite satisfactory to me when considering my contributions in the nurturing of the oldest professional body of anthropology in India created by the Indian anthropological stalwarts of early 1920s and onwards, called "The Indian Anthropological Society (IAS)". As the General secretary of IAS during 2012-19, with the help and support of our president and other council members, I tried my best to make IAS a visible and vibrant organization. Nevertheless, we know we need to traverse a long way, still.

My association with the Indian National Confederation and Academy of Anthropologists (INCAA) has also been long as a member of its Governing Council, and I have tried my best to justify the position to the best of my abilities. Apart from the two professional anthropological bodies of India, my life-membership of the Indian Statistical Institute, Indian Science Congress Association have provided me opportunities to even have possibilities for education beyond anthropology. Furthermore, my opportunity to work with the Forum for Medical Ethics Society, Mumbai as its member and a member of its managing committee enriched me in the matters of academic ethics having parallel with anthropology as well as supportive to the ethics related activism. My life-membership of the Forum for Ethics Review Committee in India, Mumbai provided me opportunity to witness various conferences that dealt with several dimensions of ethics review process cross-cutting disciplinary boundaries. Needless to say, this endeavour academically enriched me a lot.

Unlike the university quota system, a faculty at ISI cannot have many research fellows at a time. ISI research fellows are based on ISI entrance test and also ISI intra-mural project based. Again, the flow of UGC sponsored fellows intending to work with ISI faculty was not very regular. Throughout my research career, I could find opportunity to supervise till date seven Ph.D. Scholars, singly or jointly. My first Ph.D. student, Dr Sovanjan Sarkar is now a faculty in the Department of Anthropology, Vidyasagar University, West Midnapore. Others, except one, who have been awarded Ph.D. are engaged in different types of jobs in the state or central government and elsewhere. One good thing is that all of them are professionally well placed.

In 1998, after attending the World Congress of Anthropology in Williamsburg, Virginia, USA, I had the opportunity to visit The Department of Anthropology, Ohio State University (OSU), Columbus as an invited guest of Professor Dauglas E. Crews. My purpose of visit to the OSU was to consider making a collaborative research plan with Professor Crews. Our collaborative research plan became successful, when Sharon R. Williams, then a graduate student of Professor Crews got an opportunity to work for her doctoral thesis among the Bhutia women of Sikkim. Her project was a part of a larger ISI funded project investigating effect of modernization on health and well-being of tribal populations in Sikkim. The title of her Ph.D. thesis was "Energy Balance, Health and Fecundity among Bhutia Women of Gangtok, Sikkim, India" which was awarded by OSU in 2003. Dr Williams is now working in an US Science and Technology Policy Institute in Washington, D.C.

In 2016, I attended an international conference on ageing in Atlanta, Georgia, USA. After the conference, I visited the Department of Anthropology, Temple University, Philadelphia, USA as an invited guest of Professor Charles A. Weitz. During the visit, Professor Weitz and I discussed and decided to develop a collaborative project proposal on heat stress in West Bengal and its effects on the elderly life in relation to urban and rural settings. In 2019, Professor Weitz, on an American Institute of Indian Studies (AIIS) fellowship visited ISI as a Visiting Professor to implement our collaborative project. This project is now completed and three papers are already published utilizing the study results. In the meanwhile, we are planning to develop further, a collaborative proposal to continue this research on heat stress adaptation among some communities in West Bengal in the perspective climate change and health.

V

I retired from ISI on 31 October 2019. Despite my retirement my academic journey has not stopped. I am currently serving as the Research Director of the Indian Anthropological Society and contemplating undertaking and/or organizing research activities for the IAS. I remained engaged also in teaching a part of postgraduate course in Anthropology, as a guest teacher in Bidhnnagar Government College, Kolkata for the last two years.

My forty years of working life at ISI and four and a half years of retired life puts me in a situation of introspection, and taking stock of successes and failures of my professional life and how successful I have been to become a good human being, too. Fact remains that I couldn't do many things in life and I intend to do some of these things in the years to come. Certainly, all throughout my life, I tried my best to do good to the people, leave a sweet taste in everybody's mouth and to lead a honest, and ethical way of life. I have with all sincerity have always advised my students to lead that kind of life, too.

My Books

1985: A. Basu and B. Mukhopadhyay(eds.). *Human Adaptation to Environment*. Calcutta: Indian Anthropological Society.

2003: A.K. Ghosh, J.K. Ghosh and B. Mukhopadhyay (eds.). *Sustainable Environments: A Statistical Analysis*. New Delhi: Oxford University Press.

2004: A.K. Ghosh, J.K. Ghosh, and B. Mukhopadhyay (eds.). *Sustainable Environments: Ecological, Economic, Sociocultural and Statistical Aspects*. Kolkata: Indian Statistical Institute.

2013: I.J.S. Bansal, S.M.S. Chahal and B. Mukhopadhyay (eds.). *Studies on Biological Anthropology: Biocultural Dimensions*. Jhargram: INCAA.

2023: S. Biswas, B. Mukhopadhyay and R.K. Das (eds.). *Writings on Indian Anthropology and Anthropologists: Celebrating 100 Years of Teaching Anthropology in India by the Indian Anthropological Society*. New Delhi: Concept Publishing Company (Pvt.) Ltd.

7

An Anthropologist by Choice

Ranjana Ray

Introduction

My father and Dr B.S. Guha, the famous anthropologist, indirectly played a major role for me to take up anthropology. My father was neither an anthropologist nor famous but his influence was great in choosing of a career. He was insistent about education to his three daughters equally to his son. He would tell us bed time stories from my very early childhood days. As long as I remember besides other classics, Jules Verne was his favourite. The stories had long lasting impressions on me. I was quite a good student in school winning some prizes every year, so that in the end of my school days, I had scored enough marks to get admission in Lady Brabourne College, the most prestigious women's college in Calcutta. In our times one had to score really good marks to get hostel accommodation. I stayed in the hostel and completed Intermediate Science examination with good marks. Now the time came to choose a subject for graduate honours course in science stream. Unfortunately, Lady Brabourne College in 1960 did not have option for honours course in science. My father would not allow his daughter to a co-education college and I needed hostel facilities. Again, my father absolutely admired the conservative atmosphere of the Lady Brabourne College and hostel, a legacy of Fazlul Huq, founder of the College, initially for Muslim girls. Dr Rama Choudhury, the famous philosopher and educationist was principal of the Lady Brabourne College at that time. She was elder sister to Mrs Uma Guha, wife of Dr B.S. Guha, founder of the Anthropological Survey of India. She suggested that I may take Anthropology as honours subject. I had found Hooton's *Up from the Ape* book in our college library. A look into its pages made me decide to go for Anthropology.

University of Calcutta in those days had provision for teaching honours subject at the postgraduate departments under the science faculty. At my time option was Anthropology, Psychology and Physiology. One had to take admission at an undergraduate college for pass courses and for honours class at the university departments. One of my friends and I chose Anthropology. Three others chose Physiology. By that time Botany honours course began at Lady Brabourne College. Five of us mentioned above did not opt for Botany but continued with our respective honours courses in our chosen fields. It happened that each of us had two subjects in our pass course. The classes were held at Lady Brabourne College. Anthropology honours classes were taught from 9 a.m. to 12 noon. Physiology honours classes took place from 2 p.m. to 5 p.m. Only two hours were left for our teachers at Lady Brabourne College to give us lessons in pass courses. I bow my head down in great respect for those teachers. They never grudged for the extra work and time they had to give for us. I secured star marks for my pass subjects as well and was awarded book prize. Such was the devotion of my teachers.

For honours classes we were escorted by a guard from the hostel, who sat on a stool downstairs until our honours class was over. Then we were escorted back to the college inside its walled off premises. It may sound hilarious for the present generation but that was our time.

Studying Anthropology

The department of Anthropology in University of Calcutta had completed hundred years in 2021. Even in those days it was a holistic study of man comprising of three major branches; Physical Anthropology, Social Anthropology and Prehistoric Archaeology. The department was located at 35, Ballygunge Circular Road in Southern part of Calcutta in an old mansion located in the middle of an immaculate garden, donated by Late Tarak Nath Palit, an Indian lawyer and philanthropist. From 1964 the department moved in a newly constructed eight-storied building in the same campus. Anthropology was in the third floor. It still occupies the same floor but at present with the expansion of the original building, it has acquired more space.

As an honours student we enjoyed our time in the old building with its quant structure and atmosphere. In those days Anthropology shared parts of the building with Botany and Zoology. There was a small lake with ornate steps leading to the water. We spent time sitting on the steps during our lunch break. Our ethnographic laboratory was on the first floor overlooking the lake. One of the renowned professors of anthropology, whenever dissatisfied with any of our works, would throw away the note books on the bank of the lake and it was our duty to run down and retrieve them. This was a kind of reprimand for us to do better job next time. In the same room we had our anatomy class. A famous anatomist of our time taught us anatomy. He kept a femur bone ready at hand for hitting anyone who did mistake in identifying any of the bones picked up by him and there was no gender bias for the victims.

My teachers in anthropology in those days were great men. In a way I was under the guardianship of Dr Sasanka Shekhar Sarkar, friend of one of my zoology teachers at Lady Brabourne College. Others were Professor K.P. Chattopadhyay, Dr T.C. Das, Professor M.N. Basu, Professor T.C. Ray Choudhury, Professor G.S. Ray and Professor D. Sen. Dr Makhan Lal Chakraboty taught us anatomy as a guest teacher. All of them are famous for their contribution in the field of anthropology. In the year 2019, I had an opportunity to visit Olduvai Gorge. There I saw the spot where of Zinjanthropus was discovered by Mary Leakey on 17 July 1959. In 1960 in our first year undergraduate classes, Dr Sarkar taught us Zinjanthropus and the significance of its discovery for the contemporary theory of human evolution. At that time there was no internet and website facilities. This reminded me once again how great and devoted were our teachers.

In addition to theoretical knowledge, laboratory and fieldworks were given equal importance. In our time we also had museology in our curriculum. In fact, Department of Museology in University of Calcutta had its root in our department. Anthropology department always had and still have laboratories and museums for each of the three branches of the discipline. We had to have training in drawing and describing of ethnographic specimens and prehistoric tools. Each student had to learn somatometry and craniometry. There were enough replicas of fossil crania to learn about different fossil men. Fieldwork was important. In the undergraduate level we carried out fieldwork in some tribal villages. We were given initial training of living in unfamiliar terrains and to collect data from unfamiliar people without creating any problem. My degree in Bachelor of Science with Anthropology honours was completed in 1962. There were eight seats in honours in the university at that time.

Four more students having distinction marks in their Anthropology pass course level in B.Sc. were admitted to the postgraduate course in the university. We still continued in the old mansion but we were deprived of the teaching of Professor K.P. Chattopadhyay, Dr T.C. Das and Professor T.C. Roy Choudhury. They superannuated. Professor P.K. Bhowmick and Professor Biswanath Banerjee joined the university and taught us social anthropology. Both of them took us to the field at Lohardaga near Ranchi. Prehistoric Archaeology was given as special paper in 1957. Dr Asok K. Ghosh was one of the first students with special paper in prehistoric archaeology. We had him as a teacher in our M.Sc. Class.

In 1962 postgraduate was for two years. We had final examination at the end of two years. We were taught all the three branches with equal emphasis. Out of the eight papers only three were optional. I chose prehistoric archaeology for special paper. I was fortunate to be a student of D. Sen, who not only had given us understanding of the theoretical aspects of prehistory but also had guided us for exploration and excavation in the field. My friend Bharati Debi and I had opted for prehistory that year. Professor Sen and Dr Asok Ghosh took us for fieldwork in Sini area along Sanjay River Valley. Under his guidance and with the supervision of Asok K. Ghosh two of us carried out excavation at Barudih and had explored sites along the tributaries of Sanjay. We discovered rich Palaeolithic, Microlithic and Neolithic sites. The Barudih mound was excavated systematically. Not only did we learn to analyse stratigraphy and relate cultural remains to geo-chronology but our teachers gave us lessons in ethnoarchaeology with the study of living examples from the Ho villages located close to the mounds.

Barudih excavation was a landmark for Neolithic culture of eastern India. It yielded Neolithic tools, pottery and rice in stratified context. There was also some charred rice, which were dated later on by radio-carbon method. We got our postgraduate degree through fun, adventure and great wealth of knowledge and blessings from our revered teachers.

Making of an Anthropologist

We had to wait for three months for our result. I had won a gold medal. Real time for academic career started after that. Before taking up any long-term research topic, my first work was done on Palaeolithic culture of West Bengal and among the potter's community of West Bengal. Both the works were published in the *Bulletin of Cultural Research Institute* with joint authorship with Dr Asok Ghosh and Professor G.S. Ray, respectively. I opted for Ph.D. Degree and had received Junior Research Fellowship from UGC. Professor D. Sen suggested that I work under the guidance of Dr Asok K. Ghosh. Topic Chosen was Mesolithic culture. Within one year of research, I received a Federal scholarship from the Government of USA. I was awarded East West Centre Fellowship for graduate study at the University of Hawaii at Manoa. My mentor there was Professor Wilhelm G. Solheim and my adviser was Professor Richard Pearson. From them I gained expertise in excavation of beach sites. Other than studying at the university, Bishops Museum was also storehouse of learning about Pacific and Southeast Asian archaeology. However, my adviser felt that I had better take courses in social anthropology because my knowledge of prehistory was up to the mark at that time. Fellowship those days were lavish. It paid for my travel, tuition, accommodation, food and even for books and stationeries. We had option for studying for one semester at any university of our choice in the mainland US. While returning home we were provided grant to visit places of our choice.

My Ph.D. thesis was on Mesolithic Culture of India. I followed the terminology bladelet for microlith made by punch technique. The term was devised by Dr Asok Ghosh on the basis of typo-technology and resultant form of the blank. He had devised the terms for the Palaeolithic on the basis of form of raw material. Palaeolithic culture was divided by him into pebble-core, Flake and Flake-Blade element sequentially; pebble-core being the earliest cultural stage. Meanwhile I completed one personal event. Got married and raised two daughters. In 1974 I got a job as a lecturer in the Department of Anthropology, University of Calcutta. Then onwards both research and teaching went hand in hand for me. I would like to mention that during my tenure as head of the department, I had got Departmental Special Assistance Programme from University Grants Commission for next few he successive years for my department at the University of Calcutta. I got the idea, advice and help for this from my colleagues and senior professors in the Department of Anthropology, University of Delhi. As a coordinator of the programme, the results of the researches conducted by the faculty and scholars, on the given thrust areas were published in book forms, edited by me. A journal of the department was started with grant, which is still continuing by the worthy faculty of the Department of Anthropology. Under the programme we could invite foreign scholars from abroad to enrich the department with wider contacts.

Research in Anthropology

My research was diverse in nature. Some were of my own interest. Others were done in interest of my students. I had done extensive exploration and some restricted trenching for my Ph.D. Research in Eastern India. Since the topic was on pan-Indian context, I visited some of the anthropology departments in India to study the microliths of Mesolithic stage. Best experience was at Deccan College. Professor H.D. Sankalia provided me with all facilities and even after the normal working hours I was allowed to study the various materials housed at the laboratories. I think I was extremely fortunate to receive the blessings of Professor Sankalia. He was an amazing personality, always ready to help any interested person. The outcome of my doctoral research not only resulted into the thesis but I had papers published in both national and international journals and proceedings.

My Ph.D. was on the mode of ecological adaptation during early Holocene times in India. The work was in line with Binford's theory that claimed that assemblage variation is an indication of different ways in which technology was organized to perform a task. These activities were mainly considered as maintenance task for procurement and distribution of food and raw material from the environment. Attempt had been made for standardization of attributes for classification of Mesolithic tools. The clusters were tested against diverse environment of the Indian subcontinent, in order to understand Holocene cultural adaptation with blades and bladelets. It was published in Asian Perspective. Understanding of the population of Mesolithic people through their culture was done.

Below is a brief account of various researches that I carried out. These are not given in chronological order of the time for conducting the research but on the context of cultural time scale.

Research on Mesolithic culture is not mentioned separately because it relates to my Ph.D. Research. Some researches were done with scholars, which were presented as doctoral theses and degree were granted to them under my guidance.

Palaeolithic Culture

As already mentioned, one of my first paper published was in West Bengal. Subsequently I had conducted research on Palaeolithic culture of Orissa (now Odisha) and Jharkhand, especially with geochronology of Acheulian and middle Palaeolithic cultures. Study was made on mode of cultural change with transition from lower to middle Palaeolithic culture in India. The transition was interesting involving emergence of new traits, extinction of some and continuity of other cultural traits in the form of tools from lower to middle Palaeolithic culture. In view of the raw material used and source of the same, research was done on petrology of Palaeolithic tools collected from a site Jamar in Pallahara region. It came out that Palaeolithic men were much choosy about the raw materials. They selected suitable stones for making tools and had to travel a few kilometres to get them, although their habitation ground was strewn with various stones. Fieldwork was carried out in the Punjab plateau in search for Palaeolithic culture.

Neolithic Culture of Eastern India

I had conducted intensive research in Neolithic culture of eastern India. It began with Barudhih excavation and analysis of the pottery, microliths and celts from the excavation. Meanwhile I had analysed collection of Neolithic celts from Pacific region housed in Bishops' Museum Hawaii, U.S.A., under the guidance of Professor Roger Green under East West Centre Fellowship of the University of Hawaii, 1967-68. Analysis of potsherds collected from Ban Cao site, Thailand, was done on the basis of attribute analysis under the guidance of Professor W. G. Solheim and Don Bayard, Department of Anthropology, Hawaii University, 1967. I was also fortunate to have worked in the same laboratory and with guidance from Chester Gorman.

A reconnaissance and survey along the Sanjai River Valley from its source to its confluence with River Subarnarekha was conducted in collaboration with Professor Peter S. Bellwood of Australian National University. This area had scattered information but this work had thrown a comprehensive light on the cultural pattern of the region. In 2018 I was invited to Oslo University in Norway to study prehistoric tools, the collection was made by Rev. P.O. Bodding, a Norwegian missionary. From the beginning of his stay in India, Bodding with help of his Indian associates started to collect and analyse material objects of everyday life and those of ritual significance to the Santals. He also compiled the Santali oral heritage in the form of texts. The Ethnographic Museum at Oslo University was given custodianship of a huge collection of prehistoric and ethnographic objects and manuscripts donated by him between 1901 and 1935. With the expertise on Neolithic tools, it was a pleasure for me to classify them. A summary of the same came out in the *Journal of the Asiatic Society*.

I had also done research on origin of rice for confirmation that *Oryza sativa,* the domesticated variety of rice in this part of India was an outcome of selection of Oryza, a cereal with non-shattering seeds, by the Neolithic farmers. The *Oryza sp.* was collected by the Mesolithic gatherers and for domestication they had chosen *Oryza sativa.* It was also established that Neolithic culture did not evolve and spread in the pan-Indian context but Mesolithic ways of life with hunting gathering continued as cultural back water in the hills, plateau and forested areas in India. Some of the present-day tribes bear the legacy of prehistoric primitive cultural continuity.

Pallahara region had attracted me to carry out the annual fieldwork with the students. The geography was attractive and I had the facility of staying with the group of students at the town where my brother was running an NGO. Exploration was carried out previously at this area by G.C. Mohapatra. I followed his footsteps and discovered a few sites in the area. Once while travelling from Pallahara to Jashipur I stopped at a place, which somehow attracted me and near the village Kuanr I discovered a very rich Chalco-Neolithic site. The site had a more or less similar situation as Barudih. The site was on a mound surrounded by a stream of the tributary of River Baitarani. The site yielded celts made of altered basalt; potsherds; large number of stone tools comprising of scraper, knife, blade, points and quite a good number of microliths. Some brass ornaments and crucibles were the important finds. Trial trenching along the cliff and collection through grid had given good idea about the activities of early men at the site. The metals were sent to the Mineralogy Department of Jadavpur University and it turned out to be brass, an alloy of copper and zinc. Zinc was abundant in eastern India and tin was rare. Similar situation existed in Southeast Asia. Instead of bronze, the first alloy made by men was brass. Kuanr is one of the important Chalco-Neolithic sites in eastern India. Work was done on rock art of India. It was on methodology for analysis of rock art on the basis of attribute analysis.

Ethnoarchaeology

With a view to reconstructing prehistoric culture a number of studies had been conducted among present-day communities. A few are mentioned here. It was to understand the technique of pot making that an intensive study was made among the potter's community of eastern India and the findings were used to understand prehistoric pottery. An interesting finding was made in this respect that potters usually burn their pots in a communal kiln. Surprisingly afterwards each of the potter's handicrafts could be identified with the help of their thumb measurement; the potters do not put any mark, such as signature or any symbol on the pots and while taking out the pots from kiln in our long experience of fieldwork never saw any dispute over such identification.

Megaliths have always drawn interest of anthropologists. For my research the tribe Bhumij of eastern India were selected. Bhumijs were quite an important group of eastern India. They had their own king and kingdom until British had subjugated them. Bhumij practices megalithic burial. Their socio-economic milieu is connected with this practice. They practice both cremation and burial. Cremation does not have a fixed place but the ashes and charred bones are buried and a dolmenoid structure is built on it. Each village has its burial ground with specific line for clan groups. The practice is also connected with ancestral worship.

Brass objects were found from Knuar, Orissa and to find out the technology of contemporary brass workers, we looked among the Sitharia communities living in Pallahara region. These people made brass objects in lost wax process. A study of the crucible, slugs and brass objects confirmed the method of making brass objects by lost wax process. Moreover, it is interesting to note that the brass makers at present conform to a caste.

Research in Other Branches of Anthropology

Tribal study is done in some sectors. Mother and child care among the Kheria and Bathudi living in the Simlipal forest area of Orissa was chosen because both the tribes are living in common environmental zone but were practising different subsistence patterns. Kherias were gatherers and shifting cultivators, whereas Bathudis were settled agriculturists. Some works were also done on health status of tribes living in Simlipal forest area. This was done with the help of anthropometry and food intake, using weighment method.

The deltaic region of West Bengal with its mangrove environment has given rise to a group of people locally known as Meendhara. Primary occupation of these people is catching seeds of prawn for selling to the middle men for a bigger enterprise of aquaculture of prawn. The study has given in interesting picture on the emergence of social group based on economy which is of recent origin because of the demand of prawn in global market. *Meen* catching is done in shallow brackish water by the women and children of the area, which puts them into dangers of diseases for constant emersion in brackish water and prey to sharks and crocodiles. Children are to pick out the *meen* from the net out of other catches. The job needs sharp eyes. There is no fixed time for going in the water with hand nets. It depends on tide. Children can hardly go to school. Even if the boys can be spared, not the girls. Other important work in the coastal Bengal was done to see how far women were practising family planning.

Being a woman myself woman's study had an attraction for me. I am also part of the faculty of the Women's Studies Research Centre of University of Calcutta. Major topic of research was "women and violence". Gerontology has taken an important part in anthropology. Research was conducted among tribal women in rural West Bengal and urban women from Kolkata.

Interest on criminology was created among us by Professor P.K. Bhowmick. I took up study of convicted tribes from some of the prisons in West Bengal to find out the nature of crime committed by the tribal people of the state. It came out that the most heinous of the crime committed by the tribal people were murder of a witch in groups under the guidance of a tribal shaman (*janguru*). In the respective societies theft may be considered as a crime but not the murder of a witch. The convicted tribals even for a petty theft had to go through purification ceremony but those convicted of murder of witches were lauded when they returned to the village after serving the prison terms.

For a long time, I had been giving courses in Indology in the Ramakrishna Mission Institute of Culture and Research and had written chapters for the textbook, *Bharat Tattva,* on prehistory and pre-Vedic cultures of India. Uniqueness of India is found in its traditionalism. There are a number of cultural elements in our society, which has its root in prehistoric and protohistoric period are still continuing in the modern Indian Society. These are mostly connected with ritualistic and religious aspects.

Membership of Learned Societies

I am life member of a number of societies in India, most of them are anthropological. I am member of the executive committee of International Union for Prehistoric and Protohistoric Science (UISPP), and member of the heritage commission of the same. I became the life member of the Asiatic Society in 1968 and at present I am elected as the Anthropological Secretary of the Society. This gave me farther scope for research and organizing both national and international seminars on behalf of the society. As an outcome a number of edited volumes were published, mainly on the proceedings of the seminars. However, I always had the opportunity of organizing seminars both in India and abroad.

Last Words

Though I have formally retired as University Chair Professor from the Department of Anthropology with the Emeritus Fellowship but am still continuing with my research and other duties as an anthropologist. I took up the study of anthropology with a romantic image but the romance is never lost. I love being an anthropologist and hope that I have made some contribution for mankind and its posterity. I never thought of writing about myself until I had this request from the most renowned contemporary anthropologists Professor Vinay K. Srivastava and Professor P.C. Joshi. I convey best wishes for all anthropologists, past, present and future.

My Books

2003: *Unknown Women: Aged, Widowed, Tribal and Urban*. Jointly with Paromita Das Gupta and Soumitra Basu. Calcutta: Classique Books, College Street.

2004: *Selected Portraits: Aged, Weaker Section, Women and Disabled.* Jointly with Dr S.K. Sengupta. Classic Books, College Street.

2004: *Re-discovering the familiar: An Anthropological Approach.* Calcutta: University of Calcutta Press.

2005: *Adapting to Changing Environment: Studies in Anthropology*. Calcutta: University of Calcutta Press.

2009: *Status of Prehistoric Studies in the Twenty-First Century in India*. jointly with Vidula Jayswal. BAR International Series.

2011: *Development, Displacement and Marginalisation.* Seminar and Public Lecture Series. Kolkata: The Asiatic Society.

2013: *Darwin and Human Evolution*. Jointly with D.J. Chattopadhyay and Samir Banerjee. Kolkata: The Asiatic Society.

2017: *Archaeological Heritage Policies and Management Structures.* Jointly with Erika M. Robrahn-Gonzales, Aboulaye Camara, Pascal Depaepe, Asja Engovatova and Vidula Jayaswal. Archaeopress.

2019: *Tribal Health Care System: A Tribute to P.O. Bodding.* Kolkata: The Asiatic Society.

8

My Journey into Anthropology

Nadeem Hasnain

Coming into anthropology was accident for me. As per preference of my parents, I was pursuing science stream with physics, chemistry and mathematics. The goal was to become an engineer. However, my heart lies elsewhere. Literature was my first preference. I dropped from B.Sc. course against the wishes of my parents and got admitted in Lucknow University for a B.A. Degree. I never heard of anthropology before filling up admission form. It was under the advice of my neighbour, a professor of economics, that I opted for anthropology. The first few classes that I attended won my heart. It was like love at first sight. I never looked back.

When I go into memory lanes to trace the factors or reasons behind my style of practising anthropology, I find that my family background, to a great extent, is responsible for it. We come from a medium *zamindar* family of landlords from eastern Uttar Pradesh. This region was notorious for the tyranny of landlords against the peasants and agricultural labour, bonded or otherwise. The exploitation of the poor peasants is still fresh in my mind. My father being a police officer did not live in our ancestral village and farming activities were supervised by my uncle who was not as kind to the poor peasants as my father. The child in me revolted against this injustice and exploitation and that is how I developed a strong sympathy for the poor, disadvantaged, marginalized and oppressed sections of the society. This was largely responsible behind my choice for a topic dealing with an oppressed group of bonded labour for my Ph.D. thesis. I will always be grateful to my mentor and guide late Professor KS Mathur for allowing me this topic despite the fact that this was not his area of interest/specialization.

My childhood experiences have a strong bearing on my style of writing and practicing anthropology. Moreover, the writings of Verrier Elwin and the legendry Bangla author Mahashweta Devi have played an important role in my life as an anthropologist. A statement of Elwin that I frequently quote in my lectures and classes is: "The essence and art of anthropology is love without which nothing is fertile and nothing is true". The writings of Mahashweta Devi through her novels gave me not only new insights to understand tribal societies and their problems but also courage to stand for and support the oppressed Adivasis in a time when the present government dubs their sympathizers as "Urban Naxals". She insisted that I bring out a revised edition of my book *Bonded for Ever* and also its Hindi translation to reach wider readership. She promised to write preface of the book which she did. It was because of her encouragement that I visited the field again after twenty-five years to write a new introduction of the book. That is how her writings and personality moulded my style of writing.

As already stated, my entry into anthropology was a sheer accident but once I entered into it at the undergraduate level, I decided to pursue it and make it my career. Besides my strong commitment for the weaker sections of the society, I had a strong dislike for the persons who mocked and ridiculed other people and cultures and glorifying their own. I knew later that it was "ethnocentrism".

During my student days I was initiated into Marxism/socialism and till date I continue to have great respect for this ideology though unlike many others I have never been a rigid Marxist because I always held the view that change may be enacted into the idea and practise of Marxism with the changing circumstances and times. To several of my Marxist friends my stand that "Marx the man, was greater than Marx the philosopher" sounded blasphemous. Another idea or concept that has impressed me deeply is cultural relativism. I strongly believe that sociology and social anthropology are unique in the fraternity of social sciences and one of the reasons behind this uniqueness is their emphasis on cultural relativism which inculcates respect for other cultures. It tells us that a society is not necessarily monolithic. When I look at the Indian society and its immense diversity—linguistic, ethnic, religious, and the wide range of customs, traditions, values and lifeways, the idea of cultural relativism teaches me to be not only tolerant to the diversity but to respect and celebrate it. I strongly believe that whosoever does not accept this diversity and respect by heart has not accepted the idea of India. Cultural relativism opens new vistas and avenues of knowledge. It tells us that every culture is valid in itself because every culture proposes solutions to the problems people face. If one sits as judge and passes moral judgement based on one's cultural values, this is sheer ethnocentrism. Non-judgemental appreciation of the strengths and weaknesses of human societies has been the hallmark of anthropology as I understand. I am so happy to see both of my children—son Aseem who teaches sociology at the California State University, Fresno and daughter Samta, an innovative lighting designer in London have imbibed this anthropological point of view. They are totally free from all sorts of prejudices and narrow mindedness. We as parents are happy with their upbringing.

The concept of "Culture of Poverty" has also impressed me immensely. Though Oscar Lewis developed it in the context of urban poverty and slums, I thought that its basic postulates may also be applied in the rural/tribal setting. I have applied it in the rural-tribal setting of a cis-Himalayan population of Kolta and my Ph.D. examiners Scarlett Epstein and L.P. Vidyarthi appreciated it.

The sociological-anthropological implications of secularism have also contributed to molding my personality and thought process. The popular Indian connotation of secularism is *sarva dharma sambhaav* but it does not talk about rationalism and scientific approach. I understand that societies are not born secular. Instead, they have to undergo transformation from traditional—religious to secular and the process of secularization is responsible for its transformation. Any society that wishes to become a modern society has to be a secular society imbibing rationality in its thinking process. I understand that a secular and modern society is not against religion per se but it has to fight superstition and intolerance as well as bigotry and obscurantism.

I have no pretension that I have made very significant contribution to the subject but at least on one count I can rightfully claim that I along with two of my fellow anthropologists N.K. Vaid and Vinay Kumar Srivastava have contributed substantially in popularizing anthropology among the lay educated persons especially those opting for anthropology in civil services examinations through our classes for the civil services aspirants and writings. Thousands of aspirants for various examinations are introduced to anthropology every year not merely as a discipline but also as a "point of view". Obviously only a small percentage of them are finally selected and enter into various services but the remaining hundreds and thousands of them undergo changes in their attitude to the society at large; they get sensitized to "other cultures" and weaker sections of the society.

Indian Muslims have been a relatively neglected population in Indian sociology and anthropology and only a few scholars have published books on them. Shia Muslims being a significant minority, did not catch the attention of scholars in India before me. Even to this day, I don't find any full-fledged study of the Shias of India. Though bonded labour has been studied by many but for the first time the concept of "Culture of Poverty" has been applied in my study on bonded labour. *The Other Lucknow* is the first and the only ethnographic profile of Lucknow. "Changing face of Lived Islam in India" is based on the research project I did as senior fellow of ICSSR. Till date, I don't find any field-based study of "Lived Islam" in the context of Indian/South Asian Muslims and for that matter very few in the world.

During the period 2006-08, I got an opportunity to teach, lecture and present papers in USA. For 2006-07 I was invited as

Fulbright "Scholar in Residence" in USA and attached with St. Lawrence University, New York, a well-known liberal arts University of USA. At the end of my tenure, the same University invited me as visiting professor to teach in the Department of Global Studies and Department of Religious Studies besides taking classes occasionally in the Department of Anthropology. During this period, I delivered lectures in some other universities besides presenting papers in conferences and seminars.

My journey in anthropology continues even after retirement from Lucknow University in 2014 and I think I am academically more active and productive in my writings, classes for the civil services aspirants and social activism.

My Books

- 1982: *Bonded for Ever*. Harman Publications, New Delhi.
- 1986: *Tribal India*. Palaka Prakashan, New Delhi.
- 1998: *Indian Anthropology*. Palaka Prakashan, New Delhi.
- 2004: *Indian Society and Culture: Continuity and Change*, Jawahar Publishers, New Delhi.
- 2014: *India's Current Social Problems*. New Royal Book Company, Lucknow.
- 2016: *The Other Lucknow: Ethnographic Portrait of a City of Nostalgia and Undying Memories*. Vani Prakashan, New Delhi.
- 2019: *Muslim at Crossroads: Changing Face of "Lived Islam" in India*. New Royal Book Company, Lucknow.
- 2021: *Shia Muslim of India: Religion, Society and Culture*. New Royal Book Company, Lucknow.
- 2021: *Sociology of Marginalized Communities and Weaker Sections in India*. Sage Publications, New Delhi.
- 2021: *Indian Society: Themes and Social Issues*. McGraw Hill, New Delhi.
- 2023: *Society and Social Institutions*. Sterling Publishers, New Delhi.

9

Writing About Self

Mayanglambam Mani Babu

Early Life: Education, Family, Taking Anthropology as a Subject

Born on 17 October 1956 in Eroisemba village under Imphal West District (Manipur), I am the youngest of the three children of my parent. Amidst a humble surrounding, I grew up as a fond child in the family under strict supervision of my mother (M. Baruni Devi). Seems to be an ordinary mother and illiterate housewife—she was a role model to me who had the greatest influence in my life, inspiring me to grow without any barrier. My father (M. Ibomcha Singh), a renowned performer (*lairik thiba*) of his time of the Manipuri narrative art form locally termed as *Lairik-Thiba-Haiba*, was also a pillar of my strength, who always motivated me to never give up on my dream and to keep working hard.

Early education started in the village school, and I was only of average grade, but owing to my seriousness in studies many contended me as a good student. After my matriculation (in 1972) from Uripok Secondary School, Imphal, I went to Oriental College for Pre-University Science Course and then earned my B.Sc. degree in 1978 (with Honours in Anthropology) from D.M. College of Science, Imphal (both colleges were affiliated to Gauhati

University, Assam). In fact, my entry into "anthropology" was not by my choice but by compulsion. I had never heard of such a subject before, and I was not an exception also. By that time, many undergraduate students offering anthropology in D.M. College of Science (the only college in Manipur offering Anthropology in the undergraduate course) were not much aware of the subject. And, a general trend during those days among the students (and as well as their parents) who seek to admit in science undergraduate course, was to get admission themselves in D.M. College—either in the subject combination of physics, chemistry and mathematics (the nomenclature of the subject combination used by that time was "royal science") *or* botany, zoology and chemistry (termed as "bio-chemistry"). And I was not an exception who attempted for "bio-chemistry". However, since the admission process was on "merit basis" and the mark secured by me in the last university examination could not accommodate well within the cut-off mark for the subject combination that I preferred to opt,—I was to go with the subject combination of anthropology, botany and zoology (nomenclature as "bio-anthro"). After admission and before attending classes in anthropology, I even changed to geology in lieu of anthropology and even attended classes. But due to some reasons, came back to anthropology. And I feel myself fortunate to be one of the students of first batch of "Honours" course in anthropology.

After receiving B.Sc. (Honours) degree in anthropology in 1978, I completed Master of Science in anthropology from Gauhati University in 1980 with specialization in prehistoric archaeology. By that time the great student's unrest prevailed in Assam over the so-called "foreigners' issue", which disturbed the academic atmosphere, and obviously all the examinations were delayed. Our P.G examination which was to hold in 1980 was held in 1982, losing two years' duration.

Doctoral Work, Teachers, Fieldwork, Career

After post-graduating from the Gauhati University in 1980, my teaching career in anthropology began since 1983 in the Departments of Anthropology, D.M. College of Science and later in Oriental College, Imphal. In June 2007 I joined Manipur University, Imphal as an Associate Professor in Anthropology, and superannuated as Professor and Head on the last day of the last month of 2021.

Besides other fields of anthropological archaeology, I conducted ethnoarchaeological fieldwork on the different pot making populations of Manipur (namely, Thongjao, Chairel, Nungbi, Oinam, etc.). Extensive work within the processual and post-processual ethnoarchaeological frames was done among the Andros for my doctoral dissertation, and got the degree in 2005 from Manipur University. Before coming to ceramic ethnoarchaeological study for my Ph.D. degree—I registered for my research work in two instants, both on megalithic studies of Manipur, first in 1985 in Gauhati University and later in 1989 in Manipur University. However, due to myriad factors I could not complete my work, and those were the "dark days" in my academic journey that still lingers on.

My primary research areas of interest include those that comes within processual and post-processual archaeological paradigms, such as engendered archaeology, embodied archaeology, settlement and landscape archaeology, and cognitive archaeology, to name a few. Besides, issues with ceramic ethnoarchaeology, lithic typo-technology and Stone Age prehistory of Southeast Asia, are among my research interest. Six scholars have awarded Ph.D. under my supervision and three are pursuing.

Contribution to Anthropological Research, Papers, Books

Enthusiasm of writing articles began during the terminal period of my M.Sc. Course, which embarked with two articles in 1980. With the publication of two books to my credit, I have published more than *four dozen* research papers in peer-reviewed national and international journals, *two dozen* chapters in edited volumes. And also delivered more than *forty* "invited talks" on different fields concerning prehistoric archaeology, and attended more than *two dozen* international seminars/workshops/conferences. Also published popular science articles related with anthropology in the local Manipuri journals.

1.1 *Special Lectures Delivered*

- Special lectures delivered as Visiting Fellow in the Department of Anthropology, Vidyasagar University, Medinipur, Kolkata (W.B.) under UGC merged Scheme during XII Plan: during 16-17 January 2014. Lectures delivered: 04 (Issues with Lithic Systematics, Archaeological Theories: Processual and Postprocessual Paradigms, Ethnoarchaeology, and Cognitive Fluidity of Prehistoric Art).
- Special lectures delivered as visiting faculty at the Department of Anthropology, West Bengal State University, Barasat, 24-Parganas (N), Kolkata during 28-29 August 2014. The lectures comprise—(i) Lithic Study, (ii) Hoabinhian Culture: Significances in Indian Prehistory, (iii) Ethnoarchaeology as Archaeological Paradigm, and (iv) Palaeolithic Art.
- The Professor Dharini Sen Memorial Lecture (on "Prehistory of Human Cognition: Extracting Mind from Artifacts") at the 46th Annual Conference of Indian Anthropological Society and the International Seminar (8-10 November 2016) held at Manipur University (Imphal), organized by the Indian Anthropological Society, Kolkata, the Department of Anthropology, Manipur University, Imphal in association with the Anthropological Society of Manipur and Indira Gandhi Rashtriya Manav Sangrahalaya, Bhopal.
- Special lectures delivered during 15 March 2021 to 26 March 2021 as Visiting Fellow in the Department of Anthropology, Panjab University, Chandigarh under the UGC-CAS-II (PG & UG Programme). Delivered 7 (seven) *on-line* and 2 (two) public/open lectures) The two Public Lectures delivered are:

(i) "Cybernetics, Processualism and Ceramic Ecology: A Case Study in Manipur",

(ii) "Cognitive Fluidity and Semiotic Behavior: The Prehistory of Human Mind".

- Delivered lectures in a number of UGC-sponsored Refresher and Orientation Courses (in Anthropology and other allied subjects) of different Departments of Manipur University, Imphal.

1.2 *Content Writer*

Content writer in the PG e-Pathshala—Contributed as Content writer in the e-PG Pathshala project undertaken by the Ministry of Human Resource Development (MHRD), Government of India, on four modules for *Paper: 3-Anthropology* (Archaeological Anthropology).

1.3 *Membership*

1. Also held memberships with various academic bodies, such as, life member: Indian National Confederation and Academy of Anthropologists (INCAA), life member: Indian Science Congress Association (ISCA), Patron member: Anthropological Society of Manipur (ASM), life member: Indian Anthropological Society, Kolkata, life member: Palaeo Research Society, Ghumarwin (Himachal Pradesh) etc. to name a few.
2. Member of Board of Post-Graduate Studies, Departments of Anthropology, Gauhati University; Assam University (Diphu Campus); Dibrugarh University, Assam; Rajiv Gandhi University, Itanagar (A.P.).

Contribution Beyond Anthropology, Notable Student

Grew up as a quiet, shy and even as an introvert boy, I took part very occasionally in the school-level extra-curricular activities, such as one-act plays and dramas, but not in sports. My first love was in literature—reading short stories, novels and poems. Sometimes participated in the state-level high school recitation competitions. Writing poems in my early school days was followed by short stories, some of which were published in the local weekly/monthly journals. Also took part in the State Level Short Story Writing Competitions. I use to give radio talks on A.I.R. Imphal on different areas (concerning more with anthropology), and also wrote more than a *dozen* "radio features" broadcasted in the A.I.R. Imphal.

Besides being a postgraduate student (1978-80) from Gauhati University and by virtue of being associated with the student organization [the Gauhati Manipuri Students' Association (GMSA), Assam] in the capacity as its Secretary General (1979-82)—I had a good opportunity to be part of the Working Group of Manipuri Community in Gauhati University Campus (which strongly urged for a "full-fledged University" in Manipur) rubbing shoulders with a number of Manipuri teachers in the University and Manipuri research scholars as well. While serving as Senior Lecturer in Anthropology at Oriental College, Imphal—I also associated with the National Service Scheme (N.S.S.) of the College in the capacity as a Programme Officer (December 1996—May 2007).

Current/Post-retirement Activities

My superannuation from the university service as Professor and Head of the Department of Anthropology was on the last day of the year 2021. However, I have been reinstated as guest professor in the same department. Though not fully freed from teaching domain, I feel myself relieved from the earlier busy schedules. Indeed, my retirement is from the university service, and not from anthropology. Now, I do hope that all my halfway tasks—such as, books in the pipeline of their publication—be accomplished flawlessly. And hope that the Almighty will usher me the strength in engaging and fulfilling my desire to work for the cause and development of prehistoric archaeology, especially in this part of the country. And let my arousal to many young archaeologists (of the area) to delve into the myriad archaeological issues, lying almost unexplored in this archaeologically-strategic part of the globe, be endured.

My Book

2006: *Anthropology of Manipur: Archaeological, Biological and Cultural Dimensions*. Imphal: Momothayai Books.

10

Bridging Anthropology, Science, and Management

My Life's Odyssey

Arbind Sinha

My Early Life

In my early years, I was an ordinary student who traversed from mathematics to biology to zoology and finally landed in anthropology to complete his master's. Anthropology as a subject was quite alien to me when I applied and was placed on the second list of chosen students. I was a typical rustic boy, straightforward and honest. During the entrance test, when I had to answer the question, "How did you become interested in Anthropology?" I looked at the form of Lopa (who later became my classmate), who wrote, "From the beginning, I have been interested in the study of culture, and this is the best subject". Perhaps Lopa was familiar with anthropology, but I was not.

Between my graduation examination and the announcement of results, I spent two weeks with Vinoba Bhave (the Gandhian social reformer and proponent of the "Bhoodan" movement). Vinobaji advised the audience to "cultivate a habit of living with minimum requirements" in one of his evening speeches. It appealed to me, and I internalized it. It was extremely helpful to me when I began studying anthropology and conducting fieldwork in rural and tribal areas.

Learning Anthropology

The anthropology course was going well. A turning point came in my life. Ranchi University's Department of Anthropology was headed by prominent anthropologist Professor LP Vidyarthi. Professor Vidyarthi was appointed as the Chairman of a Committee on Tribal Development, and he was to travel to Andaman and Nicobar Islands to collect field data from the tribes of the islands. He intended to take with him one Ph.D. scholar and three first-year students. I was in my final year of college, preparing for our final examinations, so there was no way for me to join the team. However, I took a chance and used all of my strategies to persuade Professor Vidyarthi to accept me in the Island research team. I recall how angrily he reacted and asked, "If I take you to Andaman, who will appear for the exam, no-nonsense, not possible?" I convinced him that I would study for the examinations while on fieldwork in the Islands. Finally, he agreed to let me on the team, and it was an incredible opportunity to accompany Professor Vidyarthi on his six-week expedition to the Andaman and Nicobar Islands. The group included Vijoy Sahay and Aroon Kumar.

We visited over a dozen inhabited islands and thoroughly studied the sociocultural lifestyles of the Andamanese, Onges, and Nicobaris. Professor Vidyarthi was an outstanding field researcher, which I must underline. We travelled and worked from morning to evening, and he was always one step ahead of us.

His time management skills were remarkable. During the Islands trip, I became the tour manager and was responsible for keeping all travel plans and communication in order, as well as maintaining updated records of field expenses. It was a life-changing experience for me. Professor Vidyarthi taught me how rigorous the fieldwork should be and how meticulous the accounting must be. For me, the most important learning was getting closer to aboriginals and thinking about their developmental issues.

Back home, I wrote to Shri Jay Prakash Narayan (a social reformist known as JP) about the necessity of initiating an exclusive development effort for the island's tribal communities. JP forwarded my letter to Shri Thakur Prasad Bang, the then-President of Adivasi Vikas Sansthan, and advised me to follow up with him. This concern about development is still very close to my heart.

The Department of Anthropology at Ranchi University organized the SC Roy Centenary Celebration in November 1971, when I was in my final year, and I was in charge of reception and accommodation for the participants. This enabled me to meet most of the leading anthropologists of India, including Dr Binod C. Agrawal, who had recently returned from the United States after getting his Ph.D. from the University of Wisconsin and had joined the Indian Agriculture Research Institute (IARI) in New Delhi. I also met the first-year students of the Department of Anthropology, University of Delhi (Vinay Srivastava was one of them) during the 1971 conference in Ranchi. We discussed a lot about the fieldwork. This made me realize how important were the six weeks of rigorous rural and urban study for an anthropologist where we had to stay in another region of Bihar.

During the wait for the results, I worked on a tribal development project called Operation Self Help, which was managed by Rotary International, Riska (UK). I spent three months in a tribal village for this assignment. My two colleagues were likewise assigned to areas nearby. Ms. Hazeline Lutz, a Master's student from Chicago University (USA), came to stay in the village where I was working, and we had a great time exchanging ideas on the use of anthropological knowledge for the betterment of society. The exposure to the island and the experience of living close to the tribe helped me comprehend that the knowledge gained from field studies must be used to help people who are less fortunate. The concept of "Action Anthropology" was becoming more ingrained in my thoughts.

Professor Vidyarthi was awarded a project on the "Sacred Complex of Kashi' by the Indian Council of Social Science Research in 1972 (Vidyarthi, Saraswati, and Jha 1979). Four of us from our batch (M.N. Jha, B.N. Sahay, Omkar Prasad, and I) were selected for this project and lived in Varanasi, Uttar Pradesh, for nineteen months. It was an urban ethnographic study of people participating in religious practices in and around Varanasi's Kashi Vishwanath (Shiva) Temple. I studied the religious performances that take place on the Ganga's bank (Ghat). The local resource was Dr Baidya Nath Saraswati, a well-known anthropologist, and the Project's Deputy Director. I admire Dr Saraswati for his scholarly rigour and humanitarian principles. I am grateful to him for teaching me even a little bit of it.

We completed the Sacred Complex study and wrote papers on our research findings. The papers were presented at the project's final Seminar in October 1973. In my paper, I suggested splitting "Sacred Specialists" into "Sacred Specialists" and "Sacred Associates". Professor Vidyarthi was visibly upset that I did not embrace his concept of "sacred specialists", but the session's Chairperson, Dr Binod C. Agrawal, appreciated my interpretation and strongly supported me. This is my contribution to the body of knowledge on Sacred Complex study.

I made contact with Dr Agrawal once again. He informed me that he is going to join the Indian Space Applications Centre—Indian Space Research Organisation (ISRO), Ahmedabad, and that there may be an opportunity for me to work there.

Applications of Anthropological Knowledge: My ISRO Days

In early 1974, I joined the Space Applications Centre (SAC-ISRO) as a Research Associate to work with the Indian Space Research Organisation's Satellite Instructional Television Experiment (SITE). I was posted to Bihar, one of the states selected for the SITE project. On a framework of defined parameters, the team had to select villages suitable for the installation of satellite-linked televisions.

After the completion of the village selection survey, I was assigned to conduct a comprehensive evaluation of the one-year SITE project by staying in one Bihar village for 18 months—my second longer ethnographic research following the one I conducted in Varanasi city. This was a positive deviation from the regular survey approach practise for any large-scale evaluation in India. The task involved staying in one village for three months before the programme to study people's perceptions, twelve months during the SITE programme transmission to study reception and response, and three months after the programme culminated in studying the continuity of change brought about by development programmes beamed directly to SITE villages via satellite. Following the principle of "living with the bare necessities" helped me in this situation. ISRO thoroughly documented what I and seven other anthropologists who did holistic research in six other villages learned.

An Advisory Committee for this nation-wise study was formed to guide, support, and supervise these investigations, and members included luminaries such as professors. L.P. Vidyarthi, Sachchidanand, K.S. Mathur, Gopala Sarana, and Lakhan Mahapatra. It was a three-year project that I worked on from January 1974 to March 1977. After the experiment came to an end, SAC-ISRO created one position of anthropologist, and I was selected as a Research Associate resulting from tough competition. The journey proceeded, and I was promoted to Scientist "SC". I got permission to use part of the data I collected for SITE evaluation for my thesis. I received a Ph.D. and later reworked my thesis and converted it into a book, which was published in 1985.

I got a double promotion—from Scientist SC to Scientist SE—in recognition of receiving a Ph.D. degree and having a published book to my credit. I progressed through the ranks to the level of Full Professor at any university. Many people found it difficult to imagine that an anthropologist could work as a scientist at ISRO, which deals with space science and technology.

While at SAC-ISRO, I worked on a number of nationwide projects spanning practically the entire country, focusing on development communication, disaster communication, and the Science-Society-Technology interface. My focus was always on providing cultural knowledge and communication skills to national development, specifically for the countryside.

In December 1978, India hosted the Tenth International Congress of Anthropological and Ethnological Sciences (Xth ICAES-1978) for the first time in a developing nation, under the leadership of Professor L.P. Vidyarthi, President of the International Union of Anthropological and Ethnological Sciences (1973-78). Dr Agrawal and a half-dozen other SAC-ISRO members were given the task to work for the Xth ICAES for between six and ten months. Dr Agrawal was the Executive Secretary, and I was appointed as Assistant Secretary of the Organising Committee. It provided me with a tremendous opportunity to work with all of the renowned Indian anthropologists of the time and to interact with the who's who of world anthropologists. Professors I.P. Singh, S.C. Tewari, and JS Bhandari were always a blessing to me. It was a good experience working with Dr Surinder Nath, Dr Vardesh Channa, P.C. Joshi, Vinay Srivastava, S.L. Malik, Anup Kapoor, Naresh Vaidya, Lalit Kashyap, Kanak Mittal, Elizabeth Zakaria and many others.

The experience of team management and account keeping that I gained during my trip to Andaman and Nicobar in 1971 helped me in effectively organizing the Xth ICAES. Special mention to Professor Demitri Shimkin from SIU, USA, which helped me in getting us the most attended session of Xth ICAES—Young Anthropologists Look at the World Anthropology, Professor Sol Tax from USA, who reinforced my idea of Action Anthropology, and Professor Hebbe Vessuri from Venezuela with whom I spent some time when she was quarantined at Delhi airport for not having required health certificate, and we talked about the rigour of teaching in developed countries.

SUNCOM 1982—the International Symposium on Problems of Development of Underprivileged Communities in Third World Countries was held in New Delhi in December 1982, and I worked as the Executive Secretary under the Presidency of Professor L.P. Vidyarthi.

As Additional Executive Secretary, I was also actively involved in organizing an international conference of the International Association for Media and Communication Research (IAMCR) in 1986 in Delhi and had the opportunity to work with Professor Y.V. Laxman Rao, then-Director of the Indian Institute of Mass Communication, Professor A.J. Kidwai, Chairman of MCRC, Jamia Millia Islamia; Professor K.E. Eapen, and Professor D.P. Patnaik. During the conference, I had enjoyable discussions with professors. Everett Rogers, Bill Melody, and George Gerber—the doyens of communication. Dr Rohan Samarjiva and I became good friends.

During my time at SAC-ISRO, I was awarded a residential research fellowship that allowed me to live in Stockholm and give lectures in various locations throughout Sweden, and I was part of an Indian delegation that spent more than two months at the University of Regina, Canada, working on a project to introduce computers into Indian universities.

Finally, the curtain came down, and I took voluntary retirement by the end of 1996 after more than twenty-two years of qualifying service with ISRO, Government of India.

Enriching Knowledge with TALEEM and the Danish Embassy

Dr Binod C. Agrawal and I left SAC-ISRO, Ahmedabad, to establish TALEEM Research Foundation, which Mr Subhas Chanda, Chairman, Essel Group (ZEE Network), chairs. I worked there as a Professor from October 1996 to May 1998, with the majority of my involvement in media and health-related studies.

I joined the Danish Embassy in India in June 1998 and stayed there for more than two years. My primary responsibility was to strengthen the Government of India's National Blindness Control

Programme, for which the Danish government provided both technical and financial assistance. I coordinated with bureaucrats from the central and state governments and learned their way of working.

Karnataka state of south India was the project State for our project. With my anthropological instinct to understand the ground realities, I lived in Bidar district for a month and spent most of my time in a few villages of Bidar to thoroughly understand the process and outcomes of health communication—my third ethnographic experience. I learned a lot about the programme's and people's communication gaps. I tested the concept of the "Human Channel of Communication (HCC)" in villages in Bidar and other villages in South Bihar (now Jharkhand). I realized that if the HCC is strengthened, it can help to accelerate the pace of any development initiative. It became my primary focus in communication teaching, research, and publishing. I returned to TALEEM in the mid-2000 and later joined the Mudra Institute of Communications Ahmedabad (MICA) in June 2002.

Returning to College with Holistic Ideas

My 19-year tenure with MICA; 13 years (June 2002 to March 2015) of regular employment as Professor, Dean, Associate Director, and In-charge Director, seven years as Adjunct Professor and Advisor (May 2017 till date), and two years as Director-General of Shanti Business School, Ahmedabad, helped me understand the business and management of education.

In mid-2012, the Government of India appointed me as Chairman of the Technical Advisory Committee on Environment, Water, Sanitation, and Health (E-WASH), National Council of Science and Technology Communication (NCSTC), for a three-year term. My experience of heading this committee was not very good. Currently, I am the President of the Association of Development Communication, a worldwide organization, and also serve as the President of the Jharkhand Anthropological Association.

My Significant Contribution to the Discipline

My background as a person from a developing area, ethnographic field studies in urban, rural, and tribal areas, and my island study all impacted my ideas and sparked my interest in action anthropology. I often use my anthropological understanding of culture and communication techniques to solve people's concerns. These concerns are always expressed in national and international forums, as well as in my publications.

Some Interesting Narratives

When my book *Mass Media and Rural Development* was published in 1985, something amazing happened.

In acknowledgement of my book, I received a research fellowship from Stockholm University's School of Journalism and Communication and travelled to other Scandinavian nations to give talks. In one of my meetings in Copenhagen, I was explaining how television may be used to help rural development. The Director of Television Research of Denmark Television remembered something and claimed he had read about it and went to his study area and picked out my book. We talked about it at length.

Dr Binod Agarwal, my Ph.D. thesis supervisor and senior at SAC-ISRO, applied for research funding from the Institute of Culture and Communication in Leister (UK) in late 1986. He was given the grant with the caveat that "he had recently read a publication from an Indian Scholar—Arbind Sinha, and he wanted Dr Agrawal to follow the same anthropological approach of study." Dr Agrawal took that as the highest compliment he could receive as a teacher.

My field research-based study on "The Disaster Warning Process: A Study of the 1981 Gujarat Cyclone" was published in the London-based journal *Disaster* (1984). I sent a cyclostyled copy of my paper to many scholars, but no one responded. However, when it was published from London, I had numerous praises and requests for reprints from India and other countries. It provided me with another opportunity to apply my knowledge of anthropology and communication to disaster management.

My note on "Human Channel of Communication" to minimize the health communication gap (1999), based on my ethnographic study in Bidar district, was recognized globally. After reading this note, one of my old friends, a well-known Indian communication expert in the United States, wrote to me, praising my concept and asking if I was the same person who was working with SAC-ISRO, and we reconnected. Another significant achievement is my work, *Covering the Last Mile: A Challenge in Health Communication in India* (2016).

Apart from travelling to various countries, I lived in Stockholm (Sweden), Manchester (UK), Regina (Canada), and Tallahassee (USA). These were part of my fellowships, my participation in the national delegation, and official trips and invited talks at various universities across the world. I broadened my cultural understanding of these places where I spent more time.

I wrote and edited six books, provided book chapters, and published over a dozen papers in national and international magazines.

> There will be many more Arbinds to hit the ground further.

My Books

1985: *Mass Media and Rural Development.* New Delhi : Concept Publishing Company.

1986: Binod C. Agrawal, S.R. Joshi and Arbind Sinha (eds.). *Communication Research for Development: The ISRO Experience.* New Delhi: Concept Publishing Company.

1986: Binod C. Agrawal and Arbind Sinha (eds.). *SITE to INSAT: Challenge of Production and Research for Women and Children.* New Delhi : Concept Publishing Company.

1999: *Health communication in India: The Challenge* (Concept Note). New Delhi: DANIDA.

2002: Binod C. Agrawal, Arbind Sinha, and S.B. Sharma, (eds.). *Remote Sensing Applications in Brackish Water Fisheries: A Socio-Economic Study.* New Delhi: Concept Publishing Company (Pvt.) Ltd.

2004: *Critical Review of Existing Materials vis-à-vis the Project Objectives: Why and How to Do it?* (Teaching module being used for their training). New Delhi: Commonwealth Educational Media Centre for Asia.

2008: *Mass Media and Education*, invited Course Module for Block-4 of MES-014 on "Societal Context of Education" course. New Delhi: Indira Gandhi National Open University, pp. 31-44.

2011: *Kathabarta* (a compendium of teaching modules developed by Arbind Sinha on different dimensions of Health Communication as Facilitator's Guide), Bhubaneswar: National Rural Health Mission, Government of Odisha.

2022: Sudhakar N. Rao, and Arbind Sinha (eds.). *Culture, Communication and India's Development.* New Delhi: Concept Publishing Company (Pvt.) Ltd.

11

Traversing From History to Archaeology, Anthropology, and Museum Studies

A Narrative of Multiple Identities

Kishor K. Basa

It was about 10.30 a.m. on 30 January 1980. I had reached the Department of Anthropology, Utkal University to join as a lecturer. I was on the first floor. I saw one dignified lady climbing the staircase. I could know that she was Dr Usha Deka. I wished her and introduced myself. Polite but blunt, she said, "I don't like a student of history joining my department. If you have done so, you must have an M.A. in Anthropology." I was stunned and shocked. But later I realized how much was a well-wisher she was.

Biographical Outline

As a student I was a rank holder. In the High School Certificate Examinations, 1973 I stood first in Odisha (and my identical twin brother stood 10th and thus we both created a record) being awarded the Surajmal Saha Memorial Gold Medal. I was first class first in B.A. History (Hons.) examination, 1977 in Utkal University and was awarded Professor Ghanshyam Das Memorial Gold Medal. Then I did my M.A. in History specializing in Ancient Indian

History and Archaeology from University of Delhi in 1979 with an A grade. My exposure to social anthropology in my M.A. was confined to two areas: state formation and anthropological approach to religion. Then came an advertisement in Utkal Anthropology Department for a lecturer in prehistoric archaeology either from Anthropology or from Ancient Indian History and Archaeology background. I got the position in 1980 and superannuated from there in March, 2018 on completion of sixty years.

After my joining, at the suggestion of Professor L.K. Mahapatra I underwent practical training in archaeology for three months at Deccan College, Pune under the guidance of Dr V.N. Misra. In Utkal I started reading anthropology. I found social anthropology very interesting and clarified my doubts from Dr N.K. Behura, an excellent classroom teacher. In 1984, on one afternoon Dr Deka gave Rs. 50 to a peon to fetch an application form from the university, insisted that I should fill it up and sit for the M.A. examination. By that time, I had read the entire course in social anthropology and Indian society. I did not enjoy much the reading of physical anthropology. Dr S.K. Ghosh Maulik and Dr Basanti Rath helped me to complete physical anthropology practical while Dr K.C. Tripathy my prehistoric archaeology dissertation and practical. Dr Deka used to say that I won't have any difficulty in becoming a reader, but I would not be a professor without having a basic degree in anthropology and hence her insistence.

I won a Government of India scholarship to undertake Ph.D. in archaeology from the Institute of Archaeology, University College London from 1986 to 1991 on the topic *Early Westerly Trade of Southeast Asia with Special reference to Glass Beads* under the supervision of Dr Ian Glover. I was a UGC Visiting Associate (1994-96) at Deccan College, Pune working on tribal mortuary practises in Odisha from an ethnoarchaeological perspective and availed the Indo-French Cultural Exchange Programme at Ecole Francaise d'Extreme Orient, Paris in 1997. I won Commonwealth Academic Staff Fellowship at Department of Archaeology, University of Cambridge during 1999-2000 and worked with

Dr Dilip K. Chakrabarti—who had taught me archaeology in University of Delhi. I carried out research on *Social Theory and Indian Archaeology: A Historiographical Study*. I became a Professor in 2001 and Head of the Department from 2001 to 2003.

I was appointed as Director, Indira Gandhi Rashtriya Manav Sangrahalaya, (IGRMS), Bhopal from 2004 to 2008, Director, Indian Museum, Kolkata from December 2008 to December 2010, and Director, Anthropological Survey of India for a year in 2010. I was President, Anthropological and Behavioural Sciences Section, Indian Science Congress in 2007 and spoke on Globalisation and Cultural Heritage in the Third World. I was President, Archaeology Section of Indian History Congress, 2007 and talked on Social Theory and Indian Archaeology during Colonial Period: A Historiographical Study. My presidential address in the annual conference of Indian Society for Prehistoric and Quaternary Studies in 2011 was on Anthropological Perspectives on Prehistory and Protohistory of India. I have delivered twelve memorial lectures in different parts of the country.

After my superannuation, I became a Senior Tribal Domain Expert in the Special Development Council, Odisha from April 2018 to April 2019. I also availed Tagore National Fellowship at IGRMS Bhopal working on Anthropology and Museum in India. I was the Member Secretary and later Chairman of the Indian National Confederation and Academy of Anthropologists (INCAA)—largest body of professional anthropologists in India. I also became the Vice-Chancellor of Maharaja Sriram Chandra Bhanja Deo University (formerly North Odisha University). At present, I am the Chairperson of the National Monument Authority of India and was also Director General of the Archaeological Survey of India.

Fieldwork

My fieldwork was of three types: studying bead collections in museums in various countries, undertaking archaeological exploration and excavation in Odisha, and documenting tribal mortuary practises for ethnoarchaeology. For Ph.D. my primary study was on the glass beads from the iron age site of Ban Don Ta Phet, Thailand dated to about fourth century BC. After studying them in London, I went to Thailand and Malaysia to study the glass beads from excavated sites available in various museums and thus to create a data base for glass beads for both metal age and historical period for mainland Southeast Asia. For comparative purpose I studied such collections in various museums and excavations in India for two months in 1988. I also carried out analytical study of some glass beads by using EDAX method. Thus, I argued that glass beads were an important item of trade exported from India to Southeast Asia based not only on the basis of typology, but also on similar chemical compositions (Basa 1991). While studying beads of Bangladesh, I and S. Rahman reported the recovery of high tin Bronze-knobbed vessels from Wari and their implications for maritime trade.

With regard to Odishan archaeology, I had reported the recovery of Palaeolithic cultures from Burla, Palallhara, Parjang and Kalabadia, Mesolithic cultures from Duburi-Tamaka area (with Daitari Sahoo), Sundargarh and Rairangpur, Neolithic cultures from various sites in Mayurbhanj with a trial trench at Bajpur in central Odisha. Along with R.K. Mohanty of Deccan College, we excavated a Neolithic-Chalcolithic site at Bang-Harirajpur, which had yielded three skeletal remains—one man, one woman and a child—evidence of circular hut, a copper pendant, plant, animal and ceramic remains, implying the emergence of village farming communities in coastal Odisha. Besides, a small-scale excavation was undertaken at the Iron Age site of Malikhoja in Angul district and at the Early Historic site of Gourangapatana on the bank of Chilka Lake. Moreover, punch-marked coins were recovered and reported from Ghumal in Khadkhai River Valley in Mayurbhanj (along with Basanta Mohanta). In ethnoarchaeology, I studied the tribal mortuary practises of the Gadabas and Parajas and their implications for megalithic traditions. While earlier emphasis was usually on rituals, survey of burial/cremation ground was introduced as a methodological innovation for documentation.

Odishan Archaeology

Apart from the publications on Odishan archaeology based on fieldwork stated above, I published on history of archaeology, culture and politics in colonial Odisha, archaeological heritage summarizing the excavated sites in Odisha, its maritime archaeology, its cultural relations with Southeast Asia from an archaeological perspective, emergence of complex society in Odisha, ethnoarchaeology, etc. In a paper "Imagining Orissa: Archaeology, Art History and Cultural Identity," the role of archaeology in identity construction of Odisha during colonial and post-colonial periods were critically analysed. The various aspects included appropriation of Jagannath for political legitimacy, use of Odishi dance, Kalinga style of architecture, Puri-Kushana coins, rock art, square patterned early historic cities, etc. This provided a post-modern perspective to Odishan archaeology.

Archaeology of Trade

While my Ph.D. was on early westerly trade of Southeast Asia, I had also compiled the evidence of Indo-Roman trade. The recovery of Roman coins from Mayurbhanj in north Odisha and from two sites in the undivided Koraput district—the latter was drawn attention by me—implied indirect contact with Roman Empire. The recovery of one piece of Turquoise Glazed Ware—originating in Gulf area—at Gouranga Patana implied Odisha's participation in Indian Ocean trade network during eighth-tenth century AD. Besides, various archaeological approaches and ethnographic models for trade and exchange were critically studied.

Archaeological Theory

World System Theory

While working on the westerly trade of Southeast Asia from *c.* 400 BC to *c.*500 AD, I studied it from a world system perspective.

Wallerstein developed the world system approach in his study of the development of capitalism in Europe, since the units such as tribe, community and nation state were too small and not truly independent entities. My approach was a modified version of the world system theory. First, while Wallerstein considered politics and economics, in my version ideology and cosmology was also included. Second, while Wallerstein in his world system emphasized the primary role of politics until sixteenth century and that of economics for the subsequent period, in my view the respective role of politics and economics were considered in terms of spatial contexts. Third, the terms core/centre and periphery were used not as fixed and absolute concepts, but as relative to different spatial contexts. Lastly, periphery in antiquity was not passive. From the world system perspective, the Indo-Southeast Asian trade operated at three levels. At a pan regional level, India was the centre (or multiple centers) and Southeast Asia was the periphery (or multiple peripheries) which involved economically, what Rowlands called, "unequal exchange". The nature of relationship between the two was primarily economic, partly ideological and cosmological, but hardly political. At a regional level, with regard to the Southeast Asian coast as the centre and its interior as periphery, the relationship was more economic than political, ideological and cosmological. At a local level in Southeast Asia the relationship between the chief as the centre and members of his group as periphery, the relationship involved primarily a political domination which was ideologically legitimated by the belief of the powerful "soul stuff" (indigenous to Southeast Asia) and also by Buddhist and Hindu cosmology. Of course, this ensured an exchange of inalienable wealth from the chief for the alienable surplus from the low rank and thus, in a way, secured an economic return. But, in this case, economy, ideology and cosmology were embedded in what was primarily a political dominance. Thus the centre-periphery relation between the chief and his group members was best understood by hierarchy and exchange. Unlike Wallerstein's modern world system, it was argued that periphery in ancient world system was not a passive entity because of inadequate communication system, availability of options for trade transaction and the emergence of the concept of "localization" against the all-pervasive influence of "Indianization" . Thus, theoretically I tried to contextualize the centre-periphery relationship in an ancient world system. This contributed to post-processual archaeology.

Historiography

Historiography was another major aspect of my theoretical engagement which was mainly in five areas. In my discussion on social theory and Indian archaeology during the colonial period, it was argued that the Western engagement with India's past was not a monolith, rather was characterized by Orientalism of William Johns, Utilitarianism of James Mill, Romanticism and Hegel's universal history. While Orientalism and romanticism were in praise for India's grandeur of the past, James Mill was critical of the ahistorical Indian tradition. Hegel believed that historical process was inexorable. It was James Mill who wrote the *History of India* comprising three periods—Hindu, Muslim and the British. Although different in perspectives, the colonial approaches provided legitimacy, directly or indirectly, to colonial rule. Emerging from the late nineteenth century, the Indian Nationalist School incorporated the periodization of Mill with the sympathetic attitude of the Orientalists and Romanticists. In that sense, the Indian nationalist school was a derivative of colonial discourse; however, it became a different discourse by challenging the colonial historiography and by providing an ideological basis for the anti-colonial struggle of Indian nationalists under the leadership of Mahatma Gandhi.

Second, I undertook a historiographical review of about 100 years of Indian writings from 1889 to 1990 on early history and archaeology of Southeast Asia. It was discussed in three phases—pre-nationalist, nationalist and the writings after India was free. The pre-nationalist phase was characterized by an accommodative tone with the British civilizing mission, while the nationlist phase, especially during 1920s-1940s, witnessed a proliferation of literature on all-pervasive influence of Indianization of Southeast Asia, which was Greater India, reducing it as a passive recipient of Indian ideas, artefacts and civilizational impact. From 1960s onwards, the tone was subdued considering both mutual give and take between India-Southeast Asia cultural interaction.

My third example is a historiographical study of Odishan archaeology—pre-colonial, colonial and work after India became free. During pre-colonial period, there were references to temples, sculptures, forts, etc. in some late medieval texts and Western travel accounts. The colonial period (1803-1947) witnessed the birth and proliferation of archaeology in its broad sense—prehistory, sculpture and architecture, epigraphy and numismatics, forts and bridges. While James Prinsep deciphered Asokan inscriptions, James Fergusson for the first time provided a historical and chronological perspective to Odishan monuments, which was used and modified by scholars like R.L. Mitra and R.D. Banerji. Banerji even talked of a distinct Kalingan style of architecture. While V. Ball, the father of Odishan prehistory reported Palaeolithic artefacts from four places during 1870s, the first excavation of a Palaeolithic site in India was conducted by Nirmal Bose and Dharani Sen during 1940s. In order to counter the colonial discourse R.L. Mitra used the Odissan monuments for reconstructing nationalist discourse. The debate between Mitra and Fergusson became so bitter that Fergusson wrote a book with special reference to Mitra pouring venom against him, even linking it with the Ilbert Bill. During post-independent period, the early historic urban centres of Sisupalgarh and Jaugarh were excavated by ASI. I also published a summary of all excavated sites. Scholars of Utkal, Sambalpur and recently of Ravenshaw Universities, Odisha State Archaeology, State Museum, Orissan Institute of Maritime and Southeast Asian Studies, Deccan College, Pune as well as some German and American scholars contributed to various aspects.

An important theoretical point I had made was colonized as colonizer. There are two examples. First, the Indian nationalist school argued that during early centuries AD while the Britishers were not so developed, Indians were civilizing Southeast Asia. This created a problem, because, what is a nationalist perspective for Indians became a colonial perspective for Southeast Asians. Thus, the colonized Indians (vis-à-vis colonial British scholars) behaved as a colonizer for Southeast Asians. Second, with regard to Odisha, Rajendra Lal Mitra used its monuments for developing Indian nationalist perspective. However, on the issue of whether Odia is a separate language, Mitra thought it a part of Bengali and in that sense the colonized Mitra (vis-à-vis Fergusson) became a colonizer for Odishan heritage, especially its language.

Fourth, my paper "Situating V.N. Misra in Indian Archaeology: A Historiographical Account" was a comprehensive review on one of the well-known prehistorians.

The last study on historiography was on Indian beads under various subheadings—typology, technology, importance in trade and exchange and symbolism and in that sense, "small is useful" .

Anthropological Perspectives in Archaeology

There are four aspects of my study on this theme. I argued for two types of diffusionism in Indian archaeology. In the Irano-centric (or West Asia-centric) diffusionism of Sankalia, culture change in India was because of diffusion of traits from Iran or West Asia. In the framework of the modified diffusionism of Mortimer Wheeler, "ideas have wings and more liable to flit airily about our prehistoric as about our historic landscape, with a baffling intangibility or disguise" because "it takes a million years to develop a species, perhaps a million seconds to develop an idea" .

The second is the application of "new" or processual archaeology—developed by Lewis Binford—in India which was not necessarily a replica of the Western viewpoints. Influenced by Radcliffe-Brown's structuralism and Redfield's anthropological works on India, S.C. Malik was the first Indian archaeologist to talk in terms of a processual archaeology in India. However, unlike Binford, Malik did not reject inductive method, accepted the limitation of the nature of archaeological data and the relative nature of archaeological knowledge and emphasized "anthropological" approach to archaeology without ignoring history. He spoke on the importance of ethnoarchaeology and thought of the "regional cultural continuities" in terms of the "cultural-ecological and processual explanation". He also visualized the prevalence of the caste system in Harappan society by arguing for "a very early beginning" of one of the most important social institutions of later India "that characterize Indian style". Malik emphasized reinterpretation of archaeology in an anthropological perspective, but he did not use it in any fieldwork. For Sankalia, "New Archaeology" was a set of techniques and methods to tackle problems in the field. Sankalia was not, especially while discussing "New Archaeology", theoretically as much rigorous as was Malik. The strength of Malik was the weakness of Sankalia and vice versa. K. Paddayya combined a strong theoretical outlook (like Malik) with an intensive fieldwork (like Sankalia) in south India. He has made significant contribution not only writing on Processual Archaeology as a whole, but also in terms of making comprehensive reviews on their application in India—ethnoarchaeology, site formation processes, middle range theory, etc.

The third aspect is ethnoarchaeology. While a comprehensive review was made for Odishan ethnoarchaeology, fieldwork was conducted on the mortuary practices of the Gadabas and Parajas near Similiguda emphasizing their implications for understanding Megalithic traditions. An ethnographic study was also made on pre-industrial iron smelting in Mayurbahnj.

The fourth aspect is my study on the implications of globalization and nationalism for Indian archaeology. While globalization had implications for tourism to archaeological sites and the increasing interest of the Indian diaspora in Indian heritage, I argued for three types of nationalism in Indian archaeology. While the works of Dilip Chakrabarti stand for secular nationalism stressing on India as a geographical entity, the second type is religious nationalism emphasizing the primacy of Hindu nationalism in interpreting archaeology. The third is the cultural nationalism based on archaeology in various states which gives legitimacy to ascendancy of regional parties in India.

Anthropology

There are four aspects. The first is my presidential address in the Anthropological and Behavioural Section of Indian Science Congress in 2007 on the theme Culture and Development in the Third World. Here an emphasis was put on the role of culture as an input in sustainable development. Second, I was the General Editor of a series on Intangible Cultural Heritage of India where 9 volumes on different aspects of ICH have been published by different authors/editors. Third, a volume has been edited on anthropological impact assessment of development initiatives by Ajit Danda, myself and Kamal Misra. Fourth, I was one of the editors on a volume on M.N. Srinivas and another on plural nature of anthropology showing anthropology's relations with other disciplines in India.

Museum Studies

It has two aspects, (a) my work as Director of two leading museums in India—IGRMS, Bhopal and Indian Museum, Kolkata and (b) my publications relating to museum studies. With regard to the former, Veethi Sankool—the indoor museum building in IGRMS, was inaugurated in March 2005. Subsequently, a number of open-air exhibitions like traditional technology, house types, etc. were added. A volume was edited by me on the importance of specialized museums in India. A journal—*Humankind*—was started from IGRMS from 2007.

In a review on anthropology and museums in India, I had studied the trends and trajectories of museums in India from a colonial construct to post-colonial engagements. Set up in 1814, Indian Museum was the first museum. Some important features of museums during colonial period were as follows:

(a) there existed a tension between, on the one hand, the role of museum as an instrument of public education about the diversity of natural and cultural heritage in a scientific and objective manner and, on the other hand, the people's perception of the museum as *jadughar* (a "house of magic") or *ajaib ghar* (wonder house).

(b) The history of the Indian museum and the intellectual history of modern India almost coincide because of the linkage of different official government surveys—geological, archaeological, zoological and botanical—with Indian Museum.

(c) Museum visit as a part of pilgrimage in India is a typical Indian response and, in that sense, introduction of a Western metropolitan concept called museum in a colonial context is not a passive process.

(d) Besides, museums, like anthropology and archaeology, indirectly legitimized colonial rule as a civilizing mission by displaying the master pieces of antiquity implying a great Indian past and a backward "present" in colonial India.

The changing perceptions about museums from about mid-twentieth century onward were also pointed out by citing the works of some Indian scholars as well as discourses in the West. For example, just before India became free, T.C. Das in 1943 argued that museum should exist for the people and not for scientists alone. Giving primacy to economic museums—dealing with agriculture, commerce and industries—he argued that in a poor country like India, such museums should "carry their exhibits to the very doors of the people instead of asking them to come to the museums". Das suggested a network of three different varieties of museums: central museums, local museums, and circuit museums. In 1972, Sachin Roy proposed for a museum of man in India to promote tolerance and human understanding, to interpret natural and cultural history of India, to use the past for a "greater realization of the oneness of India" , to nourish scientific and humanistic studies as a complement to each other; to present anthropology as an integrative study of the cultural, physical, and prehistoric aspects of human life; and to give equal emphasis to the three aspects of museum services that he regarded as vital: collection, display, and the organization of educational activities. In the museum of man, "boosting of the folk art and popular traditions can be admirably combined with education, in the sphere of the cultural heritage of a country, in a museum dealing with anthropology and culture" . Writing in the background of "New Museology" and post-modern perspective, Kalyan K. Chakravarty advocated passionately that museums in India cannot ignore the fact that biological, genetic, molecular, and cultural reductionism were introduced in the wake of external colonization, that this destruction of diversity has been commensurate with making living communities into museums of objects and submerging Indian identity under a uniform homogenized set of options. According to him, the biggest challenge for a museum in India is the psychological and infrastructural difficulties of bridging the hiatus between the art in the museum and the living country of India. He argued that museums in India have to realize that so-called disadvantaged rural communities are curators of their own *in situ* museums and that their habits form the fabric of Indian history. He worried that the survival of the identity of rural communities is crucial to the survival of Indian identity and about the relevance of the museum project.

In the West, New Museology developed as a discourse from 1970s onwards critiquing the elitist nature of museum and pointing out that it was the community which is the main custodian of cultural heritage while the curators act as facilitators.

With this background, Indira Gandhi Rashtriya Manav Sangrahalaya, Bhopal began from late 1970s not with any artefacts in position but with certain ideas only. The Tribal Habitat was the first open air exhibition complex opened to the public in 1988 with its unique feature of presenting houses from different communities that had been constructed by the respective community with raw materials brought from their local area. Other open-air exhibitions include Himalayan Village, Coastal Village, Desert Village,

Mythological Trail, Traditional Technology. Involvement and participation of communities in the making of the museum is an important feature. Strident efforts were made in the museum to face twin challenges of contemporary museums—bringing communities to the museum and taking museum to the communities. The former includes activities such as Do and Learn, Sacred Grove Festival, Balrang Festival, Celebrating Regional Cultures of India, National tribal Healers Workshop, Shaswati (a programme on Women and Cultural Heritage), workshop on Diaspora and Museum, Umang—a programme for differently abled children, and an innovative project called Parvarish (with an NGO) to introduce museum as a place of non-formal learning. Taking museum to communities involves travelling exhibitions on sacred groves, rock art of India and tattoos, etc. seminar and workshops on intangible cultural heritage, workshops in Gujarat and the Bundelkhand area of Madhya Pradesh to document and promote the importance of traditional water-management traditions, workshops to promote the literary traditions of "marginalized" communities and healing traditions of tribal communities, etc. Thus, IGRMS promotes national integration, not by homogenizing culture but by celebrating cultural diversity with an inherent message of tolerance toward the other. The goal of developing scientific temper is emphasized not by high-tech science but by the dynamic and innovative aspects of traditional knowledge systems. A number of activities at IGRMS relate to the vulnerable sections of society including women and children. New and emerging issues in museology relating to identity, gender, diaspora, and differently abled people are also addressed. In IGRMS the curator acts as a facilitator to identify the space, while the communities are involved in curating the display.

To conclude, archaeology was the link between history I studied as a student and the discipline of anthropology I carried out as my profession. However, anthropological theories have helped me understand their creative engagement in Indian archaeological contexts as well as their implications for museum studies in India.

I have argued that application of western concepts in Indian archaeology and museum is neither a replica nor a passive process. Besides, my experience in both theory and practice of museum studies is another aspect of my professional life. Only posterity will evaluate whether I am an academic polyglot or otherwise.

My Books

2000: *Archaeology of Orissa*. South Asia Books.

2006: K.K. Basa, P.K. Misra and K. H. Bhat (eds.) *M.N. Srinvas: The Man and His Work*. Jaipur: Rawat Publishers.

2007: *Museology: A Comprehensive Bibliography and Webliography*. New Delhi: Serial Publications.

2010: *Multiple Heritage: Role of Specialised Museums in India*. New Delhi: Serial Publications.

2012: Kamal K. Misra, Ajit K. Danda, Kishor K. Basa (eds.) "Plural Nature of Anthropology: Golden Jubilee Lectures". *Journal of Indian Anthropological Society.*

2015 K.K. Basa, B. Francis Kulirani, K.K. Misra (eds.). *Tribes and Analogous People In India: Contemporary Issues*. New Delhi: Gyan Publishing House.

12

Reflexive Ethnography and Embodied Experience

Kamal Kant Misra

At the outset, I wish to confess straight from the shoulder. I would prefer to name this piece of writing as reflexive writing, where personal experience is coupled with careful observations about people, places and events that I studied, and critical thinking about my experiences as an anthropologist. As I had to be inextricably a part of the research process in the matter of the selection of the place, the people, the time, the subject(s) of study, and observing and interviewing hundreds of informants, I never dare to claim to be "a disembodied researcher", and hence, what I write here should not be taken at its face value. I completely acquiesce to what Clifford Geertz writes about his autobiography in his *Works and Lives: The Anthropologist as Author* (1988):

> "My own advice to anthropology departments is that this volume be kept in a locked cupboard, with the key in the possession of the head of the department, and that the students be lent it only when a strong case is made out by their tutors."

I would make an identical and candid request to the readers that as autobiographies like the present one could be reflexive for its ethnographer-author, but has to be essentially an embodied experience, belonging to the genre of "storytelling", it should not be taken heuristically. But thinking that these "stories" however obfuscating they might appear, also enlighten to a certain degree the future anthropologists and ethnographers, I conceded to the request of Late Professor Vinay Shrivastava and Professor P.C. Joshi to write this chapter. But as a reflexive writer, I take a "subject position" as it is necessary to use a personal narrative style, my only request would be not to construe this misadventure as my arrogance or imperiousness.

I shall not delve into narrating my career graph in greater detail, except hinting from the margin that I had my Anthropology and Sociology training at Utkal University, Bhubaneswar; Jawaharlal Nehru University, New Delhi; and the University of Kent at Canterbury, United Kingdom. But for forces beyond my control, I had to abandon my training as a professional town and country planner from the Indian Institute of Technology, Kharagpur, for which, of course, I do not regret. Under trying circumstances, I had to leave the course just one semester before completion. I must emphasize here that my training as an anthropologist is still not complete and I have had the privilege of learning a lot from three prestigious fellowships in three different countries and two continents: the Commonwealth Academic Staff Fellowship in the UK, the Fulbright Scholar-in-Residence Award in the USA, and the Guest Researcher Invitation in Norway. My anthropology training was further sharpened, when I got associated with Indira Gandhi Rashtriya Manav Sangrahalaya, Bhopal; the Anthropological Survey of India, Kolkata; and the Utkal University of Culture, Bhubaneswar in the capacities of director of the former two and the vice-chancellor of the last one. Even in the dreadful time of the COVID-19 pandemic, I continue to sieve out my anthropology learning from many postings on several social media platforms and participating in numerous webinars, which are the order of the day.

I started my professional career as a Lecturer in Social Anthropology in 1978 at Utkal University and there was no looking back till my superannuation in 2019 from the University of Hyderabad. I taught mainly anthropological theory, ecological anthropology and linguistic anthropology along with other subjects, depending upon the requirements at Utkal, Hyderabad and Austin College, Texas, USA. My anthropological fieldwork started in Odisha, and in the course of time, was extended to Arunachal Pradesh, and then to the undivided Andhra Pradesh. I had the privilege of studying the Juang, the Khampti and the Konda Reddy in some detail. I had very brief encounters with many other tribal communities in different parts of India from Arunachal Pradesh to Kerala, and one in the reserve of the USA, the Cherokee Indians. Nevertheless, I had a strong predilection to study contemporary Southeast Asian religion and culture, particularly of Bali (Indonesia), as between 1978 and 1988, I was teaching a course on Southeast Asian Studies to an interdisciplinary group of masters students at Utkal University from the Departments of Anthropology, History and Geography.

My first fieldwork dates back to 1975, when I set out to study the Juang, a Particularly Vulnerable Tribal Group (PVTG), inhabiting the hills of the Kendujhar district of Odisha. This was a group fieldwork with about sixteen of my classmates studying the Juang and each one of us writing a dissertation for the part fulfilment of the M.Sc. degree. We were under the supervision of Professor N.K. Behura and Dr B.K. Behera, both of whom were on the fieldwork trip with us for the entire period of thirty days. We were very modestly accommodated in three large halls at the Residential Ashram School, Janghira, about 35 km away from the district headquarters of Kendujhar, under the Harichandanpur Block. Although word restriction for this chapter would not permit me to discuss about the logistics there, suffice it to say that it was indeed a hard time for many of us. Getting up early in the bitterly cold mornings, extremely coercive and tiring travel for fieldwork during the daytime, and spending devilishly cold winter nights under the asbestos roof of a school building was extremely challenging. Therefore, Professor Behura adopted an innovative method to make us get up early every morning. He bought a hen from the Janghira weekly market (obviously from the mess money paid by us) and left her in one corner of our dormitory, whose harsh clucking sound was an unfailing wake-up call every morning around 4 a.m.. The idea was innovative, and funny though.

On the second day of our fieldwork, I was asked to visit the village Nalapanga, which was about 2 km from the base camp. I was introduced to the village headman or *pradhan* as a university student by the Ashram School Headmaster, Shri Rasananda Sahu, and was told that I needed their cooperation in writing about their culture and way of life. I chose a newlywed couple as my key informants and started addressing them as my elder brother (*ka*) and sister-in-law (*kuli*). Over time, I got several father's elder brothers (*atirai*), father's younger brothers (*dadi*) and aunties (*atirare*). The flow of information was instant and voluntary. Since I arrived Nalapanga during the harvest season, and *ka* and *kuli* were busy harvesting paddy and finger millets from their shifting cultivation field (*taila*) on the hill slope, I was invariably accompanying them with the collection of ethnographic information and helping them as well. In the afternoons, I was meeting some of the older people at the village youth dormitory (*majang*), to whom I was addressing as grandfather (*aja*), and was having long unstructured interviews on various dimensions of the Juang culture and society.

The objective of my research for the dissertation was to contribute to the ongoing debate on whether or not tribal societies were fundamentally egalitarian. It was proposed by Meyer Fortes and Evans-Pritchard (1940) from their African fieldwork that tribal societies were "economically homogeneous, equalitarian and segmentary". Contrary to this view, Marshal Sahlins argued that egalitarian societies were misnomers and simply did not exist. He contended that

> "Theoretically, an egalitarian society would be one in which every individual is of equal status, a society

> in which no one outranks anyone. But even the most primitive societies could not be described as egalitarian in this sense" (1958).

This being the background, I was asked to examine whether the Juang society could be classified as "egalitarian" or "differentiated", if not "hierarchical and stratified", as it happens in a typical cephalous society with a central political leadership enjoying all powers and privileges. I argued in my dissertation that although age, sex and personal characteristics were well-recognized universal features of minimal stratification criteria, beyond these criteria social differentiation existed in many tribal societies, the Juang being no exception. If I was to cite just one example, I might say that in *taila* cultivation although land ownership was communal and all eligible households were allotted swidden plots according to their needs, the plot allotted to the village headman (*pradhan*) was almost at the centre of the entire patch, which was relatively safer and protected from the attack of the wild animals, compared to the plots at the fringe of the patch. There were other privileges granted to the other village functionaries like *nigam* (priest), and *dangua* (village messenger).

The Juang political structure also identified an extraordinarily capable and articulate male as the tribal chief (*sardar*). The Juang settlements in Kendujhar were divided into four territorial clusters (*pidha*), namely Jhadakhanda, Rebena, Kathua, and Satakhanda. The *sardar* of a *pidha* was venerated by all the members belonging to the *pidha*. Like the village head, the cluster head and his family enjoyed many privileges, both religious and secular. I adopted participant observation and semi-structured interview methods to gather data and argue that true egalitarianism even in tribal societies was rare to find, although these might not be rigidly stratified with numerous prescriptions and proscriptions that were found in caste societies. The problems confronted in collecting empirical data were ethical. It was difficult to reveal the nature of differentiation and discrimination in the Juang society to my informants, which the Juang were not prepared to accept. Therefore, much caution had to be taken during the fieldwork, lest the reality hurt the sentiments of my informants. Besides Nalapanga, I also visited Budhakhaman, Khajuribani and other neighbouring villages for cross-verification of data, beginning with the third week of the fieldwork period. At a later date an abridged version of the dissertation was published in a paper with the title, "Dynamics of Inequality in an Unstratified Society: A Case Study of the Juang".

My M.Phil. dissertation submitted to the Centre for the Study of Social Systems, Jawaharlal Nehru University, New Delhi was on the topic, "Social Structure and Agricultural Growth in India: A Sociological Study". Since it was not mandatory then in JNU that the dissertation had to be empirical-based, my supervisor, Professor R.K. Jain was kind enough in advising me to complete the work with the analysis of secondary data. There were other problems relating to my job then. The dissertation was based on an extensive review of available literature on caste, class and the Indian agricultural scenario. The core theme of the dissertation was to examine class consciousness in Indian agriculture as suggested by many economists and rural sociologists, following the persuasive analysis of Lukàcs. I decided to critically look at the dichotomy between "class-in-itself" and "class-for-itself", and their emergence in the post-Green Revolution scenario in India. Alongside this, I also intended to examine the role of traditional social institutions like *jajmani* in rural India, contributing to the maintenance of rural social structure in agricultural societies. From the available literature, I concluded that in Indian agricultural society, despite its capitalistic orientation, the emergence of class consciousness in the typical Marxian sense was far from being set in motion, and the *jati* dynamics still played a credible and decisive role in Indian agriculture with the *jajmani* relations still in vogue in many pockets of India. An abridged version of this dissertation was published as occasional paper No. 6 with the title, "Caste, Class and Indian Agriculture", by the DSA Department of Anthropology, Utkal University, Bhubaneswar in the year 1996. Subsequently, several other publications relating to Indian agriculture were published by me, and co-authored by my student, Dr Niharranjan Mishra in journals like *Humankind* and *Indian Anthropologist.*

When I was teaching Southeast Asian Culture and Society at Utkal University between 1978 and 1988, I had almost decided to take up my doctoral project in one of the Southeast Asian countries, preferably in Indonesia. My childhood memory of sailing off paper/ banana peel boats on the occasion of "Bali Yatra" or voyage to *bali* on the full moon day of Karttik (October-November), metaphorically reminiscing the flourishing maritime trade relationship between the ancient Kalinga and the Southeast Asian countries had inspired me to probe further into the veracity of this celebration. Further,

> "Bali Jatra festival of Orissa has some parallel with "Masakapan Ke Tukad" festival of Bali where similar floating of toy boats in memory of maritime ancestors is made. Likewise, "LOYKRATHONG or LOY BRAH PRAHDIP" festival of Thailand consisting of ritualistic floating of boats in the month of December has [enormous] similarity with [the] Orissan custom." (Mohapatra 2007).

But despite all possible efforts, it was not possible for me and I had to settle down to the study of the Khampti of Arunachal Pradesh for my Ph.D. project. It was facilitated by the generous award of a Senior Research Fellowship (Cultural) by the Anthropological Survey of India, then headed by Professor A.K. Danda. When I took over as the Director of the Anthropological Survey of India, I tried my best to repay this huge debt by working hard for the Organization but without revealing this to anybody except my late wife. Besides other works, I ensured that the headquarters building of the Survey (it did not have its own HQ building till 2010) with an estimated cost of nearly 72 crore of Rupees be constructed in Kolkata instead of working from a borrowed building from the Indian Museum, Kolkata.

In October 1985, I prepared myself for fieldwork in the distant Lohit Valley. I reached Guwahati via Kolkata. It was a long train journey those days. One of the acquaintances had informed me that Shri Raj Kishore Pradhan from Bhubaneswar was the Deputy Director of the National Commission for SCs and STs in Guwahati looking after the entire north-eastern region, and could be of much help. Shri Pradhan indeed was very kind in welcoming me to Guwahati and arranging my accommodation in Guwahati as well as the Inner Line Permit (ILP) to enter Arunachal Pradesh. From Guwahati (then Gauhati), I boarded an evening bus to reach Tinsukia early in the morning. I checked into a small lodge closer to the Tinsukia bus station. After breakfast, I reached the bus station to enquire about the timing for buses running between Tinsukia and Tezu, the district headquarters of Lohit district. I was aghast with the information that only one 35-seater passenger bus ran between Tinsukia and Tezu per day, which was run by the Arunachal Pradesh State Transport Service. There was no timing for arrival or departure, as the bus had to come from Tezu daily. If it came on a particular day from Tezu, it would return; otherwise, one has to wait for the next day for the travel.

After waiting for two days, the bus from Tezu reached around Noon at Tinsukia and departed at 1 p.m. I was advised to alight from the bus on my way to Namsai, as it was the subdivision (now a district) in which most of the Khampti inhabited. The bus started rolling towards Dumduma, Kakopathar and halted at the Dirak check-gate for verification of the ILPs. After verification, the bus reached Namsai around 4.30 p.m. via Mahadevpur, the Circle headquarters of the Lekang Circle. It was almost the time for sunset. I reached the PWD Guest House close to the Namsai bus station and rested for the night with the kind help of the Extra Assistant Commissioner of Namsai, Mr Pillai.

It was a bitterly cold night at Namsai. I had the then-District Industries Officer of Lohit share my Guest House room for the night. Instantly we became friends and he volunteered to help by introducing me to the ex-MLA of the area the next day. As planned, I accompanied the District Industries Officer the next morning to meet the ex-MLA, Chow Khouk Manpoong, at his residence in the village Manmow by the side of NH 52. Chow Manpoong was a graduate of those days speaking fluent English and living in a sprawling wooden bungalow with his wife, surrounded by an orange garden. After I introduced myself, he explained how important it was to study the Khampti, which was a tribe with a rich cultural history and a developed language with scripts of its own. On my request, he volunteered to spare one of his abandoned houses across the road for my stay and conduct fieldwork in Manmow and the surrounding villages. Chow Manpoong kindly asked his men to make a permanent bamboo bed with the help of split bamboo, on which I spread my bed during the initial days of fieldwork. There were flies and insects all around, and nights were particularly very cold and scary. The shelter was close to the Manmow Government Secondary School. There was an army barrack nearby and a wayside small restaurant for tea and snacks. For the initial few days, I had to live on snacks, tea and local oranges; and visited Namsai weekly once for a sumptuous meal of rice and fish covering a distance of about 10 km both ways by walk. I took the help of a teacher, Shri Jha, from the Manmow Secondary School to get introduced to a few young males of the village to help me in my research. Initially, my presence in the village was looked at with suspicion and data collection was difficult. Further, I became sick due to cold weather, living with insects and reptiles and without proper food. I decided to shift my base camp to some other place.

At that point, Shri Jha, who hailed from Bihar, disclosed a piece of welcoming information. He revealed that in the village Kherem, which was about 35 km from Manmow, there was a teacher from Odisha and his name was Shri Behera. The very same day I wrote a letter in the name of Shri Behera (as his first name was not known to Shri Jha) requesting his help as a fellow Odia and sent the letter through a truck driver. Public transport then between Manmow and Kherem was unavailable. However, there was no way to ascertain whether the letter reached Shri Behera or not. After about two weeks, one afternoon someone knocked at my door. When I opened the door, I found a young man smilingly introducing himself as

Shri M.C. Behera from the Kherem School, whom I had requested help. When he saw my living condition and deteriorating health, he took pity on me and proposed that I should move to Kherem with him immediately. He said, he had a small official accommodation, which he was occupying with his daughter, Meena, who was studying in Standard VI then, while his wife and other children were living in Odisha. I gladly accepted his proposal as it was like God's boon. With all gratitude, I must say that Shri Behera not only offered me shelter for more than a month but also cooked and fed me for the entire duration until I decided to move on to the village Mimi. During this time, he helped introduce me to one of my trusted and best informants, Chow Thanin Mansai of Kherem, and also helped me with fieldwork in Kherem and surrounding villages. Through the generous help of Shri Behera I established excellent and life-long rapport with many friends in the Khampti country including Chow Kamin Langkhung (Momong village), Chow Suliksa Namsum (Deka Raja of Momong village), Chow Kemang Namsum (*Chowman* of Mimi village), Chow Chilakan Munglang (in-charge of the Archives of Chowkham village), Chow Niku Mansai (Kherem village) and several other friends, whose time and patience largely contributed to my understanding of the Khampti society and culture. I also encountered the most tragic and untimely death of my friend, Chow Niku Mansai (Kherem village), during my stay there. My fieldwork was enriched by my Khampti friends from many villages along the Mahadevpur-Wakro corridor, to whom I owe my sincere gratitude. Shri Behera was also instrumental in my memorable visit to Hayuliang, Khupa and Chameliang villages on a later date on an ethnographic expedition among the Mishmi, which are now under the Anjaw district of Arunachal Pradesh.

My stay in Mimi was hard enough, yet academically very productive. For a very long time, I stayed in the village Primary School, and cooked my food, thanks to Shri Sharma, the village school teacher from Nalbari in Assam, who helped with logistics as well as fieldwork. One of the memorable experiences during the prolonged fieldwork in Lohit Valley was accompanying Khampti friends on hunting and fishing expeditions, elephant riding as a means of transportation, and attending *sangken* and other religious functions in the Khampti belt. The Khampti king, Chow Khamoon Gohain (Namshum) of Gunanagar, who was also the first nominated M.P. from the entire NEFA in 1952 for two consecutive terms, Chow Chandret Gohain of Chowkham, who was the first M.P. of the Union Territory of Arunachal Pradesh in 1972, Shri P.K. Mohapatra, a teacher from the Chowkham Secondary School, Shri Diwakar Tiwari, Junior Engineer with CPWD at Chowkham, and several other friends in more than thirty Khampti villages made my long fieldwork in two different spells very productive. I tried my best to learn the vocabulary and endeavoured to communicate in Khampti language as far as practicable. Finally, I came out with the Ph.D. thesis on Khampti elite and social transformation, the abridged version of which was published as *Tribal Elites and Social Transformation* by Inter-India Publications, New Delhi in 1994.

The thesis could be placed under the broad theme of Political Anthropology. Around the time when the study was undertaken, many tribal societies in north-east India, including the Khampti, were in a state of transition from kingship to local self-governance with elected representatives. My study particularly focused on how the traditional power centres in the form of *chowfa* (traditional community chief) (King) and *chowman* (village headman) (popularly known as *gaon burha* as the Assamese usually address) still wielded power even in the modern democratic process and were elected as people's representatives because of their ascribed status as well as control over the resources. This resulted in a discreet division within the Khampti society between the pro- and anti-chieftaincy sentiments. But more importantly, I was looking at the role of these elites in contributing to the transformation of their society in all possible spheres. Interestingly, I noticed that although in their individual capacities, the governing elites were contributing to changing their society, a collective effort was missing because of narrow factionalism, thereby retarding the pace of transformation in the Khampti society to a large extent.

Even after the completion of my Ph.D. work, I was almost in touch with my informants and well-wishers either by visiting Lohit or through other means of communication. In the year 2010, I developed an interest in re-studying the Khampti after a gap of twenty-five years, for which I visited Chowkham. By that time Shri Behera had obtained his Ph.D. on the Khampti and relocated himself to the Arunachal Institute of Tribal Studies under the Arunachal University (now renamed as Rajiv Gandhi University), Itanagar. As a result, I was deprived of his warm hospitality at Kherem, which he extended in 1985. Although word limitation for this memoir will not allow me to elaborate further, suffice it to say that there were prodigious changes in the Khampti physical and cultural landscapes between 1985 and 2010. Once very affluent Chowkham village had lost its glory, which was the richest village in Asia in the 1980s. The roaring sounds of hundreds of monster trucks carrying timber to Assam round-the-clock were silenced due to the 1996 ban on timber felling by the intervention of the Honorable Supreme Court of India. Dozens of plywood and veneer industries were closed down and instead, tea gardens and manufacturing industries were coming up in the region. Communication of all kinds had improved significantly, private English-medium educational institutions were added to the government-run schools, etc. However, the strong community solidarity and kin network among the Khampti had declined in tune with the noticeable trends in the rest of India. The completed re-study manuscript is awaiting its publication.

I moved to the University of Hyderabad as a Reader in January 1989 and it was difficult to visit north-east India frequently. Like Utkal University, in Hyderabad also I had to accompany the students for their fieldwork in different pockets of the undivided Andhra Pradesh. I tried to muster courage and learn Telugu to at least minimally communicate with the informants during short fieldwork trips. I was awarded a few research projects and it was necessary to conduct fieldwork with the research assistants, for short periods though. I decided to work on the Konda Reddy, mostly distributed in the districts of East and West Godavari on both banks of the River Godavari, and also sporadically in Khammam and Srikakulam districts. They were traditionally swidden agriculturists living on hill slopes or foothills, and speaking Telugu with a different accent. I developed an interest in studying the interface between the Konda Reddi culture and ecology in general, for which I visited Vakkuluru village under the Maredumilli Block, several times between 1990 and 2015. I developed an interest in the study of Indigenous Knowledge (IK) and ethnoscience and frequented Rampachodavaram, Maredumilli, Addateegala and their surrounding villages, either alone or with my scholars for collection of first-hand data. My conversation with broken Telugu was always enjoyed by the informants and I had more than expected data at the end of each fieldwork trip. Dr Sivaramakrishna, Dr Narendra, Dr Anil Kumar, Dr Koteswara Rao, Dr Bikku, Late Shri John Victor and many other friends and well-wishers had academically contributed to several books, papers and reports I published on IK during this period. I owe a lot to them for their affection and voluntary help in my academic pursuits.

My association with two great institutions, Indira Gandhi Rashtriya Manav Sangrahalaya and Anthropological Survey of India between 2010 and 2013 with a large number of anthropologist friends working there facilitated group fieldwork in several parts of India, organizing several seminars and workshops, training programmes and publication of books, in-house journals, newsletters, brochures, etc. New galleries, new house types and dormitories, renovation of existing infrastructures in IGRMS, etc. were undertaken. During my tenure at AnSI, I expedited the publication of many excellent reports submitted by many leaned anthropologists of the Survey, revived the *Journal of Anthropological Survey of India*, the *Newsletter* and preparation of several documentaries on communities and their ingenuities as a new landmark in Visual Anthropology. I also initiated an ambitious project on re-studying about fifty villages, which were studied about half a century ago by many renowned anthropologists from India and abroad. I am told, the re-study on Bisipara has already been published. I tried my best to academically contribute as much as possible to these two great institutions as their Director under the Ministry of Culture, Government of India, despite many hurdles.

In 2016 I was appointed Vice-Chancellor of the Utkal University of Culture, Bhubaneswar for three years. When joined on 20 October 2016, I reviewed the academic and financial health of the university. It was working in Unit-2, Bhubaneswar, in a small and dingy campus at the heart of the city, closer to the Central Market Complex and the old bus station. But a brand-new university building and two hostels were already constructed and inaugurated in May that year. When I enquired about the reason for not moving into the new sprawling campus, my colleagues and students expressed the distance/accessibility as the reason. However, I was determined to move to the new campus on the outskirts of the city as I had the privilege of working on a huge campus of the University of Hyderabad with about 2,700 acres. The same evening, I visited the new campus, liked it and decided that the vice-chancellor's office would start functioning there on 9 November 2016. There were protests, resentments, etc. to which I did not budge. I arranged transport between the old and the new campuses for the students and the staff at the university cost to start with. Gradually people realized how satisfying it was to work on a larger, spacious and pollution-free campus than on a crowded and tiny campus. I also made the new campus and the hostels wi-fi enabled, digitized admissions and examinations, conducted convocations every year, started Foundation Day Lectures, exposed the students and teachers to luminaries in the fields of visual and performing art, etc.

At the twilight of my career, when I look back on my association with anthropology for nearly half a century, I find it immensely satisfying. Anthropology has given me recognition much beyond my expectations. On several occasions, I had represented my country in many different international forums as an anthropologist. Many awards from the President of India to the Asiatic Society were conferred on me because of my involvement with anthropology and I owe a lot to my discipline.

My Books

1987: *Social Structure and Change among the Ho of Orissa*. New Delhi: Gyan Publishing House.

1994: *Tribal Elites and Social Transformation*. New Delhi: Inter-India Publications.

2000: *Text Book of Anthropological Linguistics*. New Delhi: Concept Publishing Company (Pvt.) Ltd.

2001: *Peoples and Environment in India* (edited with M.L.K. Murty). New Delhi: Discovery Publishing House.

2005a: *Indigenous Knowledge, Natural Resource Management and Development: The Konda Reddi Experience*. New Delhi: Pratibha Prakashan and Bhopal: IGRMS.

2005b: *Anthropology, New Global Order and Other Essays* (edited). New Delhi: Concept Publishing Co.

2007a: *Recent Studies on Indian Women* (edited with Janet Lowry). Jaipur and Delhi: Rawat Publications (Reprinted in 2010).

2007b: *Traditional Knowledge in Contemporary Societies: Challenges and Opportunities* (edited). New Delhi: Pratibha Prakashan, and Bhopal: Indira Gandhi Rashtriya Manav Sangrahalaya.

2007c: *Rehabilitation and Resettlement in India: The Tribal Emic Perspective* (with D.J. Narendra Bondla). Secunderabad: Centre for World Solidarity.

2011: *Rock Art in India: A Selected Bibliography* (with Sudhir Shrivastava, and Md. Rehan). Bhopal: Indira Gandhi Rashtriya Manav Sangrahalaya and Delhi: Serials Publications.

2012a: *Cultural Pluralism: The Indian Scenario* (edited with S.A.A. Saheb and B. Francis Kulirani). Bhopal: Indira Gandhi Rashtriya Manav Sangrahalaya and Delhi: Gyan Publishing House.

2012b: *Anthropological Impact Assessment of Development Initiatives* (edited with Ajit K. Danda and Kishor K. Basa). Jhargram: INCAA.

2012c: *Displacement and Rehabilitation: Solutions for the Future* (edited with Nihar Ranjan Mishra). Bhopal: Indira Gandhi Rashtriya Manav Sangrahalaya and Delhi: Gyan Publishing House.

2012d: *Plural Nature of Anthropology* (edited with Ajit K. Danda and Kishor K. Basa). Kolkata: Indian Anthropological Society.

2012e: *Tribal Movements in India: Visions of Dr K.S. Singh* (compiled and edited with G. Jayaprakasan). Bhopal: Indira Gandhi Rashtriya Manav Sangrahalaya and New Delhi: Manohar Publishers and Distributors.

2012f: *Bio-Cultural Development of Scheduled Tribes: Policies and Issues* (edited with P.K. Misra and H.K. Bhatt). Bhopal: IGRMS, Mysore: Anthropological Association, and Jaipur: Rawat Publications.

2013a: *Amazing Arunachal Pradesh: Land, People, Culture* (with M.C. Behera). Bhopal: Indira Gandhi Rashtriya Manav Sangrahalaya and New Delhi: Aryan Books International.

2013b: *Gendering Material Culture: Representations and Practice* (edited with Subhadra Mitra Channa). Bhopal: Indira Gandhi Rashtriya Manav Sangrahalaya and Jaipur: Rawat Publications.

2013c: *Indian Religious Practices: A Selective Bibliography* (with Mohammad Rehan and Ravindra K. Gupta). Bhopal: Indira Gandhi Rashtriya Manav Sangrahalaya and Delhi: Gyan Publishing House.

2013d: *Ethno-Medicine in India: A Selective Bibliography* (with Mohammad Rehan and Ravindra K. Gupta). Bhopal: Indira Gandhi Rashtriya Manav Sangrahalaya and Delhi: Gyan Publishing House

2014: *Dissent, Discrimination and Dispossession: Tribal Movements in India* (edited with N.K. Das). Bhopal: Indira Gandhi

Rashtriya Manav Sangrahalaya and New Delhi: Manohar Publishers and Distributors.

2015: *Tribes and Analogous Peoples in India* (edited with K.K. Basa and Francis Kulirani). New Delhi: Gyan Publishing House.

2016: *The Particularly Vulnerable Tribal Groups in India: Privileges and Predicaments* (Chief Editor). New Delhi: Manohar Publishers and Distributors.

2017: *Villages in India: From "Little Republics" to "Ontological Existents"* (Professor S.C. Dube Memorial Oration, 2017). Jhargram: INCAA.

2018: *Exploring Indigenous Knowledge System in India* (edited with Gnanapragasam Lazar). New Delhi: Mittal Publications.

2022: *Rural Taboos of Odisha: Unveiling the Silent Practices* (with R.C. Malik). Bhubaneswar: Utkal University, Global Centre for Rural Studies. Also published in Navaneeta Rath *et al.* (eds.) *The Panorama of Odisha's Rural Culture: A Kaleidoscopic View*. New Delhi: Mittal Publications.

13

Autobiography

Amitabha Sarkar

I was born on 5 December 1952 in Calcutta to a businessman's family. My father Late, Naresh Chandra Sarkar was an engineer and contractor and mother Smt. Alaka Sarkar—a housewife, I have one brother, Samitava Sarkar. My early childhood education was at Bengali School, Darbhanga, Bihar and later at Kolkata, initially from Narendrapur Ramakrishna Mission Ashrama. I completed my B.Sc. (Honours) in Anthropology in 1972 from the University of Calcutta and then Masters in Anthropology in 1974 from University of Calcutta. During graduation at University of Calcutta I came in contact with Professor B.N. Banerjee of the Department of Anthropology which changed my vision in understanding the society and culture; with his inspiration I read number of anthropological monographs and acquired a skeletal idea of anthropological fieldwork and its systematic expression through writing.

I joined Anthropological Survey of India in March 1977 initially as Senior Technical Assistant. Prior to that I was a bank employee where I worked for about six months and then left for the job of Anthropological Survey of India at Udaipur, Rajasthan. I retired from Anthropological Survey of India as Superintending

Anthropologist in December 2012. During my official tenure I was Manageing Editor, *Journal of Anthropological Survey of India*, All India In-charge of Publication & Printing Division and All India In-charge of Photography and Cine Division.

During my tenure at Anthropological Survey of India, Udaipur, I carried out my Ph.D. dissertation work among the Dhodia of South Gujarat for a period of six month at a stretch in the villages for collection of empirical data on Dhodia community. In 1986 I received the Ph.D. degree from University of Calcutta. My Ph.D. work was guided by Professor Biswanath Banerjee, one of the *sishya* of Professor Nirmal Kumar Bose. The title of my Ph.D. dissertation was "Impact of Industrialization among the Dhodia of South Gujarat". The chief findings of my thesis were—

> "it is evident that the changes which have taken place in the way of life of the Dhodias of the impact village as well as in the industrial township for the last two generations are more around the periphery than the core of their traditional cultural life".

During my association with AnSI, I carried out several fieldworks in a number of research projects since 1977-2012 in Rajasthan, Gujarat, West Bengal, Chhattisgarh especially in undivided Bastar district, South Bihar (now Jharkhand), Malkangiri and Koraput districts of Odisha.

Some salient features of my field impressions are illustrated here. The study of ethno-science among the Abujh Maria—a half clad tribal group as well as a PVTG of Chhattisgarh as a co-worker with Samira Dasgupta. The work deserves a noteworthy contribution in the domain of anthropological research; how the celestial world of Abujh Maria is having a deep influence on their terrestrial life. Studies were done among the Toto—a PVTG of West Bengal and the Asur—a PVTG of Jharkhand. Both the tribal communities were studied holistically, jointly with Dr Samira Dasgupta, and especial emphasis was given on their belief system, world view and ethno-medical practises, where use of local herbs/

plants/tubers were used for ailment which were documented being Traditional Knowledge System.

The study focusing on Dussehra festival of Bastar shows how centripetal social force is active which brings harmony of various tribal and non-tribal communities in one platform and ultimately existence of harmonious environment occurs. Further, it is also informed that I had initiated a research work along with Samira Dasgupta on State Formation of Bastar with special emphasis on role of Danteshwari Mata—the tutelary deity of Bastar Maharaja; one section of such work is already published from New Delhi, 2010 entitled "Religious Belief and Practices: Portrayal of the Integrative Process" in 2010 from New Delhi.

Further, I have also studied Bonbibi cult at Sundarbans—who is appeased by all section of ethnic groups (including Muslims and Christians) of Sundarbans being survival strategy in such dreaded terrain of mangrove where the existence of Royal Bengal Tiger is very much in evident. Here, cultural syncretism has been observed.

At the end of my official carrier, I have carried out a study on social audit assessment along with six other members of Anthropological Survey of India. The team was multi-disciplinary, where there were two cultural Anthropologists—Dr Samira Dasgupta and myself. I took the maximum pain in designing the project, including methodology and data collection. Finally, this work was published under the caption "Fuming Forest" from New Delhi, 2014 and earned a notable review observation where with empirical data the social situation of Jungle Mahal (study area) was analysed and presented and "Foreword" of the book was written by Professor Vinay K. Srivastava. In spite of number of hurdles, being associated with a government set-up during my official carrier, only two scholars were awarded Ph.D. degree where I was co-guide of those scholars.

In spite of my official superannuation from Anthropological Survey of India, I keep serving the discipline—anthropology by virtue of my vast exposure to various field situation in different eco-cultural zones of our country and a study has been made among the

Kandh-Pano community of Odisha jointly with Samira Dasgupta for establishing social identity through empirical data and the same is also published from New Delhi in the year 2016.

It is also found that following the principle of Professor N.K. Bose in his study "Peasant life in India: A Study in Indian Unity and Diversity", I have also attempted to identify some cultural attributes of Indian communities in various eco-cultural zones in the form of little traditions. I presented those in published form to establish that in spite of variation, there is a strong pulse of harmony among all ethnic groups and which is identified as Indian diversity are signature by great heritage.

Lastly, it is to be mentioned that with my active initiation and with the help of Dr Samira Dasgupta, I was able to document the contribution of Indian anthropologists during 1920-2019 and published three volumes of Doyens of Indian Anthropology (1920-2019) wherein contribution 69 Indian scholars were documented (2019, 2020, 2021). There is also a publication where I am one of the co-editors of the volume, entitled *Retrospect of 100 years of Indian Anthropology* (*1920-2019*) where development of the branches of the discipline are dealt till date with expected new dimensions of anthropology (2020). I am now involved along with Dr Samira Dasgupta in preparing a manuscript on "Folklore of Corruptions in the Eyes of Anthropologists." The idea is inspired from Professor Gunnar Myrdal—a Swiss Nobel laureate. The present volume tries to deviate from the traditional colonial hang over but through churning of ethnographic data this book envisages in understanding the folklore of corruption practices in our country which were gathered and generated by virtue of participant observation by the present anthropologists.

My Books

1993: *TOTO: Society and Change* (*A Sub-Himalayan Tribe of West Bengal*). Calcutta: Firma KLM Pvt. Ltd.

1993: *DHODIA:Industrialisation and Change in a Primitive Community.* New Delhi: Gyan Publishing House.

1996: *Spectrum of Tribal Bastar.* Delhi: Agam Kala Prakashan. (Jt. Author Amitabha Sarkar and Samira Dasgupta.)

1996: *Fundamentals of Social-cultural Anthropology.* Calcutta: Firma KLM Pvt. Ltd. (Jt. Author B.N. Banerjee and Amitabha Sarkar.)

1999: *Frontiers of Social Anthropology.* New Delhi: Gyan Publishing House. (Jt. Author Samira Dasgupta and Amitabha Sarkar.)

2000: *Ethno-Ecology of Indian Tribes: Diversity in Cultural Adaptation.* Jaipur: Rawat Publications. (Jt. Author Amitabha Sarkar and Samira Dasgupta.)

2005: *Reflection of Ethno-Science: Study on the Abujh Maria.* Delhi: Mittal Publications. (Jt. Author Samira Dasgupta and Amitabha Sarkar.)

2010: *Religions Belief and Practices (A Portrayal of the Integrative Process).* New Delhi: Agam Kala Prakashan, (Jt. Author Amitabha Sarkar and Samira Dasgupta.)

2011: *Mal Paharia Culture at the Crossroad.* New Delhi: Agam Kala Prakashan. (Jt. Author Amitabha Sarkar, Samira Dasgupta.)

2012: *Traditional Knowledge in Indian Society,* ed. Amitabha Sarkar, A.V. Arakeri, Suresh Patil. Kolkata: Anthropological Survey of India.

2012: *Rhythm of Tribal Culture: An Unveil Saga.* Germany: Lambert Academic Publishing (e-book released on 19.10.12) (Joint Author Samira Dasgupta, Amitabha Sarkar.)

2013: *Traditional Wisdom and Sustainable Living: A Study on the Indian Tribal Societies,* ed. H.R. Mandal and Amitabha Sarkar. New Delhi and Kolkata: Anthropological Survey of India and Gyan Publishing House.

2014: *The Fuming Forest: An Analytical Critique.* New Delhi: Mittal Publications.

2016: *Indigenous People: In Search of Identity (A Quest for Social Identity of Pano or Kui Domanga).* New Delhi: Mittal

Publications. (Jt. Author Amitabha Sarkar, Samira Dasgupta, Dhananjay Senapati.)

2016: *Dimensions of Anthropology* (*A Prismatic Panorama*). New Delhi: Kalpaz Publications. (Jt. Author Amitabha Sarkar, Samira Dasgupta).

2016: *Attributes of Culture* (*Reflection of Cultural Itineraries from a Multi-Cultural Nation*), eds. Amitabha Sarkar, Samira Dasgupta, Naba Kumar Duary. New Delhi: Aayu Publications.

2018: *Little Tradition in a Culturally Pluralistic Nation*. eds. Dr Amitabha Sarkar, Dr (Mrs) Samira Dasgupta. New Delhi: Aayu Publications.

2019: *Doyens of Indian Anthropology* (*1920-2019*), eds. Amitabha Sarkar and Samira Dasgupta. Delhi: Agam Kala Prakashan.

2020: *Doyens of Indian Anthropology* (*1920-2019*), Part-2. eds. Amitabha Sarkar and Samira Dasgupta. Delhi: Agam Kala Prakashan.

2020: *Retrospect of 100 years of Indian Anthropology,* (*1920-2019*). eds. Biman Kumar Dasgupta, Samira Dasgupta & Amitabha Sarkar. New Delhi: Aayu Publication.

2021: *Doyens of Indian Anthropology* (*1920-2019*), Part-3. ed. Amitabha Sarkar. Delhi: Agam Kala Prakashan.

2023: *Folklore of Corruption: In the Eyes of Anthropologists*. New Delhi: Maya Publishing House.

2024: *Bastar: The Polity of Subalterns in State System*. Delhi: Agam Kala Prakashan (Co-Author).

14

My Journey into Anthropology

Reminiscences and Reflections

Subhadra Mitra Channa

I remember growing up in a house that was full of books; there were books on shelves, on chairs, on tables and we even slept with books under our pillows. My father was a professor of English literature and passionately fond of books. He could, as his students later told me, "bring Shakespeare alive in the class room". From childhood he imbibed the love of language and literature into me and I happily absorbed it. I was the third and last child in the family, with a brother, eight years my elder and a sister, twelve years senior who played the roles of little parents to me, more than that of siblings. We lived in a bungalow in University of Delhi campus with plenty of space for my play, but from a very young age, my love was for books. My father closely monitored my readings, ensuring that I had read all of Dickens, Scott and Jane Austen, and almost every other classic of English literature as well as those translated from other languages, like Dumas, Hugo, Dostoyevsky, Pushkin and many others. I was and still remain a book worm. In childhood I also suffered ill health that kept me at home and discouraged me from outdoor activities, books remaining my best friends and companions.

I went to a fairly elite school run by British missionaries, some of whom were still around when I was schooling in the 1950s and 1960s. School was a delight. I was very happy in the kind of schooling that was considered appropriate for girls of good families in those days, that also meant we were educated not for careers but to be good housewives. There were classes for "domestic work" and we knitted and sewed and embroidered and sang songs and played games most of the time. But there were some serious studies and I soon discovered that the one major talent that I had, was for writing. The first time our history teacher came beaming into the class and asked, "who do you think has written the best essay?", the entire class in unison, chanted my name, to my utter surprise.

When time came for us to choose our stream, the teachers advised my parents to send me into the arts section, but at that time I was enamoured of science and wanted to do science along with most of my friends, who were also "good in studies" . I loved biology and was quite comfortable with the other science subjects except for physics. However, when at my school board examinations, I scored high marks, with distinction (at that time it was considered prestigious to get more than 75% marks) in all science subjects; the family well-wishers rallied around to push me to study Physics Hons. Those were not the days when one questioned one's parents. I had wished to join medical school as I loved biology, but my brother was already passing out of his medical school and my mother did not wish me to do the same. She thought the regime was too harsh for a delicate girl like me. I wished to do English literature but that to did not go down well with my parents, so physics it was. Although initially I was quite enthusiastic, but by the end of the third year by the time I graduated my B.Sc. Hons in Physics, I did not wish to continue. My father too had realized that I was not meant for the hard sciences. He then suggested I do anthropology. "Do what?" I was surprised, I had not heard of this subject.

From his vast library, my father chose several books, *The Golden Bough* by James Frazer, *Anthropology* by Edward B. Tyler and several others. He also made me read, *Idea of a Social Science* by

Peter Winch. I was delighted. The subject seemed very absorbing and involved reading very interesting books that were close to literature. My father spoke to the then Head of the Anthropology Department, in University of Delhi; Professor I.P. Singh, who had been his former student. I was admitted and soon found out that I was doing a subject close to my heart. I was vastly impressed by the teachers who were teaching in the department at that time, like Professor J.D. Mehra, who made learning supremely exciting. I was delighted that my interest in writing could be fully utilized in this subject, where one needed expressive writing skills. At the end of my first semester, I found that I had topped the class. My friends were more excited than me and this was another plus point. In anthropology I have found life-long friends. The department of anthropology was small as compared to the large departments such as of physics and chemistry, but it felt like home. Teachers were strict and indulgent at the same time. Several of them were superb teachers, especially Professor Abhimanyu Sharma, Professor S.C. Tiwari and Professor D.K. Bhattacharya, who made their subjects fascinating.

I knew I was set in my profession. I wanted to be an anthropologist and an academician at that. I met my husband, Dr Vardesh Chander Channa, in the department itself. He was a Ph.D. scholar when I was doing my masters. When I too joined Ph.D., we began to interact more. I was deeply impressed by the brilliance of his mind and his suave manners and upbringing. He came from an elite family and had been educated in some of the most prestigious institutions in India. We became involved in some common project where we had to spend a lot of time in the library. He proposed to me inside the Arts Faculty Library (as it was then known). He was also the one to introduce me to my Ph.D. field area.

Vardesh was doing his fieldwork in the Old Delhi area, also known as the Walled city of Shahjahanabad, a city built by the Mogul emperor Shah Jahan, in the seventeenth century. Like all old cities it was enclosed by a wall and gates, some of which are still standing. Like most old Indian cities, it also had its designated caste-based plan, accommodating the service castes in enclosures that ensured that their services were available to the high castes, without intruding upon their ritual purity. Vardesh was doing his fieldwork at the other end of the spectra, with upper caste Aggarwals of the Old City. The said Aggarwals are among the early settlers of the city, who dominated the trade and economy of urban city, from the time of the Moguls. Bayley has described the peopling of the early cities of India by the merchant castes, who also relied heavily upon the migration of the service castes to the cities from the countryside. The accidental discovery of a community of washermen (*dhobis*) revealed that there was a closed community (*biradari*), who claimed that they were part of the city right from the time of its establishment. They called themselves the *sheheri dhobi*s.

Initially the choice of this community was mainly dictated by their easy availability, concentration in a small geographical area and the friendly and inviting attitude displayed by them. One of my earliest informants was a person who was a kind of important person in the *biradari*, being a successful wrestler and body builder, a bone setter and indigenous healer, along with being a *dhobi*. Through him, I gained easy entry into the *biradari*, who became like my second order kin over the next six-seven years and with members of which, I still maintain close relationships. I have discussed my emotional and personal transformation as a result of my close association with a marginalized, low caste community, categorized as "untouchable" by many of the upper castes, who used their services.

Another aspect, even more personalized that pushed my theoretical concerns was the treatment that was meted out to me as a woman anthropologist, who was also married and a mother. The very teachers, who had given me excellent marks as a student were not convinced that I could teach in the department of anthropology. For many years I struggled to find a legitimate place for myself but although I received prestigious doctoral and post-doctoral grants, a teaching post was denied to me. I was given ad hoc positions and made to teach many courses, but when it came to a permanent post, I was never found suitable.

After many years of struggles I was finally appointed as an Associate Professor, but the resentment against my appointment was so high that I was made to wait one full year before I could actually join my designated post. The rejections and the hostility, the humility and the utter disregard for my scholarship, just because I was a woman, a wife and a mother, pushed me to think about gender as an important aspect of social life. From the 1980s onwards I had been re-analysing much of my data from a gendered perspective, and am today well known globally, for my work on gender.

In 2000, I received the prestigious Charles Wallace award in Social Anthropology and went to the Queen's university at Belfast. Exposure to British scholarship, a chance to present at the ASA conference in London and a visit to the Oxford University, set me up for my international scholarship. I attended the World Conference Against Racism at Durban in 2001, on a Ford Foundation grant, and my international publications began on a regular basis. The papers that I had read at the ASA and at Durban were both published, as were many others. The work with *dhobi*s had involved me with Dalit issues and combined with my interest in gender, and the personal experience of being severely discriminated against, made me explore the larger dimensions of marginality and exclusion, both as a structural and as a cultural phenomenon.

I visited Paris on a French government fellowship as a visiting professor in 2002, and in 2003, was awarded the Fulbright visiting teacher fellowship to teach a semester at Auburn University in the USA. Later in 2008-09, I was again awarded the Fulbright resident scholar fellowship, to teach for two semesters in the USA. From 2000 onwards I have visited many universities across the world and from 1998, I have been attending the IUAES conferences regularly. From attending these conferences, I have picked up many friends, not only for academic purposes but for personal friendships as well. My regular visits to the American Anthropological Association annual meetings is to both—meet friends and to absorb some of the ongoing theoretical concerns. My life has been enriched through my academic work and I have evolved into a cosmopolitan person, at ease in most parts of the world. Anthropology taught me to be respectful of all cultures, and fieldwork has taught me to adjust to all kinds of life situations.

In 1997, I received a small grant from the University Grants Commission to do a project, for which I chose a remote community of shepherds, high in the Himalayas, who were cross-border traders. I spent several summers at these high altitudes, and was fascinated by the data I could gather. Couple of students accompanied me and supported my research, while working for their own degrees. My work on the Himalayan borders helped stimulate the publications of several prestigious papers and also brought me some recognition. My full-length ethnography about the Bhotiya community that I have studied, was published by Oxford University Press as a monograph. I retain my interest in the study of high-altitude Himalayan pastoralists and have visited other locations in 2008, studying the border communities at Kinnaur in Himachal Pradesh.

Over the many years of my professional life, I have published and researched on a variety of topics and issues. But throughout my academic life, I have been an involved scholar, one who never deviated away from a critical perspective. From my early encounter with the *dhobi*s, I became sensitive to the practise of inequality and the life of the marginalized. From suffering discrimination at the personal level, I became sensitive to issues of gender and of being rejected only for some vaguely ascribed characters, over which I had no control. My travels to Britain and to South Africa sensitized me further to racial discrimination. In my mature period of scholarship, I have theorized the concept of marginalization and the marking of bodies. My chapter in the Routledge Companion to Contemporary Anthropology, "Selves and Codified Bodies" summarizes much of what I have wanted to say as an academic. The personal and the theoretical, have intersected in my works that in a way reiterate the subjectivity of the anthropologist as recognized in post-modern theory. To look for a grounded and indigenous perspective on gender, I have searched the Indian texts, literature and worldview to create a South Asian perspective on gender.

The environment again played an important role in shaping my academic perspectives as I am a staunch advocate of environmental sustainability and a critic of the present-day market driven life-style. To educate the young generation about environmental issues, I taught in the School of Environmental Studies for more than a decade, doing my personal readings to learn up the subject more fully. It must be mentioned that ecological anthropology was developed in the Department of Anthropology, University of Delhi by my husband, and I taught it for many years.

Having suffered discrimination as a student, my one mission had been to be fair to all my students, as much as was humanly possible. Many students have come back to me to tell me that my encouragements have served to shape their confidence and prepared them for a successful future. At the end of the day, it is the great love and respect that I have received from students that has made all my struggle worth the while. I rose from a neglected anthropologist to hold some of the most important positions in global anthropology. I remember while attending my first international conference in the USA, feeling awed by the keynote speaker. About a decade later, I found myself as the keynote speaker at a major anthropological event, in China, speaking before an international audience of more than 5,000. Today I hold many positions, am often invited for lectures, keynotes, and for contributing my writings to many projects. Yet the most satisfactory aspect of my entire academic career has been classroom teaching and supervision of research scholars. In 2016, I was awarded the best serving teacher award by University of Delhi, a proud moment for a person who had to fight hard to get a teaching position in the same university. But even now, a message from an old student, a card, a phone-call and a teacher's day message, makes me feel as if my life has been worth the while.

My Books

1985: *Tradition and Rationality in Economic Behaviour*. New Delhi: Cosmo.

2013: *The Inner and Outer Selves: Cosmology, Gender and Ecology on the Himalayan Border*. Delhi: Oxford University Press.

2013: *Gender in South Asia*. Cambridge: Cambridge University Press.

15

Me and My Journey in Anthropology

Sekh Rahim Mondal

Early Life

I was born on 1 September 1951, in a suburban village named Purbo Buri Khali, located under Bauria Police Station, in Uluberia Subdivision of the district of Howrah in West Bengal, India. I am the eldest son of Rejia Begum and Sekh Abdul Hakim Mondal. My family genealogy suggests that our ancestors were used to live in the said place more than for last 500 years. My ancestors were well known in the locality as many of them used to serve the role as heads of villages called Morol of the surrounding areas. Thus, we used to enjoy respect from both the Hindu and Muslim villagers. We are ethnically the Shaikhs, but received the title "Mondal" from the local authorities, as a result the local people started to called us "Morol", which is still continuing. Once both of my paternal and maternal ancestors were the big landowners thus carried the tradition of landed gentry class. I was born and brought up under such a joint family tradition and socialized accordingly. I feel it is important to note here that my maternal parental village was also under Uluberia subdivision of the district of Howrah, but located comparatively in remote area which is now a fringe village. While my paternal village was initially a fringe village but now under an urban municipal area, which is also a noted industrial setting of Bengal. The differences between the nature of my maternal and paternal villages which I noticed my early age later helped me to grow my interest in anthropology.

Education

My initial education was started at home under my grandparents. I had completed my basic primary education (I-IV) from Burikhali Kadamtola Primary Vidyalaya, which was established by my ancestors long back before my birth. After completing Britti Pariksha (IVth standard), I took admission in "Fast Gloster Upper Primary School" and completed Vth and the VIth standards from this school. For my high school education I went to Burikhali Kshetra Mohan Institution and took admission in Class VII and finally passed School Final Examination (Class X standard) from this school.

After completing my high school education, I took admission in Uluberia College in Science stream and obtained Pre-University (PUSc.) Degree from the University of Calcutta. The next phase for my higher education faced some trouble. Initially I took admission in B.Sc. at Narasinha Dutta College with the combinations of botany, zoology and anthropology. At this stage my father wanted to put me in medical science. To fulfil his desire I took admission in Pre-Medical course. As I already started to study B.Sc. course and was getting interest on it, so I left the Pre-Medical course for completing B.Sc. degree. But my father was not much happy with my decision for my studies in general stream. However, he was happy when I passed B.Sc. with highest mark in anthropology from the University of Calcutta. I did my under graduate fieldwork in a remote village of Howrah district and prepared a field report on "Technology of Paddy Cultivation in Southern West Bengal". This was my first rigorous fieldwork in anthropology.

After graduation I took admission in the Department of Anthropology, University of Calcutta, for my P.G. course. I got the

M.Sc. degree in anthropology with specialization in Social-Cultural Anthropology from the said university and stood first in first class.

At the time of my P.G. classes I came in contact with many veteran anthropologists of the country along with my own departmental teachers. I was lucky enough to be a student of this iconic department and taught under the veteran teachers of University of Calcutta at that time. The most important among them were Professor M.N. Basu, Professor G.S. Roy, Professor D. Sen, Professor Tulika Sen, Professor P.K. Bhowmick, Professor Biswanath Banerjee, Professor A.R. Banerjee, Professor A.K. Ghosh, Professor S.K. Sengupta and Professor M.B. Bhattacharya. I also got some Professors of other universities like as teachers viz. Professor I.P. Singh, Professor Andre Beteille, Professor Gopal Sarana, Professor L.K. Mohapatra, Professor S.N. Rath, Professor B.M. Das, Professor A.C. Bhagaboti, Dr Amal Kumar Das, Professor A. Basu, Professor Alok Ghosh etc. who used to visit to the department as visiting professors, visiting fellows and guest faculties during my student days. It is also to be noted here that when I was in 1st Year M.Sc. course the Department of Anthropology, University of Calcutta celebrated the Golden Jubilee function (fifty years) and being a student I got the opportunity to see and interact with many stalwart anthropologists of the country and abroad. The academic environment of anthropology of University of Calcutta of such a nature during my student days actually created my interest in anthropology for higher studies in this discipline. During my 1st Year M.Sc. Course, I went to Seraikella of Bihar (now Jharkhand) along with my other batch mates to conduct field studies on physical anthropology, pre-historic archaeology and socialcultural anthropology together. We did intensive field studies among the Hos and prepared three field reports on

(a) "Darmatographics Studies among the HOS of Seraikella",
(b) "Pre-historic Cultures of Seraikella" and
(c) "Environment, Economy, Society and Culture among the HOS of Seraikella".

Those studies were conducted under the supervision of Professor A.R. Banerjee, Professor D. Sen and Professor S.K. Sengupta, respectively. During our fieldwork the then museum keeper of the Department of Anthropology, University of Calcutta, Professor Atul Chandra Bhowmick helped us in many ways to collect and analyse the prehistoric tools and other museum objects collected from the field. I got interest in both physical and cultural anthropology, but finally selected social-cultural anthropology as my special paper. During second year of my M.Sc. many of my teachers encouraged me to do research on Muslims of West Bengal, due to lack of much anthropological research on the said community at that time. As a result, I did fieldwork among the Muslims of some villages of Midnapur (WB) and prepared a dissertation paper on "Kinship and Social Structure among the Muslims of Midnapur", under the supervision of Professor Biswanath Banerjee, who was one of the great admirers of Professor N.K. Bose and Surajit Chandra Sinha. This dissertation paper was examined by two external examiners, viz. Professor Surajit Chandra Sinha and Professor N.C. Chowdhury. Both of them were very pleased with my initial anthropological work on Bengal Muslims and suggested me to continue such study for my Ph.D. degree.

Being influenced and motivated by my teachers and other well-wishers I entered into the field of research after completing my M.Sc. At first, I obtained S.C. Roy Fellowship from Asiatic Society of Calcutta and joined as S.C. Roy Research Fellow under the supervision of Professor S.C. Sinha (Then Director of AnSI) and started to work on Muslims. Within a few months, I got two more fellowships one from AnSI and other from UGC. At this stage Professor Sinha left Calcutta and joined as Upacharya (Vice-Chancellor) of Visva-Bharati, Santiniketan. He suggested me to accept UGC Research Fellowship and to continue my Ph.D. research under my university teacher Professor B.N. Banerjee. Accordingly, I started my research work on "A Comparative Study of Hindu and Muslim Villages of an Industrial Setting in West Bengal". The study was not simply an ethnographic study of two villages, but touched upon the issues of social structure, social interaction, social organization and social processes among the inhabitants of those two distinct villages. In this study I devoted my attention not only to explore the similarities as well as differences in social behaviours and culture patterns of two apparently different social categories of peoples (socio-religious communities), but also to discovers the missing links as well as the existing links amongst them and how those links bind them to live together in a harmonious way at a particular space. The study was also focused to discover the nature of problems faced by the two different socio-religious communities living side by side in the backdrop of dominant—minority social milieu. During this research I got tremendous helps and support from Professor S.C. Sinha, Professor P.K. Bhowmick, Professor A.K. Ghosh and Professor M.K.A. Siddiqui. I successfully completed my Ph.D. from the University of Calcutta. This thesis was considered as a pioneering anthropological work on Muslims of West Bengal. This in later phase I have extended and enriched in various ways through further research and writings.

While in University of Calcutta as a research scholar I got an opportunity to visit Andaman Islands with a batch of fieldworkers for conducting field studies in Port Blair and neighbouring areas. The team was leaded by Professor P.K. Bhowmick, Professor A.R. Banerjee and Mr Romendo K. Ghosh of the Department of Anthropology, University of Calcutta. Out of this visit, we got the chance to study some refugee settlements in and around Port Blair. We also visited and studied the Great Andamanese settled at Strait Island. We also studied some Nicobarese families living in Port Blair. After returning from Andaman Island Professor Bhowmick told us to prepare and publish some papers on the basis of our field visits of Andaman Islands.

Being a student of anthropology from U.G. to P.G. levels and then at the level of Ph.D. research, I got tremendous support from my teachers of both the college and the university as well as from the scholars of other research institutions like Anthropological Survey of India, Indian Statistical Institute and Cultural Research Institute,

Calcutta. Those in many ways helped me in my professional journey in anthropology.

Career, Position and Association

My professional journey in anthropology started with the joining in the Anthropological Survey of India during first half of July 1978. I was there in this esteemed world-famous research institution up to middle of September 1981. During my shot stay at AnSI I got an excellent opportunity to learn anthropology much more deeply for practising in professional life. The very rich library of the said institution was a great help for me. I also got the scope to discuss and consult with many anthropologists of AnSI, who had versatile knowledge in fieldworks and writing of monographs. The then Director Mr H.K. Rakshit and Deputy Director Professor A.K. Danda, Mr K.A. Razzaqe, Dr M.K.A. Siddiqui, Dr Biman Dasgupta, Dr B. Roychowdhury, Dr M. Dutta, Mr S.K. Sengupta and many others were of a great help for my academic exercise at that stage.

While in AnSI, I did a long three months fieldwork among the tribes of Tripura for the national project on "Tribal Education in India" and prepared the report along with my co-researchers. I was also associated with some other research projects those were on process at that time. At this stage I was able to publish some research papers, those helped me for my entry in teaching profession at later stage.

Since my student days, my ambition was to be a university teacher. But in spite of my repeated attempt I was not able to secure such position even though I performed well in selection committees. The reason was unknown to me at that time, but later realized when I became firmly established in my teaching carrier.

After repeated attempt, I got the teaching position in the Department of Sociology and Social Anthropology at the University of North Bengal in second half of September 1981. I served this university for long thirty-five years as teacher in various positions and also as administrative heads of various offices of this institution.

I was formally retired from my university service in 2016. But later started to serve the said institution as guest and visiting faculty in some social science departments, which is still continuing.

Initially I joined as a lecturer in the Department of Sociology and Social Anthropology (SSA) of the University of North Bengal and then got the position of Reader in 1986 and which was continued till December 1998. During my long association with the department of SSA I taught many courses of both Social Anthropology and Sociology and the most important among them were the courses on concepts and theories, qualitative research methodology, Indian Rural Societies, Modernization and Social change and Societies of north-east India, etc. For some years I also served as Head of the Department of Sociology and Social Anthropology and during my tenure of headship Professor A.K. Danda joined as professor in the said department. It is to be noted here that the famous INCAA also started to form at that time.

In 1999 I got the position of the University of North Bengal. As a result, I formally left the department of SSA but continued teaching for some more years. I joined as Professor and Director of Centre for Himalayan Studies in January 1999. This was basically an UGC Sponsored Research Centre within the University System devoted primarily for research studies and teaching for research oriented courses like M.Phil. and Ph.D. programmes. Gradually I adopted with this new center of my university and started to do project works including teaching of M.Phil. and other research related courses. In due course university introduced a multi-disciplinary P.G. course in this centre in the name Strategic and Area Studies to which I introduced the relevant anthropological and sociological papers and courses. The most important among them were Anthropological and Sociological Theories in Area Studies, Anthropology and Sociology of Globalization, Research Methodology and Peoples, Societies and Cultures of Himalayas. I used to teach many of those courses along with my other colleagues.

During my service in CHS, a new responsibility was assigned to me by the then Vice-Chancellor Professor P.K. Saha, who suggested me to start the full-fledged Department of Anthropology in NBU and appointed me as Professor and Head of the Department of this new department. The department was started in 2000 with a very meagre infrastructure with two young newly-appointed teachers. It is to be noted here that these two new lecturer positions were sanctioned earlier by UGC for opening of a new Department of Anthropology in University of North Bengal under the initiative of the department of SSA for the interest of the students.

After taking the charge of the Department of Anthropology I started to prepare the syllabus and took other necessary steps to start the M.Sc. Course and Ph.D. programmes with the help of my two young colleagues and visiting faculties. Courses were started, and I had to take the responsibilities of teaching many courses along with my academic duties at CHS and other university responsibilities. At that time, I invited many teachers of other universities throughout the country to deliver lecturers or to act as examines of practical courses to popularize this new department. Meanwhile, I was able to manage some more posts from UGC and recruited the teachers for the expansion the department. By this time various committees were constructed, several projects were launched and funds were managed, to work on them. In addition, several seminars and workshops were also conducted for the growth of this new department. I left the Department of Anthropology during September 2008, after serving almost long eight years as my additional responsibility of teaching and headship. At the time of my association in the Department of Anthropology I took the initiative of establishing an another research centre under the university in the name of "Centre for Studies in Local Language and Cultures of North Bengal (CLLCNB)", as directed by university authority. This centre was created in 2001 as per desire of the then Chief Minister of West Bengal Sri Buddhadeb Bhattacharya for studying the tribal and folk cultures of North Bengal. I served this centre as founder director for almost four years in addition to my routine duties in CHS and Anthropology Department of NBU.

After being relieved from the Department of Anthropology and CLLCNB I totally concentrated on my unfinished research projects and teaching of courses in CHS and this was continued till the last days of my formal retirement in 2016. Being one of the senior teachers of the university I had to handle many official responsibilities and to act as members in different statutory bodies like Executive Council and Faculty Council. Several times I served the university as campus In-charge as a senior faculty.

As a teacher of NBU, I had several research scholars from the departments of SSA, CHS and Anthropology. A total of fourteen scholars successfully completed their Ph.D. degree under my supervision. About twenty M.Phil. scholars have completed their dissertation paper under my guidance.

During my long teaching career, I not only taught in the University of North Bengal, but also taught in other universities in India and abroad. At least eleven foreign counties I had visited in connections with my academic activities. I supervised not only the scholars of my own university but also of other universities of India and abroad who came to University of North Bengal as visiting scholars.

When I was in the University of North Bengal, thrice I got the post of professor in other universities, but not left my own institution for the sake my students. Once I also got the position of professor for establishing a new Department of Anthropology in an African Country. But this was not materialized for some official reasons.

I took the membership in various professional bodies as a "life member". The most important among them are "Indian Anthropological Society (IAS)", "Indian Anthropological Association (IAA)", "Indian National Confederation of the Association of Anthropologist (INCAA)". I was also the ordinary members for some years in other professional bodies like "Indian Science Congress Association (ISCA)", Ethnogrpahic and Folk Culture Society (EFCS), Indian Sociological Association (ISA), Sociological Association of Bengal, International Institute of Asian

Studies, International Union of Anthropological and Ethnological Sciences, etc.

Awards, Recognition, and Felicitation

For my better result in M.Sc. Anthropology. I owned the Gold Medal and Book Grant Award from the University of Calcutta (1972). I received Life Time Achievement Award from the Department of Anthropology, University of Delhi (2018) for my varied nature of anthropological works. I got the award for my works on Muslims in India from the Institute of Objective Studies, New Delhi. For my research works on disadvantage women in India award was given to me by Asian Resource Foundation, Bangkok. KITS and KISS felicitated me for my experience on the studies of tribes, peasants, urban-industrial societies, mountain communities and Muslims. Honour was also given to be by Indian Science Congress Association for delivering invited lectures on "Anthropology and Contemporary Challenges".

Research and Writing

Throughout my entire professional life of almost four decades, I have conduced and completed fifteen research projects, and published six books and 117 research papers. Since major part of my teaching profession was in both the Departments of Sociology and Anthropology, I did research on both the fields of enquiry. I have conducted extensive and intensive field studies on various issues and problems among tribe communities, caste groups, peasants, urban industrial workers, religious minorities, mountain societies, inter-ethnic and inter-community relations, gender inequality, globalization and other emerging issues of contemporary reference. For all such studies, I did fieldworks in the states of West Bengal, Bihar, Sikkim, Tripura and Andaman Islands. I also gathered the experience of conducting field studies in Nepal, Bhutan, Bangladesh, and Maldives. In this section I shall highlight about some of my research works. I have already mentioned that I was the principal Investigator and Director of many research projects sponsored by UGC, ICSSR, Action Aid, and Many other funding agencies of national and internal reputations. The results of many of my research projects were published in the form of books and research papers.

I have studied many tribal groups of Bihar, West Bengal (both southern and northern parts of the state), Sikkim and Tripura, with particular reference to State of their socio-economic condition and relation with the neighbouring non-tribal groups including the emergence of their identity crisis and ethnicity. I also did an interesting study on detribalization process of many *kirati* (social groups of Sikkim and Darjeeling) and noted the historical process of tribe-caste continuum as well as the recent trend of its reversal to tribal status process again. On the basis of archival data as well as through my field visit, I have conducted a study on ethnic and cultural profile of Eastern and Western Himalayas and identified two distinct tribal cultural zones of Indian Himalayas. Those I have designated as "*Jum* and bamboo cultural area" of East and North-East Himalaya, and "pastoral cultural area" of Western Himalaya. This was published in the prestigious journal *Science and Culture.*

So far caste societies are concerned, I have studied various caste groups of urban and rural areas of northern and southern West Bengal. The most important caste groups of North Bengal, which I have studied is the "Rajbansis" a largest Scheduled Caste group of North Bengal. It is also to be noted that the Rajbansis are the most important and only mongoloid caste group of West Bengal. I also did researches on several caste groups of Nepalese origin living in North Bengal and Sikkim.

While studying tribes and castes my primary focus was not only to examine their social and cultural life, but also to identify the issues of their social cohesion and social conflict in respect to inter-ethnic and inter-caste relations in the backdrop of historical and developmental issues.

My major research works was on Muslims in India, for which I had conducted field studies both in southern and northern regions of West Bengal and adjoining states like Bihar, Tripura, Assam, and other adjoining states. I also conducted research on Muslims living in Nepal, Bhutan, Tibet, Bangladesh and Maldives. Through those researches, I have tried to understand not only the unique sociocultural attributes of Indian Muslims but also explored the social and cultural attributes of South-Asian Muslims. Interestingly I have noticed that the Muslims living in India as well as in South Asia are simultaneously follow both the great traditions of Islam as well as the local traditions of their habitat to which they live in. the bio-social hybridization and cultural syncretism are the most important features of Indian and South-Asian Muslims.

In addition to my vast research works on tribes, castes and Muslim groups, I have tried my best to do some works on various emerging issues of anthropological significance. The most important among them were cultural globalization, environmental management, refugees, border societies, development and change, cultural syncretism, third gender and many others.

In course of my teaching and research, I also wrote some papers on history and growth of anthropology in India as well as on contemporary methods and perspectives of anthropological research.

Epilogue: Desire and Hope

India is a land of diversities, varied biological, social and cultural groups are living in this vast country science time immemorial. "Unity in diversity" is the constitutional ethos of India. One of the prime focus of anthropology is to study all forms of human diversities. India is a gold mine for anthropologists. The professionals of this discipline have a great role in nation building process and development of this country.

Throughout my long professional life, I have experienced a lot, both joys as well as pains. In spite of ample opportunities of anthropology, quite often I had to face some acquired questions both from anthropologists and non-anthropologists about the future of the discipline. To me anthropology in post-colonial India confronting with the two major issues and problems, viz. its relevance and its representations. We are celebrating the 100 years of teaching and research of anthropology in India. We have proved that our disciple is neither dead, nor dying rather professing. But for the issue of representation, we have to go a long way. We are still far away from not only to represent all the groups living in this country through our massive research, nor we are able to show the significance of the diversities of the country. Moreover, we are still not much concern about our professional responsibilities for the society by touching upon the issues of contemporary relevance through which the country is confronting.

I feel there is an urgent need of a new anthropology for dealing with the contemporary issues with which the peoples are struggling for survival and development. For this new anthropology we have to invent and invest new theoretical perspectives, new methodological tools and open mind to understand the realities and problems of the peoples and country as well. In twenty-first country the prime concern of Indian anthropology is to come out from its colonial/ Western past as well as neo-colonial and neo-traditional present for shading its real relevance and true representation. The waves of reflexive and critical anthropology is also knocking our door. Thus, the time demands to reconstruct and deconstruct our discipline as it stands today at the cross road for its journey in the twenty-first century.

My Books

1991: *Stratification, Hierarchy and Ethnicity in north-east India.* New Delhi: Daya Publishing House (Jointly Edited with R.K. Bhadra.)

Dynamics of Muslim Society. New Delhi: Inter India Publications.

Muslims of Siliguri. New Delhi: Institute of Objective Studies (Genuine Publications).

Educational Status of Muslims. New Delhi: Inter India Publications.

Rural Muslim Women. New Delhi: Northern Book Centre.

2009: *Jari Embroidery: A Study of Traditional Craft and Craftsmen in Bengal.* New Delhi: Kalpaz Publications.

16

How I Became an Anthropologist

Tanka B. Subba

In writing this autobiographical essay on how I became an anthropologist, I have been inspired by two similar articles, one written by M.N. Srinivas (1997) and the other by Fredrik Barth (2007), both of which were published in the much-regarded *Annual Review of Anthropology*. I never met them in any of the anthropological or sociological conferences in India or abroad, nor did I ever correspond with them, but in a rather strange way I bring them together, albeit unwittingly, in my doctoral research. But let me come to that a little later.

Early Life

I wish to start my story of becoming an anthropologist from my graduation days. I went to a college called Kalimpong College which was located about 8 km away from my home and to reach the college I needed to walk uphill for about 2.5 hours and downhill about 1.5 hours. When I joined the college in 1974, I had no idea what subjects I should take. So, I tagged along with a close friend of mine, not because he was better informed than me, but because we had studied together in the same school. We finally opted for a major in Political Science and took English, Nepali and Philosophy as our elective subjects.

The college was housed in a building which was used as a wool godown till the Sino-Indian conflict of 1962. Until then Kalimpong was a prosperous town, as it was a "contact zone" in the Himalayas for traders and international spies alike. Wools came from Tibet via the all-weather Jelepla Pass on mules and were stored in that building and the same were graded before they were repacked and exported to the USA via Kolkata. The wools were re-loaded on mules and transported up to a place called Geil Khola, where a meter gauge train came from Siliguri to pick up the same.

Our classrooms were separated by the same gunny bags that were once used for packing wools, which meant that they were not sound-proof and students sitting in the adjacent rooms could be seen through some of the holes made by students to pass small pieces of paper containing love messages, as there were no mobile phones to do that those days. We also had the benefit of listening simultaneously to two, and at times even three, lectures sitting in the same classroom. Come afternoon and the lecturers had tough times to be audible to students, what with the Tibetan songs and drum sound coming from the ground floor of the same building, which housed a school for Tibetan refugee children. But I must say that we had two excellent teachers out of the four for the major subject and I did well in a paper called Political Sociology. In fact, that was the only paper in which I scored a first class, but the overall grading was a sober second class. It could certainly be better if my days did not pass by commuting and doing household chores like cooking and grinding maize or husking paddy in the evenings after dinner. I also almost missed the B.A. Part I examination on account of severe blood dysentery. I was released from the hospital just a few days before the Part I examination started. I had my notes on the hospital bed but I could not read them on account of a rather noisy General Ward where I was given a bed.

But it was not for this particular performance in Political Sociology that I chose to do my master's in Sociology & Social

Anthropology. I didn't even know that such a department existed in North Bengal University from where I finally did my master's and doctorate degrees. One senior student from the same college where I studied was doing his master's in Political Science. It was he who advised me to go for Sociology & Social Anthropology. He also informed me that the subject was new and a "famous" professor was appointed as head of the department. On the very first day, as I was going to my classroom, someone held me from behind and asked where I was from and which school I passed out from. I told him the names of the school and the place. He then asked me to see him later, which I did at the earliest opportunity, and after meeting him I felt thankful to the senior student from my college for giving me the right advice. I never regretted having changed my tracks from Political Science to Sociology & Social Anthropology, except once briefly to which I shall return a little later.

Doctoral Research

As soon as the M.A. Part II examination was over, I got a chance to work on a project on tribal handicrafts in Sikkim for a couple of months. When the project was over, I made carpet designs on graph paper and sold them to make a living for a couple of months. In the meantime, with the help of my supervisor Late Professor N.C. Choudhury, I got a research fellowship of Rs. 400 per month from the Christian Institute for the Study of Religion and Society (CISRS), Bangalore and about a year later a UGC Junior Research Fellowship of Rs. 600 per month. I completed my fieldwork in about twelve months and the first draft of my thesis was ready on completion of two years of my tenure as a research scholar. But, as luck would have it, it took another three years to get my result. First, my supervisor did not read my thesis for one year and five months, but when he finally read it, he just took five days to say that I could get it typed and submitted. During the long wait, I often regretted having opted for Sociology & Social Anthropology but channellized my frustration to writing the report on what I had done for one year under the CISRS fellowship, which the institute kindly published in the form of a book titled *The Quiet Hills* (1985). When my thesis was finally through, I revised it in the form of a book and published it under the title *Dynamics of a Hill Society* (1989).

My Academic Contribution

Preposterous though it may sound, I think my master's thesis on land and politics was not only something that gave me the first ever publication in *The Eastern Anthropologist* (1983) but perhaps deserves a brief mention under my academic contribution. This thesis showed that the informal as well as formal leaders were from the landowning class and none was from the sharecropping or agricultural labourer class. I collected the data on both formal and informal leaders using the sociometric method.

My Ph.D. thesis was on the relationship between caste, class and agrarian relations in the Nepali society of Darjeeling and Sikkim. Whatever I read about caste in Indian societies showed that it had both economic or political dimensions, but there was hardly any work that brought out the relationship between caste and physical environment. For instance, Srinivas wrote on how Dalits lived in the peripheries of the village and how they were not even allowed to pass through the main street. But in the Darjeeling-Sikkim Himalayas, the physical environment had a strong relationship with caste or ethnic relations, and hence the study was close to Barth's study of Swat in North Pakistan. I selected villages at different altitudes and aspects to see if this was true. The thesis clearly indicated that caste relations were more meaningful in lower altitudes, east or south facing slopes, and valleys where irrigated lands were available than in the higher altitudes or north facing slopes.

After Ph.D., I joined the Centre for Himalayan Studies at North Bengal University as a Lecturer in 1985, instead of joining the Department of Anthropology, North-Eastern Hill University, and registered myself for a Tibetan language course taught by my colleague Ugyen Lama, who has now founded a monastery not so far from the same university. We also had, amidst us, Dawa Norbu whose books on Tibet and the Tibetans were some of the most widely read and quoted and who later died as a professor of Jawaharlal Nehru University. Although Tibet was part of the mandated area for our Centre it was inaccessible. So, I decided to work on Tibetan refugees with the objective to know about Tibet through the Tibetan refugees. Michael Aris, the husband of Aung Sui and one of the best-known historians on Bhutan, once asked me discouragingly about what new facts I could hope to bring out after so much had been published on the Tibetan refugees. I might have faltered for an answer then, but what I found and wrote in my book (1990) was perhaps not so unimportant. My research showed that the racial, cultural, religious and linguistic proximities made the adaptation of Tibetan refugees in Darjeeling and Sikkim a lot more successful than their adaptations in Odisha and Karnataka, where they lacked such proximities.

In 1991, I was reappointed by NEHU. This time as a Reader in the same Anthropology department. By then, I had begun to feel politically stifled on the campus of North Bengal University and I was looking for an opportunity to leave. So, on 3 September 1991, I joined NEHU. Strange though it may sound, my identity as an anthropologist actually began here. Until then I was attending the All-India Sociological congresses regularly but after this, I did not receive the notices for such congresses, despite being a life member of the Indian Sociological Society, which I think was due to change of postal address than anything else. This coincided, at the time of my joining, with a rather acrimonious relationship between the Departments of Sociology and Anthropology at NEHU. One year after I joined, the teaching programmes of the two departments were totally separated, and I was given the responsibility of revising the syllabus of my department. As I started working on the syllabus, I realized how little I knew about the branches of Anthropology other than Social Anthropology, as I understood next to nothing about Physical Anthropology and Prehistoric Archaeology. Having done my master's from a Department of Sociology & Social Anthropology I had never read about other branches of anthropology. So, my acculturation as an anthropologist actually began at NEHU. Thus, in more senses than one, I became an anthropologist only after joining the Department of Anthropology in NEHU in 1991.

When I joined NEHU, I wast awarded the prestigious Homi Bhabha Fellowship for two years. One of the conditions for accepting this fellowship was that I would have no teaching or administrative responsibilities during my tenure as a Homi Bhabha Fellow. The conditions were accepted by NEHU on paper, but out of five teachers in the department one was on leave and teaching at the University of Trinidad & Tobago, and one other retired soon after I joined. Thus, I not only had to teach three papers in each semester but also take care of administrative works assigned by the then head of the department, besides being forced to take students for their fieldwork training during the winter vacations. Obviously, my proposed fieldwork for this fellowship was badly hampered. Although I submitted the report to the Homi Bhabha Fellowships Council in Mumbai within the stipulated date I was not happy with the limited time I had for my fieldwork. However, the paperback (1999) that I published out of this research has been giving me some royalty every year for the past two decades.

I think one of the strengths of this work was the use of vernacular sources of literature which are rarely used by anthropologists today. The other reason why this book is often referred to is because it mainly deals with the ethnic movement that swept the hill areas of Nepal, Darjeeling and Sikkim, in 1990s seeking various kinds of protection under the constitutions of Nepal and India.

Beyond Anthropology

Having done my master's in Sociology & Social Anthropology and the first job being a Lecturer of Sociology at the Centre for Himalayan Studies, North Bengal University I was already at the margins of anthropology. As a faculty member of the Centre for Himalayan Studies, which was an interdisciplinary centre for doing research on the Eastern Himalayas, I came in close contact with my colleagues who were from history, geography, political science, economics and language backgrounds. I also worked closely with one colleague outside of the centre in the area of sociolinguistics. Further, I continued my academic collaboration with one scholar from the field of English literature and we jointly published a few articles. It was only after joining the Department of Anthropology in September 1991 that I truly began to learn about anthropology and was soon identified as an anthropologist. This process of becoming an anthropologist could have started in February 1985 but for my decision not to join NEHU at that point of time in my life the same was postponed to till September 1991.

Notable Students

Out of a dozen-odd students whose Ph.D. theses I supervised about half of them are doing quite well in their professions. One of the early doctoral students of mine is now an Associate Professor at the Centre for Indigenous Cultures, Central University of Jharkhand; the next who worked on reproductive health is employed in the health sector in Ireland; the third is my colleague in the department and now a professor with expertise in the field of food as well as archaeology; the fourth is an Associate Professor of Anthropology at Pondicherry University; the fifth is an Assistant Professor of Anthropology at Sikkim University with the rare expertise in Linguistic Anthropology; the sixth is the former Principal of Sacred Heart Theological College in Shillong and an established author in his own capacity; and the last is an Associate Professor of Anthropology at the Royal Thimpu College, Thimpu. Academically speaking, the last-mentioned doctoral student of mine has published his articles in some of the best journals in the world and has some of his books published by reputed international publishing houses. He has already emerged as one of the foremost scholars on India's north-east. I am glad that he has gone far ahead of me in terms of scholarship and quality of publications. I also pin a lot of hope on one of the doctoral students currently working on social media under my supervision. He has the penchant to deal with quantitative data, which is quite rare in the field of cultural anthropology.

International Collaborations

My first international collaboration started when I was a Lecturer at North Bengal University. I was chosen as the Country Tutor by Benqt G. Karlsson, much against the advice of some of my senior colleagues. He is now a professor at the Department of Social Anthropology, Stockholm University. After I joined NEHU, I was again chosen as the Country Tutor by Erik de Maaker, who is now Associate Professor at Leiden University, the Netherlands. Besides these two scholars, I had a close collaboration with Professor Andrew Russell of Durham University, Dr Uwe Skoda of Aarhus University, Professor William Sax of Heidelberg University, Late Professor Georg Pfeffer of the Free University of Berlin, Professor Frank Heidemann of Munich University and Dr Philippe Ramirez of the National Centre for Scientific Research, Paris.

Life after Retirement

It has been almost two years since I retired, but neither anthropology nor anthropologists have abandoned me so far. While I also do not intend to leave anthropology, I wish to make forays into anthropologically interesting areas of other disciplines. I wish to reflect on the four-decade long academic journey I had and write/ lecture about the lessons I learnt and the lessons others could learn from my experiences. I also wish to travel to some of the places within the country as well as outside as long as my health permits. The purpose of the visits would now be to renew my relationship with my friends and acquaintances, trying to connect with their children and grandchildren, and share moments of joy and laughter with them rather than see the places per se or simply deliver some lectures as before.

My Books

1985: *The Quiet Hills: A Study of Agrarian Relations in Hill Darjeeling*. Delhi: ISPCK.

1989: *Dynamics of a Hill Society: The Nepalis in Darjeeling and Sikkim Himalayas*. Delhi: Mittal Publications.

1990: *Flight and Adaptation: Tibetan Refugees in the Darjeeling Sikkim Himalaya*. Dharamsala: Library of Tibetan Works and Archives.

1992: *Ethnicity, State and Development: A Case Study of Gorkhaland Movement in Darjeeling*. New Delhi: Vikas Publishing House.

1999: *Politics of Culture: A Study of Three Kirata Communities in the Eastern Himalayas*. Hyderabad: Orient Longman Ltd.

17

My Journey as an Anthropologist

P. Venkatarao

Like many others in the discipline, I am an accidental anthropologist. At a young age, my goal was to become a scientist. As a child, I used to learn about impressive stories of great scientists and their inventions. I landed in my graduation class with zoology as a major subject. I heard the word anthropology for the first time while studying biological evolution in zoology classes. At that time, it appeared to me that anthropology (human development) started where organic evolution ended. In the first year of postgraduation in anthropology, we learnt archaeological, biological, and cultural dimensions of anthropology. In the beginning of the second year, the choice of specialization was very clear for me to move to social anthropology. The credit for this goes to my teachers who were able to convert someone who wanted to be a scientist to shift to social sciences. On the first day in the anthropology class, there were four periods of one hour duration. One after another faculty members came and introductions followed telling the teacher about our personal and academic background, hobbies, and what made us prefer anthropology discipline for postgraduation over other disciplines. The teacher Dr D.L. Prasada Rao (a student of Professor Aiyappan and Professor

N. Subba Reddy) who came into fourth hour was an exception to this pattern. He straight away started the introduction to the subject without asking any questions. His approach impressed me. Two years later I joined under his guidance for my Ph.D. and followed his example of teaching style when I became a lecturer. The study period was 1974-76 partly including the days of turbulent National Emergency where campus life was different.

I had my first initiation to fieldwork as part of the requirements of M.A. Programme. We did fieldwork in the Eastern Ghats of Andhra Pradesh, studying Koya Dora, a subtribe of Koya tribe. After completing the postgraduation, first exposure to data collection was in a survey conducted in the slums of Visakhapatnam. The work involved collection of socio-economic data for formulating a rehabilitation programme for the slum dwellers. Research scholars visiting the student's fieldwork camp for a day or two has been in practise with us at Andhra University. The tradition of research scholars helping each other during fieldwork and thesis writing was a common practise. Visiting the field areas of fellow research scholars in physical anthropology and excavation sites of the prehistory teachers and research scholars gave many insights in to their work. One thing I learnt is to not leave a willing informant, however exhausted you are; thinking that you can contact him next day. Next day or next week or next month you may not able to talk to him. So, extract whatever information possible on the same day is the message. My supervisor, Professor D.L. Prasada Rao used to attach junior scholars to senior scholars finalizing their thesis to assist them. This used to be a good learning experience. I assisted my seniors M. Suryanarayana, G. Prakash Reddy, V. Sudarsen, N.V. Kameswara Rao, M.V.T. Raju and immensely benefited by the experience. As young research scholar I used to volunteer for seminar work in all departments. I remember writing my first seminar paper on "Adult Education Programmes in a Tribal Area" in 1978 sitting in the university vehicle waiting for picking up delegates outside Waltair Railway Station.

My first experience of anthropological fieldwork was working in a research project for a biological anthropologist Professor Ajit Kishor Ray (Toronto University, Canada) who initially received training in India under Professor N.K. Bose. This fieldwork involved collection of genealogies using networking method among caste groups known for high incidence of consanguineous marriages. As I collected large number of genealogies, my supervisor suggested to me to consider Kinship as a research topic for my Ph.D. I started reading about alliance theory, decent theory and so on. Later the interest shifted to study of urbanization in the fringe villages of Visakhapatnam city. Later, study of interethnic relations among the tribes of Eastern Ghats emerged as prospective area for me. For my pre-Ph.D. examination, I made a presentation on the concepts of ethnicity and ethnic groups. But, I had to shift from this topic also when I received a University Gants Commission's Junior Research Fellowship to study tribal development programmes. That was the time when Integrated Tribal Development Projects started functioning. When I first went to fieldwork, I did not go with any clear plan. My supervisor told me to go to the field and stay there for some time. I was to discuss with him after my return on what could be my research focus. Fieldwork in those days of scanty transport and communication facilities was a memorable experience. In my Ph.D. work, I focused on the role of leadership and the functioning of development functionaries. Apart from other things, I tried to understand the integration envisaged in the formulation of the Integrated Tribal Development Projects (ITDA in Andhra Pradesh) and the actual achievements. Apart from covering the ITDA area, I focused on two tribal villages for micro-level understanding of the processes. When I started writing my thesis, my supervisor posed a question that "what for you are comparing two villages?" Not able to convince my supervisor, I used data from only one village for my thesis titled "Institutional Framework for Tribal Development Case study of a Tribal village In Andhra Pradesh" . There was a long waiting period of eighteen months for the award of Ph.D. The delay was due to refusal of one examiner Professor Gerald Berreman who was involved in a controversy with Indian government at that time. Professor Aiyappan who was examiner also took some time.

After completing M.A., I did not to heed to the advice of well-wishers to write the civil services examination of UPSC. My goal was to complete Ph.D. and enter academics. As a Ph.D. student, I was helping civil service aspirants in their preparation for competitive examinations. After submitting Ph.D. thesis, the looming uncertainties of career forced me to make an attempt to make use of my last chance to write civil service exam. It was my first attempt at the age of 28 and achieving a rank of about 500 in the one lakh initial aspirants gave me immense satisfaction and confidence. But, when I was to join an allied service, the teaching job in Hyderabad central university came my way. With little hesitation, I preferred sticking to anthropology. This must have disappointed my relatives as there are many in academics in the family and none in a government job.

I started my teaching in the combined Department of Sociology and Anthropology. There were limited number of anthropology courses and more courses from the sociology stream. As a beginner I had limited choice in teaching and had to teach some sociology courses including a full course on Social Psychology. With the usual friction in the combined department, sociology and anthropology got separated, and I shifted to my original choice of anthropology.

As a research scholar, I published papers areas related to my Ph.D. topic of tribal development. Based on my fieldwork, I published papers on education, cooperatives, Panchayati Raj Institutions, and natural resources in the tribal areas. I also worked on secondary materials such as children's tales, proverbs, films, matrimonial advertisements resulting in publications. After I became a faculty member, the advice given to me from my teacher was to specialize in an area of anthropology and not to continue as a general anthropologist. As I worked on tribal development for my Ph.D. degree, development anthropology, anthropology of communication and medical anthropology were suggested to me. In Anthropology Department, I was teaching most of the courses as we started with only two regular teachers. I designed a course in development anthropology as elective after addition of more faculty members. One of the compulsory courses that I was teaching namely, economic anthropology became my second elective course after it was shifted from compulsory courses to an elective. When I started admitting Ph.D. students, I allowed them freedom to select their research topics. The students selected topics falling in to different areas such as tribal development, marginalized and nomadic castes, ecological adaptations, common property resources, ethnic identity, religion, peoples' movements, games, agrarian issues and so on. This made me to work along with the students and helped me to expand my horizon. But I could get labelled as a specialist in a given area. However, five students obtained Ph.D.s under my supervision on topics related to agriculture. My research publications were on diverse topics and in different areas of anthropology on my own and along with my students. Whenever I went for fieldwork along with M.A. students, I moved with the students and collected data that is of my interest. I used material based on such work for my seminar presentations and published papers. For example during students fieldwork among Chenchus in Nallamalai forest, a paper on ageing, from students fieldwork among Lambadas in Telangana, a paper on the consequence of shift from dry crops to irrigated agriculture can be mentioned here.

Starting with Ph.D. work, my focus has been on understanding the dynamics of development in the backdrop of the constitutional objectives and government policies in tribal areas. Assessment of the existing policies towards Scheduled Tribes and PTGS to arrive at the adequacy of the policies in dealing with specific problems of the groups has been a preoccupation. In the recent decades legislations like PESA and Forest Rights Act, and the recent Land Acquisition Act have joined the existing interests. Another area of research interest has been the Social and cultural dynamics of Scheduled Tribe communities under contact with non-tribal society, and various other forces. An edited book tilted *Tribal Development*

Policy and Practice included different articles published by me on diverse areas of tribal policy and the implementation carried out by governmental institutions and programmes. Like in other parts of India, In Andhra Pradesh and Telangana also, differences between tribes and castes have been essentialized by the colonial writers. However, there are variations and disagreements on the identification of groups and sub groups. The tribal scenario showed dynamic, permeable and shifting boundaries. Clubbing of sub-groups, failure to identify sub groups, ignoring local specializations and divisions are some of the factors responsible for the confusing situation with regard to subdivisions. I explored the issues related to labels used by tribal groups and subgroups in the projection of self-image and identity, among some of the tribal communities of Andhra Pradesh. Based on my own fieldwork and other available studies I highlighted the varying levels of continuity between caste society and tribal communities in Andhra Pradesh. The presence of hierarchy, commensal relations, and other caste like features; the links with great tradition as reflected in origin myths, folklore, etc.; tribal labels having caste prefixes and suffixes; number of Hindu beliefs and practises existing in different communities reveal the continuity and contact between non-tribals and tribals in Andhra Pradesh.

Receiving of University Grants Commission's Research Award in the year 1999 enabled me to carry out a comprehensive survey of studies carried out on tribal areas in Andhra Pradesh which got published as a book titled *Dimensions of Transformation in Tribal Societies with reference to Andhra Pradesh*. In this book, the works available on different tribes have been dealt with in terms of tribal profiles, inter-tribal relations, impact of non-tribal contact, land alienation, credit, marketing, forest-tribal interface, unrest, government policies and programmes etc. Andhra Pradesh and Telangana regions formed my focus and the role is played by anthropology in tribal development in the post-liberalization scenario was brought out in paper presented by me at the International Congress of Anthropological and

Ethnological Scenes held at Kunming in China. The concern about role of anthropology and future of anthropology in India is reflected in some of my publications. The decline of enrolment in anthropology departments, especially in south India and downsizing of departments due to various reasons, very few new department coming up is a matter of concern. The cherished ideal of the holistic integrated discipline of anthropology with all four major branches flourishing remained only as ideal. I argued that specializations existing with one or two faculty members cannot do justice to the requirements of students, leave alone introducing them to expanding frontiers of anthropology by teaching advanced courses. Prescribing uniform specializations structures, without ensuring uniform faculty strength is detrimental to the growth of the discipline. I made a plea for tolerance towards diversities existing in various anthropology departments.

In the initial years of stay at Hyderabad University, I developed interest in the study of the aged and ageing and carried out a research project for ICSSR. What interested me are the problems of the aged in rural and tribal areas, where the conditions are different from that of the aged in urban areas. Apart from writing on ageing in rural and tribal areas, I also enrolled my field as an adjunct faculty in the inter-disciplinary Centre for Research and Education in Ageing. Except one student, I could not motivate any of research students to take up study of the aged. Similarly, another area in which I had developed interest and taught for decades is economic anthropology. When opportunity came for delivering Dr K.S. Mathur memorial lecture organized by Ethnographic and Folk Cultural Society I dealt with the status of "Economic Anthropology in India". Like ageing, in this area also only a couple of students pursued research for their degrees. The trends emerging in the post-liberalization period, the consequences of globalization received attention have come out in my publications. The policy of liberalization including a rapid shift towards commercial agriculture had several consequences for the tribal agrarian scenario. Along with traditional anthropological topics, I also took interest in the contemporary trends and published papers on topics like post-modernism, liberalization and globalization. My first research project was a restudy of a village near Hyderabad which was earlier studied by Dr M.V.T. Raju as part of SITE project of ISRO. This work got published recently jointly with Dr Binod C. Agrawal and others. My interest in restudies drew me to other scholars who did restudies. This led me to undertake an overview of the research done by Scarlett T. Epstein and publish a paper in *The Eastern Anthropologist*. Professor Epstein appreciated my effort and suggested that I should join with Professor Panini (JNU) in bringing out an edited volume of her works by including my paper. While Professor Panini and I were grappling with the issue of obtaining permission from the copyright holders of her papers, the sad demise of Professor Epstein resulted in shelving the project. Apart from the work of Professor Epstein, I also took interest in the contributions of other scholars. Papers on contributions of C.V.F. Haimendorf and N. Subba Reddy got published in the journal *The Eastern Anthropologist*.

There are many unfinished projects and plans to be pursued subject to getting opportunity. Coming from a rural background, educated in Telugu medium up to graduation, trained in a not so high-profile Anthropology Department under a modest research supervisor, I made an attempt to make my presence felt among fellow social anthropologists in India. When I look back at my journey as anthropologist, I derive satisfaction that I was instrumental in the progression of many students who are occupying positions in places of repute.

My Books

2019: Joint author with Binod C. Agarwal *et al. Television Revolution in India*. New Delhi: Concept Publishing Company (Pvt.) Ltd.

2020: P. Venkatarao and Ajaya P. Sahoo (eds.). *Indian Diaspora and Transnationalism*. New Delhi: Serial Publishers.

18

On Becoming An Anthropologist

My Story

Deepak Kumar Behera

Early Life, Education, Family, Taking Anthropology as a Subject

I was born in Sambalpur/Odisha in the year 1956. I had my schooling in C.S. Zilla High School, Sambalpur. I graduated from G.M. College (now G.M. University) in the year 1976. My father retired as an Executive Engineer, Department of Minor Irrigation, Government of Odisha. My mother was a housewife who remained busy in taking care of her eight children. I was a well-known cricketer in the Sambalpur, the captain of G.M. College cricket team. I also represented Sambalpur University and under-21 C.K. Naidu Trophy (Junior Odisha) in cricket. I was a left-hand off-spinner and hard heating middle order batsman. I had no idea of anthropology until I graduated from G.M. College, Sambalpur with Botany (Hons.). I thought of shifting from botany to anthropology in order to gain some extra time to concentrate on cricket. I was un-attentive in the very first class I attended in the P.G. Department of Anthropology, Sambalpur University, for which I was severely reprimanded by the then Professor and Head of the Department. The latter gruffly told me that anthropology would be simply beyond my reach and I should better seek for some other career option instead of wasting time. I felt quite mortified and took it as a challenge to prove my teacher wrong. I quickly shifted my focus from cricket to anthropology. I borrowed some cricketing principles and started applying those to anthropology. Those were: hard work, determination, confidence, concentration and courage. This innovative strategy started paying off rich dividends to me eventually. I became the topper in my batch in the year 1978 and was awarded the University Gold Medal. Finally, the same subject anthropology helped me to gain recognition both at the national and international levels. I have visited more than twenty-five countries through forty-three overseas tours in different academic connections. Some of those countries are: USA, Mexico, Brazil, Germany, Italy, The Netherlands, France, England, Belgium, Switzerland, Ireland, Denmark, Sweden, Norway, South Africa, Australia, Israel, Palestine, Japan, Singapore, Poland, South Korea, China, Nepal and Bangladesh.

Doctoral Work, Teacher, Fieldwork and Early Career

I was a UGC Doctoral Fellow in the Department of Anthropology and Sociology, Sambalpur University, for the period 1979-83. I did my doctoral research on the theme "Ethnicity and Social Interactions among the Christians of Western Odisha" under the supervision of Professor Satya Narayana Ratha, the then Professor and Head of the Department. A modified version of my thesis was published in the form of a book. I joined as a lecturer in the department in 1985. I became a Reader and then full-time Professor in the same Department of Anthropology, Sambalpur University, in the year 1992 and 2000, respectively. I was a former Professor and the Head of the Department of Anthropology, Sambalpur University, India for long sixteen years. I served in various academic positions in the department for more than thirty-five years.

I had done extensive fieldwork among various tribes living in different remote areas of Odisha. I accompanied the postgraduate students to the field as many as twenty-one times. The strong fieldwork tradition of the Department of Anthropology, Sambalpur University, is well-known to the anthropologists in India and abroad. I was a student-friendly teacher. I had twofold interest in teaching and research. Those are: (1) Tribal Studies and (2) Anthropology of Children, Youth and Childhood. Besides, I have made some contribution to anthropology of development and gender studies. I could establish academically rewarding contacts with many Indian and overseas anthropologists. More than 300 overseas scholars and students visited the Department of Anthropology, Sambalpur University, under my dynamic leadership. The Department of Anthropology, SU signed MoUs with seven overseas Department of Anthropology under my leadership. Anthropology students and scholars from Europe, America, Africa, Latin America visited the Department of Anthropology Sambalpur University under my initiatives.

I was a Fulbright Visiting Professor at California State University at Long Beach during the Fall semester 2007-08. As a Fulbright scholar, I taught a course titled, "Childhood in a Changing Context (With Special Reference to South Asia)" to the graduate students of the university. As the recipient of DAAD fellowship, I was a Guest Professor in the Department of Anthropology at Karl Eberhard University, Tubingen, Germany, during April-July 2013. I was also a Visiting Professor in the Department of History and Area Studies, Aarhus University, Denmark (2011), Department of Anthropology, University of Free State, Bloemfontein, South Africa (2001, 2003), Department of Anthropology, University of Durban-Westville, Durban, South Africa (2001), Institute of Psychology, Federal University of Rio de Janeiro, Brazil (2004) and Maison des Sciences de L'Homme, Paris and CNRS-EHESS, Toulouse, France (2006).

Besides Fulbright and DAAD fellowships, I was the recipient of the prestigious Carlos Chaga Foundation Fellowship, Brazil, National Research Foundation Fellowship, Republic of South Africa, German Research Council Fellowship, Germany, Indo-French Academic Exchange Fellowship, India/France, Indo-Israel Academic and Cultural Exchange Fellowship, India/Israel.

I was the recipient of the prestigious Sarat Chandra Roy Memorial Gold Medal by the Asiatic Society, Kolkata (the oldest educational institution in Asia) for my outstanding contribution in the field of cultural anthropology in India for the year 2016 (award received in 2017).

Seminal Contribution to Anthropology, Important Papers, Books, etc.

I have to my credit more than 130 research publications in reputed journals and edited volumes. Most of my publications are in the fields of "tribal studies" and "children and childhood". Of the twenty-two volumes authored/edited by me, eight published volumes of the series Contemporary Society: Tribal Studies (Concept Publishing Company, New Delhi) are jointly with Professor Georg Pfeffer, Institute of Ethnology, Free University of Berlin, Germany.

My publications have appeared in reputed publishing companies such as Routledge, Springer, Anthem, Elsevier, Pearson, Orient Longman, Kluwer International, Trans-National, Manges, Greenwood Press, Concept, etc. I have delivered distinguished invited lectures at Hebrew University of Jerusalem, Israel, Tel Aviv University, Israel, University of Orange Free State, South Africa, University of Durban West-Ville, South Africa, University of California at Santa Cruz, University of Illinois at Chicago, University of Utah, Logan (famous Brownbag Lecture), University of Arizona, Tucson, USA, INNSO, UANL, Monterrey, Mexico, etc. I also delivered the prestigious Jubilee lecture (Anthropology Section) in the 100th Science Congress held at University of Calcutta in January 2013. I was the editor of the *Journal of Social Sciences* (New Delhi) during 1997-2002. I successfully completed more than a dozen research projects funded by University Grant Commission, New Delhi, Indian Council of Social Science Research, New Delhi, Ministry of Welfare, New Delhi, Winrock International, Indo-Canadian Shastri Foundation, WHO, UNDP, German Research

Council, etc. I served as a member of the Executive Board of World Anthropology Association (International Union of Anthropological and Ethnological Sciences, IUAES) for two consecutive terms, i.e. for the period 1998-2009. I was a member of the Permanent Council of IUAES for a long time.

I was the founding Chairman of the IUAES International Commission on Anthropology of Children, Youth and Childhood. The Commission was officially recognized by the Permanent Council of the IUAES at the Göttingen Inter-Congress on 19 July 2001. One of its most important objectives is to encourage research about children, in which children are themselves active agents as opposed to being just objects of study as they were most often in the past. I am the first anthropologist to promote this subfield of anthropology in India. As the Founder Chairperson of the International Commission on Anthropology of Children, Youth and Childhood, I organized more than a dozen panels and sessions relating to children and youth in different IUAES Congresses and Inter-Congresses. The Commission under my leadership (Chief Organizer) organized an IUAES inter-congress on the theme "Childhood in Changing Context" at KISS/Bhubaneswar/Odisha/India in November 2012. More than 300 overseas anthropologists from forty-eight countries participated in this Inter-Congress. The Commission has brought out so far four volumes focusing on "Anthropology of Childhood".

Administrative and Institution Building

Using my anthropological skills, I started gaining recognition as an academic administrator. I am currently serving as the Vice-Chancellor of Kalinga Institute of Social Sciences, Deemed-to be-University, Bhubaneswar, Odisha. I also served as the Vice-Chancellor of Sambalpur University from 18 January 2018 to 17 January 2021. Prior to that I was the Vice-Chancellor of Berhampur University from 1 August 2013 to 31 July 2016. I was also appointed as the first Vice-Chancellor of Rajendra University, Balangir, a newly established state-funded University in Odisha. I am the only anthropologist in India to become the Vice-Chancellor of four different universities. Under my leadership, Berhampur University became the first state-funded university in Odisha to obtain "A" Grade by NAAC. I played a significant role in helping Sambalpur University secure "A" Grade by NAAC. I was instrumental in signing of seven numbers of MoUs by Sambalpur University with different overseas universities and seven other MoUs by Berhampur University with overseas and Indian universities/institutes. I was a member of the Governing Council of Association of Indian Universities (AIU) continuously for three consecutive terms (from 2013 to 2016).

I was on the Advisory Board of the Centre for India Study at Aarhus University, Denmark. I was a member of the Advisory Committee of the Indian Council of Social Science Research, Eastern Regional Centre, Kolkata, for more than six years. I am a member of the Medical Advisory Council of India functioning under the National Medical Commission of India. I was the Director-in-Charge of the "UGC Centre for the Study of Social Exclusion and Inclusive Studies", Sambalpur University.

I maintain a strong academic network both in India and abroad. Under my initiative, some students from the Department of Anthropology, Sambalpur University, went to different European universities for pursuing their studies for a semester under "Study Abroad Programme of Erasmus Mundus Action 2". I was also instrumental in bringing many overseas anthropology students for their study at the Department of Anthropology, Sambalpur University.

Contribution Beyond Anthropology, Notable Students

Twenty-six scholars have received their doctoral degrees, and one her post-doctoral degree working under my supervision. The revised versions of a dozen theses of my scholars have already been published in the form of books. Some of my scholars have been working as professors, associate professors and assistant professors in different anthropology departments in India. Some are senior central government bureaucrats (IAS and Allied Services, Census of India), state government bureaucrats (OAS) and some others are practising anthropologists. I am also a member of the Editorial Board of the Indian Journals: *Oriental Anthropology, Social Change and Journal of Social Sciences.* I have collaborated with more than fifty overseas social scholars in different research and publication projects. I am a manuscript reviewer of Oxford University Press, Cambridge University Press and Sage.

Current/Post-Retirement Activities

I am the General President of the newly-formed Anthropology Association titled, "United Indian Anthropology Forum (UIAF)", the most vibrant, registered anthropological organization in India. I am trying to bring all the anthropologists of the country to a common digital platform. The Forum is very vibrant. As the Vice-Chancellor of KISS-DU and the President of UIAF, I have successfully organized the WAC-2023 jointly with UIAF and in collaboration with Department of Anthropology, Utkal University, Department of Anthropology, University of Delhi and Department of Anthropology, Sambalpur University. I am coordinating the UIAF website activities with the support of some senior members of Governing Council of UIAF. The Forum is in touch with all the major anthropological organizations and departments in the country. I am trying to popularise a new subfield of "anthropology of children and childhood" in India. I have been working in this subfield (still little known in India) for over three decades.

My Books

1996: *Contemporary Society: Childhood and Complex Order* (jointly with Georg Pfeffer, Free University of Berlin, Germany). New Delhi: Manak Publication Ltd.

1997: *Contemporary Society: Tribal Studies, Vol. II (Development Issues, Transition and Change)* (jointly with Georg Pfeffer, Free University of Berlin, Germany). New Delhi: Concept Publishing Company (Pvt.) Ltd.

1997: *Contemporary Society: Tribal Studies,* Vol. I (*Structure and Process*) (jointly with Georg Pfeffer, Free University of Berlin, Germany). New Delhi: Concept Publishing Company (Pvt.) Ltd.

1999: *Contemporary Society: Tribal Studies* Vol. IV (*Social Realities*) (jointly with G. Pfeffer of Free University of Berlin, Germany). New Delhi: Concept Publishing Company (Pvt.) Ltd.

1999: *Contemporary Society: Tribal Studies* Vol. III (*Social Concern*) (jointly with G. Pfeffer of Free University of Berlin, Germany). New Delhi: Concept Publishing Company (Pvt.) Ltd.

1999: *Gender and Society in India,* Vol. II (*Rural Studies*) (jointly with R. Indira, Director, Centre for Women Studies, Mysore University). New Delhi: Manak Publication Ltd.

1999: *Gender and Society in India,* Vol. I (*Urban Studies*) (jointly with R. Indira, Director, Centre for Women Studies, Mysore University). New Delhi: Manak Publication Ltd.

2002: *Contemporary Society: Tribal Studies* Vol. V (*The Concept of Tribal Society*) (jointly with G. Pfeffer of Free University of Berlin, Germany). New Delhi: Concept Publishing Company (Pvt.) Ltd.

2005: *Contemporary Society: Tribal Studies* Vol. VI (*Tribal Situation in India*) (jointly with G. Pfeffer of Free University of Berlin, Germany).New Delhi: Concept Publishing Company (Pvt.) Ltd.

2007: *Childhoods in South Asia.* New Delhi: Oriental Longman and Pearson Education.

2007: *Children and Youth in Global Metropoles.* (jointly with Professor Margaret Trawick of Massey University, New Zealand). New Delhi: Manak Publication Pvt. Ltd.

2008: *Contemporary Society: Tribal Studies* Vol. VII (*Identity, Intervention and Ideology*) (jointly with G. Pfeffer of Free University of Berlin, Germany). New Delhi: Concept Publishing Company (Pvt.) Ltd.

2009: *Contemporary Society: Tribal Studies* Vol. VIII (*Exchange in Tribal India*) (jointly with G. Pfeffer of Free University of Berlin, Germany). New Delhi: Concept Publishing Company (Pvt.) Ltd.

2013: *Contemporary Society: Tribal Studies* Vol. IX (*Tribal Health*). New Delhi: Concept Publishing Company.

2014: Children and Young People in a Changing World. Special Issue of *Oriental Anthropology*, Guest Edited (eds.) Behera, Deepak Kumar, Spyrou, Spyros, Luithle-Hardenberg Andrea, Gabriele Alex.

2015: *Contemporary Society: Tribal Studies* Vol. X (*Tribal Children and their Childhood*). New Delhi: Concept Publishing Company (Pvt.) Ltd.

19

My Anthropological Voyage

P.C. Joshi

I was born in a hill village of Uttarakhand named Khairakot in Manan, which is located between Almora and Kausani in the district of Almora. My village was located on the banks of River Kosi and one had to cross the river from Khosari on the main road to reach the village. Manan is a very picturesque location with Kosi River nearly touching the road out there. A very scenic Shiva Temple almost in the middle of Kosi River makes this place very attractive. Among four brothers and a sister, I was the second son; my sister being the youngest of all. My village had a shrine of Bhagwati Goddess and a place called *dhooni* which was used for night long *jagar* trance séance. Our family deity Golu's shrine was located across the river at a place called Pathri. We were a family of hill farmers, surviving on hard work to cultivate agricultural fields and raising cattle. I distinctly remember my mother working very hard in the fields and then threshing paddy to remove paddy husk while I was in the village. My early education was in government schools in Hindi medium. In the school, I used to consider English to be a very difficult subject. Although I topped in my board examinations of class fifth and eighth, I passed my higher secondary examination with average marks, two marks less than the required percentage which could have made me eligible to join pre-medical course. Since I could not get into pre-medical, I decided to go for B.Sc. and the choice was to opt between B.Sc. general in which I had to study three subject and B.Sc. Honours course in which I were up specialize in one subject. A clerk at the science faculty suggested that I may take anthropology which was offered as honours course which I accepted, although, I must admit that I had heard of anthropology for the first time in my life. I later discovered that this subject was most appropriate to my taste and interest.

My experience as an undergraduate student of anthropology was a memorable period of my life. In my student days, the Department of Anthropology was a very lively place bubbling with exciting activities and new experiences. For the first time in my life, I had among my classmates' students hailing from all parts of India. The department boasted of students from north, far south, east and west. Students from West Bengal made maximum number of students of the department during those. Among my notable teachers, who left an unforgettable and lasting impression on me were Professor J.D. Mehra, Dr Abhimanyu Sharma, Professor D.K. Bhattacharya, Professor S.C. Tiwari and Professor I.P. Singh. All of them had their own characteristic style of imparting knowledge to their students. Among them, Dr Abhimanyu Sharma is most notable for his sheer dedication and innovative teaching style which made even a dull student take keen interest in the subject. Professor J.D. Mehra, my M.Sc., M.Phil. and Ph.D. supervisor had his characteristic style of interpretation and argumentation and Professor D.K. Bhattacharya, who had the ability to enter into the private self of students and motivate and guide them to the path of scholarship. While Professor Mehra was my supervisor, Professor Bhattacharya was a true mentor and motivator and I consider myself lucky to have such great teachers.

One thing that I had always found exciting in anthropology is its fieldwork tradition. Our teachers in DU had always placed fieldwork at top and were always ready to take students for fieldwork to teach them the nuances of a good anthropological investigation.

I distinctly remember going for B.Sc. anthropology fieldwork with Professor I.S. Marwah and Professor H.K. Kumbnani in the year 1975 to Chakrata to work amongst the Khasas of central Himalayas. This fieldwork was extremely exciting and I felt that a trip of two weeks was not enough to learn the nitty-gritty of anthropology. I therefore went for a private fieldwork in the summer vacation of 1975 to Chakrata to taste the joy of fieldwork. This private fieldwork was conducted in the most inaccessible part of Jaunsar-Bawar where I had to walk for a full day to reach the village from the motor road. It was the time of Emergency imposed by Mrs. Indira Gandhi, a time when the entire area was in the grip of uncertainty as the government has decided to inject penicillin to all adults for venereal disease, abolishment of bonded labour and family planning drive. Unannounced, I landed in the village and literally forced myself on the village head, who had a son trained as doctor. While the villagers were quite courteous and helpful, they greatly feared me as they disclosed it to me later. In fact, once they even thought of killing me to avoid unnecessary trouble. I stayed with a school teacher named Rakesh master and started my fieldwork focusing on survey of lower caste erstwhile bonded labours and marital stability as divorce was quite common. I presented the results of this fieldwork on situation of divorce in the area to the 64th Indian Science Congress of 1977 held at Bhubaneswar, Odisha.

My fieldwork has mostly been confined to Central Himalayan polyandrous community known as Khasas of Jaunsar-Bawar, one of the most studied communities by University of Delhi and Lucknow University. I have worked for my M.Phil. and doctoral degree in this community and have learned the finer nuances of social anthropology in the company of these people. However, I have also worked among the Kashmiri Muslims of Badgam, the Jats of western Uttar Pradesh, the Dasnami Sadhus of Hardwar, the Oraons of Jashpur Nagar, Chhattisgarh, the Himachali of Junga and Sirmaur and the Bhils of Mount Abu in Rajasthan, earthquake effected Bhuj, flood affected Bahraich, Uttar Pradesh, Cyclone affected Sundarbans in West Bengal and made films on

German village Mauer besides villages of Vietnam and Philippines. While doing my fieldwork among the Jats of western Uttar Pradesh assisting Professor Elwyn Lapoint of Eastern Washington University in early 1980s, I was introduced to a re-study as he had done his first fieldwork in the early 1970s. The re-study has its own charm as the people know anthropologist who almost enjoys primary group relationship with the community members. I therefore, enjoyed the fruits of Lapoint's rapport while assisting him. I got the chance to organize a re-study when I was conducting capacity building programme for the young faculty in Anthropology Department of University of Delhi in 2013. Under their fieldwork training, I decided to take them to the celebrated village studied by Oscar Lewis nearly sixty years ago. The village was pseudonym as Rampura village by him. When we entered this village, it took quite a while for villagers to know who we were and why we were visiting them. But once we met some of the villagers who were little kids at the time of Oscar Lewis's visit, the situation suddenly changed. The nostalgia of people in re-visiting their childhood and the village folklore came alive all of a sudden. Late Professor Indera Pal Singh, who had participated in Oscar's fieldwork as a research student and taken nearly forty black and white photographs was alive at that time and shared with the team his experiences. For example, we learnt that Oscar when visited the village suffered severe diarrhoea on eating food in the village. To our team, finding out the current condition of the locations depicted in the photographs was a memorable experience. We organized a special seminar in the DU's Department of Anthropology where Professor Singh was invited to our presentation of the Rampura village. Professor Indera Pal Singh himself presented the re-study of Daleke village studied by him in the 1950s.

In my master's practical examination, Dr K.S. Mathur of Lucknow University had come for my *viva voce* and was impressed by my performance as he asked Professor S.C. Tiwari to send me to work under him for my doctorate among the Khasas. When Professor Tiwari told me about this, I considered it to be a good opportunity and went to Lucknow in the summer of 1977 to work under him. He asked one of the research scholars, Dr Ashok Kumar Pandey to host me in the university hostel till I take admission. Thus, in the summer of 1977, I spent my time in Lucknow to be a research student under Dr Mathur. The Department of Anthropology at that time was a very vibrant place with very active research scholars like Nadeem Hasnain, B.P. Joshi, A.K. Pandy, Mili Deb and many more active scholars. Dr Mathur was himself a very charismatic personality who played an important part in organizing of Lucknow Mahotsav of 1975-76. However, I had to leave Lucknow due untimely death of Dr Mathur. I joined University of Delhi which had started M.Phil. programme and before Ph.D., it became compulsory. I joined M.Phil. programme and was also given the UGCs Junior Research Fellowship to pursue my research. Although, the amount of fellowship may look meager from today's standard, I felt that I was most privileged to receive this fellowship. As we were the first batch of the M.Phil course, the department took more than one year to clear us but fortunately for me, I got a seat to do Ph.D. under Professor J.D. Mehra immediately after doing my M.Phil. In those days, only Professor Mehra was eligible to register students for Ph.D. in social anthropology so it was quite difficult to do Ph.D. in social anthropology in University of Delhi.

I completed my Ph.D. under Professor Mehra with Professor A.C. Bhagwati, Professor Gopala Saran and Professor Owen Lynch being my Ph.D. examiners. While doing my Ph.D. and staying in Gwyer Hall, one day I chanced upon a beautifully carved acheulian hand axe on the Delhi ridge, discovery of which became a huge media event. With Professor D.K. Bhattacharya, I scanned the ridge for more tools and later published a paper in the *Eastern Anthropologists*. After submitting my Ph.D., I worked briefly with Professor Ashish Bose as his assistant and in the summers of 1985, I got my first job as lecturer in anthropology at the then Garhwal University (now known as H.N.B. Garhwal University). I joined this department which was without any faculty as my predecessor Dr A.P. Singh had suddenly left the department to join Lucknow

University. I had to shoulder the daunting task of rebuilding the department. To be very frank, Anthropology in Garhwal University at that time was known as an insignificant department. I faced the challenge of establishing a department amidst giants like botany, zoology, physics, chemistry and many other well-developed departments. I started my journey of teaching with two students only but within three years, the student strength grew to more than a hundred with start of masters and research programmes as well. I made anthropology popular by regularly hosting conferences and seminars. I myself would actively participate in the intellectual activities of the campus bringing my unique anthropological perspective in the debates and discussions. I would also make sure that I keep involving well-known personalities in my academic programmes. Thus, people like Chandi Prasad Bhat, Sunder Lal Bahuguna, Gaura Devi, Jagat Singh Janglee—the noted environmentalists of Uttarakhand were part and parcel of my seminars.

I also started participating very proactively in the social and cultural activities of the campus. With some like-minded dynamic teachers of the campus like R.K. Kala and D.R. Purohit, I embarked upon eco-conservation activities and aligned with the Dasoli Gram Swarajya Sangh. We formed an association named Daliyon Ka Dagariya (The Friends of Trees) which received the prestigious Indira Vriksh Mitra National Award in the year 1987. Many students trained by us in the late 1980s and early 1990s joined national and international NGOs and are at present in leadership positions. Throughout my stay in Garhwal, I tried to make anthropology and anthropological perspective a popular discourse by continuously keeping the local media informed of my activities.

I lived in Garhwal for nearly twelve years and then moved to a neuro-psychiatric teaching hospital in Delhi in the newly-created position of Associate Professorship in Medical Anthropology. Working in this institution, called Institute of Human Behaviour and Allied Sciences, was a very different kind of challenge as I was continuously trying to find a place for medical anthropology amidst the clinical specialists. The challenge was not only in finding a place but also changing the positivistic mindset of the psychiatrists and neurologists. My major task involved interacting with the patients and establishing community linkages as there was strong stigma attached to a psychiatric institution. I organized a "Happiness Fair" in the institution in which the community was truly involved in the programmes of the institute. In the wake of Bhuj earthquake of 2001, a mental health team was sent by the institute to comprehensively study the mental health impact of disaster and to identify the mental health service needs. This study was conducted by a multidisciplinary team consisting of psychiatrists, clinical psychologists, psychiatric social workers and medical anthropologists. It liberally made use of anthropological methods like free listing, pile sorting, social mapping and focus group discussions. I joined the Department of Anthropology, University of Delhi as professor of social anthropology in the year 2003 and have since taught a generation of students, some of whom are now in senior positions. I had primarily taught the specialization of medical anthropology and research methodology to the students in DU.

I started my serious research career by learning about the health-related beliefs and practices. The idea to work in the area of medical anthropology was incidentally given to me by Professor Bhattacharya who thought this subfield of anthropology needs to be explored. Professor Mehra had in past guided couple of masters and a Ph.D. (uncompleted) in medical anthropology. My master's dissertation was on ethnomedical beliefs and practices of a village in Kashmir. While I was doing my M.Phil. and working for my dissertation on medical anthropology, I got a chance to interact with the doyens of medical anthropology—scholars like Charles Leslie, Arthur Kleinman, Ronald Frankenberg, Arthur Rubel and A.L. Basham, who had come to participate in the 1978 Xth ICAES and its post-plenary session at Pune in Maharashtra. It also gave me an opportunity to meet scholars like Professor R.K. Mutatkar, H.K. Bhat and other Indian medical anthropologists. The decision to take up medical anthropology seriously as career was taken after the ICAES. I therefore pursued my study of medical anthropology in the central Himalayan region and wrote many papers based my researches. Being involved deeply in the eco-system restoration in the Himalayas also gave me a chance to pursue Ecological Anthropology as well. When I joined the neuro-psychiatric institute in Delhi, it was but natural that I take up some studies on the issue of mental health. While joining University of Delhi, I seriously became interested in exploring the anthropological perspective in disaster risk reduction and development of methods and tools to study disasters. In University of Delhi, I also develop keen interest in the study of antibiotic resistance by studying varied population of Delhi.

I had been the Head of the Department in all the three institutions where I had worked. In fact, I had joined Garhwal University in 1985 as a Lecturer and Head of the Department and attended the Academic Council meeting immediately I had joined the university. Staring from two students in the under graduation to start with, I had established a full-fledged masters and doctoral programme with nearly 350 students when I left the department in 1997. In Garhwal, the challenge was not only to increase the student intake but was also to establish space for anthropological knowledge amidst domination of science and art subjects in the campus.

In University of Delhi, I had been very keenly associated with organization of conferences and seminars on variety of themes involving other faculty members in the task. I had also taken many national and international projects. I would like to especially mention the European Union funded Microdis project which was a consortium of multiple partners across Asia and Europe. I acted as the Asian Coordinator of the project and steered the Asian researches of the project having 5 million Euro funding. I assumed office of the Head of the Department in January of 2019 and became the Pro-Vice-Chancellor of University of Delhi in June 2020 and subsequently the Vice-Chancellor In-charge. As VC, I was instrumental in initiative long pending promotions of teaching and non-teaching staff members of university departments and colleges. In fact, I can proudly say that the position of professorship in the DU colleges was possible due to the bold decisions taken by me.

My contribution beyond anthropology is in two fields, namely environment and child labour. The work on environment started while I was in Garhwal and through the NGO "The Friends of Trees" I guided the activities of this group. We took up various action projects under the banner of this NGO but also organized many lectures and conferences to create awareness among the young and budding students of Garhwal University. In the field of child labour, I had intervened through the international organization Goodweave which provides certification to the carpet and apparel industry based on their child safety practices and works in the rehabilitation and education of the children found engaged in working for carpet industry. Currently, I am the trustee of Tri Impact, a NGO working for the welfare of the workers, especially in the unorganized sector. I have also joined the United Indian Anthropological Forum to take up advocacy work for the subject of anthropology and have been instrumental in opening of anthropology in some states of India.

My international collaborations have primarily been in the area of disaster research through the Centre for Research on Epidemiology of Disasters. I had closely collaborated with international institutions such as Heidelberg University, Northumbria University, Indonesia University, Hue University, Hanoi University, Xavier University, Philippines and Catholic University of Louvain. I have been local supervisor for many Fulbright doctoral and young faculties coming from different universities of United States of America.

At present, after my superannuation, I am involved in advisory positions in various organizations. I am the Ombudsmen and Chairman, Academic Audit Committee of the Kumaun University, Nainital; Chairman, Project Advisory Committee, IGNCA, New Delhi; Chairman, Academic Advisory Committee, IGRMS, Bhopal and Chairman, Empowered Committee, Delhi Biodiversity Parks. My professional positions include being President, Society for Indian Medical Anthropology, Mysuru; Vice-President, United Indian Anthropology Forum and Vice-Chairman, INCAA. Among my students, some have retired as professors and directors in research institutes. My early students Professor Beena Saklani retired in 2019 after active service in H.N.B. Garhwal University. Another of my research student Dr A.P. Mangla retired from Indian Council of Social Science Research long back. My doctoral students are teaching in various colleges of University of Delhi, besides working in places like Ambedkar University, H.N.B. Garhwal University, Allahabad University, Kalahandi University, National Tribal University and H.S. Gaur University, Sagar.

My Books

1990: P.C. Joshi and Anil Mahajan. *Studies in Medical Anthropology*. Delhi: Reliance Publishers.

2004: A.K. Kalla and P.C. Joshi (eds.). *Tribal Health and Medicines*. New Delhi: Concept Publishing Company (Pvt.) Ltd..

2006: Debarati Guha-Sapir, Lian Parry, Olivier Degomme, P.C. Joshi and J.P. Saulina Arnold. *Risk factors for Mortality and Injury: Post-Tsunami Epidemiological findings from Tamil Nadu*. Brussels: WHO Centre for Research on Epidemiology of Disaster.

2011: N.K. Ganguly, R. Lakshminarayan P.C. Joshi *et al. Situational Analysis: Antibiotic Use and Resistance in India. Global Antibiotic Resistance Partnership*. Washington DC: The Centre for Disease Dynamics, Economics and Policy.

2013: *Explorations in Indian Medical Anthropology* (Vol. II): Disease, Health and Culture. (ed. H.K. Bhat, P.C. Joshi and B.R. Vijayendra). New Delhi: Concept Publishing Company (Pvt.) Ltd.

2013: *Explorations in Indian Medical Anthropology* (Vol. I): *Illness, Health and Culture*. (ed. H.K. Bhat, P.C. Joshi and B.R.

Vijayendra). New Delhi: Concept Publishing Company (Pvt.) Ltd.

2013: *Relevance of Traditional Medicines in Global Era.* New Delhi: Icon Publications Pvt. Ltd.

2020: *Covid Crisis: Social Science Perspective.* (ed. Abdul Matin, P.C. Joshi and B.I. Laskar). New Delhi: Om Publications.

2021: *Recent Advances in Medical Anthropology.* (ed. P.C. Joshi and C. Mahajan). New Delhi: Concept Publishing Company (Pvt.) Ltd.

2022: *Biographical Account of Indian Anthropologists.* (ed. P.C. Joshi and Prasanna K. Nayak). New Delhi: Concept Publishing Company (Pvt.) Ltd.

20

An Enigmatic Student of Anthropology

Naresh Vaid

How to Write About Myself, that is the Toughest Question I am Facing Today

I tell my students, who are mostly professionals but have opted Anthropology for the Civil Services Examination: "When you write your first answer in 200 words, it may take even two hours to write and you may still not be satisfied with your attempt." Before starting, you just look at the plain paper and try to understand what it says. It stares at you and says, "You know nothing. Why you want to spoil me besides wasting your time." Today, I have understood how difficult it is to express what has not been attempted before.

"Self-praise is no recommendation", they say and writing about oneself simply means that only. I can talk about my failures and the lessons learnt therefrom, the turn of events that brought me where I am today, the persons who helped me in my journey and those who created hurdles in my way. I can share my idiosyncrasies and my restlessness. My anguish, hopes, aspirations and desperations. By asking me to write about myself (as I am among the chosen ones), Professor V.K. Srivastava has not done justice to me; rather, he himself can write better, more accurately and in a flamboyant language. Yet, with all humility, let me make an attempt. (In one of my couplets I have said: *If they can, why can't I. If they can't, let me try.*)

Enter the Dragon (named Anthropology)

After doing my premedical from DAV College, Chandigarh, and failing to get a seat in a medical college with scholarship (doing MBBS without scholarship was beyond means for me), I decided to join an undergraduate course in Panjab University, Chandigarh. I had a number of options but I wanted to study a discipline which was as close to man as possible. I scanned through the definitions of various disciplines and anthropology was the natural choice. That is how I entered the Department of Anthropology, Panjab University, Chandigarh as a first year student of B.Sc. (Hons.). There are rich memories of my four years and a half in completing my M.Sc.

The most fascinating aspect of the department was the teachers whom I can never forget. Though I can praise volumes about their contribution in my life, I must mention one—a Guest Faculty—Professor I.J.S. Diwan (hope, I remember the name correctly), Head, Department of Anatomy, PGI, Chandigarh and former Principal, Rohtak Medical College. He taught us Anatomy through Gray's Anatomy (which even medical students don't read today) in a style which I remember even today. More importantly, he inculcated in us the importance of punctuality. He would be present at the door of classroom five minutes before time and would wish everyone coming late. In a couple of days everyone started coming on time.

The department, founded by Professor S.R.K. Chopra specialized in Biological (Physical) anthropology, while Social-Cultural Anthropology was taught only by D.D. Kapur Sir. Learning was real fun but there was one itch, i.e. in M.Sc. (Hons.) there was no wider choice and all of us had to take up two courses in First year—Advanced Physical Anthropology and Bio-Statistics. In M.Sc. (Hons.) Final Year, each one of us had to write a dissertation based on our individual fieldwork and a Guide was assigned to each one of us by Professor Chopra. My journey in Anthropology, in fact, started from here as Dr J.C. Sharma was allotted to me as Guide.

Now came the interplay of internal politics of the department. Dr Sharma and Professor Chopra were not in good terms; rather Dr Sharma, despite being number two in the department, was pitted against everyone else. Obviously, I too, being his student, was to bear the brunt in the time to come. Dr Sharma turned out to be a very good human being and an excellent guide. He fully helped me not only in my fieldwork but in the whole process up to submission of my dissertation. Meanwhile, I also completed Diploma in Translation (English-Hindi, but why I did it, I don't know) that proved quite helpful when I became a journalist later.

I submitted my dissertation in October 1976. One day, in the evening, Vinod, my classmate, and myself visited Mr Kuldeep Bhatia, who, despite being a research scholar, had taught us genetics. When I sought his advice, he was very straight forward, "Naresh, either you leave Anthropology or leave this department, as you have no future in this department". He explained to me in detail why he was saying so.

I received my M.Sc. (Hons.) final results on 4 December 1976. I had secured just one mark less than 59 per cent. As per rules, the University could give 1 per cent as Grace Marks, if a student applied for the same. But scoring just one mark less smacked of malice. I applied for re-evaluation (from internal sources, I came to know that I had been given 24 per cent marks in one of the papers. Those days, the university never declared marks for each paper) but the university had no rule for re-evaluation. I had to fight it out (it is a long story) and finally, after two years, I was the first one in Panjab University to secure First Division through re-evaluation.

In-between, Professor S.C. Tiwari of University of Delhi, the teacher of my Guide, came to take my M.Sc. Viva Exam. After the Viva he asked Dr Sharma: *Ye Ladkaa Mujhe De Do* (Give this boy to me).

"Yes, Naresh! What do you think"? Asked Dr Sharma.

"You know better, Sir", I replied; and my fate was sealed.

Dilli Chalo

If Chandigarh was a Sea, Delhi was an Ocean with huge department with all facilities and conducive environment. I met many of the would-be famous Anthropologists on Day-1 itself—(now Late Professor) V.K. Srivastava, being one of them I can remember right now for his wit and interest in Urdu poetry. I introduced myself to Dr S.C. Tiwari, who gave me a seat to sit in his room. I also met Professor I.P. Singh, the Head and Mr J.S. Bhandari. The reason for me being called by Professor Tiwari was that he had taken up a UGC-funded project to study "Three Isolated, Endogamous Communities" of Uttarakhand in UP with himself as the Principle Investigator and Mr Bhandari as Investigator. To carry out the project, he had appointed four research scholars, one of which had left the project and I was to fill in the gap. Dr Tiwari promised me that I could use the data generated in the project for my Ph.D. (I was, however interested in studying my own community "Mohyal Brahmins" and registered the same as my topic for Ph.D. It was then decided that, if need be, I may change my Topic to use the data generated from the project.) But that was not to be. Subsequently, I, on my own, with the support of Senior Research Fellowship from Anthropological Survey of India, studied Tolcha and Marchha Bhotia of Chamoli in Uttarakhand.

Of the two researchers of Physical Anthropology, only I had the experience of sero-genetic research (in my M.Sc.) while the other one (who hailed from Delhi only) never even had held a syringe in his hand. Yet, after completion of fieldwork, he was given the data on genetics for his Ph.D. That is why I conducted fresh fieldwork in Chamoli. The other scholar, now armed with doctorate, was subsequently appointed in the same department while I was still analysing my data.

The Turning Point

That day I realized that I had no future in this department too. I took a decision quickly—forget the thought of academics and look elsewhere. I strode into the unknown territory of journalism, sometime as a regular job, some other time part time; on assignment basis and even on contract basis. I started teaching Anthropology to M.Sc. students staying in my hostel (I still remember two of them, i.e. Amarendra Mahapatra and Pankaj, the youngest son of Professor Vidyarthi) and also to those who wanted to join Civil Services with Anthropology as their Optional, but without charging any fee from them.

However, I must admit, I had quite fruitful time spent with Dr Tiwari and in his room. All teachers would approach him as and when they wanted and discussed their experiences with him. I developed very close relations with Dr P.K. Datta, Dr Abhimanyu Sharma, Dr D.K. Bhattacharya, Professor J.D. Mehra, Mr Marwah, Mr Kheda, Dr Kayastha, Dr Surinder Nath, and Dr S.L. Malik. Professor I.P. Singh, the Head, was always approachable. I also benefitted a lot through personal discussions with Professor Baker, Professor Mawalwala, Professor de Wilde, Professor Wolanski, Professor Mrs. Heath and many others.

Though initially trained in Physical Anthropology, I wanted to be an anthropologist, not merely a Physical Anthropologist. After a year or so after I joined a job as a journalist (by then I had become a casual visitor to the department), once Professor Singh spotted me in the department and called me to know what I was doing those days. I told him. He advised me to tread cautiously or "I may jeopardize my chances in academics" . But when I asked him, "Do you really see my future here anytime soon?" Professor Singh didn't say anything. My apprehensions were confirmed once again.

In one of such casual meetings Professor Singh narrated one incident to me. In a meeting to seek Special Assistance Programme for the department in Chandigarh, Professor Chopra cited me as a brilliant student who could not be absorbed in the department due to lack of funds. I believed Professor Singh, according to him, he too was present in the meeting. Interestingly, again, according to Professor Singh, he cited my example later on to seek the status of Advanced Centre.

I had shifted my residence to Timarpur but was a regular visitor to the hostel where I guided juniors in preparing for Civil Services Examination. In 1984, I got an opportunity to coach anthropology students at S.N. Das Gupta College, the oldest in this industry and my efforts resulted in my first success through Rajiv Sinha. But one thing was always lurking in my mind that why people don't know my fascinating subject and get attracted towards it.

Till October 1984, I was associated with journalism when I decided "enough is enough" and I decided to start a consultancy/ coaching institute to train civil services aspirants. I left journalism and it took me almost eight months to start my "business" . Initially, it was a fun. I guided students at several places: In a hostel in IIT, in a house in R.K. Puram, to a friend at her house in Tagore Garden, in my hostel PG Men's Hostel and my Institute in Shalimar Bagh. To the surprise of everyone, including myself, 17 of my students qualified for civil services in the first year itself. There was to be no looking back thereafter.

As a journalist, I had developed the habit of writing on daily basis. Most of my writings were published with different pseudonyms as no one was ready to publish me so often. I presented and published some research papers too, three of which were presented in X-ICAES, in one of which I was the first author. (I never had the habit of keeping a record of my works and I do not have proof of most of my claims.) But, as a businessman, my journey has been quite fruitful as more than 2,000 of my students have joined central civil services and many more in state civil services.

Return to the Dragon

The Bhotias, in general, had a long-lasting impact on the way I thought and acted. These people, after their trade with Tibet ended abruptly in 1961 (because of the border tensions), adopted a new way of life turning to education. By 1970s, when I conducted fieldwork among them, they still cherished the memories of lucrative trade with Tibet as also the dangers involved. I absorbed their simplicity in my life as also looking at things as a matter of fact. I can cite several instances of their generosity despite themselves being in trouble. As for my learning, I acquired working knowledge, not only of their own languages but of others too which they spoke. I also learnt some of their history, geography and culture through their folk songs (I enjoy melodious songs in any language and memorize them by heart. Then I ask meaning of each word. Thus, through one song, I could learn 50-100 words of that language) and I feel, learning a language through its songs is the easiest way to learn that language). My identity with them became so jumbled up that they gave me one of their own names "Narua"; back in Delhi, my friends started calling me "Bhotia".

In 1985, when I started my consultancy, Vaids ICS and it became an instant success, I decided to pay back to the people back in Pithoragarh. I started an NGO, SMM-TRE'N'DS in the memory of a friend, a student of M.Sc. who lost his life drowned while conducting fieldwork in Jagdalpur in Bastar. Subsequently, another friend, Mr Pawan Rana, an M.A. in Political Science, also formed another NGO, Experiments in Rural Advancement (ERA) with myself as the Founder Head and himself as the chief functionary. My visits to Pithoragarh were not as frequent (mostly twice-a-year), but he established himself permanently (at least for the next two decades) in Pithoragarh. My role was mainly limited to discussion of projects and their progress, and, to a limited extent, funding. Today, Pawan Rana is an established name in voluntary sector. Even now I help NGOs and individuals with my limited resources and sharing my limited experience in theory as well as in practise. For the last eight years, I have been trying to make the life of Birhor of Jharkhand better.

Here, I want to make one thing clear. I don't impose my will on the people and whatever I do is neither charity nor an obligation thrust on them. I do because I can; and because I can afford. I also do because I enjoy doing it. To explain it is quite painful for me as that is not a part of my nature. Anthropology has given me much more than what is enough for me (besides, I am not sure if I deserve it) and I must "invest" it the way I deem fit and the way my anthropological wisdom directs.

The Lull

Business-wise, I was doing quite well and I also involved myself in writing as well pursuing others to write textbooks in anthropology as I realize that one way to promote a discipline is through basic text books. Professor D.K. Bhattacharya (*An Outline of Indian Prehistory*), Professor Nadeem Hasnain (*Tribal India, Indian Anthropology*), Professor Surinder Nath (*Forensic Anthropology, Nutritional Anthropology*), Professor Abhik Ghosh (*Meetings With the Other*) promoted Anthropology through their books while Dr V.K. Srivastava contributed articles in a popular magazine *The Toppers' India*, with myself as publisher-editor. I also pitched in with my contribution in English as well as in Hindi (self-translating) while helping in translation of books (into Hindi) by Professor Bhattacharya and Professor Hasnain.

The syllabus of Anthropology for Civil Services Examination was revised upward in 1995 but it had no effect on its popularity among students. It was revised again in 2001, that too in a way that it threatened the beginners (I can say that it was done deliberately as, after the revision, one of the experts sent me a message: "Now let us see how you run your shop"). I was shocked. How out of jealously people can destroy the popularity of a discipline that has been their bread and butter for decades! The move by UPSC made a severe dent in my popularity as well as earnings. I, by many of my well-wishers, was advised to look for alternatives. I was offered handsome alternatives too; but I never ever thought of leaving anthropology for sociology or for an editorial job. The popularity of Anthropology dropped so low that in 2008 just more than 200 candidates opted anthropology compared to over 3,000 in 1994.

Return of the Dragon

In 2008, fortunes of anthropology changed, and mine too. Two things happened. First, UPSC started its website where it started uploading the performance of various subjects; and second, Iva, daughter of Professor V.S. Sahai, secured all India third rank with anthropology as a subject. There was no looking back thereafter. Then onwards, Anthropology has helped the career of hundreds of aspirants so much so that in 2017 all India 1st, 3rd and 7th rankers tasted success with Anthropology, of which 3rd ranker Sachin and 7th ranker Ayush were my students. In 2018, Akshat and Shreyansh both my students secured All India ranks 2nd and 4th. Immediately next year, my student Shubham topped the list of successful candidates.

Self-Praise is…

> "I love anthropology because I'm insatiably curious. Anthropology uniquely spans the arts, humanities, social science and natural sciences, and touches all fields of human endeavor or inquiry. Human origins? Uh huh. Human rights? Certainly. Ontology and the nature of being? Got it. Genome sequencing? Check. Poetics and aesthetics? You bet. Cross-cultural psychology? Please. Climate change? Down cold. Migration and displacement? Daily. Social media? We study that. Diversity and the many ways of being human? Obviously. Religion and spirituality, food security, human trafficking, ancient pottery, how humans communicate, Northwest Coast art, or family relations among baboons? Yes to all. Anthropologists

> study what makes us "us", in all its complexity. It can be hard and frustrating, challenging and contentious, surprising and often fulfilling—but it's never boring."

Sachin Gupta, a student of mine had sent me above WhatsApp message on 30 March 2018. He had faced "Interview", i.e. the final stage of Civil Services Examination, 2018. I circulated this message in two WhatsApp groups of anthropologists of Delhi and Chandigarh respectively, but without much comment/criticism/ appreciation. After a month, when the Final Results were declared, Sachin had secured All India Rank III. Praise started pouring in instantly. Moral of the story: For most of the people, individuals and their identity are important, issues and ideas are not. But whenever I have expressed myself, I find myself being rubbed on the wrong side. I had written over a hundred articles in various magazines and newspapers. (Interestingly, my first popular article was "Existence of Mankind in Danger" with major inputs from my knowledge of anthropology). I was also publisher-editor of a popular magazine, *The Toppers' India* for several years, editor of another magazine *MTG Current Currents*, etc.

I, however, consider relaunch of *Manav*, the only journal of anthropology in Hindi and published by Ethnographic & Folk Culture Society (EFCS), Lucknow (that remained defunct for many years due to "n" number of excuses given by the governing body) as an achievement. Professor Nadeem Hasnain, Secretary, and myself director-publications (interestingly, I remained director-publications for several years without being given any task of this nature) of EFCS decided to revive it. We roped in Dr Yogesh Atal, who had recently returned from UN and was not too busy, as editor and with myself as managing editor. Subsequently, for many years, I remained its editor. Besides, I really felt elated when Professor B.K. Roy Burman would address me as "promoter of anthropology".

I had published my first anthropological book *Economy and Social Relations* in 1990 that struck controversy immediately as, in the Preface, I had written,

> "...Anthropologists had ample time and opportunity—some of them had made an impact on world Anthropology, others have been honoured nationally and/or internationally. But the narrow, parochial attitudes towards humanity have rarely, if at all, let them grow beyond thinking about themselves."

Again, another controversy started with my "*Who Cares for Tribal Development*" as I began the Preface with a few lines from the 29th Report of the Commissioner for Scheduled Castes and Scheduled Tribes, Dr B.D. Sharma:

> "What should one say about a system in which the Constitution itself has bestowed on the President and Governors unlimited powers for protection and welfare of the tribal people, yet they have not been able to save the people from exploitation and oppression of their own servants, and THIS HISTORIC TASK HAS BEEN ACCOMPLISHED ONLY BY THE NAXALITE IN SOME AREAS?"

The only book of mine that did not raise a controversy, perhaps, is "Social Cultural Anthropology", the reason of which I think is Professor Vinay Kumar Srivastava, the least controversial and the most respected anthropologist of our generation, who has written Foreword of the book. I have never been a slave to any "ism" ; that is why I have neither many friends nor many adversaries. I don't believe in Left, Right, Centre, Left of Centre, Right of Centre, etc. thought and the only "ism" I believe in is *rationalism*. I support, if I can, anyone or everyone who is active, has some ideas, is interested in doing something to improve the lot of others. Besides, I have never been in competition with anyone. That is why, I cannot boost of anything. I have enjoyed isolation of COVID-19 during which time I am midway in my survey of "Behavioural Changes due to Lockdown caused by COVID-19" that I, most likely, will complete by September-end. I have written two research papers about Indian anthropology and Indian anthropologists. I have tried to help some of those bearing the brunt of Lockdown. I have also published a book *The Truth about Caste* after thorough research.

I forget to mention one thing which I must. With the initiative of Professor K.C. Malhotra, Dr Lalit Kumar and I conducted a course in Anthropology in Management and Marketing in a management institute SOIL of Gurgaon. It was a great success because of which the Institute not only has decided to continue next year too, but also has started canvassing for its promotion in other sister organizations. If all goes well, but COVID-19 stalled the progress. The last event in my journey so far has been my active participation in World Anthropology Congress held at KISS, Bhubaneswar (2023) where I proposed to "Debunking the Colonial Constructs of Caste & Tribe". Hopefully the world will agree with me one day.

The Only Wish

In 2020, I decided that before I hang my boots, I'll build an All India level school for tribals in Madhya Pradesh to develop leadership in them and to create nation-builders, protecting the rights and identity of their own people. I have already purchased 10 acres of land for the same. Hopefully the school will start functioning by the end of 2025. I need your blessings for the same.

My Books

- 1991: *Economy & Social Relations*. Palaka Prakashan, New Delhi.
- 1992: *जैविक मानवशास्त्र*. Palaka Prakashan, New Delhi.
- 1993: *Evolution of Genus Homo*. Ashtam Prakashan, New Delhi.
- 1996: *Who Cares For Tribal Development*. Ashtam Prakashan, New Delhi.
- 1997: *जनजातीय विकास–कुनबा डूबा क्यूँ*. Ashtam Prakashan, New Delhi.
- 2003: *जनजातीय विकास–मिथक और यथार्थ*. Rawat Publications, Jaipur.
- 2004: *Who Cares For Tribal Development*. Mittal Publications, New Delhi.

2007: *सामाजिक सांस्कृतिक मानवशास्त्र* (सह-लेखक) छत्तीसगढ़ राज्य हिन्दी ग्रन्थ अकादमी. Raipur.

2013: *In Search of Ourselves*. Palaka Prakashan, New Delhi.

2022: *The Truth About Caste*. Garuda Prakashan, New Delhi.

21

A Trajectory of Multiple Truths and Diverse Realities

The Living of Anthropology

Vineetha Menon

I was born in a small village called Pampakkuda in Kerala as the third child of a Block Development Officer during the days of community development in India, a year after states were formed in India on linguistic basis. A simple rural life was the beginning of my life journey. I do not remember much of those days except through narratives on some early photographs and occasional nostalgic reminiscences of my mother. My birth took place at home, something that is unthinkable in today's Kerala for a middle-class person. Mother had narrated her experience of how her older sister had provided comfort and assistance to her when she was in labour pains. The village did not have much medical facilities in those days and our family, like most others in the village depended on a local Ayurvedic *vaidyan* for most health problems although in any case of dire situation we were lucky to get the health advice of my mother's eldest brother who was a biomedical doctor in the Army. Later when my father took up a post in the state department of Agricultural Income Tax and Sales Tax and as a state government official got transferred to different places, I too became very mobile with my family and learned to adapt to the changes that came along. New schools, new friends, new dialects spoken, new forms of cultural celebrations and ethnic mixtures in the neighbourhood, even the pace of life changed with the places. The dialect in Thrissur district which is known as the cultural capital of Kerala where I spent some of my adolescent years, was very different from the colloquial Malayalam spoken in rural Thiruvananthapuram, while the urban part of Thiruvananthapuram that had a large floating population of government officials and professionals who preferred to stay on in the capital city besides the traditional residents spoke a mixture of various dialects that had no distinct character to it. Education and cultural upbringing colored the diverse dialects of these people. In the coastal areas, the fisherfolk too spoke very differently. As a child I did not come across anyone who lived in the forest region.

In the village of Pampakkuda, Thiruvananthapuram city and Thrissur town, three major places where I spent my childhood, the festive occasions were also different. While the capital city of Thiruvananthapuram had the vestiges of Travancore royal family heritage also, the temple festivals sometimes shared aspects of Tamil culture and traditions as some parts of present Tamil Nadu were part of the then Travancore state. Muslim mosque and Christian churches were also part of the central landscape of Thiruvananthapuram. But government buildings like the Secretariat and the legislative assembly, hospitals and educational institutions and the different types of markets like the big Palayam market and the small wayside vendors convey an understanding of everyday life being very heterogeneous and complex. This heterogeneity and complexity were not only due to the influences of interactive traditions, culture and heritage but also because of the nature of markets, proximity to structures and practices of governance, schools, markers of knowledge, power, authority and discipline that people experienced in different ways and measures. In Thrissur, the Thrissur Pooram, a major festival brought three temple festivities under one umbrella; two temples of female deities ritualistically competed in festivities in front of the male deity Shiva in the name of Vadakkumnathan. Contesting, competing and co-operating female spiritual energies under the surveillance of the male adjudicating power was symbolic. The festivities were religious but also of the pride of entire *desams* (localities) transcending religions and very cultural as well; it drew lot of tourists from all over the country and internationally transcending locales. The Christian churches were equally powerful in Thrissur. The Christian architecture, commercial and educational institutions also contributed to the cultural flavour of Thrissur and all these dynamics of diversity were distinct from that of Thiruvananthapuram, the capital city where Christian Church, Muslim Mosque and Hindu Temple stood in close proximity.

In the village of Pampakkuda, the transforming rurality under committed community development initiatives and a modernization urge were very striking as I retrospect. I was way too young to appreciate all that then but looking back now, these strike me as significant. I don't remember any religious festivals of Pampakkuda village although I am sure there would have been many but what I recall of that village are the agricultural and dairy fests, poultry raising, etc. In fact, our family album has some pictures of my mother interviewing some women in their poultry farms, may be as the wife of the Village Block Development Officer. I remember her as being genuinely interested in these livelihood activities that were state promoted although to her, it was a passionate hobby and interest in fellow women.

When I look back on that childhood, I think I was surrounded by pluralities in everything, from language, dress, food, healing systems, housing patterns and architecture, things valued and abhorred. Tolerance and inclusion were not words that needed to be used in any superimposing way; coexistence and harmony and cooperation even while differences existed was a lesson that I unconsciously imbibed from that everyday childhood experiences that I had in different parts of Kerala. I do not know if it was the same for my siblings too. Memory is a curious thing that can be selective, embellishing certain things and pushing to background certain other things. As an anthropologist who is trained to pay attention to many of these differences and similarities and different realities of life, I might be recalling memories selectively, interpreting them with anthropological sensitivities that my siblings may not share in the same way or intensity. I am however, certain that being something or someone was not an important thing in my childhood but giving the best in whatever one engages in was instilled in me as something very honourable to strive for. Both my parents were hardworking and had strong senses of right and wrong. While mother was a jovial homemaker who tried to give priority to my father's wishes, in her own inimitable ways she exercised lot of authority in the household decision making and also intervened on our behalf to negotiate with father on what we children feared might not meet with his approval. I was not told to become someone but there was an insistence that I should never fall behind in my studies. Education was the first priority for children. It was during my secondary school leaving period that I was confronted with the question of choice. In the latter half of my final school year, father got transferred back to the capital city where school admissions were extremely difficult even at the beginning of an academic year. After much recommendation on my behalf, I was admitted to the prestigious government girls' high school in the city on the condition that I would surely obtain a first class. That was when I started feeling the pressures of learning for the first time in my life. I struggled with my books and managed to keep my word and obtained a good first class. It was then that medicine and engineering surfaced as threats to my existence. All intelligent children are expected to get admission for science or mathematics groups, but I was certain that I cannot do dissection of frogs and cockroaches and so naturally, science and medicine were scored off from my choice of courses to pursue; as for mathematics and calculations, I was not at all good in them. By a logic of exclusion, I narrowed down my choice to history, economics, and politics, least prestigious choices coming under the third group. My parents were disappointed but I prevailed and started learning Indian History,

World History and Economics and later, graduated with Economics as my main subject.

By the time I got my bachelor's degree, civil services had become an attraction, first for my elder brother who went to Jawaharlal Nehru University in New Delhi for his postgraduation in economics. Having learnt from him that economics postgraduation in JNU was heavily mathematical, I decided to opt for sociology for my postgraduation as sociology could be taken as one of the papers for the All India Civil Services Examination. Once in JNU campus, life took a different turn; books and the library took over and threw out the window my dormant and faint civil services dream. That policy, administration and governance are not the concern of just those in civil services was a lesson that came to me much later. After my postgraduation, I had to take a break from academics; during this time, I worked as a journalist in my hometown in Kerala. Meantime, family life beckoned me and soon life took a different turn. Life's eventualities took me to British Columbia, Canada where I came to meet two well-known Canadian anthropology professors. One was Professor Brenda E.F. Beck, who was a student of Louis Dumont, the French structuralist and a scholar who did much work in Tamil Nadu. In her works, Brenda Beck combined structuralism and symbolism with a dexterity. The other person was Kathleen Gough Aberle whose work among the matrilineal Nair of Kerala made her question if a universal definition of marriage was possible. Her strong stand against America's position in the Vietnam war had later led her to raise questions about anthropology's relationship to colonialism and its funding interests and led to many uneasy debates in the discipline. Kathleen Gough's husband David Aberle, the renowned linguistic anthropologist, whose work among the Navajo (Dine) people of the Southwestern United States has made this people very visible was among my teachers for whom I had great respect. Aberle's doctoral thesis on "The Reconciliation of Divergent views of Hopi Culture through the Analysis of Life History Material" was under the guidance of none other than the very well-known anthropologist Ruth Benedict whose name is linked to the culture-personality school of thought in anthropology which probed into model personality and culture and led to the "nature-nurture debates". Aberle's work *The Peyote Religion among the Navajo* is still a classic in the field. He taught me Anthropological Theories at the University of British Columbia. Both David Aberle and Kathleen Gough were involved in many civil rights and social justice issues. Kathleen Gough was not teaching but affiliated to the University of British Columbia. As Aberle's student from Kerala, she had graciously invited me to lunch and we had an afternoon long discussion on divergent practises of matriliny in different parts of Kerala and among different communities.

As a beginner in anthropology, I doubt if I fully appreciated the great honour and opportunity, I was being bestowed upon to learn from these well-known anthropologists. Terms like engaged anthropology, public anthropology, action anthropology, advocacy anthropology, etc. were not heard of in those days. The term that was popular then was only "applied anthropology" which was later pitted against "academic anthropology" but the Aberle couple independently and jointly did succeed in raising their anthropological concerns as public concerns for debate and could well have qualified to be termed forerunners of public anthropology or engaged anthropology. In UBC, as a postgraduate student, my interest was limited and confined to understanding cultural value portrayals and their meanings in a comparative perspective. Closely supervised by Brenda Beck, my exposure was mostly to symbolic interpretations and structuralism. Nevertheless, I also had been introduced to the comparative understandings of medical anthropology. More importantly, I began to consciously appreciate that divergences existed and that "truth" has different manifestations and that vantage points coloured human perceptions. All this has helped me to consciously look for multiple perspectives and their meanings and logic in my later years.

The move from Jawaharlal Nehru University to University of British Columbia helped me to understand how academic disciplines get structured in different institutional settings differently and how the knowledge generated in different structural contexts with different perspectives on their perceived utilization shape up differently. I also learnt that comparing knowledge systems as more scientific and professional may not be as useful as trying to understand why and how certain types of knowledge get privileged in certain historical, cultural, and structural contexts. I consider these very valuable insights that shaped my later anthropological orientations. The courses I learned in the Centre for the Study of Social Systems in Jawaharlal Nehru University for my postgraduate degree in sociology, like family, kinship, religion, etc. were more accommodatable in the Department of Anthropology in the combined department of Anthropology and Sociology in the University of British Columbia. In those days, UBC sociologists concentrated more on industrialization, urbanization and other such issues. Plurality, comparative understandings, structures and meanings and processes that created knowledge systems and cognition and human agency were seeping into my unconscious through these experiences and exposures even when I was not conscious of them then. University of British Columbia had a very huge anthropology museum developed beautifully by its Director Professor Michael Ames who was also my teacher. The huge totem pole that stood outside the museum was my first exposure to the North American Indian Cultures. In hindsight I now feel it a quirk of fate that I confronted North American indigenous populations before I confronted the tribal lives in India. It is through such a circuitous route that I came to learn about Adivasi lives in Kerala and elsewhere in India and started to get to know these diverse lives. The greatest advantage this has given me, I think, is to be able to see India's scheduled tribal people as part and parcel of a transforming India even as anthropologically I study them exclusively in-depth. It has also helped me escape seeing anthropology as merely tribal studies even when structurally, the Department of Anthropology in Kerala State (University of Calicut and later, Kannur University) was sanctioned for the study of regional tribal aspects and hence, within the institutional setting, I had to concentrate on study of Kerala's tribal cultures.

It seems strange that after three decades of teaching in an anthropology department in Kerala, I still have to enter into dialogues with several people to correct their narrow perception of anthropology as tribal studies or of fossils and primitive people and vanished cultures. The interdisciplinarity and transdisciplinarity of anthropology and its quest for comparative and holistic understandings have made a deep impact on me. Biographical sketches of the anthropologists who laid the theoretical and conceptual foundations of the discipline show that many of them had very interesting backgrounds that shaped their anthropological contributions and research questions. Take for instance, Franz Boas, known as the father of American Anthropology under whom anthropologists like Ruth Benedict, Robert Lowie, Margaret Mead, Ashley Montague, Paul Radin, Edward Sapir, Alexander Goldenweiser, etc. got trained and did their Ph.D., each one influencing anthropology in his or her own right. Boas's doctorate was in Physics, and he studied geography and conducted geographical expedition to native Canada, attracted by the language and culture of Baffin Island Inuit populations. Then he became a museum curator. His interest in geographical and environmental factors and on language and culture led him to inquire into the diffusion of ideas through interactions of populations. Similarly, Malinowski's early training was in mathematics and physical sciences. He came into anthropology through an accidental reading of the Golden Bough by James Fraser and was in New Guinea because of this new found interest and the accidental marooning there. Anthropology too takes a circuitous route through various cultures in different parts of the globe, and the comparative and cumulative wisdom of humans everywhere is part of the corpus knowledge of the discipline.

The revisit into the pathways of my life lived so far makes me feel that my understandings and appreciation of anthropology have been shaped by the life events that I sketched above in somewhat of a patchy manner although I did not realise then that I am travelling towards anthropology. Only in retrospect that I now see how the makings of the anthropologist in me and the person who I am today are very inter-related and mutually shaping.

Contributions

A researcher's contributions to the discipline and to society stem centrally from the research questions and the purposes of research s/he has outlined for herself and the orientation and consciousness s/he has as to why the knowledge is being created. The knowledge accumulated in the pursuit of that research question get disseminated through various platforms and to different audiences as the data collected for any research is much larger than can be used in a single research output. I have discussed these relationships in knowledge production and its use in an earlier reflexive paper. I have tried to show in that paper that it is not unusual in research to see that knowledge produced through one research project or programme gets disseminated in different parts in different forms. So, outlining one's contributions is a difficult and complex task. I see my contributions in different ways: in the production of anthropological knowledge; in institution building; in interdisciplinary research and in practise and policy. These are not mutually exclusive but are often interpenetrative.

My first major anthropological fieldwork was among the Kanikkar in the forests in Trivandrum division; this did not result in a published book but is available in microfiche in the Canadian National Library as a Ph.D. thesis that was submitted to York University. A few published papers have also come out of this one-year fieldwork. These are contributions in the field of medical anthropology and also cross listed in tribal studies. The published papers varied in the themes from the functioning of plural medical system in Kerala, viewed as contesting healing power and knowledge of different health care systems, politics of maternity and fertility control in the context of the Scheduled Tribe Kanikkar community, and health-seeking among the forest-dwelling people, to symbolic aspects in the Kani indigenous curing ritual in what is perceived as life-threatening situations of illness. Fieldwork among an ecologically significant coastal region in the northern part of Kerala where livelihood and cultural practices markedly differ from most other parts of Kerala produced two major research papers: one drawing attention to multiple vulnerabilities—of sociocultural marginality, gender and old age in an ecologically significant area that differs markedly from other parts of Kerala. One of these papers presented in an international conference on rice-fish farming held in Can Tho, Vietnam added a new dimension to the economic analyses of rice-fish farming areas by bringing to fore the marginalized lives of a Scheduled Tribe population that depended on traditional technology for catching diverse fish varieties. A study of their indigenous knowledge of rice cultivation in a field which gets periodic saline intrusion due to its proximity to sea and the people's seasonally shifting livelihood to fishing as saline water is allowed to enter rice fields after harvest was a study of ecological anthropology too. The elderly women's livelihood vulnerabilities as commercial aqua farming of prawn was being state promoted could be persuasively presented in Can Tho before an international audience of development economists and policy experts as a human cost to be counted when the focus was only on economic cost benefit analyses.

The second paper from the same field site was an expanded one done as interdisciplinary collaborate work between an economist, statistician and anthropologist and used an institutional framework. Regional debates on the ecological and economic costs of destruction of mangroves in opposition to commercial monoculture of prawn were stimulated by the second paper. Scientists and officials from the government departments of agriculture and fisheries engaged with the issue in a development debate seminar although no consensus could be arrived at. Nevertheless, everyone conceded that there are grey areas on which further clarity and more research was required. In the area of development, policy issues in relation to settling a nomadic tribal population and issues that emerge when a forest dwelling Scheduled Tribe's health culture interacts with the market are significant. The paper titled "Responding to Policy: Challenges in the Practice of an Anthropologist" is also worth mentioning; it provides insights into anthropological contribution towards policy. A paper on disaggregated data's importance to inform policy has highlighted that aggregated data of a region can lead to myopia on marginal existences. Interdisciplinary collaborations with economists have led to some research papers in peer reviewed journals. The themes related to varied aspects of agriculture and livelihoods in the context of reforms. The collaboration outputs are in the form of published papers: on livelihoods and coping strategies in an agrarian village; agrarian distress and livelihood strategies; distress debt and suicides among agrarian households; lease farming in Kerala; reforming agriculture in a globalizing world; and case study of dynamics of irrigation institutions. Collaborations with management expert Kulbhushan Balooni furthered interest in irrigation schemes. In this collaboration the enquiry was on issues of self-reliance vs state responsibility in sustaining lift irrigation systems based on a study in Kerala.

In the area of family and kinship, the study of a matrilineal community of Nambudiris in Northern Kerala transforming into patrilineal kinship to integrate with the patrilineal Nambudiri groups in the rest of Kerala was published in the *Journal of Comparative Family Studies*. My own identity as a matrilineal Nair engaging with this topic raised interesting reflections on the multiple dimensions of the "self" and "the other" in anthropology. Aging in a transforming society as an anthropological concern comes to fore in the cross-cultural enquiry into the dignity and abuse of elderly.

Reflections on the practise of anthropology, research as empowerment, ethnography in the study of changes, and on knowledge in applied anthropology are contributions asking for critical look in these areas of anthropological knowledge production.

In institutional building, one of the two major contributions I may mention are in the establishment and development of the only anthropology department in Kerala, as its founder head.

Now in Kannur University, the department was started in the University of Calicut. The contributions are not just academic but also in the infrastructure development and networking with other anthropologists and anthropology departments. Interactions with the south Indian universities of Mysore, Dharward, Visakhapatnam, Madras, Pondicherry, and Hyderabad brought robustness to the new department with limited human resources.

The second contribution to institution development that merits mention was as coordinator of the UGC Special Assistance Programme in the Department of Anthropology, Kannur University. During this period, the department further strengthened its collaborations with anthropologists from other Indian universities also, especially from University of Delhi, University of Hyderabad and Chandigarh University.

In public anthropology or engaged anthropology, contributions were made in the capacity as a permanent jury in a social reality show titled "Green Kerala Express" and described as the first-ever social reality show, intended to find the best models of sustainable development put forward by local self-governments of Kerala. This programme was organized by Kerala branch of Doordarshan Kendra, India's public television broadcaster Kerala and C-DIT, Kerala for the Kerala Ministry of Local Self Government, the Suchitwa (Sanitation) Mission and the Centre for Development of Imaging Technology (C-DIT). It was a daily 30-minute interactive show which started in February 2010, focused on sustainable development models developed by the local self-governments. The local government authorities (panchayats) were evaluated based on their performance in sectors like water and land management, sanitation, environment, health, energy, social security, women's empowerment, education, agriculture, and food security among other aspects.

International Collaborations

Opportunities for my international collaborations opened up through my research collaborations with Professor K.N. Nair, an economist who was the Director of Centre for Development Studies (CDS), Thiruvananthapuram and head of the Kerala Research Programme on Local Level Development. I accepted the invitation to join CDS as a Visiting Fellow and joined KRPLLD, on deputation from Kannur University. With this collaboration with KRPLLD, I became part of a larger international collaborative research network of Multi-Annual Multi-Disciplinary Research Programme, promoted by the Research and Communication Division of the Netherlands Ministry of Development Co-operation. I also became a senior researcher in a major research project entitled "Coping Strategies in the Western Ghats: Threats and Opportunities of Economic Globalization and State Decentralization". This project was sponsored by the Swiss National Science Foundation/University of Berne/Geographical Institute/ University of Zurich under National Centre of Competence in Research North-South Research Partnership, from 1 April 2002 to 2006. I also collaborated in the research project on Knowledge Utilisation: A Comparison of Some South Asian Projects funded by the Netherlands Ministry of Development Cooperation. Under this, ten research projects funded by the KRPLLD were assessed for their social impact, capacity building of scholars and institutions, utilization of knowledge from the project by stakeholders, policy makers, and communities. The findings were disseminated in international workshops for comparing lessons.

I also completed research partnership with the Development Study Group, Department of Geography, University of Zurich under the Swiss National Centre of Competence in Research North-South (NCCR-North-South), under Swiss National Science Foundation, Berne. Under this partnership, C.P. Vinod, a Ph.D. scholar working under my supervision in Kannur University successfully completed his Ph.D. with project fellowship. A publication collaboration within this research collaboration with Sanjay Barbora, Ganesh Gurung, Karin Astrid Siegmann and Susan Thieme led to a comparative paper on migration (Barbora et al. 2008). Anthropological knowledge gets enriched through such comparative understandings as it helps us ask different and sharper questions in our in-depth study of a society or culture.

Another gratifying international academic collaboration was with the Department of Anthropology, University of Adelaide through Kannur University with regard to my local guidance to a Ph.D. scholar registered in the University of Adelaide in medical anthropology and Ayurveda; The scholar—Bronwyn Jayne Hall—successfully completed her Ph.D. with Dean's commendation. Learning from others and constantly reflecting on experiences and lessons learned enrich anthropological insights as well as the anthropologist. Of this I am convinced from my reverie of my living of anthropology and living as an anthropologist.

My Books

2005: *Alleviating Poverty: Local level Processes and Case Studies from the Developing World* (co-editors: P.R. Gopinathan Nair and K.N. Nair). New Delhi: Rainbow Publishers.

2007: *Social Change in Kerala: Insights from Micro-level Studies* (co-editor: K.N. Nair). New Delhi: Daanish.

2008: *Confronting Violence against Women in Kerala: Engendering Kerala's Development Experience* (co-editor: KN Nair). New Delhi: Daanish.

2008: *Water Insecurity, Institutions and Livelihood Dynamics: A Study in Plachimada, Kerala, India* (co-authors: K.N. Nair & Antonyto Paul), New Delhi: Daanish Books in collaboration with Centre for Development Studies, Thiruvanathapuram.

2012: *Ecology, Indigeneity, Resource Conflicts and Adaptations: Empirical Studies from India* (edited volume). New Delhi: Concept Publishing Company (P) Ltd.

2019: *Chronology and Events: The Sociological Landscape of Changing Concepts.* (co-editor: Susan Visvanathan). New Delhi: Windshield Publications.

22

The Journey of an Accidental Anthropologist

A Memoir

Abhijit Guha

In this autobiographic article, I have narrated the story of my induction into anthropology through a series of accidental incidents, which led to some unprecedented outcomes. These accidental incidents included my encounters with the Adivasis living around my own university campus, who enjoyed our campus land as a common pool resource and got alienated from this geo-cultural space owing to the establishment of the Vidyasagar University campus. Another accident was my chance meeting with a peasant leader fighting against governmental land grab in the vicinity of Medinipur town for industrialization. On hindsight, I view these accidents crucial to my career as an anthropologist to which I look back as an unending auto-ethnographic journey.

Prologue

Imagine a young man of 29, educated at Kolkata during the tumultuous 1970s was suddenly dropped in a small town in West Bengal as a teacher in a newly-founded state university. Imagine further that this young man had no previous experience of teaching, let alone living permanently in a rural area, and he lived there as a permanent resident, within a university campus, surrounded by villages and of course, wide open countryside. That was me and it was 1987. Viewed from an anthropological perspective, the campus and my full-time residence was ideal for conducting participant observation and fieldwork, and I did that too, although accidentally. I did not know that I was doing fieldwork.

I joined Vidyasagar University on 6 December 1985, and became a permanent resident of the campus since July 1987. I saw the university growing up brick-by-brick and I also grew up within the rural milieu, slowly, sometime without even knowing the changes that had occurred within me. It was, simultaneously, a painful as well as a joyous journey in all sense of the term. I missed my friends, *addas*, cinemas, theatres, book fairs, little magazines and my cerebral life in Kolkata. Culturally, I was uprooted. I could only share my pains with my wife for she too was displaced like me. But our memories of Kolkata were not dead; those were in fact relived as our sons grew up at Medinipur. They listened to our ways of living at Kolkata, which we visited with them for three to four times in a year. I have seen my sons growing up jubilantly within the beautiful campus of the university, which was also developing from an embryonic stage to its present state. My life at Vidyasagar University from the very beginning was wedged up in the locality where I would station myself permanently for the next twenty-seven years. That finally yielded many accidental and fruitful events in my academic career and social life. I will narrate some of them in this memoir.

Marginal Native?

It was impossible for me to think of Vidyasagar University as a separate entity from the Medinipur town and the district. But then, it was again a painful experience for two reasons. The typical urban middle class Kolkatans, my friends, relatives and others had a vague idea about Medinipur. Many thought that the place where I lived was near to the sea-side tourist resort named Digha now located in Purba (East) Medinipur. Still others even thought that I worked in Vidyasagar College of Kolkata. I have also heard a number of intellectuals referring to "Midnapore University" as my place of work. Renowned sociologist, Ramkrishna Mukherjee once asked me whether the university where I teach was adequately "urbanized" or not? All these were, disgusting for me. Equally nauseating was the view of some local elites who expressed concern over the recruitment of inexperienced young teachers, like us, who have become founders of postgraduate departments at a university which had just disassociated from the Great University of Calcutta! Initially, I felt like a marginal person and many of my friends and well-wishers suggested that at the earliest opportunity, I should leave Vidyasagar University. A good number of my best friends and colleagues who were academically sound too left the university. These disenchanting events, instead of alluring me were shocking in the process of my socialization at Medinipur as well as Vidyasagar University. At this juncture, I could vividly recall my personal communications with my teacher Professor Surajit Sinha with whom I was associated for doing my Ph.D. as an Indian Council of Social Science Research doctoral fellow at the Centre for Studies in Social Sciences in Kolkata. Just after joining Vidyasagar University, I wrote to Sinha describing my daily struggles of working and adapting to local conditions. He gave a very interesting reply, which I believe is valuable even now. Let me quote

> I am very glad that you are already quite busy running the show single handed for developing what the university has labelled as a Bridge Course. Please be careful that the course should be manageable, precisely formulated and play a decisive "bridge" role and not a "buffer" role.

Few years later, during the late 1990s, when I got thoroughly entrenched in the local milieu of Medinipur, I met Sinha at the Indian Museum Hall in Kolkata. By that time, my Ph.D.

registration at University of Calcutta under his supervision had expired. He asked: "What are you doing now at Medinipur?" I promptly replied: "Sir, I am now writing in a little-known Bengali daily named *Upatyaka* published from Medinipur town." Sinha looked at me and in his characteristic style (I always regarded him as a "stylist anthropologist") and uttered: "This is the right kind of thing you are doing. You should do it more." I was surprised with this kind of accolade from one of the great anthropologists in India. Sinha's occasional comments, encouragements and particularly his Bengali writing on the potentials of Viswa Bharati University were my great source of encouragement.

A Flashback

My anthropological journey began in 1974 when I had to opt for an honours course at the undergraduate level at the University of Calcutta since I could not get a chance in any well-known and popular science subject with my kind of school leaving marks. I was not a very good student and secured only a mediocre second division in the Higher Secondary Examination in West Bengal. I later felt and still feel that it was a blessing in disguise! I fell in love with anthropology but not when I just started after leaving school. One of my brilliant friends who chose to study economics suggested me to take anthropology since it was "off-beat". It was an accident and I am still grateful to him. I liked my teacher Professor Asoke Kumar Ghosh at the University of Calcutta who, in his first classroom encounter enquired all of us about why we had chosen anthropology and congratulated those students who confessed that they had taken anthropology since they could not get honours in physics, chemistry or other biological sciences. Obviously, I was one of those who told the truth.

Time passed and more I was socialized in anthropology more I became a disbeliever in what I was being taught in the classes until I chose a cognitive study on Bengali kinship in my M.Sc. dissertation. I read the book by two American scholars (Ralph Nicholas, an anthropologist and Ronald Inden, a historian of the

University of Chicago) on Bengali kinship and agreed to differ with them on substantial grounds based on my own fieldwork in Kolkata. Much later, I could publish a paper out of this dissertation in the *Journal of the Indian Anthropological Society* (hereafter *JIAS*) in 1989 two years after I joined at Vidyasagar University. Another beneficial accident occurred during the mid-1990s. I was teaching General Anthropology to the then M.Sc. Part I students and spent a substantial part of my reading time on bio-social anthropology, wrote a paper in *JIAS* with my students on the trends of bio-social anthropology at the global level by collecting data from *Man*, *American Anthropologist* and *Current Anthropology*. During this period I was greatly influenced by three biological anthropologists, D.P. Mukherjee, Pranab Ganguly and Amitabha Basu and I used to read *Current Anthropology* and *Population and Development Review* (*PDR*) regularly during this period. In 1993, I read an article in the March issue of *PDR* entitled "On the Darwinian View of Progress" by Amartya Sen and disagreed with his reading of Darwin and challenged his philosophical arguments against Darwinism with my readings on bio-social anthropology. I wrote a full-blooded four page critique at *PDR* in its December 1994 issue and hey presto, it was published, and Amartya Sen also had to give a rejoinder in the same issue! My entrenched reading in the library of a rural university in the pre-internet era on evolutionary biology under the guidance of the physical anthropologists of India paid its dividends in the international academic arena.

At this juncture of my journey, I should digress a little to narrate my journey through bio-social anthropology in early part of my career. Let me begin with A.L. Kroeber from whom I derived support in my debate with Amartya Sen. In his lesser known 1915 article *Eighteen Professions* published in the *American Anthropologist* Kroeber began with two interesting paragraphs. The first one is Anthropology today includes two studies which fundamental differences of aim and method render irreconcilable. One of those branches is biological and psychological; the other, social or historical.

The second paragraph starts with a more interesting sentence, which ran as follows:

There is a third field, the special province of anthropology, concerned with the relation of biological and social factors. This is no-man's land, and therefore used as a picnic-ground by whosoever prefers pleasure excursions to the work of cultivating a patch of understanding. Some day this tract will also be surveyed, fenced and improved.

My real interest in anthropology began with a picnic on this "no-man's" land under the influence of Professor D.P. Mukherjee at the Department of Anthropology, University of Calcutta during early 1980s. With D.P., I used to have long debates on the possibilities of doing researches on the relationship between social structure and fertility among various communities in India, although I did not proceed further in this line and instead took up Bengali kinship as my preferred area of research. But then again, I lost interest in kinship studies owing to the fact that under some unavoidable circumstances, I was dropped in a cultural and political milieu of a rural university to pursue my career as a teacher of anthropology in erstwhile Medinipur district of West Bengal.

I however, learnt two important lessons from my excursions into the bio-social studies (Kroeber's "no man's land") and kinship (a common land in anthropology) which were: (i) Indian anthropologists should no more remain successful "apprentices" (to borrow a term from Surajit Sinha) of their Western masters and (ii) we should concentrate more on the non-traditional and policy focused problems under interdisciplinary frameworks. The unique location and cultural milieu of Vidyasagar University provided me the opportunity and I plunged into a no man's land which of course was not envisaged by Kroeber.

Two accidents

Case I

During the mid-1990s three students of the Department of Anthropology at Vidyasagar University went to do fieldwork for their M.Sc. dissertations in a village named Paschim Amba, only 8 km from the Medinipur Railway Station. They selected a hamlet inhabited by the Koras and started measuring human bodies and collected data on family, marriage and kinship following the standard anthropological methodology. In one usual afternoon in the department, when we were discussing about the colourful Kora marriage ceremony, a student remarked, "The colour and pomp of Kora marriage will soon go away since their lands are being taken over for a big pig iron industry of the Tatas".

The remark of the student was a sufficient jolt for me and on one Sunday morning in 1995, I landed up in Paschim Amba where I first met a peasant leader named Trilochan Rana who was then leading a militant movement against the acquisition of agricultural land for private industries by the state government. In Trilochan Rana's house we met a good number of peasants hailing from Amba, Mahespur, Kantapal, Gokulpur, Baharapat, Shyamraipur and other villages of the area. Very quickly, they started to narrate quite enthusiastically the gloomy story of how their lands have been taken away for the industries. Trilochan Rana depicted how they were trying to protest against this kind of anti-peasant policy suddenly adopted by the Left government in the wake of liberalization in India. Ironically, Mr. Rana, who was a former Naxalite, took refuge under the Congress party to organize this peasant movement. "But sir, how coming from a university you can help us in this struggle for survival?" At that moment, I could not give any direct answer to this straightforward and pointed question.

While returning to Medinipur I was thinking of the possible course of my individual action on land acquisition. Should I take up research on this problem? In fact, I had to struggle within myself for a long time on this issue simply because it was not just passing through the railway station Gokulpur twice a week like the service-holders commuting from Kolkata to Medinipur. Anyway, after my maiden visit to the field many events occurred and I had to go to those villages several times accompanied by the students. During this period I took two firm decisions. One was to do my Ph.D.

dissertation on this problem and the other was to support these dispossessed peasants by writing popular articles on the various adverse effects of land acquisition on the socio-economic life of the enterprising Sadgope cultivators and poor Lodha and Kora families living on both sides of the south-eastern railway track between Medinipur and Kharagpur railway stations. Gradually, a feedback with the peasants developed and while collecting data I took an active part in organizing a public meeting within Paschim Amba in collaboration with the district unit of the Association for the Protection of Democratic Rights (APDR).

Finally, what I could ultimately sustain was continued research on land acquisition for development projects by combining field and archival materials and dissemination of my research findings in various academic and popular forums. The methodology of my research can hardly be called "purely anthropological" let alone "neutral" since my holistic perspective did not end in the village but went far beyond into the files, notes, and gazette notifications at the Land Acquisition Department of the District Collectorate to the West Bengal Assembly Proceedings. My accidental entry into such a politically sensitive field site was made possible by the peasants who were organizing a movement against the decision of the government to acquire their fertile land for an industry.

Case II

Let me begin with a tribal man—of a village—bordering my university campus. He was about sixty, when I first met him in 1987, a dark-skinned lean man, strong enough to pedal a three-wheeler cycle rickshaw with passengers in the town. He narrated his childhood when the present campus of Vidyasagar University was the village common land. Raghunath told me several times, "The land of your university is the grazing fields of our cattle, our women collect fuel from your ground and our children play here. We defended our village from the attacks of the robbers with our bow and arrow and village unity, but now your guards are creating problems for us." He died begging on the streets in the year 1994.

In 1997, the university authority employed a private security agency to guard the campus from the "encroachers".

Our Munda neighbours ("encroachers"?) to whom Raghunath belonged, were poor and illiterate and alcoholism among the men was found to be one of the major social evils of the village. The women, particularly the older women were also found to drink local rice beer. Whenever we went for fieldwork in the village, the villagers complained about the absence of irrigational facilities and problems encountered by them in grazing their cattle and collection of fuel for their domestic needs.

Despite their poverty and illiteracy, the Munda villagers were found to be peaceful, good-humoured and sometime they outwitted me during conversations. I will narrate one such conversation.

On one occasion, when I asked some Munda women and men about the reason behind the occurrence of a solar eclipse, they recounted from a myth which narrated the story of a Munda man who in the remote past could not meet the payments to be made to a traditional midwife belonging to a low Hindu caste group. On the day of a rare solar eclipse, which took place in India on 24 October 1995, I asked an old woman of Muradanga: "Are the dues to the midwife still unpaid?" The Munda woman replied: "Oh! Yes, how can other people pay for him? The eclipse recurrently takes place owing to that original sin." I, however, kept on like an anthropologist and continued with the question: "But why then does the eclipse go away and the sun reappears?" After a few moments, came the reply in the form of a question: "How can the eclipses (*grahana*) recur unless they go away?" I was outwitted by the poor and illiterate Munda neighbour.

Ergo

I however could not remain satisfied only with these ethnographic snippets from the campus. My point of departure lay in viewing the physical and the cultural space named "university campus" by situating the case study of Vidyasagar University in a theoretical and global context. I gradually became an accidental anthropologist of my university campus! My anthropological subjects in the cultural space labelled as "campus" ranged from the Vice-Chancellors to the indigenous tribal people who were viewed as "encroachers" by the university community while the latter looked at the campus as part of their traditional village common land. Ironically, the aims and objectives of my university were to build up research and teaching towards the development of the tribal and the underprivileged people of the region in which the university is located. Thus campus anthropology and study of land grab which came accidentally in my anthropological journey have an underlying unity and that is the essence of this memoir. Would you call this journey anthropological? I will not mind if you don't!

My Books

2007: *Land, Law and the Left: The Saga of Disempowerment of the Peasantry in the Era of Globalisation*. New Delhi: Concept Publishing Company.

2015: Santanu Panda and Abhijit Guha Edited. *"Criminal Tribe" to "Primitive Tribal Group" and the Role of Welfare State: The Case of Lodhas in West Bengal, India*. New York: Nova Science Publishers.

2016: *Tarak Chandra Das: An Unsung Hero of Indian Anthropology*. Delhi: Studera Press.

2022: *Encountering Land Grab: An Ethnographic Journey*. Routledge.

2022: *Nation-Building in Indian Anthropology: Beyond the Colonial Encounter*. Routledge.

23

Journey of a Grassroot Anthropologist

A.K. Sinha

Early Life, Education, Family and Taking Anthropology as a Subject

I come from a middle-class family. I have two brothers and a sister among whom I was the youngest. My father worked as an accountant in the railway department of North-Eastern Railway, Samastipur.

I completed my early education from a missionary school and secondary education from King Edward Higher Secondary School, Samastipur. I pursued B.Sc. Zoology (Hons.) in Samastipur College, Samastipur, which was affiliated to L.N. Mithila University, Darbhanga, Bihar. Back in those days, the sessions used to begin very late because of which my family wanted me to pursue my M.Sc. Zoology from Ranchi University (then Bihar), which presently falls in Jharkhand State. I took their advice and reached Ranchi to join this course, however, I could not find my name among the first list of students who were admitted to the course. One of the professors suggested me to apply for admission in anthropology as he was sure that my name would appear in the second or third list of admitted students, which would give me a chance to transfer to my first preference, which at that time was zoology. This is how my venture with anthropology began. As suggested by the professor I applied for admission to the Department of Anthropology, Ranchi University, Ranchi and decided to visit my elder brother who lived in Jamshedpur back then.

After a few weeks, I got a letter from the university that I had been selected for admission to the Department of Anthropology and was asked to enroll within a week. I decided to go ahead with the same. Upon reaching Ranchi, I met Dr V.S. Upadhyay, who was in-charge of admissions, and pursued him to enlighten me about the subject of anthropology. He helped me gain perspective on the subject and also informed me how it was less opted for and hence there was less competition. Thereafter, I decided to buy the syllabus for the course and again come back to Jamshedpur as my classes were to begin only after fifteen days.

I started to deeply study the syllabus and found myself greatly influenced and fascinated by the subject, which convinced me to opt for studying anthropology for my masters. Fieldwork was a tradition those days, and it was a part of our second-year curriculum, the duration for which was 30-45 days. Every year, the fieldwork was usually conducted in tribal areas. However, at our time sacred complex was hugely popular and therefore we went to Joshimath and Badrinath for fieldwork. All students were divided to two groups: one was headed by Dr V.S. Upadhyay and another had gone to Rishikesh along with Dr M. Jha. I was a part of the former group, which comprised six boys and six girls and first visited Joshimath and then to Badrinath where we stayed at Kali Kamliwala Dharamshala. The memories of the fieldwork are still very fresh in my mind. It was during this time that our proximity with our teachers grew.

We used to discuss social issues and sometimes personal lives too with our field supervisor. We used to cook our meal by ourselves. Every evening, after our return from the field, we had to submit two copies of our field report to our teacher, which was returned the next day with comments and suggestions. On days when we had any difficulties, our teacher accompanied us to the field. This was the time when my relationship to anthropology strengthened, and I gained interest to pursue Ph.D. After the return from the fieldwork, guides were allocated to students and I was fortunate enough to write my M.Sc. dissertation titled "Pilgrims of Uttarakhand with special reference to Joshimath and Badrinath" under the esteemed guidance of Dr K.N. Sahay.

Early Career, Teachering, Fieldwork and Doctoral Work

By the time I passed out of my masters, I had a basic idea of what the subject is, and my interest to pursue a Ph.D. in the subject arose. I approached Dr K.N. Sahay for the same. I should mention here that I was never a very bright student but was extremely dedicated and hardworking, and my hard work was always appreciated by my teachers. Dr Sahay asked me to visit him at his house on a Sunday at 9 a.m. As intimidated as I always was by his presence, I could not muster enough courage to ask him his address. I then approached Dr A.P. Sinha for help, who was a research associate at that time and had been a Ph.D. research scholar under Dr Sahay. I found out that Dr Sahay then resided in House No. 3K/48, Bariatu Housing Colony, Ranchi. Dr Sinha had also very specifically asked me to reach on time. I reached his place a few minutes before 9 a.m. and was warmly welcome by him. During our conversation, he inquired about my family and social life and then asked if I liked sweets. Considering it an offering, I promptly said "yes sir, but I don't wish to have it right now". He responded by instructing me to write a brief account of sweets and present it to him in the following week at the department. As time passed, everything seemed to fall in place and within three-four months, I was able to prepare a synopsis. As per the regulations, after signatures from the Head of Department and Dean, the synopsis was to be submitted to the Research Degree Committee for approval. I was positive about everything. Following the procedure, I took the synopsis to the Head of Department Dr L.P. Vidyarthi to get his signature. Upon looking at the title of my synopsis, he blatantly asked me "where would you be able to find the job of a confectioner". I was left discouraged after this encounter and approached Dr Sahay. He asked me to keep faith and mentioned that such difficulties are bound to happen in the course of my research with him. He was very direct in giving me the liberty to find another teacher to guide me if I was easily scared by such events, but I was always sure about him being my guide. Later I got to know that Dr Vidyarthi and Dr Sahay were co-brothers but they didn't get along very well. This experience was my first encounter with academic politics.

Back in those days, the only department that taught anthropology as a full course in Bihar was under Ranchi University and evidently, the department had a huge number of research scholars and it was common for scholars to find themselves amidst departmental politics, however, no one dared to complain about their experiences. Despite the power being in the hands of the Head of the Department and all internal conflicts, I was enrolled under the supervision of Dr K.N. Sahay. After beginning my research work, I ensured to get my work by him, even if it was just as little as a page. Being aware of my not-so-strong hold over English, Dr Sahay always corrected my English and gave his suggestions. He even taught me English translation tuitions on Sundays along with his second son whom he lovingly addressed as Buchchu. As days passed, our relationship grew and he treated me like a member of his family, so much so that I used to ride back from the department back to his home with him every evening. We both used to travel using bicycles as there was hardly any traffic back in those days. It became a routine to have a discussion about anthropology and related topics with him every evening at his place. I covered the distance of 9 km on my bicycle back from Bariatu to Doranda, where I lived in a rented room. This routine ride was truly an enriching experience for me. During those days I learnt about not only the subject but I became aware of my social surroundings and ups and down of life.

Coming back to my synopsis, I was supposed to cover twelve districts each from Bihar and West Bengal for my fieldwork.

During my research the library access was permitted from National Library, Calcutta. Hostel stay was provided to each scholar at the rent of Rs. 2 per day by the National Library. I had applied for the ICSSR Fellowship and Professor Surajit C. Sinha was the Honorary Director those days. Upon meeting with me, he was very impressed by my topic of research. He allowed me a fellowship for three months, every year for a period of three years. He always provided me with very useful suggestions while I was there. During my library work in Calcutta, I got to know about Dr L.P. Vidyarthi's untimely death. It was shocking. To translate the folklore during my thesis writing period, I had to take help from a translator, however, my supervisor helped me at each stage of my work. By the time I was done with my thesis work I felt as I was a member of his family. He taught me the real "Anthropology of society". Due to his extra fondness towards me and my respect for him, our relationship was often described as that of a cow and her calf by members of the department. He even designed the cover of my thesis. Due to lack of computers at that time, most of my work was done manually. I submitted my thesis titled "Anthropology of Sweetmeats: Its Tradition and Diffusion with Special Reference to Bihar and West Bengal" in the department under the chairmanship of Professor A.B. Saran.

I was supposed to get six prints of the thesis and thus each page was typed manually two times. Every word had to be typed carefully as everything was done by hand and any mistake would make the work even more difficult. When I went to submit my thesis, merely by looking at thickness of my thesis that weighed 5.1 kg, Professor Saran jokingly said to not put it on the table fearing it might break the table. Similar thoughts were presented by Professor Surajit Sinha when I submitted him a copy of my thesis. Right after finishing my Masters, I got an opportunity to work with Dr V.S. Upadhyay as a Research Investigator in the project titled "University Education and Tribal Society" with a fellowship of Rs.700 per month. After completing this project, I did another project with him titled "Sociocultural Implication of Leprosy in Tribal Bihar". This was the time when I acquired sufficient knowledge about Medical Anthropology. The money I saved by doing these works were extremely helpful during my Ph.D. but the fear of delay in my Ph.D. work, the load of duties assigned by my supervisor and the Principal Investigator of the project, Dr V.S. Upadhyay, were a lot and fulfilling all these roles together seemed like a tough task for me and thus I had to deny working with him for the third time, which did upset him a little.

From my early years, I have been taking up opportunities to work closely with people. After I submitted my Ph.D. thesis, I got a chance to work as a Research Investigator in the Centre for Advanced Study in Anthropology, Ranchi University for which I had to go to Andaman and Nicobar Islands for the fieldwork. It took me four nights and three days via ship to reach Port Blair from Calcutta. The area of my work was Baratang Island. During this period, I also visited Nicobar Islands and Straight Islands and had an opportunity to live with the Great Andamanese for three days and two nights.

I have also conducted fieldwork among Sauria Pahariya of Bihar when I was in Ranchi. Later I got an opportunity to work in Madhya Pradesh among the Birhor tribe of Raigarh district and the Bharia of Patalkot of Chhindwara district as well.

On 16 April 1989, I joined the Department of Social Anthropology and Tribal Development, Guru Ghasidas University, Bilaspur, Madhya Pradesh (presently Chhattisgarh). Dr D.N. Tiwari was the serving Vice-Chancellor those days and the sessions started in July, therefore, as per the order of the Vice-Chancellor, I worked as a Coordinator for the Centre of Evaluation till sessions began. Only M.Phil. and M.Sc. courses were taught there. Classes were held in the department from 10 a.m. till 5 p.m. with a lunch break from 1 p.m. to 2 p.m. I also took a paper on "Tribes and Forests" in the Department of Forestry. These were the days when university was in its establishing phase and had very small number of students, i.e. approximately twenty. It was also situated in a tribal dominated area. I was involved in various academic activities, such as translating anthropological content to Hindi.

I joined as a Reader in the Department of Anthropology, Panjab University, Chandigarh on 16 April 1998. During my initial days at Panjab University, I was supported and helped by Professor B.G. Banerjee, Professor R.N. Vashistha and Mr C.J. Edwin. Dr Shalina Mehta and Abhik Ghosh were other Social Anthropology teachers in the department. Initially, I had a few problems in shifting the mode of my teaching from Hindi to English but I found my way. The first ten years here were very good. Dr Ghosh and I did a lot of fieldwork in Himachal Pradesh and Haryana. We used to go for fieldwork for ten days in a month, and sometimes Professor Banerjee and Professor Vasishtha accompanied us as well.

Seminal Contribution to Anthropology, Important Papers, Books, etc.

My association to anthropology and its various subfields has always encouraged me to venture into diverse areas. I have about 190 research papers and seventeen books, including edited books and the books that I have co-authored to my credit written in diverse areas of anthropology. Here, it is not possible to talk about all of them here, however, a few important ones should be mentioned.

The first book I ever published was based on my Ph.D. work, it was published in the year 2000 titled *Anthropology of Sweetmeats*. This was empirical research done in several parts of India. This was the first time in Indian anthropology where an attempt had been made to study the varieties of sweetmeats since the days of Indus Valley Civilization. I tried to explain how diffusion could be studied with help of a cultural trait. I also used the "W" formula, which was also used by Gifford and Kroeber (1937) and Saraswati (1978) in their respective studies.

Next important contribution was the book titled *Panchayati Raj and Empowerment of Women* which was published in 2004, this book aimed to familiarize the readers with the institution of Panchayati Raj. The book presents a detailed description of the women from Haryana and an understanding of the Panchayati Raj. It is based on historical context simultaneously examining contemporary issues.

In 2006, I published a Hindi language book titled *Chhattisgarh Ki Aadim Janjaatiya*, which was first of its kind in a way as it talks about ethnographic account of primitive tribes from Chhattisgarh.

In 2008, I published *Reinventing the Watermill in the Himalayas: The Gharat in History, Traditions and Modern Development* with other faculty members. This book was a sincere attempt to look at traditional watermill or *gharat* of the Himalayan region in order to create an understanding of its importance.

Another book *Ayurveda: A Traditional System of Medicine in India* was published in 2013, where myself, Dr B.G. Banerjee and Dr K. Gurpreet Singh have critically examined the major issues and themes in pursuit of medical anthropology and explored the traditional and indigenous systems of medicine focusing on north India.

In 2013, along with scholar Sukhbir Singh, I co-authored a paper titled "The Health-Seeking Behavior of Leprosy Patients: An Explanatory Model", this paper was set to assess the health-seeking behaviour of leprosy patients. I am happy to write here that the paper was awarded first prize in Ackworth best published paper in 29thBiennial Conference of Indian Association of Leprologists at PGIMER, Chandigarh.

In 2014, along with Dr K.D. Sharma and Dr Lemessa Mergo from Ethiopia, I published an article titled "Sacrifice, Vow and Ritual Feast among the Ormo of Horro Guduru Hinterland (Ethiopia)" was published in esteemed journal *Anthropos*. The paper considered three contexts namely sacrifice, vow and ritual feast in light of various anthropological theories.

In 2018, myself along with my scholar, Dr Avanee Khatri have also published a book *Digital India Today: Discourse and Rural Users in the Information Age*. This book is an endeavour towards examining the validity of relationship between information and communication technologies and economic development that has been constructed in the discourse of knowledge in rural context, based on empirical research conducted in Khanyara village of block Dharamshala in district Kangra, State of Himachal Pradesh in India.

In the year 2022, a book entitled *Visual Merchandising and Consumer Behaviour in Shopping Malls* was published with Dr Ramandeep Bawa and Dr Rita Kant that presents the importance of malls in the lives of millennial shoppers and paints a comprehensive picture of the way visual merchandising influences consumer behaviour in shopping malls.

Recently (2024), a book *Climate Change and its Impact on the Community: An Ethnographic Study* was published along with Dr Jagriti Mehta and Dr Maninder Kaur. This is a compelling and insightful book that provides a unique perspective on the impact of climate change on the horticultural community, offering valuable lessons and recommendations for creating a more sustainable and just future.

My research papers (along with scholars) have also been published in international journals like *Annals of Human Biology; The Family Journal: Counselling and Therapy for Couples and Families; Perspectives in Public Health*, etc.

Owing to my hold over Hindi language, I have had opportunities to translate the work of eminent anthropologists in the past. This has been extremely satisfying for me as I enjoy doing them. This not only gave me exposure with the important works in anthropology but also expanded my knowledge about anthropology at different stages in life.

Administration and Institution Building

In 1988, I was actively involved and had put in my hard work in capacity of Research Investigator, in the Curriculum Development in Anthropology and Sociology, developed and sponsored by University Grants Commission, New Delhi. The coordinator for this was Professor A.B. Saran, who was Head of Department of Anthropology and Director, Centre of Advanced Studies in Anthropology, Ranchi University.

Since the time I joined the Department of Anthropology, Panjab University in April 1998, I have been actively involved in several departmental activities. From 1998 to 2006, I published twenty-six papers and nine books as author and co-author. When I was a Reader, the department provided me with the opportunity to organize a seminar in the year 2007. An edited book for the same has been published titled *Bio-social Issues of Health* which included themes of health and disease, nutrition, human growth and development, health and mental health and contemporary issues in tribal health and care of the aged.

For the period of 2011-16, I was actively involved in the promotion of the department to UGC Centre for Advance Study (CAS)-I along with Dr K.D. Sharma. During this period, I served as the Chairperson and Coordinator for CAS. I was promoted as professor in the year 2006, from this period onwards I have written and have co-authored more than 100 papers and written eight books. I was fortunate enough to work as member and secretary for various committees appointed by Panjab University and also Department of Anthropology, Panjab University, Chandigarh.

The highlight to the Department of Anthropology "Museum of Man" was also established during this period. I and Dr K.D. Sharma played a vital role in its establishment. Under my chairmanship, I ensured to process the promotions of the non-teaching staff of the department that were pending since long.

I also organized a national workshop "Situating Social Impact Assessment in Development Milieu: A Holistic Approach" in the year 2019 on 8-9 March. The event was attended by more than 100 renowned personalities in the field both from and outside Chandigarh, and many research scholars and participants. The book entitled *Social Impact Assessment in India: Learning from the Field* was published in 2023 by SAGE Spectrum.

Contribution beyond Anthropology, Notable Students

Other than this I had the opportunity to work in several research projects. From 1998-2003, I took up nine research projects.

Further, I have completed three major research projects, funded by University Grants Commission as Principal Investigator.

First project I undertook was a minor research project titled *Madhya Pradesh ki Adim Janjati: Birhor Ek Janvritshashtriya Adhyayan* which was sponsored by Guru Ghasidas University, Bilaspur, Madhya Pradesh, in the year 1979-99.

From 2008-10, I was a principal investigator for a UGC major research project titled "Social Problems of Leprosy Patients: A Concern and Challenge for the Society". Next, I again undertook a major research project in the capacity of Principal Investigator from year 2015 to 2018 titled "Making Sense of Diabetes: Bio-sociocultural Dimensions and Its Management in Chandigarh", funded again by UGC.

In the 2016-17, the Department of Anthropology, Panjab University, Chandigarh was selected as a nodal centre for conducting Social Impact Assessment studies. From this period onwards the department has completed a total of ten Social Impact Assessment projects, five of which I have undertaken as a Coordinator/Principal Investigator which were funded by Greater Mohali Area Development Authority, two by Government of Punjab and two by Chandigarh Administration, respectively (of about Rs. 1.75 crore in total).

Under my supervision, twenty-eight scholars have completed their Ph.D. in various areas such as tribal studies, education, women studies, religion, migration, design anthropology, population studies, medical anthropology, business anthropology and media anthropology. Presently, four out of eight research scholars under my supervision are pursuing their Ph.D. in the field of medical anthropology.

In the past students have secured government jobs and some have been appointed as lecturer. A student who completed his Ph.D. in Business Anthropology has been successful in his endeavour and now settled overseas. Scholars are working in the field of anthropology as researchers and teachers both nationally and internationally and in administrative services.

Current Activities

I was recently appointed as the editor to the journal *South Asian Anthropologist* (ISSN: 0257-7348) for which I would be working further on. In the same tenure I plan on working on some pending projects that previously could not be completed due to time constraints and other engagements. I am working on writing a book in Hindi. I was superannuated from my active service from October 2023.

Currently I am working as an ICSSR Senior Fellow. Other than my academic engagements, I try to devote my time in studying religion and decipher meaning and sense of the written texts purely out of my personal interest.

24

The Setting Sun and Fading Memories

Nabakumar Duary

Anthropologists always refer field research as a *rite of passage* by which an individual becomes a fully qualified member of the profession. This experience and first-hand knowledge give a unique scope in academic world as well as to reach to the commoners. But here I am writing as a contemporary anthropologist and this is my maiden input autobiography in this unique volume. Here I have tried to share my anthropological journey from my fading memories and field notebooks.

Family Background and Childhood

I was born in a joint cultivator family on 18 November 1965 in Shikharpatrabar village, a coastal settlement on the bank of Orissa Coast Cannel of Contai Subdivision in undivided Medinipur district of West Bengal. My mother Late Nupur Rani Duary is a housewife and my father late Bibhuti Bhusan Duary as a Pharmacist. My grandparents were late Srimati Kadamini Devi and late Darshanchandra Duary. Darshanchandra was a famous Hindu idol maker. I am the eldest son among the five offspring to my parents. My nick name is "Nutu", a popular character in the *Sahajpath* book of Kaviguru Rabindranath Tagore. My official name Nabakumar is borrowed from a young idol of Bengali character in *Kapalkundala* novel of Sahitya Samrat Bankim Chandra Chattopadhyay. My grooming up in a joint family was with my loving grandparents, two uncles (*kaka*), two aunties (*kakima*) along with five parental aunts (*pisi*). I have gradually learned many things from the nature, village society and of course from my family. I travelled through the green trees-shrub, mud path, agricultural field under the open sky; went to educational institutions on bare foot with my classmates and other school going children. My childhood has been cherished with my sweet memory of my happy friends, family members and relatives. I enjoyed very much from playground to pond, from *pathshala* to schools. I usually studied in the morning and evening with kerosene lamp on mud floor in the southern veranda of our house. I heard many folk stories and Hindu mythology from my grandmother in night. I was very much interested in art and craft work since my childhood. I also helped my family in different agricultural activities from my teenage in plantation to paddy threshold. I went for weekly market, village fairs and festivals walking through miles after miles of muddy path with playmates, senior family members to listen to folk songs, devotional songs, *tarja gan, kavi gan* and to see puppet dance, folk drama, *yatra, palagan,* magic show, and so on.

Education

I started schooling from Kakhuria Sushilabala Prathamik Vidyalaya (Estd. 1961) in March 1968 and passed class four in December 1972. I was admitted in class five in Dhanghara Jnanendra Vidyapith (Estd. 1950) on 1 January 1973 and passed Madhyamik Pariksha (Secondary Examination) in July 1980. I got admission in Haria Siva Prasad Institution (Estd. on 15 January 1917) in August 1980 and passed Higher Secondary Examination in September 1982. I completed my graduation from Habra Sree Chaitanya College (Estd. 1956) in June 1987 with honour in anthropology along with pass subjects botany and zoology. In July 1987, I got admission in the Department of Anthropology, University of Calcutta and completed postgraduation in anthropology (Estd.

1920) in November 1991 (1989 batch). My specialization is in social-cultural anthropology. The name s of my postgraduate teacher were Professor P.K. Bhowmick, Shyamal Kanti Sengupta, Biswanath Banerjee, Tulika Sen, D.P. Mukherjee, Amulya Ratan Banerjee, Asit Baran Das Chaudhury, Asoke Kumar Ghosh, Ranjana Ray and Manibrata Bhattacharya. I stayed in the school boarding and college hostel from class eight to under graduate study.

During my childhood I actively played all kinds of folk games including board games and outdoor games. I played theatre in school and received a prize in class nine in painting completion I have received merit certificate for 400 m race and javelin throw in Annual Athletic Meet, 1985 in college. I have participated in All India Science Exhibition during 6-12 November 1986 at Yuba Bharati Krirangan, Salt Lake. I received first (in collage) and second prize (in painting) in Inter-Departmental Cultural Competition and Festival "Campus 1989" of University of Calcutta during master's study.

Fieldwork Training

During three years undergraduate course in anthropology honours I took part fieldwork training in anthropology in a Santal inhabited village Jeridi near Shimultala in the then Bihar during March-April 1986. During two years postgraduate course I studied religious life of Konda Reddy, a forest dwelling tribe (PVTG) in Chitapalli and Urinka villages in West Godavari district of Andhra Pradesh (April-May 1989). I also studied a comparative technology assessment among the Munda in Paschim Medinipur district of West Bengal (May 1989) under the supervision of Professor P.K. Bhowmick. The pre-history fieldwork training was carried out under the supervision of Professor Asok K. Ghosh and Professor Ranjana Ray on the bank of Subarnarekha River near Ghatsila in Singhbhum district of the then Bihar (February-March 1989).Completed dissertation work in social-cultural anthropology in the final year of postgraduate course under Professor P.K. Bhowmick and the titled of my dissertation was "Hos in Different Setting: With Special Emphasis on Political

Organization" (fieldwork during April-May 1990 in Shikurshai village, Singhbhum, Bihar and Hoshanpur village in Medinipur, West Bengal).

Since anthropology is profoundly based on fieldwork, I voluntarily opted for anthropology subject in my own interest during graduation. I believed that it may be helpful due to my rural experience exposure and the scope to know other cultures from past to contemporary society. Some of my classmates are in teaching profession in anthropology in universities and college like Professor Dr Subrata Sankarar Bagchi, late Professor Jaydip Sen and Dr Gopal Chandra Mandal.

Work in Short-term Project and Fellowship

Immediately after my postgraduate finals exams, I got the opportunity to work in the Institute of Social Research and Applied Anthropology, Kolkata as a Project Fellow under the project "The Level of Literacy of Tribal Population in West Bengal" with funding from Ministry of Welfare, Tribal Development Division, Government of India from August 1991 to August 1992. Then, I joined as a Junior Research Fellow in the Eastern Regional Centre, Anthropological Survey of India, Kolkata on 2 September 1992 and then transferred to Field Station, Ranchi to join on 17 May 1993. During my three years fellowship, I have completed my individual research project entitle "Tribal Education in Western Border Bengal" till 1 September 1995. This project covered six blocks in three districts namely Medinipur, Bankura and Puruliya in four types of tribal inhabited villages (multi-ethnic, caste dominated and town fringe) and nine different tribal groups under the four economical categories like gather hunter (Lodha, Kheria and Birhor), bamboo artisan (Mahali), earth worker (Kora) and settled agriculture tribes (Santal, Munda, Oraon and Bhumij). I worked in a short-term project with Allahabad University in a village Churchuria under the project of Vindyaschal Thermal Power during October 1995.

Doctoral Work and Awards

I have completed my doctoral work under the supervision of Professor A.K. Haldar, Department of Anthropology, Ranchi University and was awarded Ph.D. degree in October 2001. The title of the thesis was "Tribal Education in Medinipur District of West Bengal". Here, I highlighted the literacy rate and level of education of four different economic tribal groups Lodha, Kora, Mahali and Santal. Later on, it was published in a book *Education in Tribal India: A Study of West Bengal* in 2010. The Government of India awarded Rs.10,000 for my doctoral degree. However, I am awarded Ekalabya Samman-2019 from Punyatma Dipak Narayan Dhar Bhabanisankar Singha Tarpanashram for academic contribution in the field of anthropological research.

Professional Life

I joined the Anthropological Survey of India on 29 November 1996 in the capacity of Senior Technical Assistant (Cultural) at Ranchi Field Station. It was a great opportunity to work in the world's largest anthropological organization in government sector. On 21 April 2003, I was transferred from Ranchi to the Head Office and continue as a Research Associate (Cultural) till 19 January 2024 and joined as an Assistant Anthropologist (Cultural) in North East Regional Centre, Shillong on 29 January 2024 and continue to work till date.

I have a good academic association with some well-known senior anthropologists in the Anthropological Survey of India and other organizations like late Dr Biman Kumar Dasgupta, late Dr Arabinda Basu, late Dr Mahadeb Prasad Basu, late Dr Bikas Raychaudhury, Shri T.N. Pandit, late William Ekka, Dr M.K. Raha, Dr. R.K. Bhattacharya, Professor Ajit K. Danda, Dr Jayanta Kumar Sarkar, Dr Styabrata Chakraborti, Professor V.R. Rao, Professor K.K. Basa, Dr Kanchan Mukhopadhyay, Dr Sikha Chatterjee, Srimati Bela Moulik, late Professor Ram Dayal Munda, Professor Rajat Kanti Das, Professor Gouranga Prasad Chattopadhayay, Professor Atul Chandra Bhowmick,

Professor Barun Mukhopadhyay, Professor P.C. Joshi, Professor Sarit K. Chaudhury, Professor M.C. Behera, late Professor A.R.N. Srivastava, Professor Vijoy S. Sahay, Professor Pradip K. Singh, late Professor V.S. Upadhyay, Dr Upala Barua, late Dr R.M. Sarkar and few others. I also have association with the faculty members of anthropology departments in India and abroad. Above all, I have a special close association with the daughters of two doyens, i.e. Indian anthropologist like late Ms Mira Roy at Ranchi, youngest daughter of Rai Bahadur S.C. Roy and with Alta Ahmad, New York, daughter of Dr B.S. Guha.

Fieldwork in Professional Life

Fieldwork is the strength in anthropology discipline. My experience in fieldwork is much diversified due to my interest as well as my deployment in different types of research projects of the Anthropological Survey of India. Fieldwork tradition of the Survey is unique and this field data is the main source of bio-cultural aspects of Indian population. Being a government researcher, we follow some government protocol or formalities from beginning to end in any fieldwork. After receiving the official tour order from the office, the leader of the research team apply concerning sections like General, PMI, Accounts, Store, Stationary, Photography, Sound and Reprography for issuing introductory letters, contingent advance and received different kinds of articles for long period fieldwork. All members also apply for tour TA/DA advance. The leader of team submitted the tentative tour programme to the office just before proceed to fieldwork. All team members give the authorization letters to the colleagues for receiving his monthly salary and reach to respective families. After reaching at field area first two to three days are spent in visiting concerning offices at district head quarter for intimation regarding fieldwork and trying to gather the primary information about the community to be studies and their habitat. After establishing the camp, the leader of the party informed the camp address to the respective regional head quarter of the Survey, District Magistrate and local Post Office through application. It was mandatory to send the monthly daily field dairy with certified by the leader of the research team from field camp. However, it was mandatory to take permission from regional Head before windup the camp or shifting of camp and also compulsory to inform to the Post Office and D.M. office for the said matter. Sometimes Regional Head visited the concerning field and stay with research team members.

I am deployed in many national and regional/local projects of the Survey. I have done fieldwork in different castes, communities and tribal societies in different eco-cultural and linguistic zones and in rural and town/town fringe areas as well as international border areas along with junior and senior male and female researchers for multidisciplinary research works. We were moved with number of big size metal boxes and gunny bags where carried hundreds of essential materials issued by office and with personal belongings. Some of those were all kinds of stationery items, cyclostyle household census schedules, envelops, service stamps, different types of store articles for field camp like kerosene stove, match box, torch, battery, candle, soap, all kinds of cooking utensils, thermo flask, all sorts of bedding materials, lantern, *molmol* cloth, soap, bucket, mug, water bottle, talcum powder, thread, needles, side bag, folding coat, rain coat, gift items (e.g. biscuits, ribbon, scale, pencil, etc.), first aid box, common medicines, camera, reel, tape recorder, cassettes, radio and so on. Earlier it was difficult to procure all aforesaid essential materials in field and conduct fieldwork smoothly. We stayed in field camp around two month in private rent house of the village or school building/government bungalow/guest house.

We conducted fieldwork and established rapport with the community people. During fieldwork we employed guide cum interpreter for data collection. We also participate in some government programmes, meeting, social functions of the villagers on invitation like celebration of India Independence Day/Republic Day, visited village market, different fairs and festival, participated in life cycle rituals and function. Sometimes we organized football match among village boys.

On last day we always organized camp fire function at night in presence of local officials and key informants/village or community people. We share our field experiences, play music and songs and arrange food for them. Sometimes we received *gamucha,* paintings, bow, arrows, cow-bell, crafts objects, bamboo flute and other things as a token gift of love.

I had to encounter several fieldwork hazards like transportation, physical communication, accommodation, food, illness, faced natural calamities like flood situation and living with poisonous snake. My senior research team member had treated me as a brother and developed a relation with each other. Every member followed disciplined life during fieldwork, sharing of space, infrastructure and food. We perform daily duties in camp to data collection, i.e. preparation of food to distribution, visited post to telegraph office, government offices; purchased essential commodities and taking care of fellow members during illness of any member of the team. Correspondence to the office and residence of the researchers through letter and telegram. During field area we were eagerly waited for letter from our house. Sometimes our team member received sad news or good news from his or her house and office like demise of parents/nearest kin members/beloved teachers/ transferred or promotion case and other things. We tackled that painful situation and also enjoy the good news. I have a lots of field experiences of fieldworks during my twenty-six years of professional life in the Survey.

I have conducted fieldwork in different villages and town in different parts of India under the national project and regional projects during my twenty-eight years of professional life in the Survey. My first fieldwork in service life was on Madhubani folk painting in famous three villages like Ranti, Jitwarpur and Harinagar in Indo-Nepal border district of Madhubani of North Bihar during November 1998 to January 1999 and August-September 1999 under the national project "Documentation and Dissemination of Folk Art, Folk Music and Folk Traditions".

Studied religious syncretism in three locations amongst Oraons in both Christian and Sarna religion in Sosai village in Mandar block in Ranchi district of Jharkhand from December 2002-February 2003; studied Sahebdhani sect in Brittihuda village in Chapra block, Sahebtala fair in Nagla village in Nakasipara block in Nadia district (Indo-Bangladesh international border) and Agradeep fair in Katwa block II in Barddhaman district of West Bengal during the year 2004 and among the fisherman caste in Nagaon village and Barpeta satra in Barpeta district of lower Assam from December 2006 to January 2007 and in March-April 2007 under the national project "Syncretism in India: Multidisciplinary Approach".

Conducted fieldwork among the Dom in Keoratala, Neemtala cremation ground areas and Maniktala Dom *basti,* Kolkata during June 2007 for making a documentary on Dom in Kolkata—reflecting their bamboo crafts and cremation activities their only visual anthropology training course in Satyajit Ray Film and Television Institute, Kolkata.

Studied the fishermen in Uttar Pithulia, Raghusardarbar villages, Haripur, Junput, Saratpur and Baguranjalpai *khotis* and also some Hindu and Muslim religious places in coastal areas in Purba Medinipur district of West Bengal during February 2008, August-September 2008, January 2009 under the national project "Traditional Knowledge: Tangible and Intangible Cultural Heritage".

Studied on sex workers in Sonagachi, red light area in north Kolkata in September 2011. Conducted fieldwork in Saora inhabited villages like Paonsuri, Bagmari, Bhubani, Puriasaoi, Patrapur, Andanda and Keraba in Chandragiri and Tumba Saora Development Agencies in Ganjam and Rayagada districts in Orissa during April to May 2012 under the national project of "Particularly Vulnerable Tribal Groups in India".

Studied Ward No. 9 of Jogbani Nagar Panchayet in Ararea district in Indo-Nepal border from September-October 2013 and February-March 2014; studied Indo-Bangladesh border village Matai and Indo-Bangladesh border Hat at Srinagar in South Tripura district in Tripura from August-September 2014 and December 2014; January 2015 and July-August 2015 under the *Border Area Study*.

Studied villages in core, transition, periphery areas of Panna Bio-sphere Researve like Krishna Kalyanpur, Darera, Patha, Dhodan, Palkoha, Kankra Naroli, Kharini in both Panna and Chatarpur districts of Madhya Pradesh from August-September and November-December 2016 under *Man and Biosphere Study* of the project "Bio-Cultural Diversity, Environment and Sustainable Development".

Studied traditional potter caste in Barwani district town of Madhya Pradesh from September and November-December 2017 under the national project of "Sustainability and Development".

Studied Dandasi caste in Naya Baigonbari village under Berhampur police station in Ganjam district of Odisha during August and November 2018 and studied Bauria caste in Jhallor village in Sangrur district of Punjab during December 2019 and January-February 2020 under the project of "Anthropological Study of Denotified, Nomadic and Semi-nomadic Communities".

Conducted fieldwork among the Nayak, Hari/Hari in Jhalania village in Fatehabad district, Munnawali village in Sisar district and Kalirawan village in Hisar district in Haryana during January-February 2020; Studied Chamarmangta in Khajuria and Mujhana villages in Pharenda block in Maharajganj district and Gayaspur, Karamganj and Antamau villages in Kunda block in Pratapgarh district in Uttar Praddesh during November-December 2021 and Bauria community in Bihar during February-March 2022 under the project of "Ethnographic study of 226 Denotified, Nomadic and Semi nomadic Communities".

There are a lot of changes in fieldwork tradition in the Survey like reduced duration of fieldwork, comfort able stay in hotel, avail local transportation by car, mode of communication through electronics device, method of documentation by digital camera and multipurpose smart cell phone. These changes take place due to development of science and technology as well as the implementation of government rules. Moreover, I have a good relation with some of the key informants and resource persons in both male and female in every field and correspond with each other from time to time through letters and cell phone. Even, I send my published articles and books to them by post or email for community/village people. Even some of them come to Kolkata and stay with me.

However, I also conducted fieldwork on different issues or subjects in different parts of West Bengal and adjoining states as my personal interest for writing popular articles in Bengali. About hundred articles in Bengali have been published in reputed journals, magazines and edited books. Some of these subjects are like ethnographic notes on village, fair, festival, folk song, village market, ethnographic note on river, youth dormitory, hunting festival, bow and arrow, tribal education, architecture, life sketch of the folk singer, puppet dance, snake and society, folk religion, rain making ceremony, art and crafts, traditional knowledge, folk technology, field experiences and so on.

Academic Work and Contributions

I am trying to contribute some works in Indian anthropology through publishing articles, books and making documentary films on tribes, caste and communities, on doyen of Indian anthropology and anthropological organizations for popularising anthropology subject and create interest among the young researchers in anthropology. I have made documentaries jointly like *Dom in Kokata: Craft & Cremation* (2007), *Ghotul* (2009), *Utra* (Northern wind, 2010), *An Incessant: Introduction to Anthropological Survey of India* (2010), *Tale of Two Cities* (2010), *Magic Fingers* (2015), *Song of Earth* (2015) and independently made *Beniputul* (*Glove Puppet*, 2014), *An Epic Journey: History of the Indian Anthropological Society* (2016), *Bheri Bathan* (Camp Life of the Shepherd Community, 2017), *Untiring Mind* (on Dr B.S. Guha, 2019) and Centenary Passage *Man in India* (1921-2020).

As popular writers and academician, I wrote more than hundred articles in different subjects like in genealogy and genealogist, tribal language, tribal education, gender discrimination in education of tribals, educational development, educational problems, tribal political organization in different settings, family planning practise of the tribals, tribal customs, bow and arrow and identity of tribal culture, portrait of *sal* tree in a tribal society, mortuary practise of a PVTG, ethnographic note of a PVTG, myth on *mohua* liquor of a tribal community, religious life of a forest dweller tribe, tribal dances, religious movement of a tribal society, Madhubani folk painting, *patachitra*, camp life of the shepherds, *Dash Avatar Tas* (playing cards), village market, transaction of food, beverage and ranking of space in a village market, traditional knowledge in weather forecast, traditional knowledge of fisher folk, traditional knowledge of potter, religious syncretism of Sahebdhani sect, religious syncretism of fisher folk, folk songs, folk art and crafts, puppet dance, life sketch and contribution of some Indian anthropologists, unexplored and least known stories of Indian anthropology, life-sketch, contribution of a cinematographer in Indian anthropology, book review, obituaries, reminence and so on. These are published in reputed academic journals, bulletin, magazines and in edited books from India and abroad. Some of these journals and bulletins are *Journal of the Anthropological Survey of India, Man in India, The Journal of the Indian Anthropological Society, Humankind, Indian Journal of Traditional Knowledge, Social Change, South Asian Anthropologists, Anthropos India, Journal of Tribal, Folk and Subaltern Studies, Vanyajati, Bulletin of the International Committee on Urgent Anthropological and Ethnological Research, Bulletin of the Bihar Tribal Welfare and Research Institute, Bulletin of the Cultural Research Institute, Rural India* , *Social Welfare* and so on.

I published two books namely *Education in Tribal India: A Study of West Bengal* (2010). *Biraja Sankar Guha: Centenary Year of Teaching of Anthropology in India* (2022), edited two books—*Some Aspects of Indian Society and Culture: Essay in Honour of Professor A.K. Haldar* (jointly with Pradip K. Bhowmick, 2005) and *Attributes of Culture-Reflection of Cultural Itineraries from a Multicultural Nation* (jointly with Amitabha Sarkar and Samira Dasgupta, 2016).

In-service Training and Oriental Course

I have participated in many in service training programmes and oriental course in the Survey. Some of these are "Application of Statistics and Computer in Bio-Social Anthropology" (2-7 February 1998), "Extended Horizon of Anthropology: An Interdisciplinary Approach" (5-9 June 2000). "Training in Visual Anthropology" in Satyajit Ray Film & Television Institute, Kolkata (29 May-17 June 2007), "Audio-Visual Documentation" (1-7 November 2012), "Anthropology in 21st Century", organized by International School of Anthropology (16-19 November 2015) and so on.

Professional Body, Teaching and Guidance

I am a life member of the Indian Anthropological Society, Kolkata since 1989 and I was honoured as the Joint Secretary, of the Indian Anthropological Society, Kolkata and presently Assistant Research Director of this Society and life member of the SIMA, Mysore. Occasionally, I take classes on Visual Anthropology in Anthropology Department of University of Calcutta and Gurusaday Museum. I was a guest faculty of the Integrated Rural Development and Management of the Ramakrishna Mission Vivekananda Educational and Research Institute, Narendrapur and supervised the Master's dissertation work of the students of the said department.

Participated Academic Forums

Presented several papers in local, state, national and international seminars, symposium, conferences, workshops and screening of documentaries in different parts of the country and abroad, which were organized by different educational institutions and research organizations. Some of these organizations are regional and sub-regional centres of the Anthropological Survey of India, Indira Gandhi Rastriya Manav Sangrahalaya, Indian Anthropological Society, INCAA, different postgraduate and undergraduate anthropology departments like University of Calcutta, Sagar University, Vidyasagar University, North Bengal University, Burdwan University, Rabindra Bharati Viswavidyalaya, Ranchi

University, Vinoba Bhave University, Manipur University, Cotton University, Hari Singh Gour Viswavidyalaya, Guru Ghasidas University, Visva Bharati, University of Delhi, The Asiatic Society, Sreenath College of Education (Jamshedpur) and other organizations like Maulana Abul Kalam Azad Institute of Asian Studies, Cultural Research Institute, Kolkata, Bihar/Jharkhand Tribal Welfare and Research Institute, Ranchi, Gurusaday Folk Museum, Kolkata, Institute of Social Research and Applied Anthropology, Bidisa; Kolkata Society for Asian Studies, Academy of Folklore, Kolkata, Bangladesh Folklore Research Centre, Rajshahi, Bangladesh and many more.

Association with in Other Organizations

I was an Executive Member in the Community Radio Council, Satyajit Ray Film & Television Institute, Kolkata. Presently, I am the President of the Bonsoir Art Society, Kolkata.

Participation in Rare occasions in Indian Anthropology

It was a great opportunity to participate in some of the rare occasions of the Indian Anthropology like the centenary celebration at the Departments of Anthropology, University of Calcutta (1920-2019), celebration of golden jubilee (1945-94) and platinum jubilee (1945-2019) of the Anthropological Survey of India, celebration of birth centenary (1884-1984) and 125th birth anniversary (1894-2019) of B.S. Guha, Hundred Years of Teaching of Anthropology in India (1920-2019), Birth Centenary of Professor Nirmal Kumar Bose (1901-72), Golden Jubilee of the Indian Anthropological Society, Kolkata and Golden Jubilee Celebration of Department of Anthropology, Ranchi University (Estd. 1955). I was one of the organizing members of the aforesaid occasions.

Other Activities

I have been involved in many social activities from my school life. I have participated as teacher in Extension of Adult Education Centre of Rabindra Bharati Viswavidyalaya, Kolkata during my master's. Even today I am also involved in few organizations for science activities, art and craft work, health programme and developmental work in my residential area as well as for down trodden people in different localities.

Interest

My interest is very diversified like listening of radio programme, reading of biography of any Indian personalities, love creative art work, love in both Indian classical and folk music, anthropological photography, traveling in remote area and interact to local people, like participate in evening *adda,* i.e. rendezvous with the people in different sections of the society.

Endnote

Anthropology, as a subject gave me the opportunity to see another India with in India and to see the beauty of diversity of Indian culture and languages during three decades of my anthropological fieldwork in the Survey. In this regard Dr B.S. Guha, founder Director of Anthropological Survey of India stated in his writing "...in India, an enormous field of research, both theoretical and practical, lies before the anthropologist..." I strongly believed that fieldwork is the backbone of Anthropology. It is observed that the fieldwork and research work in the Anthropological Survey of India is different to any other anthropological (educational/ research) organizations. Because, it is a national organization and all scientific staffs here deployed in national projects. Researchers go for fieldwork along with other team members of different disciplines for multidiscipline research with in a scheduled time period. Nobody allowed to visit again and again and not to publish field data without prior permission of the competent authority. However, there is a scope to see the different culture and traditions of various castes and communities in different environment. Researcher enjoys the government logistic support at field situation. On contrary, the researcher in educational institution devotes his/her life for a specific field and visits again and again and follows minimum official formalities. They use to enjoy more freedom than a government anthropologist.

I am always praying to the Almighty to give me the mental and physical strength to do more work and contribute something for Anthropology and Indian societies. My anthropological journey can be broadly be divided into anthropological research activities in a government-controlled research organization and my research activities beyond government rules and regulations. Till date this journey has been a smooth sail with devoting my time for research on official activities during office hours and spending the evening hours and weekend in my small library at my home, public libraries like Indian Anthropological Society and Ramkrishna Mission Institute of Culture, Kolkata. Therefore, my biographic writing upon minute details of my journey both in government set up and beyond it. Whenever this has been an administrative barrier to undertake a work in my office, I undertook the same at my own level ignoring the cost and time spent over it. Today I can proudly say that my film entitled *Untiring Mind* and pictorial biography book *Biraja Sankar Guha-Centenary Year of Teaching in Anthropology in India* are few such initiative which I have done for the posterity at any own cost.

I am grateful to my teachers and colleagues in the Survey, who taught me in anthropology and sharing the anthropological knowledge in anthropological discourse from class room to field training and also from camp to seminar hall. I am also thankful to my mother, wife and daughter for their kind cooperation and inspiration in my academic work. Moreover, this is the blessing of grandparents, parents and my teachers for what I have achieved in my life.

25

Do I Know the Anthropological Man at Last?

M.C. Arunkumar

The early 1980s in north-east India, especially in Manipur, was a period of confusions on the part of ordinary citizens as well as of the governments (state and central). Manipur witnessed starting of urban guerrilla of some youths having limited weapons, mainly snatched from security personnel. Earlier Manipur experienced various armed conflict of different colours and shades since early twentieth century much before what Naga armed conflict. The Anglo-Manipur War of 1891, Kuki Rebellion of 1917-19, Second World War affecting entire state, the communist armed movement of late 1940s was the series of armed conflict in the state; however, the Urban Guerrilla Move of 1980s was a new phenomenon. As, most probably, the urban guerrilla attacks in Imphal were the first of its kind in India, even in South Asia, governments did not know how to response. They used disproportionate forces to meet the guerrilla forces as well as to separate the guerrillas from the mass. Mao Tse Tung once said that the guerrillas are fishes and masses the water. Corollary to it, the *mantra* of counter-insurgency is "separate water and fish". However, the government could not evolve the method, suitable to Indian context or in the soil of Manipur, for separating water and fish. It took about a decade to understand the nature and potential of these groups. Following the counter-insurgency campaign elsewhere, especially the Malay experience, the governments suspected all the youths to be one of these phantom persons operating for one political goal, rational or otherwise. All youths were subjected to screenings, combing operations and random pick-up for interrogation. These actions of guerrillas and security personnel affected all the aspects of society; the fear psychosis, the people had during the Second World War, once again reappeared in this period of history. This state of mind was reflected in some of the poems, short stories, besides political and academic writings.

On the other hand, All Manipur Students' Union (AMSU), one of the oldest student unions in north-east India, launched a movement against foreigners who came illegally to India (Manipur). Assam also had the similar movement in those days. There was a series of strikes, *bandh*s, class boycotts, *gherao*s, and many more. The government was in a dilemma: it could not convince the students to stop the movement as well as it could not act to fulfil their demands. The state government was sandwiched. It was also true that the students of the state were under pressure of two different kinds—psychological pressure for their academic career on one hand and physical pressure from state forces to suppress the student movements on the other. The academic disturbance lasted for about one year.

Though my schooling was done in Assam, I came back to home state in those days. As a student in this period, I could not concentrate on the text books only. Outside my classrooms, there were claims and counter-claims of the historical events which were unfolded in front of my eyes. There were many waves of ideas and thoughts, ideologies and philosophy. Besides biology, mathematics, physics and chemistry, my mind was exposed to these undercurrents of current history and political debates, interpretations and propagandas. In those days, I went from one college library to another as well as to Manipur State Central Library in search of books ranging from Marxism to Anatomy (the post-mortem reports published in newspapers demands ABC of Human Anatomy), to Indian independence movements, Transfer of Powers between Indian and Britain to History of Manipur.

Like other parents, my parents also wanted me to study medical science or engineering or mathematics or life science. Against the will of my father, I wanted to study one subject from which I could understand all the subjects. I thought, at that time, life is too short to understand all the dimensions of science; and so I started searching some sort of *Philosopher Stone* of academics.

Fortunately, I came across a big sized book, entitled *Anthropology,* written by A.L. Kroeber and *Social Anthropology,* written by Lucy Mair. In the Manipur State Central Library which had about 2,000-3,000 members, generally many other books were in bad shapes as many readers borrowed them frequently. However, these two anthropological books were issued to only a few readers before me. These books took me to the world of anthropology which has all the aspects of man and his world, I thought. From prehistoric man and his tools, how was his world changed to become Manipur of 1980s. Imagining anthropology was the subject, I was looking for, I applied for the subject for my B.Sc. Honors course. Thus, I became a student of Anthropology in D.M. College of Science, Imphal.

The first ever class of anthropology in the college gave me an idea of Anthropology as Study of Man. I knew etymological meaning of the word may not give nature of the subject. Therefore, I was not convinced by the lecturer who answered my question, "majority of the disciplines like Political Science, Literatures, History, Psychology, Medical Sciences, even the economic botany deal with Man, then what is so unique of anthropology in dealing with man". The question I had in my mind might be due to typical way of thinking prevailing among youths of the volatile period. We asked questions for which we suffered and we were asked questions for which we had to be in some dark and smelly lockup rooms, subjecting to psychological traumas, if not tortures.

Later, I developed my question, what is anthropological concept of man. What is nature of anthropological man, concept of man in anthropology? My teachers in Ranchi University, one of which was Professor L.P. Vidyarthi, encouraged me to ask such questions and suggested me to read some books which were not text books such as books on theoretical anthropology, philosophical anthropology. In order to understand many other aspects of man's life, I opted social psychology as one of my optional papers in Second Year of M.Sc. Course in Anthropology. I am still grateful to all of my teachers in Ranchi University for their advices and suggestions. But I still wonder why not we teach our young students the basic question of anthropological perspective of man, the main object of our study.

Every year when I start taking class of I Semester of M.Sc. in Anthropology course, I ask my class what is Anthropology. As expected, students answer quickly "It is study of man". Being a young adult in their lifespan, they like to impress not only the teachers but also their friends in new university set-up. They are no longer in a college. Some students add some qualifying words like "totality", "holistic", "man and his works" and others add some words indicating time-scale such as "from prehistory to modern". When asked, how anthropological "man" differs from "men" of other disciplines, they all slow down giving answer. They start showing a face not familiar with other primates—a confusing face that always confuses me if I ask wrong question. But every year I enjoy starting class by creating a state of confusion. I remember the lines of Salvador Dalí, "What is important is to spread confusion, not eliminate it" and "You have to systematically create confusion, it sets creativity free. Everything that is contradictory creates life." My life as a young man started with various types of confusion and overcoming the confusion requires creativity and new horizon of knowledge. Being a student of anthropology, I always think that breaking the everyday life creates a state of confusion but is a new step towards a new order.

Anthropological man is the object of study in anthropology. He is not a mere biological being having certain number of chromosomes or having certain social behaviour. Man is not a unidimensional animal. Man has a body, a social and cultural life and an active mind, a psychic life. Man has a mind which is capable of being conscious of his own body, social and cultural life and the surrounding environment. Man is studied by psychologists, men of medical science, historians and so on; and also, by anthropologists. Unlike biologists, anthropologist studies human body not in isolation from his social life and mind; anthropologist's man is an interacting unit in a network of body-social life-mind. Again, anthropological man's mind is not an individual mind on which majority psychologists engage their mind, but a collective mind, mind of various minds. Social Life is not considered as mere life among fellow members as that of bees or ants but with other beings that influence or being influenced by other beings (including supernatural beings) and environment which change men and their life as well as is changed by action of men in search of their energies for survival and social life. Anthropological man is very busy in interaction with his life and mind and is a conscious part of nature the rest of which has no consciousness. In other words, we can say anthropological man who can incorporate nature as cultural objects (kangaroo as totem animal, Bhim as son of wind) is himself a part of nature in which nature can understand nature itself. While attending one B.Sc. class on cell division in college, my teacher irritatingly but politely asked me to let her finish her lecture when I asked her how marriage affect crossing-over of genes. Involuntarily I said, "OK". Sorry, I did not address her "Madam or Miss" which ought to be done in classroom. The class was of zoology. The dimensions may be different from those of Anthropology, I told myself.

While doing my Ph.D. course in mid-1980s, unknowingly I stared some young lady who was working for her Ph.D. in Life Science in Manipur University. In Manipur University, Life Science is Anthropology's neighbourhood; it was Psychology in Ranchi University. Gradually staring the plant pathology laboratory became my habit. Somehow, I enjoyed watching them watching some micro-organisms under their microscopes of different types and colors. There was a chain of watching (if I take the term from

Desmond Morris" *Man Watching*) or observation, the lady was watching the nature or behaviour of some microbes, her guide watched her progress in research and I watched both of them and their methods of watching or observation their specimens. The social interaction between them as well as their behaviour towards a defined goal was some of objects of my observation, if I considered myself as being anthropologist with no other motives of watching them. Suddenly, one question comes up in my mind. Could microbes understand the person who watched it? In anthropology, the observed object is three-dimensional man like the man who watched him. The observed object is not a mere combination of morphology and physiology. He has also an active mind—conscious and unconscious. Then how can you take the man you observe act naturally after all he is conscious of being watched? The man being observed went through a process of socialization (and/or enculturation) that gives various shades of stereotypes, a typical classification of the world including types of man, having stores of unfulfilled desires that shapes various reflex actions, having unconscious fixation to some shapes or otherwise. The triangular relation of body-social and cultural life-psychic life of the informant affects his behaviour with particular anthropologist. His evaluation of the anthropologist will definitely affect nature of the collected data. Unconscious preference of your love object will affect the crossing over of your genes and hence the body of your children.

In early 1980s, young men in Manipur were picked up by police or military personnel for questioning. Any unusual sound of grenades or improvised bombs or burst of bullets may take the youths in dark open space to line-up there. One by one, they would be asked certain questions, sometimes in Hindi. Knowing Hindi was life-saving skill in those days, especially in rural and hill areas where majority of the youths could not speak Hindi fluently. "What is your name?" "Mera (Mera is name of 7th Month of Manipuri Lunar calendar. This was once very popular personal name)", "What? Where is your home", "Tera (Tera is a place name where cotton trade was done in King's day, literary *Tera* is Cotton).

The Hindi-speaking sepoy might have been annoyed with *tera-mera*.

Many of youths of 1980s knew the frequently asked questions. Out of fear, they developed a number of ready-made answers. "Do you drink wine, take tobacco?" If answer is negative, the suspicion-level will raise by 5 per cent. "Do you have girl-friend?" At any cost, the answer should not be negative, even if you do not have one. If asked who she is; the answer should be "I cannot tell you, sir. Being blind-folded I don't know who are around me. She is daughter of a police officer." There is calculation in both minds of anthropologist and of the "subject" as being object of your study. The subject knows why these questions are asked and what the anthropologist would conclude if he answers in this way or that way. The anthropological or ethnographical fieldwork is a battle between two active minds in volleying questions and answers, the purpose of which is interpreted by both the parties in their own ways. Because both the anthropologist and his subject are men having three dimensions, like both the police officer who tries to extract information and the suspected youth who knows every answer may become liability on his part, are three-dimensional men.

I still remember one incident during a fieldwork with some of my PG students who specialized in Social and Cultural Anthropology, in one remote area of Manipur. My Ph.D. Guide, Professor Ch. Budhi Singh who is faithful follower of Levi-Strauss, asked one aged informant about their classification of the world and world-objects. The information thus gathered fell exactly under the Levi-Strauss schema of structural elements and their dialectics, the opposites and their unity. On the other hand, when I talked with the same informant, he started giving meaning of the symbols in their house, graveyards and textile designs in a different way but in the tune of my questioning. He knew my interest was looking at meanings associated with sexual symbols and sex-worship, of course, in a different theoretical framework. Here, my intention is not to evaluate Professor Budhi's Straussian framework or mine, what I like to highlight is the difficulty of dealing anthropological man as he is not a microbe under microscope. He is a thinking man who can evaluate the conduct of the anthropologist who thinks to study the world through him.

In another incident, when I was in a peasant village with a team of students conducting a regular fieldwork of M.Sc. I year, I made familiarity (rapport) myself with children of below 14 years of age. I talked with their language following little socio-linguistic principles, having limited vocabularies but many abusive words, using different symbols of their age-grade. Initially, they were reluctant to interact with me, may be because of age gap, my profession (teacher is regarded as being honourable person), gradually we started talking informally all sort of their village life. For an anthropology teacher, it is very difficult to overcome the hurdle of being "honourable person"; if he is still honorable person, he will not be able to reach "heads and hearts" of the informants. Your observation may be participant or non-participant, unless you occupy a position in heads and hearts of your informants, you will fail to enter the world in which your objects are spread for observation. Luckily, the children of this site were not fully trained by their socialization to hide what should be hidden from strangers even if he "occupies a position" in their minds and hearts.

I started asking them about their dreams. For about a week, I asked them to narrate their daily dreams. They narrated their dreams of eating something, boating, walking on a remote path, fishing in a river and many more, as expected. After a week, I asked them "Did you ever dream anything that you do not like to share with me?" They all giggled and on insisting, they opened their "unconscious mind" (loosely following Sigmund Freud) from which I gathered information out of which I could understand the social reality of the village.

Of course, I was aware of the ethical questions in dealing with young children even while talking with their real dreams. Here my concerned is that of the mind of my object of observation. The familiarity with them overcame their inhibition and expected behaviour with an adult stranger, thus opened the gate to give information what I sought. I still wonder what might have been in their mind about me; whatsoever the level of their mind, they had mind to know and evaluate me. My presumption at that time was that those children might not have so much readymade answers to FAQs as adult informants had. Still one of them said at time of bidding bye-bye after twenty days of fieldwork: "Oja, you are so funny". *Oja* is Manipuri word for teacher. I realized then I was being evaluated with their little minds. They had been behaving with me with whatsoever evaluation they had. It was not a simple thing but a complex phenomenon of human interaction between the observed man and the anthropologist.

Considering the nature of three-dimensional Man, we need to understand our subject matter and its methodology. By the end of this article, I realize that someone who is reading will not simply read this article to understand what I write; they will rewrite me in their mind depending on their biological and social backgrounds. Still, I would like to insist that the anthropological man, i.e. the concept of man in anthropology is very complex. We cannot define him as a product of Darwinian Evolution or a bundle of chromosomes in which Kinship rules operates or a simple equation of stimuli and response. Let me stop by putting three questions: Is man a biological machine having morphology and physiology only, is he a puppet of social and cultural grammars without having any individual desire and aspiration or is man simply an equation of stimulus and response.

26

On Becoming an Anthropologist

Subho Roy

The Beginning

I am born in a family, where of one my parents, i.e. my father was an anthropologist. He taught anthropology in Bangabasi College, Kolkata, West Bengal. This is an undergraduate college where scholars like B.S. Guha and P.K. Bhowmik taught at one point of time of their illustrious career. Right from my childhood I grew up listening to the terms, like Ramapithecus, Australopithecus, Races, Caucasoid, Santal, Oraon, Chopper and Hand Axe. My father had personal collection of anthropological textbooks. Whenever, my father used to study, I would hang around him to take a glimpse of the pictures portrayed inside the book. I remember, my father telling me stories on human evolution showing pictures of apes and fossil hominoids or about the tribal life and culture in a lucid manner. Thus, my home environment provided an opportunity to train my mind about the subject matter of anthropology.

As a Student of Anthropology

I took up graduation course in anthropology and got admission in the same college where my father taught. I took some time to compose myself among the batch mates and the seniors since they all knew that I am the son of B.N.R. Sir (Biswanath Roy is my father's name). They used to give snoopy look at me. Since I was little conversant with the terms and phrases used in anthropology, I did not find the subject alien to me at the beginning, unlike my other batch mates. In the third year of the undergraduate course, we were taken to Keonjhar district of Odisha to conduct a field study on the Ho tribal community living in Murgabeda village. Three of the teachers of the college namely Dr K.P. Chatterjee, Sri Arun K. Ghosh and Dr Ratna Bhattacharya accompanied us in the fieldwork. Prior to our journey to the field, we were rigorously trained about anthropological fieldwork and data collection methods. I was much excited with this fieldwork since from childhood I heard from my father about different shades of his experiences in conducting fieldwork. The fieldwork was scheduled for twenty-one days, but we had to return early because of political disturbance in the field area. In the field we received training to collect ethnographic account of a community using various data collection techniques. This fieldwork sparked off a lot of debate. One of our teachers, who did not accompany us, started questioning whether the studied community was Ho or Munda and why have we returned from the field because of political disturbance and why this issue of political disturbance was not addressed in course of the fieldwork. As undergraduate students we did not have answer to these questions. The debate continued and eventually, that affected our result. I was so disappointed with my undergraduate result that at one point of time I even decided to move to University of Delhi for pursuing postgraduate course. On the advice from a senior professor, I dropped the idea of moving to Delhi and took admission in the University of Calcutta.

In the first year of the postgraduate course, we conducted fieldworks in social cultural anthropology, primate behaviour and prehistoric archaeology. The latter two fieldworks were new to us. Professor A.B. Das Chaudhuri took us in Nandan Kanan, Odisha for conducting the fieldwork on primate behaviour and Professor Asok K. Ghosh joined later to supervise the fieldwork on Prehistoric Archaeology. Under the supervision of Professor Ghosh, we did trial digging in the Utkal University Campus and unearthed many lithic tools of blade bladelet culture. In course of the fieldwork in Odisha, we had an opportunity to visit the Department of Anthropology of Utkal University and to meet the then faculty members like Professor Usha Deka, Professor K.C. Tripathy Professor Supriyo Ghosh Moulik and Professor P.K. Das. Later, Professor Ghosh encouraged me to analyse the tools further and jointly published a paper (Ghosh and Ray 1990-93). I was much excited when I saw my name printed for the first time in a research paper. Professor P.K. Bhowmik took us for social cultural anthropology fieldwork to Purulia district of West Bengal. In this field we studied how successful was the implementation of rehabilitation programmes on a group of Birhor tribal population of Purulia using anthropological approach.

I took up Advanced Physical Anthropology as my special paper in the final year and joined Professor Asok K. Ghosh to do my dissertation paper on Dental Anthropology. My decision to join Professor Asok K. Ghosh became a matter of discussion among the students and faculty members in the department. During that time the students were given a chance to select their supervisors for the dissertation paper, and I find it to be very democratic. The objectives of my dissertation paper were to take metric measurements of teeth and to find out the pattern of shedding of teeth with respect to age and lifestyle factors. Eventually I qualified JRF (UGC) before the completion of my final year examination. In the final year examination, I scored 68 per cent mark in M.Sc. dissertation paper, perhaps the lowest in the batch. This might sound very odd to the contemporary students in Anthropology. I decided to join Anthropology and Human Genetics Unit of the Indian Statistical Institute (ISI) to pursue my Ph.D. programme under the supervision of Professor Amitabha Basu. My supervisor gave me the liberty to choose the topic of my research. Periodically,

I updated Professor Basu about the progress of my work. Initially, I sketched three research projects, but finally zeroed in to do my research on the mother and child health of the Hindu and Muslim communities who were living in adjacent clusters in a squatter settlement on the embankment of a canal in the city of Kolkata. The objective of my research was to investigate the socio-economic concomitants of health and well-being of two contrasting social groups inhabiting a squatter settlement in Calcutta. I used a number of health-related traits like demographic, self-reported morbidity, haematological, intestinal parasitic infestation, clinical, nutritional (including one-year longitudinal growth study of preschool children) to investigate the differences in health-related traits between the Hindu and Muslim populations residing in that area. I also collected case studies to understand the attitude, beliefs and practises of the mothers towards their own health and of their children. Professor Basu assigned Dr Premananda Bharati (who was then a faculty member of ISI) to give me hand on training in data collection techniques. I collaborated with two medical professionals (Dr Pradip K. Mitra and Dr Sukumar Basak) since some of my data types warranted medical expertise. A section of the Hindu women of this settlement was engaged as domestic help in the nearby middle-class households. I hypothesized that working women of this settlement are getting an exposure of the middle class attitude toward health. So, it was interesting for me to compare the health-related traits and attitude towards health between working and non-working Hindus and found my hypothesis to be correct. The fieldwork spanned for a period of three years (mid of 1993-mid of 1996) and could publish some articles. My take home message from this Ph.D. programme was how to formulate a research problem, to design a study, collect data on various biological variables and analyse the results. In addition, I learned how to use a mixed approach (quantitative and qualitative) in a research. Professor Basu was an erudite scholar, a person with integrity, and a generous gentleman. His personality and magnanimity attracted me and his guidance was a learning lesson. It was my long-time desire to analyse and interpret his life and works as a mark of gratitude and contribution to anthropology.

As a Professional Anthropologist

In the year 1996 and later 1998, I appeared in the interviews for recruitment in the post of lecturer in undergraduate colleges of West Bengal. In both the occasions, I failed to secure an upper berth. The subject experts found the other candidates to be superior to me. By that time, I had submitted my thesis and was desperately looking for a job. Suddenly, I got an opportunity to teach undergraduate course in Anthropology at Narasinha Dutt College of Howrah district. I took this opportunity to prove my worth as a teacher. I taught in that college dedicatedly for a year or so and also trained a group of undergraduate students in anthropological fieldwork. My job was to assist the senior teachers of the college in selecting the field site, making logistic arrangements for the students and also to supervise them in the field.

In the meantime, Professor Susmita Mukhopadhaya (Susmita di) of ISI kindled an interest in me to do research in the area of reproductive health. In fact, during the end of the last century, the concept of reproductive health took a new dimension. This was triggered off by two international conventions—one on Safe Motherhood Programme and International Conference on Population and Development of UN. Subsequently, Susmita Di received a DFID project on Maternal Obstetric Morbidity Studies (under the aegis of Safe Motherhood Programme) of six months duration (starting from mid of June 1999) and I decided to join the project. The objective of that study was to investigate the concomitants of maternal obstetric morbidity of women living in three districts of West Bengal (namely Malda, North Dinajpur and South Dinajpur). My job as a project supervisor was to recruit field investigators and to train and supervise them in data collection. Additionally, I had to interact with the government health officials for seeking their support in conducting the fieldwork. I visited no less than thirty villages and collected data on 900 mothers who have given birth to a child not less than two years old. It was the first time I had an experience to conduct an externally funded mega project deploying multiple field investigators. We analysed the data to investigate factors that significantly affect obstetric morbidity outcomes. We also conducted focus group discussion (FGD) sessions to understand how the health providers, prospective mothers, young mothers and elderly women respond to issues like early marriage, early child birth, adoption of family planning and availing public health facilities.

I started my second innings in anthropology as a faculty member in the University of Allahabad on 2 February 2000. I was the first teacher in that department who was appointed as Physical Anthropologists; the others were Professor A.R.N. Srivastava and Professor Vijoy S. Sahay. The students were very excited to find their new Physical Anthropology teacher. I am thankful to them for accommodating my bad Hindi. The students took great interest in learning human evolution, racial biology and genetics. My colleagues of the departments were very cooperative and encouraged me in getting good books in Physical Anthropology for the library and laboratory equipments and museum exhibits. I used to discuss with the students on the prospects of studying Physical Anthropology and apprise them about contemporary research trends. In one occasion, the department received financial assistance from the university to hold a National Seminar. Although the funding was little, yet we thought of holding the seminar to give an exposure to this department at a national level and also to motivate our students and scholars in anthropology. The seminar was on "Role of NGOs in Rural and Tribal Development". I still remember the enthusiasm and contribution of the students and scholars in making the seminar successful. For me, it was the first experience of organizing a national level seminar and also to get to know my colleagues who are serving in other universities of the country. My academic interaction with the faculty members of other departments of AU increased with time. Professor Janak Pandey, the then Head of Psychology Department and Pro-Vice-Chancellor of the University roped me in developing an interdisciplinary Centre in Cognitive and Behavioural Science. I was made the Coordinator of Behavioural Sciences. Later this centre organized a seminar under my convenorship (along with Professor Ajit K. Dalal) on Social Dimension of Health. In continuation with this seminar, Professor Dalal and me edited a volume on Social Dimension of Health and in the first article of this volume we (the editors) explained how socio-economic factors, health care practices, health system and perception of a community determine the health and well-being of a community. This exercise gave me ample exposure to ponder on a research topic beyond my disciplinary boundary.

I was interested in teaching and developing anthropology in Allahabad. But my parents wanted me to return to Kolkata. Thus, when an opportunity came to join the University of Calcutta, I was in a dilemma. I am still very much obliged to Allahabad University for the love, affection and respect I received from students, teachers and non-teaching community. It is true that I could not make any significant mark in research during my brief stay in Allahabad (2000-04), but in truth I wanted to develop the department. I feel happy when I see that some of my students joined Indian Institute of Technology (IIT), Indian Statistical Institute (ISI), Anthropological Survey of India (AnSI) and other institutes to pursue doctoral programme.

I joined the Department of Anthropology, University of Calcutta on 5 May 2004 and started my third innings in anthropology. In University of Calcutta, the postgraduate students come with an honours graduate degree in anthropology. Thus, the postgraduate syllabus of Calcutta was advanced compared to that of Allahabad. I spend six months to prepare myself for teaching the postgraduate course. I was assigned to teach human growth, human ecology and stress, biostatistics, demography and molecular evolution of primates. I took deep interest in teaching the history and development of Biological Anthropology, growth and ecological studies. This helps the students to generate an interest in the concerned subject matter and to understand the significance of the topic in Anthropology. In Calcutta, many students, despite their interest in Biological Anthropology, opt for other special paper because the course contains modules on statistics. I took this as a challenge and started teaching statistics in a lucid manner, citing anthropological examples. I feel happy when most of the students make successful attempts in solving statistical problems in the examination.

In University of Calcutta, I wanted to open a new frontier of research, i.e., my long-standing research interest on reproductive health. In the first year I was allotted five students to supervise their dissertation work. I remember, Bhubon completed dissertation paper on Adolescent Male Reproductive Health and Kaberi and Surupa on Menstrual Characteristics of Adolescent girls. Since these areas were new to me, I worked very hard to give shape to their dissertation works. The examiners were not happy with the dissertation topics and found those queer in anthropology. Some even questioned about biological anthropological content in those topics. I took this up as a challenge. During the year 2005-10, our department received the financial assistance of UGC (DSA, Phase III). Under this programme, each of the faculty members had to submit two research proposals. I submitted one project on Adolescent Reproductive Health and the other on Menstrual Health. Subsequently, I was able to publish few articles on menstrual health and adolescent male's sexual and reproductive health in number of reputed journals. My publications justified that studying human biology not only mean just to measure some bodily features, but also to identify the sociocultural factors that shape human biology. Simultaneously, I became interested to study family planning and decision making, menopause, breast feeding and anthropological demography. I explored my research interest and assigned these topics to my dissertation students. Subsequently, I started supervising Ph.D. students in these research areas. For example, the first student who did dissertation paper with me on menopause is Doyel Dasgupta. She compared the rural urban difference in menopausal age and menopausal symptoms. I thought of further investigating this area to explore why menopausal age, menopausal symptoms, attitude towards menopause, postmenopausal quality of life and the meaning of menopause differed across populations. I submitted a major research project at the University Grants Commission and received the grant. I successfully completed this project and trained one scholar who eventually completed Ph.D. on this topic. In course of time, I published a number of articles on menopause with my students. Our research on Menopause interested Lynnette Leidy Sievert of the University of Massachusetts. Lynnette is one of the leading scholars in menopause research and was Editor-in-Chief of *American Journal of Human Biology*. We agreed to do collaborative research on Menopause, and finally have been able to contribute an article on "Menopause" in *Routledge Handbook of Anthropology and Reproduction*. My research interest in Menopause gave me the opportunity to collaborate in writing a policy paper d with epidemiologists, clinicians and gynaecologists on the issue of "Optimising Health of Women who reach Menopause at an Early Age". This paper got published in the journal *The Lancet*.

Later, I became interested to examine the relationship between menopause and cardiovascular risk factors in a microcosm of ethnic, socio-economic, rural/urban and health disparity; and Debasmita joined me in this project.

Human reproduction takes place in a behavioural ecological context, because reproductive preferences and decisions of individuals are influenced to a considerable degree and in numerous ways by their personal life circumstances. Thus, decision in family formation became another important area of my research. I assigned Nandini Bhattacharya to pursue this project for her dissertation paper. The objective was to find out under which circumstances couples take decision to limit family size, increase birth spacing and switch over from one contraceptive type to the other. Nandini has completed her Ph.D. on Family Planning and Decision Making among the Rural Adolescent Married girls.

Modern society encourages the search for a perfect body. Concern over body weight and related behaviours are common among the adolescent, particularly girls in Western countries. This problem has now assumed alarming proportions in India. A shift towards the concept of thin body image is occurring among the urban girls, as an outcome of mass media exposure and globalization. A large section of the girls are involved in attaining thin body image which at times develop dissatisfaction over body weight. Body weight dissatisfaction gives rise to the development of body weight concern and disordered eating behaviour. We took up this burning issue as a Ph.D. research problem in collaboration with Susmita Mukhopadhyay of ISI and came up with fascinating research findings.

I became interested in Anthropological Demography when Mir Azad Kalam joined me for his dissertation work. Mir belongs to Darbhangia Khotta Muslim community. This community has migrated from Darbhanga district of Bihar to West Bengal during the reign of Emperor Akbar. In course of my discussion with Mir, I got the insiders perspective of the community, especially about their marital choice and practises. I inspired Mir to pursue his doctoral research on anthropological demography of his own community. He studied how the trend in consanguinity changed across generation, how consanguinity impinges on family relation using mixed method of research. Saptamita Pal, another Ph.D. scholar took up a research topic on the "Changing Fertility Scenario of Kolkata Metropolitan City". This work has a different kind of demographic flavour, unlike the work of Mir. It appears from the trend of Saptamita's research that Kolkata couples are seeking for lesser number of offspring as trade-off between quality and quantity and to have more leisure time for themselves. Professor Saswata Ghosh, a renowned demographer of the Institute for Developmental Studies, Kolkata collaborated in these two demographic researches. In fact, Saswata encouraged me to analyse National Family Health survey data and write research papers on the prevalence and determinants of consanguineous marriage in India and how the prevalence and determinants changed across decades.

The relationship between ecology and health, especially on the coping strategies of communities living in contrasting ecology has long been my long-time interest. So, when I floated this idea to my scholar Parna Ghosh, she came up with a proposal to study the health and health care strategies of people living in deltaic and non-deltaic Sundarbans with a hypothesis that the people living in deltaic Sundarbans, owing to their disconnection with the main land compared to their non-deltaic counterpart would have a different health status and health management strategy. Later, I found it interesting to see how migrants in their new ecological set up responds to the challenge and trade off with reproductive energetic compared to the sedentes. Myself and Monali Goswami jointly supervised a Ph.D. candidate (Joyeeta Thakur) on this topic and has been successful in publishing articles to examine how migration status is related to various dimensions reproductive health.

Studying obstetric morbidity and its determinants has been my interest ever since I became interested to research in the area of "Reproductive Health". One of my doctoral scholars, Shormona Dhara showed interest to pursue her research on obstetric morbidity and its determinants in Assam using mixed method approach. The rationale of this study is how maternal health-seeking behaviour reflects sociocultural and behavioural discourse, beyond the provisions of availability and accessibility. But hardly any attempt has been made to understand the complex framework of the determinants of obstetric morbidities, its associated health-seeking behaviour, and maternal mortality. We considered imperative to address the aetiology of obstetric morbidity and mortality and the utilization of available care, to understand the gap between demand and supply of seeking maternal health care resources in the state with the highest prevalence of maternal death. Dr Arupendra Mozumdar, an anthropologist working in the Population Council, New Delhi has a vast experience in this area of research. On my request, Arupendra agreed to jointly supervise this doctoral programme with me.

I love to do experimental research, breaking the stereotype approaches and exploring new areas. And in most of the cases, I associate a student in these types of research endeavour. For example, in a couple of research we used cultural consonance model to understand how perception of a community towards health guides health behaviour; or say for example, how people's attitude toward smoking can be studied using phenomenological approach; or may be questioning whether developmental discourse is marginalizing the aged; or in writing 100 years of history of Biological Anthropology in India; or in introspecting the discourse of Anthropology as a discipline.

In academics, as one grows, one has to think beyond his/her personal scores. Thus, when the proposal came from the Indian Anthropological Society to take up the responsibility of the Managing Editor of their organ *Journal of the Indian Anthropological Society* (*JIAS*), I thought it would be a pious job to render my service for the cause of the discipline. And I feel contended that *JIAS* is doing well with the support from the Editorial Board members and our esteemed reviewers. However, there is more to do with the growth and activities of Indian National Confederation and Academy of Anthropologists, in which presently I am the Member Secretary.

I know that I have a long way to go and many more to contribute in anthropological literature. But the most important thing which I consider anthropology warrant is to produce trained mind and a good human being who will carry forward this discipline in the next hundred years to come.

27

My Journey as an Anthropologist

Lucy T.V. Zehol

Early Life, Education, Family, Taking Anthropology as a Subject

My passion in the field of anthropology began during my postgraduate studies. However, the reason I applied to the discipline may seem naive now that I reflect back; the Department of Anthropology at North Eastern Hill University was in its formative years. Anthropology as a discipline was new and unique among my peers. I was privileged to be mentored by exceptional professors to mention a few: Professor A.P Sinha who also founded the Department of Anthropology in 1980 at NEHU and was the only lecturer in the department in its initial years and he was later joined by Professor H.K. Bhat, Professor P.K. Misra and Professor B. Saraswati.

The inceptive training of applying anthropological knowledge began with my Master's Dissertation on a preliminary survey of Mental Illness in Shillong. The discipline fit perfectly right in understanding the world in which I grew up in and the prospect of exploring the ethnographic narrative was exciting. Under the supervision of Late Professor Sinha, I completed an M.Phil. degree on the title "The Tribes of Manipur: An Ethnographic Study" and further pursued Ph.D. Degree on "Ethnicity in Manipur: Experience, Issues and Perspectives".

Growing up, I was taught to work hard and never once suppressed from pursuing my dreams (because of being a female). I have pushed my own limits each phase of my life with the surmounting responsibilities as an academician, administrator, elder sister, wife, mother and aunt. I can confidently say I have done my duties to the best of my ability and capacity. However, the due credit is to a woman, my mother known as Mrs Aneng who has been a constant pillar of courage and integrity. Her parents were hard working farmer; her father was the clan head. Every person in the family had a specific chore allocated; hers was to graze the cows and buffalos. Her daily routine included enjoying her packed lunch prepare by her mother for the day and taking the cattle to graze in the open fields along with other fellow elders to her. This was a time when our people came in contact with the Western missionaries and her brother was sent off to study theology. My mother in the later years narrated to me that she never felt the need to pursue further studies and was quite pleased and happy just as she was attending the village primary school. It was her brother who persuaded her to move out of the village.

Over the years, I've carried this narrative as an inspiration to deconstruct stereotypes of relation between men and women. My mother completed her studies and rose to become the first tribal women Gazetteer Officer in Manipur. She was equally committed to her roles as a mother and the professional demands of her work. My father instills the value of honesty and hard work and had been a pillar of strength to my mother and relatives around us.

Doctoral Work, Teachers, Fieldwork and Early Career

My doctoral work entitled "Ethnicity in Manipur: Issues, Experiences and Perspectives" has dealt with an important social category, viz. ethnicity which has acquired an extremely critical place in understanding the social structures in varies parts of the world. In a multi-cultural society of India, ethnicity is a significant element of social structure.

The thesis deals with the ethnic dimension of Manipur, and is not confined to the tribal communities only but also discusses the non-tribal social groups and their interaction. It is an analytical study and has attempted a comparative analysis of different empirical situation as obtained in Manipur. Unlike many anthropological studies, it is not an intensive field based micro-study yet as an inhabitant of Manipur I am privileged to possess "home knowledge" of the situation and is overwhelmingly presented in historical perspective and deals with people of Manipur as a whole. My challenge as a young researcher in the 1990s was that anthropologists studying simple societies have not yet developed tools for analyzing a complex society gripped by multilayered and multifaceted traditions, as in the case of Manipur. Interviewing key informants from the diverse communities greatly enrich my data. My mother and father helped me in the rapport building process during my fieldwork in Imphal as all the key informants were well known to them and they in return extended all support to me. Land phone was a very convenient tool to carry on many conversations with my informants or even cross-checks my data. One of my key informants (in his late 1990s) till date reminds me of the help he had extended to me and I am ever grateful to him.

Seminal Contribution to Anthropology, Important Papers, and Books

During the course of research, the discipline of anthropology has made me to explore the narratives of indigenous people projected to the world at large. Belonging to the first generation of women pursuing higher education, especially in the field of research allowed me to understand the importance of scientific studies that can be beneficial in producing ethnographic work from the lens of an indigenous scholar. In the initial years of pursuing research, the literature available about the ethnic communities of Nagaland and Manipur of India were dominantly written by administrator turned scholars such as J.P. Mills, J.H. Hutton, etc. In the context of the Nagas, means of passing knowledge was only through oral means of communication, these works by British administrators continue to be treasures in having recorded the lifeways of the people. However, these works do not justify the perspectives and academic research as the only means of narratives of the indigenous people.

Motivated by the need to produce empirical research from the indigenous perspective, my first book *Ethnicity in Manipur: Experience, Issues and Perspective* (1998) highlights the continuing change in the definitions of the various tribal communities in Manipur. I grew up in Manipur fairly most part of my life. At (school and other/various) social surroundings, one could clearly observe or would be engaged in discussions of the various ethnic discourses of identity, rights and definition of which group was identified by what traits or custom. Manipur being a multilingual and multiethnic as the other states of north-east India showcase a high level of coexistence amongst its people as well as extreme levels of disharmony among its people. From an anthropological understanding, this book sheds light for the upcoming researchers as to how the definitions of ethnicity evolve over time and influence in building stronger systems of harmony in the microcosm of indigenous people in north-east India.

In the 30 plus years of my profession as an anthropologist and educator but also firstly as a woman, daughter, wife and mother to two sons, there is an unquestionable need to focus on gender studies. Among the first works I published was the book *Women in Naga Society* (1998). It was made possible through the collective contribution of women and men colleagues and my husband. It is an attempt to ponder into the various aspects of women's life in the Naga Society. The status of women in the Naga Society as popularly interpreted by well-known authors such as Haimendorf mentions that "women from the more civilized parts of India will very well envy the women of the hill people as they are more free and happy". This notion on the status of women has been explored and showcased that in the recent decades, the perception of the status of women in the Naga Society has evolved from that of ascribed roles to that of her achievements.

I believe that gender studies among the Naga society are in its nascent stage as to how gender is discoursed among individuals, communities and in between the two genders. The role of women in the context of Naga society goes beyond the domestic responsibilities. I have explored this field with an anthropological lens whereby, it could be gathered that women play crucial roles in the well-being and progress of the communities as well as in the harmony among different social groups and ethnic communities. This is to be acknowledged at a larger scale in every level of social institutions in the Naga society whereby there is a harmonious inclusion of both the genders while navigating the society in terms of development policies, evolution of traditional customs and laws, welfare of the disadvantaged group of people. My papers reflect these mentioned needs and aim not to limit only among the Naga society however, provides a comparative study between the different ethnic communities across the north-east region.

I believe the role of the anthropologist is to bring to light the various lifeways of human beings and justify that there can be many ways in which a custom may be practiced and as we explore further every custom, one gets to understands the practices has values associated with a moral rational of why it is done in that particular manner. *The Legendary Naga Village* (*A Reader*): *Khezhakeno* (2009) co-authored with my husband was produced with the desire to show case that traditional Naga society was and is not at all "primitive", "savage" or "devoid of intelligence", neither in their "means" nor in the way they conceive their activities around them and the need to treat the Nagas with respect and dignity extend even today.

I have argued that the way Naga women portray themselves, their lives and responsibilities stand in direct contrast with the socially dominant representation of women. And that although the male model is not a static but an ideology that is inconsistent, incomplete and not systematic, women still have to negotiate their identity within the dominant male-focused construct.

In my paper "The Construction of Gender in the Northeast: An Anthropological Critique" (2016) I compared the Naga women to the Khasi women. Not only my students and colleagues were doing their fieldwork among the Khasi, I am truly fortunate to live and observed their way of life and their reaction to me as a Naga women-lived experience here in Meghalaya.

As per both Khasi and Chakhesang Naga (Kheza) customary laws, women are not traditionally allowed to take part in the village administration, which is traditionally considered men's domain. Apart from these similarities, the traditional Khasi and Chakhesang Naga customary laws differ in the way that they privilege women and men, respectively.

Among the Khasi, for example, lineage is passed down through the maternal line, which contribute to make women security and less dependent on their husbands to access resources. On the other hand, among the Chakhesang Naga people, descent is passed down through the paternal line and although women are given rights of use on their husband's land, they do not own the land. In case of divorce among Chakhesang Naga people, custody is given to the father and the mother has to leave the husband's house bringing with her only her clothes. The position of a Chakhesang Naga woman as per customary rights is inferior and less secure than that of men.

An investigation on gender dynamics in the matrilineal Khasi society and in the patrilineal Chakhesang Naga society allowed gaining insights in the gender division of labour at both household and community level as well as in the agricultural field. The role of women and men in the household, in the community and in the agricultural field appeared to be similar in both social systems. It emerged that both Khasi and Chakhesang Naga women were primarily involved in children care, household management, weaving and agricultural production. Men, despite being equally involved in agricultural activities, were also to a large extent engaged in non-agricultural income generating activities, such as mining, stone quarrying, basketry and furniture making.

In the Khasi and Chakhesang Naga society, community administration, management and decision making were considered men's domain, with no or very limited women's intervention. In both societies, men were considered the leaders of the household, considered to hold heavier responsibilities.

However, whereas among the Khasi people, gender division of labor seemed to be more blurred, both boys and girls being introduced to household chores and cooking, for example, among the Chakhesang Naga the household management was found to be exclusively women's task. Although male chauvinist narratives were found in both the Khasi and Chakhesang Naga society, the former appeared to be generally more egalitarian than the latter, where biases against women emerged more clearly.

By favouring women and men respectively, Khasi and Naga customary laws were noticed to support power relations that shape values, world views and attitudes towards both women and men. Through the process of socialization, men and women reinforce "culturally dominant representations that acquire their status precisely because they are consistently believed in".

It is noticed that while among the Khasi people the relationship seemed to be more egalitarian and the work and role of women in society socially acknowledged, among the Chakhesang, the relationship between women and men appeared to be more hierarchical, where women (mother, wife, sister, etc.) were portrayed as socially less relevant than men and their work was not acknowledged and valued but instead, expected and taken for granted in spite of their visibility contribution to the household and economy.

Further, when it comes to participation in the community, women are confined to groups such as the Naga Mothers' Association and the various women's church organizations and welfare committees. The present apolitical role of women contracts with the traditional position of women as mediators between warring villages where they acted as ambassadors known as *demi* among the Chakhesang or *phukreila* among the Tangkhul to resolve conflict-today this role is being played to a limited extent by the Naga Mothers' Association and other's civilian and church organization.

Administrative and Institution Building

I have been Warden of PG and Research Scholar hostels, Head, Department of Anthropology and Dean of School of Human and Environmental Sciences, North-Eastern Hill University. All experiences contributed towards administrative and institution building capacity training. I am grateful that I am able to break the class ceiling in term of being able to be the first female Head of the Department and Dean of the School of Human and Environmental Sciences, North-Eastern Hill University.

Contribution beyond Anthropology, Notable Students

I genuinely consider the perks of being a university professor is the opportunity to mentor and in turned be enlivened by the constant association with young postgraduate students, research scholars and doctoral fellows beyond anthropology. During my charge as the hostel warden, I ensured that a certain amount of trust was built between me and the women hostelers whereby, any misbehaviour/ unnecessary inconvenience was reduced.

Shillong is an agglomeration of students from different ethnic communities. My contribution beyond research would perhaps be as an advisor to the various student bodies such as Naga Students Union, Shillong, Evangelical Union, Naga Students Fellowship, NEHU, Naga Postgraduate Students' Coordination Committee and as the Women President of the Shillong Baptist Church.

I've felt the most fulfilled when I encounter my students from various batches approach me or drop in a message saying how the lessons taught in and beyond classroom have made a positive impact in their lives. Some of my students have joined teaching profession, state and civil services, NGOs, business and happy enterprising home makers … still in the making.

International Collaborations

An international collaboration with Dr Aparna Sharma, World Arts and Cultures, University of California, Los Angles (UCLA) was a learning process for me, master students, researcher scholars beyond anthropology and colleagues. It was a two-days workshop on "Visual Anthropology: Practices and Documentary Studies" that introduces researchers to the history of visual media, their uses in specific disciplinary contexts and current directions of work. The workshop draws connections between discourses around visual media from the fields of Visual Anthropology, Photography and Documentary Studies. The workshop includes seminar discussions, a visit to the Verrier Elwin Museum at NEHU and a field-based photographic assignment.

How can visual materials—photography and film—be integrated into research? What are the ways by which visual data have been generated in the production of knowledge? These questions are key to understanding how visual data can be generated and used effectively in research processes. Visual materials—photographs, moving images (film or digital video)—offer researchers additional resources that complement their written analysis in various disciplines of the humanities and social sciences. Visual materials differ from writing as they engage our senses of sight and sound. They do not only tell, but they show. This specific quality of visual media is of particular value in disciplines that involve field-based research such as anthropology. Here, photography and film can provide evidence of fieldwork; transport readers and viewers to disparate field-sites witnessing practises and ways of living that are under study. Besides offering a more immediate and situated experience of field-research, visual materials offer competing modes of knowledge and understanding.

Presently, two ways can be identified through which visual data and materials get used in research. One, generation of photographs and films as part of field-based research. Photographs and films of field-based research complement written analysis and offer readers/viewers situated knowledge about specific landscapes and cultures. A second way by which visual materials get used in research involves critical examination of the histories of how peoples and their cultural practises have been represented through photography and film. Here, the researcher asks: what kinds of knowledge and understandings do existing visual media afford in relation to the subject under study? This mode of research involves study into the impacts of visual representations on their subjects and intended audiences. These two ways of working with visual materials are not exclusive to each other. Researchers may use one or both, with varying degrees of emphases.

Current Activities

I have been appointed as the Dean of School of Humanities and Environmental Sciences at North-Eastern Hill University, 2021-24 which encompass seven disciplines under its administration.

Over the 30+ years of studying and teaching anthropology, I believe I have come a long way in learning and unlearning how I understand and demonstrate anthropology both as a relevant and essential discipline in understanding the world we live in today. Looking back on my first encounter with anthropology, it intrigued me just for the simple fact that it was a new discipline by its name and in its simplicity has allowed me to unravel the importance to highlight what is so very usual about our human nature and the way we do everything. I aim to be part of the building of the local scholarship in narrating the change and continuity of the Naga culture and traditions. I would like to further explore classic and contemporary anthropological contributions to women and gender issues in Naga society. Ever since the Nagas have come in contact with the western way of living, the rate of acculturation has been higher than the rate of revitalizing our (original) culture in forms of clothing, education, values, customs or technology. I do not see a bleak future; however, the need to pace with involving more people from all age, gender and tribes/non-tribes in research is paramount in understanding experiences in women rights/issues and the role of Nagas in nation building.

28

Autobiography

R.R. Prasad

The Prologue

It is perhaps often difficult to look back vividly into one's own bygone days and then reconstruct some meaningful chronicle of events by connecting the dots that weave the professional threads of an anthropologist's life. Despite certain limitations, it is, however, always worthwhile to indulge in such an exercise with the hope that it might reveal and unpack some valuable insights for others who are in similar professional pursuits.

My name is Rajiv Ranjan Prasad (R.R. Prasad) and I was born on 29 December 1955 in Hazaribagh, Jharkhand (undivided Bihar State). Both of my parents are deceased. I had my school education in a government school and did my graduation from St. Columba's College with Economics and History as my elective subjects. After my graduation, I had to take a decision about my higher studies. And it so happened that one internationally eminent anthropologist with whom we had family ties, encouraged me to pursue postgraduation in Anthropology at Ranchi University. Yes, that was the turning point in my career. I did my Master's degree in Anthropology in 1976 with specialization in Applied & Action Anthropology.

Beginning of Career in Anthropology

In the year 1976, I joined in a research project as Junior Research Fellow in the Department of Anthropology, University of Delhi, under the guidance of Dr S.C. Tiwari. This project was geographically located in the Indo-Tibetan borders of Kumaon and Garhwhal Himalayas of the then undivided Uttar Pradesh State. This project gave me opportunities for carrying out extensive fieldwork in the Central Himalayas and preparing the ethnographic profiles of the Bhotia and Raji Bhotias have traditionally been involved in trade with Tibet from where they brought valuables and sold out at various places in India. The Raji, on the other hand, has been eking out a livelihood from food gathering and silent barter trade. This three-year tenure for me as a Junior Research Fellow really transformed me in a manner that I could practically apply my theoretical knowledge in anthropology as a postgraduate student. It gave me the confidence that I really now I understand anthropology and also make effective and efficient application of this knowledge in writing and preparing comprehensive ethnographic reports.

While working as a research fellow in a project, I also conceptualized my idea for writing a doctoral thesis and then got registered for doing Ph.D. in Ranchi University. I submitted my Ph.D. thesis on "Economic Transformation and Cultural Adaptation among the Bhotias" under the guidance of Professor V.S. Upadhyay. I was awarded my Ph.D. degree in the year 1981. My Ph.D. thesis was subsequently published under the title *The Bhotias of India.*

When data collection work was in progress for the research project in the Central Himalayas, Professor Tiwari had encouraged me to study the status of women among the Kuthalia Bora community. I did that study and published one paper under the title "Where Women are Untouchables". This was my first entry into the gender domain of anthropological research. Similarly, during my village study among the Jaad Bhotas in Uttarkashi district, I had studied the manner in which the locally brewed liquor called *chhung* was having integral linkage with the sociocultural life of the community. This was the period when Janata Party had formed the government at the centre and had imposed prohibition across the country. I argued in my paper titled "Prohibition among Tribals", published in the *Mainstream*, that prohibition cannot be enforced among the tribals as it is intimately linked with their sociocultural life.

This was also the period when I developed interest in Medical Anthropology as my ethnographic research data among the Bhotia shed light of many sociocultural beliefs and practises which influence their understanding of diseases and their cure. I published one paper on "Obstetrical Practices among the Tribals" in the *Tribal Research Bulletin*, March 1982. And the other paper on medical anthropology was "Beliefs and Practices Pertaining to Child Birth in Bhotia Society" which was published in the *Spectra of Anthropological Progress*, 1982.

After completion of my tenure as a Junior Research Fellow, I was awarded the Senior Research Fellowship in the Department of Anthropology, Ranchi University for about six months during which I prepared a research report on the Sacred Complex of Central Himalayas.

I was still in search of a regular job as an anthropologist. This search took to me to the Foundation of Aid Industrial Recovery (FAIR), New Delhi which gave me a research assignment to prepare the socio-economic status of the pastoral nomads of Rajasthan. This assignment was rewarding for me as it not only gave me an opportunity to study the pastoral nomads but also subsequently publish a book under the title *Pastoral Nomadism in Arid Zones of India*.

Professional Career Commences

In February 1981, I was appointed as a Senior Investigator in the National Commission for Scheduled Castes & Scheduled Tribes, New Delhi where I was subsequently promoted as Research Officer and transferred to Patna in Bihar State. After serving for about eighteen months in Patna, I was transferred to the Ministry of Home Affairs, New Delhi. During my posting in Patna, I got married with Dr Sushama Sahay who was my class and soul mate while pursuing postgraduation degree in Anthropology in Ranchi University.

It is said that after marriage, one's fortune gets aligned with wife's fortune and luck as well. It turned to be true for me. In April 1984, I was appointed as Deputy Director, Cultural Anthropology at the National Institute of Rural Development (NIRD), Hyderabad. And it was NIRD wherefrom I retired in December 2015 as Professor & Head, Centre for Equity & Social Development.

At the NIRD, I got opportunities to make full use of my anthropological knowledge in the field of rural development research and training. It was here where I learnt that the field of development is inter and multi-disciplinary and I have combined the skills of disciplines allied with development in general and rural development in particular. I had to now shed my label as anthropologist primarily interested in tribal studies. I had to enter into new domains of development such as social equity, environment, humans vs wild life, gender, social and community mobilization, child labour, capacity building, financing development, etc.

In the year 1995, I was selected for the post of Director (Sociology and Cultural Anthropology) at the NIRD. Subsequently, this position was changed to Professor & Head (Centre for Equity & Social Development). Under the Colombo Plan, I was selected in the year 1989 for pursuing Master's Degree course in Economics and Management of Rural Development at the Institute for Development Planning & Management (IDPM), Manchester

University, UK. Thus, I acquired my second Master's Degree in Economics and Management of Rural Development.

Major Contributions

If I were to report my major contributions in the area of rural development with special focus on social equity, environment management, capacity building, good governance, corporate social responsibility (CSR), etc. I will certainly mention about my innumerable projects, publications (books and papers), awards and honours, international collaboration, etc.

In the NIRD I got opportunities to associate myself with research studies and organising training programme on several issues related to development which can be categorized into Sustainable Development, Corporate Social Responsibility (CSR),Participatory Development, Social and Community Mobilization, Social Assessment, Social Equity and Justice, Social Audit, Mainstreaming Disadvantaged Sections of Society, Tribal Development, Bonded and Child Labour, Natural Resources Management, Rights-based Development and Rehabilitation of Project Affected Persons. In recognition of my contribution in the field of rural development, I received the following two award namely, the Best Citizen of India Award, 2011, by the International Publishing House, 2011, for exceptional excellence in the chosen area of activity and Bharat Jyoti Award, 2011, by the India International Friendship Society, 2011, for meritorious services, outstanding performance and remarkable role.

Publications

I have to my credit fifteen books and over seventy published research papers in various national and international journals. I also developed interest in writing for the English daily newspapers, magazines and professional non-anthropological but social science journals. It is not desirable to list below all my research paper publications. However, I am furnishing below some important books.

Post-Retirement Affiliations

After my retirement from the NIRD in December 2015, I have been mostly associated as Consultant with the NIRD, NITI Aayog, GRAAM (Mysuru) and as a Trustee with one civil society organization. My life as an anthropologist has been full of adventures, opportunities, challenges, rewards, and accomplishments. There are more and more to recollect and rejoice from the past experience and absolutely no regrets. The discipline of anthropology has taught me to be more broad-minded, less critical and always ready to listen to others' perspectives. This is what life is about. Life's journey has to come to an end someday, but the wisdom dawned upon me from my anthropological endeavours would always be available to the next generations from my publications.

My Books

1987: *Change and Continuity Among the Scheduled Caste Leather Workers.* National Institute of Rural Develpopment, Hyderabad.

1991: *Tribals, Rehabilitation and Development Rural Development and Social Change* (ed. 2 vols.), Rawat Publication, Jaipur (co-author).

1992: *Social Factors in Social Forestry.* Chugh Publications, Allahabad (co-author).

1993: *Tribal Situation in Forest Villages.* Discovery Publishing House, New Delhi (co-author).

1994: *Pastoral Nomadism in Arid Zones of India.* Discovery Publishing House, New Delhi.

1994: *Bonded Labourers: A Study of Rehabilitation and Organisational Dynamics.* Har-Anand Publications, New Delhi, (co-author).

2005: *National Exposure Programme for Leaders of Self-Help Groups.* BIRD, Lucknow, (co-author).

2015: *Community Mobilization: Methods & Models.* Discovery Publishing House, New Delhi.

2015: *Encyclopaedic Profile of Indian Tribes* (ed. 4 vols.). Discovery Publishing House, New Delhi.

29

Lifetime in the Sea of Humanity

An Introspection

Abhik Ghosh

Bionote: An Introduction

Writing a note on myself for a researcher is a weird experience, where one feels odd while at the same time finding for oneself the constraints caused to put forth a set of academic ideas that need to be explicated. So, without further ado, let me begin. I am Abhik Ghosh, a Ph.D. in Anthropology from University of Delhi and a faculty from 1998 at the Panjab University's Department of Anthropology, where I sit today as I write this.

We rummage through people's lives to find those nuggets that we are interested in at the time. Through this ransacking we learn about others' lives, all in the spaces and times of our one lifetime. Through these others we live lifetimes in this sea of humanity. Also, our learning often causes us to introspect, and we come to learn more about ourselves as a human being, as a person, and as a part of other matter and living beings.

For many, introspection and subjective feelings about oneself get in the way of research and one's concept of "objective" work. However, I have often felt that introspection was a good guide to knowing, not only about oneself but about the world, even as knowledge of the world helped in knowing myself. Thus, it was a tool, as the philosophers and many symbolists like Umberto Eco would have it, as an experiential two-way pathway to knowledge. Thus, for me, the personal, the self, and thus the subjective, is not at a remove from the objective, the subject, the Anthropology that I do.

Relevant Experiences from Childhood: Practising Anthropology My Way

When I was in school, two major events shaped the trajectory of my choices. My father had a major road accident and neurological damage which resulted in his death. At the time, I wished to become a doctor, preferably dealing with neurosciences, to deal with the way his case was handled, or so it seemed to me. Second, I was strangely attracted to Human Genetics and felt future research in these fields would be personally satisfying.

So, I when I was unable to get into the MBBS Course in Delhi, I automatically applied for a Bachelor's in Botany or Zoology. I thus began my graduation with a Botany Honours degree at Hans Raj College where I had friends from Anthropology with whom I interacted. After I completed graduation, I was again unable to get into Plant Molecular Biology and thus chose Anthropology at the University of Delhi than Botany at some other place. Eventually, I hoped, this might be my ticket to studies on Human Genetics.

My Adventures in Learning Anthropology

So, I joined anthropology with many misgivings and a lot of emotional baggage. I began with questions. Thankfully, I met a mentor who could patiently listen and answer to these queries. Professor D.K. Bhattacharya kept giving me books to read, which I would finish in a couple of days and bring back with two handwritten pages of questions each time, which he would answer. It became a pattern, until it was January when he requested me to read up on the syllabus so that I could do well in the examinations! Though our interactions continued, I became more involved with the work of clearing my Masters in the second year. My interactions of that time come through with a poignancy, as I recall that many of these teachers are no longer alive. It is through their dedication that I owe the choices I make today in my researches. They included professors P.K. Seth, S. Seth, H.K. Kumbhnani, S.C. Tiwari, S. Nath, P.K. Ghosh, I.P. Singh, M.P. Sachdeva, A.K. Kapoor, S. Kapoor, R. Singh, S.M. Channa, V.C. Channa, I.S. Marwah, J.S. Bhandari, V.K. Srivastava and later S.M. Patnaik and R.S. Mann. With many of them, I have had intense discussions and details that remain etched forever in my memory. They were so successful in imbuing me with the idea of Anthropology, that by the second year of my Masters I abandoned the idea of doing Human Genetics and took up Social Anthropology. This was primarily because the testing of genetic samples was expensive and very difficult. Reagents had to be imported and took much time. It all sounded very troublesome, frustrating even forbidding. With my new-found interests in the other sub-fields of anthropology, I relinquished my idea that I would only work on Human Genetics.

Further, I also felt interested in Prehistoric Archaeology since Professor D.K. Bhattacharya enthused us in his classes. However, after my M.Phil. when I requested him to be my supervisor for a dissertation on Prehistoric Archaeology, he refused, saying that no one would give me a job and asked me to continue with doing Social anthropology. However, my old interest in Prehistoric Archaeology continued till the present, forcing me into academic pathways I could not have imagined at the time. This included teaching, researching and fieldwork on Prehistoric Archaeology and Palaeoanthropology, including a few select publications over the years.

Anthropological Ideas and Their Personal Impact

There were two areas which were very important to me. They were related to tribal studies. One was about their economy and their symbolism. The economy was an issue of interest for me since my Masters' dissertation. Symbolism was my way of finding a new way to organize social data and to classify it without falling into the trap of any theoretical perspective, per se. This brought me up into the heavy reading material of philosophy. In fact, Professor Marwah had often told us not only to read the early classics in Anthropology but also philosophical works since without them the social science theories hardly made any sense.

For my Masters' dissertation I initially wanted to do a study on some aspect of the family as a basic unit of rural society. When I eventually started reading issues relating to household and other terms also came up. One of my seniors Rahul Sen was helping me find my way through this morass by finding me references to read through for clarifications. Eventually, I asked him the meaning of "domestic group" and also "mode of production". So, we began through a set of readings on Marxism. Finding it fascinating I decided to use this model to organize ideas relating to economics and the household in a rural setting. My delays got on the nerves of my supervisor Professor I.S. Marwah. He politely said, "Abhik, I think we should meet". One day before we were to leave for the field, I laid out my plans before him. He was happy but also apprehensive about whether I would be able to collect the data. It sort of worked out in the end.

However, during my M.Phil., I started reading Philosophy and History, trying to deal with concepts and researching into Anthropology and found them to be too useful to ignore. Also, symbolism ensured that I interact with students of sociology from D'School through whose courses in symbolism I learnt much, including how their concepts differed from those in Anthropology. These strains and interests became my enduring passions.

Within the year, I was also given another interest, when Professor Bhattacharya asked me to write papers on policy matters in a column, he had created in *Indian Anthropologist* which he was editing at the time. This became a very useful reading for me as I came to realize later. Local history became a very special interest during my research, and this interest in local variations in history was something that developed from my Masters' dissertation, developed from our fieldwork in Pauri Garhwal. Eventually, I recognized that established beliefs about how people behave may vary greatly, even as we claim that they belong to the same culture. It seems like a given today; it wasn't somehow so obvious when I began.

Through my interaction with *Indian Anthropologist* and its proofreading, some of which we did as students in the department taught me much about the running, management and maintenance required for an academic journal. This stood me in good stead for a lot of work relating to proofreading and working on issues through the reputed journals in India like *Man in India*, among others. Through this and the meticulous English of Professor V.K. Srivastava, I learnt to check and edit my own papers as far as I could.

In our final year of Masters', Professor J.S. Bhandari taught us Tribal Transformation in India. For this paper he asked us to do a project. For the project, I wished to interview a few tribal people from India, but how to find them in a place like Delhi? One of my classmates claimed that two Oraon tribals from Jharkhand (then Bihar) were present in his hostel and he could request them. Eventually, I interviewed them about their experiences and changes that they saw happening in their community. Their answers formed the basis of my project report. Eventually, when I wished to work on a tribal community for my M.Phil., I turned to the Oraon for my further work.

To this eclectic mix of subjects, I added my old interest in health and indigenous medicines. In the introduction of my M.Phil. as well as my Ph.D. there is some information on neurosciences, to introduce the idea of symbolization and the mind.

Rebellion ran strong in my early years, and I often rebelled with my teachers over their use of what I felt were outdated theories, concepts and ideas. In turn, they taught me about the nuances of their work, how, through the quotidian of everyday experiences, they transcended the current lot of theories with the nuances and details of their work. Further, this sense of rebellion drew to me readings on alternative interpretations and papers on those who rejected current theoretical approaches in Anthropology. These included Stanley Diamond, Dell Hymes, and many others. It also led me to rethink ideas about the apparent, even if it was held by the majority.

Through Professor D.K. Bhattacharya as well as the teachings of Professor V.C. Channa, I was also led to studies on ecology. This has also become something of a burr that never left my side through different issues, ideas, topics and subjects. I gained much from the different issues and ideas already covered in Prehistory by Professor Bhattacharya as well as the papers we read, discussed and wrote about together. I think we both had a passion for the immediacy of the issue and it enlarged my vision of human life and living tremendously.

Over the years my interaction with senior anthropologists from India also became not just about the exchange of pleasantries but also about their ideas and publications, through which I could see many new vistas opening up. Over the years, I cannot count or even calculate the ways by which their gentle influence has impacted on my work. Through these conversations, I often re-evaluated my ideas, changing and modifying them so that these ideas were acknowledged in any work on the topic. This often led me to dwell overmuch on theory, a fact not liked by Professor Bhattacharya who thought that I needed more white hairs on my head before I could do that and still be accepted by others. Of course, sitting for sessions at different conferences, seminars and workshops opened up my mind to other ethnographies and works. To acknowledge these issues and not to acknowledge the gains I made through my interactions and classroom teaching of students would be boorish. Many questions targeted at me by students have made me rethink my analysis and the way I write about my research.

My readings were very eclectic. Apart from my readings about anthropological matters, I was also hooked to a variety of fiction as well as other readings on non-fiction. All of these give me a broadness of ideas and thought as well as knowledge that I think stood me well over the years. Some of my readings on crime fiction, informed my classes on criminology and many societal concepts, ideas and theories were illuminated through my readings in science fiction. This was especially relevant in understanding how social utopias could often fail through human misanthropy.

In my initial classes in Anthropology, I was influenced by Professor V.C. Channa's discussions on tribes, castes and Hinduism. However, I think my two influences in social anthropology were primarily those of Professor I.S. Marwah and Professor V.K. Srivastava. The many hours of discussion and brain-storming that I indulged in while they spoke to me led me to learn much more than I would have done without their encouragement and help. Their mental and cognitive maps of the subject were seemingly endless, and I could never get enough of conversation with them.

Finally, I was also impressed by the ideas that brought in good research, that is, research methodology. I was so fascinated by so many authors, that I read through many, used much, and in my reflective mode put their modifications and usages in my writing and teaching. Upcoming and new research methods would also remain interesting for me, as Social Impact Assessment has been for me recently. So, also, fieldwork, was an exhilarating and passionate experience for me, where I learnt much.

Contribution to the Subject

The contribution of any researcher is often seen by others, often after a period of some time. Hence, through the discomfort of writing about oneself, I am trying to join the dots of a life led through a series of deadlines, one after the other, where sense and meaning are often lost.

First, I would perhaps see my contribution in the arena of tribal studies, especially with respect to tribal symbolism. Economy, ecology, health and medicine would, of course, become specific aspects of such studies. Thus, for me, the emphasis on time and space in my writings were an offshoot of symbolic studies and human perception.

A similar idea is about giving recommendations through a variety of studies on policy matters so that someone might pay attention to them at some point. To this point, I may increase emphasis on being a "pressure person" (as opposed to being a "pressure group") for important issues, including again ecology, health, nutrition, as well as education.

An area of interest for me has also been the idea of conflict, cooperation and inter-community relations. These relationships have always been an arena of interest for many, but for me they have been a part of enduring relations in the past. These past relations between communities have shaped and been shaped through local histories as well as interpersonal relations. Uncovering these could be deeply important for anthropologists of the future who could use these relations in the present to predict possible outcomes. We are still at an infancy in predicting development outcomes, and this might give us an edge.

Working without pauses, especially when the papers written are often dictated through the titles of seminars, books or special editions of journals mean that one is always learning and attempting to stretch, sometimes unsuccessfully, beyond one's comfort zone. Finding the time to read and write in spite of other encroachments on one's time, like teaching, interacting with students and checking dissertations and papers, meant some pussy-footing with time and space whose effects only became apparent over time.

International Collaboration

One interesting outcome of our work on ecological studies included our involvement with the Millenium Ecosystem Assessment groups, through which our chapter on Cultural Services was put together. This collaboration resulted in a joint Zayed Award given to the whole M.A. group after the reports were put together.

Apart from this group, over the years, many individuals have contacted me and stayed in touch across the world on academic issues that have enriched my work and thinking.

A word of caution for those who might read this. For many neuroscientists, the cause of an action is often an afterthought, and much that we do is often done without thought. Perhaps, that is what all my work became, and this paper is, as Professor Mehra would have quoted, a lot of sound and fury signifying nothing.

My Book

2006: *The World of the Oraon: Their Symbols in Time and Space*. New Delhi: Manohar (republished 2021).

30

Memories and Experiences

A Wonderful Journey called Anthropology

Geetika Ranjan

Introduction

At the outset I thank Professor P.C. Joshi, the editor of this volume for giving me the opportunity to share my thoughts on my journey in anthropology as this wonderful discipline completes 100 years of teaching in India. Crossing a 100 years mark is a big achievement for any discipline in terms of teaching and learning, but the achievement is even bigger for a discipline like anthropology which overcame several hurdles in the initial years of its journey to earn a place of relevance for itself. As I wrote this article, I realized it would be an article with a difference. That's because writing this gave me the opportunity to express my own journey in anthropology, go back in time, and traverse a route sprinkled with multiple experiences. I have a career in anthropology. As I wrote this piece, I could delve deeper into the thought that a career cannot be just another compartment in the totality called life. I cannot completely relate to the often heard sentence, "I do not take my work home", because I realize that knowingly and unknowingly, an anthropologist is always doing anthropology. As a student of anthropology which I continue to be, I have enjoyed my association with the discipline which, to a very large extent has influenced my approach towards life, and my way of seeing the world.

Growing up Towards Anthropology: The Early Years

When I look back, I realize and understand that the accidental and planned happenings in my life—all leading me towards anthropology, have left a deep meaning in my existence. The experiences of my growing up years, drew me in a very organic way later towards taking anthropology seriously. I was born and brought up in the city of Lucknow. My parents, both teachers—my father, a Professor of Public Administration and my mother of Sanskrit, ensured that we, their children are raised in a simple and humanism infused atmosphere of *vidya dadati vinayam* (knowledge gives humility), which is so characteristic of a teacher's household. Beyond the realm of the house was the society outside that further schooled me to ask questions, the answers to which I found in anthropology later on. The initial years of my life, till 17 years or so, were dominated by a rather elite, class and disciplined environment offered by my school—Loreto Convent, Lucknow. My encounter with the *real* world was mainly after I passed class twelfth and entered Lucknow University. I have grown up in a society where time and again a term like caste, dominates and decides many things in the lives of the people. Talks about conflicts between castes and politicization of caste were part of my universe as I grew up. Every social institution would in some way or the other smack of caste issues. Even an educational institution like the Lucknow University, my *alma mater*, is known as the hub of Brahmin vs Thakur lobbies.

Anthropology gives me the opportunity to articulate in my writings *my* understanding and felt experiences of who *I* am and who the *others* are. "It holds up a great mirror to man and lets him look at himself in this infinite variety". Caste and religion could be a significant part of one's life experiences. I can say this through my own example. A plethora of childhood experiences of being a caste, born to a Brahmin father and a Kayastha mother, of being an adolescent in an environment infused by the Mandal Commission furore of 1990-91 and Babri Masjid demolition, some of my writings of anthropology became a means of catharsis for me. When I shifted to Shillong in 2009, I experienced living amidst a new term called "tribe". Like caste, the dynamics in the term "tribe" makes it a never-ending topic of discussion.

About two decades of being in association with anthropology, first as a student at Lucknow University, then as a teacher of the subject at Lucknow and now as one in Shillong, life unfolded new experiences before me that helped me to talk, write and practise my way of doing anthropology.

Introduction to Anthropology

After completing standard 12, I took admission in the B.A. programme of Lucknow University. Lucknow University offers pass course (and not Honours) and the three subjects (each of equal weightage) which I chose to do graduation in were English Literature, History and Anthropology. Opting for English literature and History was a natural choice as I always found the two disciplines interesting to pursue further. Taking up anthropology was purely to score well because of the practical component therein. Getting a first division in Bachelor of Arts degree without taking up a subject with practical component was considered difficult. Further, as Anthropology at Lucknow (like almost everywhere in India, except in some places of northeast India) was taught only from B.A. and B.Sc. level, and not from 10+2 stage, I felt I would not feel disadvantaged for not having a prior training in this subject, which I thought would be the case if I opted to take any other practical related subject such as Psychology and Geography, which I had not read in previous classes. Little did I know at that time, that a subject which I am opting mainly to have a good aggregate of marks would be the one which would determine the course of my life.

As a B.A. first year student, I soon developed interest in learning anthropology and my focus towards the same kept on increasing with time. The entire credit for generating this liking for the subject goes to the most wonderful teachers like Professor Gopala Sarana, Professor Banvir Singh, Professor Chitralekha Verma, Professor B.R.K. Shukla, and Professor Indu Sahai who taught me. I had the good fortune of being taught by the stalwart Professor Gopala Sarana for four years (from B.A. first year till M.A. first year). Professor Sarana's deep love for anthropology rubbed on his students as well. It was through him that we first learnt of the legend Professor Dhirendra Nath Majumdar, one of the biggest names in anthropology and founder of the Department of Anthropology at Lucknow University, the one whose exemplary efforts earned for the department of anthropology at Lucknow University, the esteemed title of "Lucknow School of Anthropology".

After completing Masters in Anthropology, I decided to pursue research towards Ph.D. in Lucknow University. My orientation in tribal studies evoked in me the desire to understand the contemporary situation of the tribes in India—how are they situated in India post 1947; the nature of dual polity in terms of the co-existence of a traditional political system vs the post-1947 modern one, directed by the blue print of the Constitution of India and; the debates around traditional leadership vis-à-vis statutory leadership. Anthropology's emphasis on the integrative nature of culture and the relevance of holistic study drove home to me the significance of anthropology's niche. My reason for pursuing political anthropology is summed up in these lines,

> "Indeed, one of the main insights provided by political anthropologists was always that the "political" cannot be so neatly separated, as the political sphere intersects with social and cultural patterns and practises."

My doctoral thesis is on the political organization of the Bhoksa, a Particularly Vulnerable Tribal Group of Uttarakhand. How political leadership, emerging leaders, latent forces behind the manifested forms of power and authority, channelize and influence the entire gamut of welfare and development, of a vulnerable group became the quest of my research?

The Niche of Anthropology

As I pursued the learning of anthropology, what appealed to me most was the discipline's focus on the field—going deeper into it, the one to one, face to face interaction between the researcher and the respondent. The discipline's focus on culture specific, people specific study, the study of the particular, through intensive, long term ethnographic research, yields the seen as well as the unseen, the manifest as well as the latent facets of the life of a people, and this makes anthropology stand apart from other social sciences. An anthropologist goes much deeper, way beyond taking a bird's-eye view picture of a people, understanding them "from the outside and from the inside".

The idea of doing "barefoot anthropology" has always been my prime focus. Anthropology's emphasis on the grass-roots level empirical study could lead to a vast and deep reservoir of knowledge about human beings. I completely subscribe to that breed of anthropologists who believe that "if Anthropologists have to make politically meaningful contributions to the worlds in which they work they must continue to make the vital connection between knowledge and action". The need of the hour is to do "ethnography that is personally engaged and politically committed". In this ongoing journey of learning and practising anthropology, I kept moving away from the view that the anthropologist should not adopt the

> "part of an administrator, developer, manipulator, 'do gooder'. The anthropologist by virtue of carrying out intensive fieldwork is equipped to construct a policy for the welfare of the people concerned. As a grass-roots level worker, the anthropologist provides the people with tools of effective political participation".

As I continued to be more and more socialized in anthropology, my respect and appreciation for the founding fathers of anthropology of India kept growing for their seminal contribution in putting anthropology of India on the global map. The pioneers of anthropology in India like N.K. Bose, D.N. Majumdar, Irawati Karve, L.P. Vidyarthi, S.C. Dube and others strove to establish the importance of anthropology as a medium of comprehensive and holistic study of a people. All kinds of societies—tribal, non-tribal, rural, urban, came within the purview of their research. While admiring and learning from the established schools of anthropology in Britain and America, they drew attention towards the growth of an anthropology of India which understood, explained and catered to India specific scenario. L.P. Vidyarthi encouraged the anthropologists not to neglect India's "Indianness". A discipline contributes significantly when it is brought down from the ivory towers of mere rhetoric and relates to the people and their lives. D.N. Majumdar, popularized the concept of what is now popularly known as "public anthropology" and in this vein he tried to relate the basic concepts of anthropology to the situation of general public. Credit also goes to him to make anthropology reach out to a large section of people by encouraging writing about anthropology in Hindi. All these stalwarts strove to establish the relevance of Anthropology to the extent and form of inspiring the likes of me to understand anthropology as a way of life.

Teaching Anthropology

When I started teaching anthropology at a Degree College in Lucknow, and later at North-Eastern Hill University, Shillong, I realized that this wonderful discipline is quite underestimated, with talks about its struggle for survival and questions on its relevance being heard off and on. Apart from other factors, one main reason behind this notion is that anthropology is lagging behind in terms of visibility and acceptability, the latter being basically from the perspective of the students. Students, after passing out class twelve, came to seek admission in B.A. and B.Sc. programmes in the college where I was teaching. They were counselled regarding the subjects they could take up. I observed that even after counselling them about anthropology, they were reluctant to take it up. The students who sought admission to B.A. and B.Sc. programmes in the college, hailed primarily from lower economic class. Many among them were first generation graduates in the making. They opted to study subjects like political science, sociology, and history as they had read these in their previous classes, or were familiar with their names. Anthropology was new, unheard of. I had a tough time encouraging students to take up anthropology. Their parents would say, *Madam, yeh anthropology hai kya? Humne to kabhi iska naam nahi suna* (Madam , what is this anthropology? I have never heard of it). When students did take admission in anthropology, it was an uphill task for me and my colleagues to retain them in the discipline. As long as the students learnt about marriage, family and kinship, they were happy and the going was smooth. But when they were introduced to physical anthropology and particularly to the practical course which involved craniometry and cephalometry, many became petrified. They felt that the subject is hard and beyond their ability to cope with. It was left to me and my colleagues to devise interesting pedagogical techniques to make anthropology a student friendly discipline. Our efforts bore fruits and anthropology came to be one of the most respected subjects in the college.

> "While many of us have come to anthropology by choice, there are still some who came to it by accident. However, in my personal interactions, I learnt that there is hardly anyone who though landed up doing anthropology quite by chance than by choice, eventually fell in love with the subject."

In the year 2009 I joined the Department of Anthropology at North-Eastern Hill University, Shillong. Through my interactions with students here, I learnt that though most of them had taken up anthropology only when they did not get admission into their preferred subject like geography or zoology, they had no regrets and were too happy to have come to anthropology.

Exploring Diverse Areas

Being in Shillong for more than a decade now, I feel fortunate to have got the opportunity to observe and understand the north-east from very close quarters. From *kwai* (beetle nut) symbolizing the culture of respect and hospitality in Meghalaya, to a mosaic of myriad cultures within cultures, India's north-east is a fertile ground to do anthropology. Between 2011 and 2016, I was engaged in an international project in collaboration with the universities of Aarhus and Copenhagen at Denmark, and with Kathmandu University, Nepal. This was funded by the international funding agency DANIDA. This dealt with the situation of the Nepalese migrants working in the coal mines of Jaintia Hills in Meghalaya. The prime focus of this research was to look into the three related dimensions of the lives of the coal mine workers—risk, remittance and return to Nepal. Meghalaya has a rich reserve of coal and the state has been in the news for a long time because of its tradition of indulging in illegal, unscientific coal mining known as Rat-hole mining. The research went around the same time when this type of mining was banned by the National Green Tribunal. The study addressed the role of different stakeholders—the government, the non-government organizations, the Jaintia coal mine owners, and the Nepalese migrant labourers working in the coal mines.

After completing the project on the migrant coal mine workers in Meghalaya, I did a sort of *ghar vapasi*, when as a recipient of the UGC Research Award, I returned to my home town Lucknow to carry out my proposed study on the lives of the girl child domestic workers. Our everyday life, and all that goes around us, are realities of life waiting to be explored anthropologically. Urban living has increased the dependency on hired helps. My study on the girl child domestic labour at Lucknow against the back drop of "Beti Bachao, Beti Padhao" tagline addresses the situation of the girls working as "maids" in the houses. How they are situated in a scenario infused with structural and symbolic violence; the responsibility of the government, their parents and employers towards them and how they have agency themselves—these dimensions were explored in this research. Apart from this study on children, some of my other works focus on certain aspects related to children and childhood such as the crucial place of child rearing practices in a culture and the ethics in studying children.

Applied and action anthropology has taken the discipline of anthropology to greater heights. My chance of doing action anthropology came about in a more conclusive way when I was engaged by the National Tiger Conservation Authority, Ministry of Forest and Environment, Government of India, in the capacity of a social science expert in a three-member committee, constituted by the Ministry to look into a village relocation programme. The programme entailed the relocation of entire villages which lay in the Tiger Reserves of Ranthambor and Sariska so as to make more space for the tiger, an endangered species, and also to minimize human-wildlife conflict. This three-member committee had two wild life experts apart from myself and our work was to evaluate the village relocation exercise, to look into the grievances of the villagers and discuss the ground level hindrances in the process of relocation. I carried out intensive fieldwork and our team submitted the evaluation report to the Ministry containing the description of the scenario, our observations, the loop holes in the execution of the programme and suggestions for the redress of grievances.

While different arenas of human living came under the purview of my curiosity which took me to the *field*, what further intrigued me was this art (or science?) of *writing cultures*. How data from the field was worded? My keen indulgence in "Writing Cultures" made way for another bent in the road of doing anthropology. My love for literature and my curiosity to learn where fact ends and fiction begins, where the two overlap and why and how literature can be a significant ethnographic source, led me to explore the engaging relationship between Literature and Ethnography. This genre motivated me further to encapsulate the essence of our dear anthropology in poetry form and this piece became the anthem of World Anthropology Congress organized by United India Anthropology Forum (UIAF) and other partners at Kalinga

Institute of Social Sciences (KISS), Bhubaneshwar from 9-14 August 2023. Sharing here the opening lines of my poem on anthropology:

I am.........Anthropology

I too came,
I too saw,
I too conquered,
but with concern and care
for the multitudes out there.
It's been a long journey
but one worth its toil

I am Anthropology

Called a colonial hand maiden in the bygone days
I steadfastly steered my way
from verandah anthropology to a barefoot one
I arose from the clouds like a bright, determined sun
Attacks made me grow more
Labels made me stronger
For I know my assets and my essence
to name a few—holism, comparison and relativism

Conclusion

Anthropology in India has traversed a long way. Almost two decades back a scholar wrote in *Economic and Political Weekly* that anthropology in India "still follows the colonial anthropologists' footsteps of studying marginalized people". Contrary to this claim, I think, in India, anthropology has for long been conspicuously evolving, going much beyond the study of marginalized people. Anthropology is breaking newer grounds, dealing with topics like migration and diaspora, eco-tourism, social media, people living with HIV (PLHIV), food, and others. At the same time, there is absolutely no reason why anthropologists should be apologetic about continuing to study the marginalized groups. The latter's changing dynamics raises several new questions—whether they are still in the margins or are coming on the centre stage? Who is mainstream and who is sub stream? These are questions which anthropologists are seeking answers to.

Looking back at my journey of reading, learning and doing anthropology for over two decades, I am engulfed with a deep sense of gratitude to anthropology. It would be unfair to say, *I took up anthropology*, because the truth is, *anthropology took me under its wings* and helped me to see human life from a humane perspective. In this journey of doing Anthropology, I experience ultimate truth in this quote by Eric Wolf "Anthropology is the most humanistic of the sciences and the most scientific of the humanities." This exciting journey continues with the blessings of my parents whose unflinching support and unconditional love encouraged me to follow my love for the subject without falling in the traps of meaningless debates about the *scope*, the *market* and the *viability*, of the subject. They very rightly drew home to me the *mantra* that if one sincerely pursues with passion the path of any discipline, limitless avenues will open. The key lies in perseverance, which ensures the successful tiding over the stumbling blocks which are natural impediments in the long and adventurous road of life.

My Books

2014: *Political Organization among the Bhoksa: A Tribe in Turmoil.* New Delhi: Pragun Publications.

2016: *Approaches to the Study of Indian Culture and Society*. New Delhi: Pragun Publications.

31

Autobiography and Contribution to Indian Anthropology

Farhad Mollick

I am currently a Professor in the Department of Anthropology, Mahatma Gandhi Antarrashtriya Hindi Vishwavidyalaya, Wardha, Maharashtra. The Anthropology Department of Mahatma Gandhi Antarrashtriya Hindi Vishwavidyalaya was established in 2009 under the leadership of Professor Nadeem Hasnain. My working experience as a head of the Anthropology Department of Mahatma Gandhi Antarrashtriya Hindi Vishwavidyalaya will always be a memorial to me. In 2011, I became the Head of the Department and continued in this post till 2020. I again took charge as a Department Head in August 2023. I am offered the academic position of Dean in the School of Humanities and Social Sciences. The Department of Anthropology comes under the School of Humanities and Social Sciences in Mahatma Gandhi Antarrashtriya Hindi Vishwavidyalaya. I have also been serving as a Dean of the School of Management since October 2023.

I was born on 3 July 1969 in my maternal village, Kaitha, in Birbhum district in West Bengal. I am the eldest son of Dr

Firojeuddin Mollick and Sitara Mollick. My father was a veterinary doctor in West Bengal. My grandfather, Kamaluddin Mollick, was a member of the West Bengal Judicial Service and one of the landlords of the village named "Kalinagar" of Uluberia in Howrah district. My ancestors migrated here from Mankur in the Burdwan district of West Bengal during the Bargi invasion. I received my earlier education from my paternal village. I passed the matriculation examination from Uluberia High School, the higher secondary examination in science from Uluberia College, and graduated in bio-science from University of Calcutta. For higher studies, I moved to Raipur of Madhya Pradesh in 1989, and it is now in the state of Chhattisgarh. In 1991, I received M.Sc. degree in Anthropology specializing in Social Anthropology from Pt. Ravishankar Shukla University, Raipur, Chhattisgarh. During my study in Social Anthropology, I came in close contact with my great teacher, Surendra Parihar. He influenced me greatly, helped build my personality, and instilled a keen interest in studying social anthropology. The department made a field trip to the "Binjali village" of Narayanpur district of Bastar division in Chhattisgarh, where I did my first anthropological fieldwork on the tribal society.

After obtaining a postgraduate degree in Anthropology from Pt. Ravishankar Shukla University, M.Phil. in Social Anthropology was awarded to me in 1992 by Guru Ghasidas Vishwavidyalaya in Bilaspur district of Chhattisgarh. I had topped the list among all successful candidates. I was then awarded Post Graduate Diploma in Industrial Relation, Labour Welfare and Personnel Management in 1992 from the Department of Management Studies of Guru Ghasidas Vishwavidyalaya. A Gold Medal was awarded to me for securing the top position. I delivered lectures in the Department of Management Studies and the Department of Social Work for several years.

A. Doctoral Work

I did my doctoral work on "Ethnicity and Tribal Unrest: An Anthropological Inquiry into Madhya Pradesh and West Bengal" under the supervision of Professor Bhawani Mohan Mukherjee from Guru Ghasidas Vishwavidyalaya. In 1989, Professor Bhawani Mohan Mukherjee, a well-known anthropologist in India, came to Guru Ghasidas Vishwavidyalaya to build-up a newly established Anthropology and Tribal Development Department as Professor, Head and Dean of the Faculty of Life Science. Before joining as a Professor in Anthropology of Guru Ghasidas Vishwavidyalaya, Professor Mukherjee served as a Reader at Manipur University and lecturer at University of Calcutta. Professor Mukherjee was offered the post of Professor in Anthropology by Mahatma Gandhi Antarrashtriya Hindi Vishwavidyalaya in 2011. I did my Ph.D. work under his guidance. Doctoral degree in Anthropology was awarded to me in 1999. I settled down in Bilaspur after marriage in 1996. My wife, Dr Ghazala Mumtaz Mollick, comes from a family in the Ballia district of Uttar Pradesh. She serves as a system analyst at Guru Ghasidas University, Bilaspur. Her constant support built my career in anthropology and insisted I settle down in Bilaspur and move to Mahatma Gandhi Antarrashtriya Hindi Vishwavidyalaya, Wardha, Maharashtra, to work as a faculty member.

In my doctoral work, I attempted to examine the social vortex theory to study tribal unrest in central India. Social vortex theory deals with social unrest depending on inequality, injustice, and disparity in social and economic aspects. The persistence of inequality, injustice, and exploitation in tribal areas is so considerable that it develops an enormous vortex. The wrath and injustice subsequently gave way to tension and conflict in society. As a result, tribes became agitated, anti-establishment, and wanted autonomy in all respects. Once upon a time, *maharaja* was all in the tribal area. Though he did not belong to their ethnic group, he was always loved and treated next to God. As soon as the princely states were abandoned and the *zamindari* system was abolished, it was left with a vacuum. This vacuum has never been bridged. I think that the Naxalites operate in this vacuum. New administrative and political institutions never fill this vacuum. So, it has to be treated carefully by gradually extending the benefits of development, health care, and education.

The result of my doctoral work was published in several articles on the Socio-Political Movement of the Tribes, namely, "Gond Revivalism and Reintegration" (1999), "Gondwana: Whether Political or Socio-cultural Realty" (1999), "Movements among the Gonds of Chhattisgarh" (2004), "An Anthropological Study on Tribal Unrest" (2007), and "Ethnicity, Social Injustice and Revivalist Movement amongst the Gond in India: Past Trend and Future Perspective" (2014). In my paper "Gond Revivalism and Reintegration," the revivalist movement among the Gond was analyzed. Special emphasis was given to their historical background and the social contact of the Gond with the Hindu society. The movement was designed to restructure the society, reinterpret its own cultural and religious values, and reject the religion and culture of other groups. In another paper on "Gondwana: Whether Political Issue or Socio-cultural Reality" (1999), I examined the Gond organization in historical depth. It was published in the journal *The Anthropologist*, vol. 1, No. 4. The Gond movement looks political, but it has all the merits of social and economic justice in an absolute sense. It has been a process to re-establish some traditional customs and introduce a new set of values reflecting purity in ideology and ritual practises. On the one hand, the revivalists outrightly reject the Hindu culture and religion, and they tend to discard their age-old drinking habits on the other. Hence, neo-tribalism is gradually emerging.

B. Career in Anthropology

After obtaining my M.Phil. degree in anthropology, I did fieldwork in various research projects like the "Monographic study of Birhor and Pando" sponsored by Indira Gandhi Rashtriya Manav Sangrahalaya and "Displacement and Rehabilitation in Coal field's areas of South Eastern Coalfield Limited", under the guidance of Professor Mukherjee. My paper on "Impact of Displacement on Tribal Economy" was selected for the "XVth Madhya Pradesh Young Scientist Award" in 2000. It was organized by Rajiv Gandhi Prodyogiki Vishwavidyalaya, Bhopal, in association with the

Madhya Pradesh Council of Science and Technology on 29-30 July 2000. Another paper on "Displacement and Resettlement: Relocates of Gevra Area" with the joint authorship of Professor Mukherjee was published in *Man and Life* 26 (3&4) in 2000. Here, we have examined rehabilitation policy intending to minimize the adverse of the project on the host communities.

In 2004, I was appointed as a Lecturer in the Department of Anthropology and Tribal Development at Guru Ghasidas Vishwavidyalaya and served in this post till 2010. In 2009, Guru Ghasidas Vishwavidyalaya was upgraded to a central university. In 2010, I moved to Mahatma Gandhi Antarrashtriya Hindi Vishwavidyalaya, another central university in Wardha, Maharashtra, to work with Professor Nadeem Hasnain, then Pro-Vice-Chancellor of the University and Head of the Department. I joined as a Reader in Anthropology. Mahatma Gandhi Antarrashtriya Hindi Vishwavidyalaya promoted me to Associate Professor in 2013 and Professor of Anthropology in 2016. Since its inception, the anthropology department has established a distinguished identity as a promising centre of tribal studies in a relatively short period. I was invited as a Speaker and Panelist in a workshop on "FRA, 2006-its implication" as a part of the National Tribal Carnival-2016 organized by the Ministry of Tribal Affairs, New Delhi. It was inaugurated by the Hon'ble Prime Minister at Indira Gandhi Indoor Stadium. My speech brought on the challenges in implementing the Forest Rights Act while bringing out the protective rights granted under the Forest Rights Act (FRA).

C. Research Project

My interest in the study of tribal health was reflected when I directed a project on "Cultural Context and Environmental Dimension of Baiga Health" financed by the Chhattisgarh Council of Science and Technology in 2006. It was followed by another project on "Health Status among Baiga" sponsored by the Ministry of Tribal Affairs, New Delhi, in 2012. Here, I evaluated their health status by highlighting the socio-economic variables of health. I also examined the cultural aspect of health to understand their knowledge system about health care and the constraints in implementing health care services in those areas. The article entitled "Child and Mother Health among Baiga: A Particularly Vulnerable Tribal Group of Chhattisgarh" (2020) was published in the *Indian Journal of Research in Anthropology* (vol. 6, no. 2). Here, I have mentioned the need to implement government-sponsored development programmes quite seriously in tribal areas to achieve Sustainable Development Goals.

My interest in tribal rights appeared when the University Grants Commission allowed me to conduct project work on "Wildlife Conservation and Issues of Tribal Right". I conducted intensive fieldwork in the tribal areas of Melghat Tiger Reserve in Maharashtra and Achanakmar Tiger Reserve in Chhattisgarh. The finding of the study was published in a paper under the title of "Conservation, Displacement and Tribal Right: An Anthropological Study on Tribal Issues in Achanakmar Tiger Reserve" published in the *Indian Journal of Research in Anthropology*, vol. 2, no.1, 2016. I applied this approach in the study of *Human Rights and Right to Health* (2012), *Tribal Rights over Forest and Land* (2014), *Tribal Rights on Land: Policy, Practices and Perspective* (2015), and *Displacement and Tribal Rights: A Study on Forest Dweller in Melghat Tiger Reserve* (2018) also.

D. Academic Contribution as a Head of the Department

I served as the Head of the Anthropology Department for about nine years, from March 2011 to March 2020. The Department of Anthropology, being the second Department of Anthropology in Maharashtra, was established in the Mahatma Gandhi Antarrashtriya Hindi Vishwavidyalaya under the guidance of Professor Nadeem Hasnain and with the keen interest of Shri Vibhuti Narain Rai, the then Vice-Chancellor of the University, in 2009. A large number of tribal populations and diverse tribal groups reside within 50 to 300 km of Wardha. The demographics of tribes paved the way for establishing the Department of Anthropology at Wardha. The department aims to explore the cultural issues of tribes from historical and contemporary perspectives and research the life and culture of the tribes of central India.

The project proposal on "Research and Documentation on Traditional Healing Practices among the Kolam and Madia Gond" was submitted to the Tribal Research and Training Institute (TRTI), Pune, Maharashtra, when I was the Head of the Department. TRTI sanctioned about Rs. 30 lakh to the department to work on Traditional Healing Practices among the nine tribal communities of the Vidarbha region of Maharashtra. The project aims to study the tribal belief system concerning disease and illness and determine its etiology and indigenous treatment methods. Ayushman Bharat's scheme emphasizes the need to integrate traditional and scientific knowledge to prevent and treat disease for sustainable options. The Astana Declaration (2018) also states that integrating scientific and traditional knowledge would strengthen primary health care. It will improve health outcomes and ensure access for all people to the proper care at the right time and at the most appropriate level of care. The Declaration emphasizes the importance of Primary Health Care (PHC) as an essential component of Universal Health Coverage (UHC). UHC has been adopted as a strategy to achieve the Sustainable Development Goal (SDG) by 2030. Health is one of the essential goals of SDG and its place in its centre. Therefore, the project includes the study of the cultural context of health and the nature of the local healing system.

E. Ethnographic Tribal Museum and Exhibition

In this context, the department planned to develop an Ethnographic Tribal Museum focusing on the tribal culture of central India in 2013. The museum's theme was decided with the fulfilment of the department's mission in view. Shri Vibhuti Narain Rai was the source of inspiration for establishing the museum at the university. The museum was developed through the remarkable efforts of Professor Bhawani Mohan Mukherjee. It is aimed at documenting and preserving cultural information, resources, knowledge and tradition, arts and crafts, musical instruments, and the material existence of different communities. A unique feature of this museum is that it shows the indigenous knowledge system used by the different ethnic groups for their subsistence using locally available materials. Ethnographic specimens of various tribal groups have been displayed to highlight their economic pursuits and depict the culture of tribal groups in central India. Ethnographic specimens and implements of cultural information, economic pursuits, arts and crafts, ornaments, and musical instruments are collected from different parts of tribal areas in central India during the fieldwork by the students. Tribal culture has also been depicted in the museum by tribal photographs of their house type, jewellary, musical instruments, dress and ornament, hunting and agricultural implements.

The museum is one of the important centres for research in various branches of knowledge, particularly in anthropology and ethnology. In continuation of its importance, the department organized attractive exhibitions associated with the Anthropological Survey of India for mass and cultural education. "Bio-cultural Evolution of Man and Tribal Culture" was exhibited on 5-7 September 2013 with the remarkable support and interest of Shri Vibhuti Narain Rai, the then Vice-Chancellor of the university. Professor Rajnish Kumar Shukla, the then Vice-Chancellor of the University, inaugurated another exhibition on "Human Origin, Evolution and Bio-cultural Diversity" on 16-19 September 2019 for the local people and students of the schools at Wardha. Museum artifacts were displayed to understand the tribal culture and the evolution of man by exhibiting models of earlier human species, displaying economic pursuits of hunting, gathering and agricultural implements, showing ornaments and musical instruments, and presenting the sketches, text and tribal photographs.

F. Seminar Organized and Publication

The department organized a couple of national seminars and completed a good number of research projects to examine contemporary tribal issues and retrieve comprehensive knowledge about the diverse groups of tribal people inhabiting different ecological settings in the country. A National Seminar on "Tribal People of Central India: Problems and Prospects" was organized on 19-20 March 2012, in collaboration with the Anthropological Survey of India, Ministry of Tribal Affairs, and Indian Council of Social Science Research. I was the convener of the seminar. Dr B.D. Sharma, the Former Commissioner for Scheduled Castes and Tribes, played a crucial role in the inaugural session of the seminar. Another national seminar on "Tribal Unrest in Central India: Causes and Challenges" was organized on 26-27 August 2013 by the department in collaboration with the Indian Council of Social Science Research and Indira Gandhi Rashtriya Manav Sangrahalaya. It aimed to bring together academia, bureaucrats, activists, police officials, artists, and other stakeholders to provide multiple voices in debating the issue of tribal unrest. Professor P.C. Joshi, the former Vice-Chancellor of the University of Delhi, commented that tribal unrest and insurgency are generally avoided in anthropological discussions. It is quite a bold step that the Anthropology Department has decided to discuss the issue of tribal unrest. Shri Vibhuti Narain Rai, then the Vice-Chancellor of the university, delivered the Presidential address, the Keynote address by Professor Nadeem Hasnain, and the Valedictory speech by Professor P. Venkata Rao (Hyderabad University). K. Vijay Kumar, Advisor to the Home Ministry for the Left Wing Extremism areas, was invited as a chief guest of the seminar. The importance of such a seminar to update knowledge in the emerging areas of research interest in the tribal revolution was highlighted in the speeches given by Professor R. Shiva Prasad (Hyderabad University), Dr Joseph Bara (JNU), Dr Ramdas D. Gambhir, Dr Vijay P. Sharma, Prafulla Samantra (NAPM, Odisha), Professor S. Kolay (Bastar University), and many others in the academic session of tribal movement through the ages, land alienation and over industrialization, politico-religious causes and policy issues, and contemporary problems and threat to existence.

I also convened a national seminar on "Displacement, Environment and Tribal Life" in collaboration with Indian Council of Social Science Research (ICSSR) on 16-17 April 2016. The seminar focused on the impact of displacement on the ecology, livelihood, socio-economic and cultural life of the tribal people. Also, it highlighted how the enforced involuntary displacement leads to social exclusion and various impoverishment risks. Professor Girishwar Mishra, the then Vice-Chancellor of the University, chaired the seminar's inaugural session. Professor Vinay Kumar Srivastava (Former Director of the Anthropological Survey of India) delivered the Keynote address. Professor P. Venkata Rao presented the Valedictory address. Professor P.C. Joshi delivered a special lecture on "Natural Resources, Environmental Protection and Right of Scheduled Tribe Communities" and Professor R. Shiva Prasad on "Who can Protect the Crop if Fence Eats It: The Plight of the Resources and Livelihoods of the Tribal and Rural Poor".

As a Course Director, I organized a three-day workshop, in association with the Indian Council of Social Science Research (ICSSR), on the Methodological Perspective of Ethnographic Research on 11-13 March 2019 for the research scholars of social sciences. The workshop aimed to enable the researchers to understand ethnographic research methods and increase their skill and competence in collecting and analyzing ethnographic data. Professor Girishwar Mishra (eminent psychologist) delivered a lecture on the "interdisciplinary relevance of ethnographic research", and Professor S.N. Chaudhary spoke on the "challenges of ethnographic research". Professor P.C. Joshi focused on *Field Research in Ethnography*, Professor Ram Gambhir on FieldWork methods, and Professor D.P. Singh (TISS, Mumbai) on the "observation method in ethnography". Ratna Dhar (ANSI, Nagpur) and Mohan Kanti Gautam (Netherlands) highlighted the importance of fieldwork in ethnographic research. The workshop was so designed that it was pretty helpful in understanding the critical aspects of the ethnographic method and anthropological perspective to avoid biases at the time of ethnographic writing. I am currently working on the cultural significance of Mohua in tribal culture and identity issues of Neo-Buddhists.

My Books

2014: *Tribal People of Central India: Problems and Prospects* (with B.M. Mukherjee). New Delhi: K.K. Publication.
2014: *Madhya Bharat Ke Adivasi Samasya Evam Sambhavanaye* (with B.M. Mukherjee). New Delhi: K.K. Publication.
2015: *Adivasi Ashanti: Karan Chunautiyan Evam Sambhavanaye* (with B.M. Mukherjee). New Delhi: K.K. Publication.
2016: *Tribal Unrest in Central India: Causes, Challenges and Possibilities* (with B.M. Mukherjee). New Delhi: K.K. Publication.
2018: *Development, Displacement & Tribal Life*. New Delhi: K.K. Publication.
2019: *Vikash Paryavaran Aur Adivasi Samaj* (with Roopesh Kumar). New Delhi: K.K. Publication.

32

My Journey

Mini Bhattacharyya Thakur

After completing my schooling in Guwahati, I had a couple of months of free time. In that lazy summer of 1978, upon reading a seemingly random array of books, the seeds of my interest in anthropology were sown. One such book was *Roots: The Saga of an American Family*, a 1976 novel by Alex Haley. The book depicted the story of how Kunta Kinte, an eighteenth century boy was sold into slavery in Africa and transported to North America. The book followed his traumatic journey and then proceeded to depict the lives of Kinte's descendants in the United States. This book captured my interest especially because of how it drew on genealogy and created a narrative of heritage and culture. It created a world of thought within me and generated curiosity about anthropology.

That summer, a meeting with Professor Sashi Dhar Goswami, the then head of the anthropology department at Cotton College, a good friend of my father, had also proved to be fortuitous. Professor Goswami passionately advised me to take up the subject arguing that anthropology was such a discipline that provided a balanced understanding of a particular society "based on its own merit". This resonated with my belief that every society is respectable and each has its own good principles as well. He also mentioned that anthropology was the only subject that could "make the familiar exotic and the exotic familiar" by decoding the uniqueness of different cultures. Impressed by such encounters—the story of Kunta Kinte and his descendants on one hand, and Professor S.D. Goswami, on the other—I took up anthropology for my undergraduate studies in Cotton College, Guwahati in 1978 along with three other subjects.

My years in Cotton College were spent learning the basics of the subject from people like Hari Prasad Mishra who made learning Prehistoric Anthropology so very interesting. And Professor S.D. Goswami, an alumnus of Lucknow University, used to teach physical anthropology. Both of them, provided me with requisite stimuli to continue with anthropology. My teachers in Cotton College took great interest in our acquiring the essence of the subject along with expectations of getting good grades. With their push, and some hard work on my part, I managed to top Gauhati University not only in anthropology (which admittedly was only offered in a few colleges at the time) but also got the highest marks among all arts graduates in 1982.

Given my grades and aspirations to pursue anthropology further, I decided to go to University of Delhi as it was known to be (and I might add, still is) one of the most prestigious anthropology programmes in India. However, this was when the Assam Movement spearheaded by All Assam Student's Union was at its peak. Given our duties as politically conscious students, I along with my classmates wholeheartedly participated in this agitation resulting in sacrificing one academic year.

So, after graduating from Cotton College with a two-year B.A. degree and a brief interlude at the recently instituted North-Eastern Hill University Shillong, I finally started my M.Sc. in anthropology in University of Delhi in 1983 after completing a year-long bridge course at University of Delhi. The department was beautifully located with the university garden in the front and the stately Vice- Chancellor's office complex in the right flank. It was a sea change from what I was used to. My earlier experience had conveyed that while anthropology was a proud and useful field of study, the departments were nevertheless relegated to dingy corners of some building. This conveyed a message that in the symbolic hierarchy of disciplines anthropology was nowhere at the top of the pecking order. However, in University of Delhi, the department occupied a place at the very core of the university campus. Immediately, for a new student like me, this was not only a source of pride but also a vindication of my belief in the discipline that I had come to cherish.

The University of Delhi Anthropology Department offered specializations in almost every major sub discipline and every teacher was a legend in their own right. I was fortunate to have been taught by Professors I.P. Singh, J.D. Mehra, S.C. Tiwari, D.K. Bhattacharyya, Vinay K. Srivastava, V.C. Channa, J.S. Bhandari, I.S. Marwah, S. Nath, S. Tara Devi, P.K. Seth, Swadesh Seth, H.K. Kumbhnani, A.K. Kapoor and Satwanti Kapoor. The M.Sc. programme was 2-years long where one could specialize in physical, sociocultural and archaeological anthropology. I opted for sociocultural branch. In my second year, when one had the liberty of selecting from many optional papers, I remember taking up courses in Indian prehistory, tribal society and peasant culture in India.

Our fieldwork for the M.Sc. dissertation was an unforgettable trip. That year in 1985, Professors I.S. Marwah and Vinay Kumar Srivastava were assigned to conduct and supervise our fieldwork. It was decided that we were going to Nagaland to study the Angami Nagas of Jotsoma village. Professor J.D. Mehra came to see us off at the station and brought boxes of pastries from Wenger's, the famous cakeshop of Connaught Place in Delhi. Mehra sir did not provide any last-minute wisdom on fieldwork but asked us to soak in the experience of the field in the company of our friends. That is how the nine students (all of girls) specializing in sociocultural anthropology, accompanied by two teachers and a field assistant, Mr Jagdish, boarded the (rather slow) Brahmaputra Mail to Guwahati. Thankfully, the journey took only a little more than two days.

The journey from Guwahati, however, was another story! On reaching Guwahati, in the morning of day 3, the whole team went to visit Kamakhya Temple as arranged by my father. After enjoying an Assamese lunch, we again boarded the train to Dimapur, Nagaland, in the evening. Early next morning, we travelled about 75 km by road, soaking in the breathtaking scenery along the NH 29. After about three hours, we reached Jotsoma village near Kohima, which was to be our home for the next three weeks. The following morning our contact person Professor Renu Suri arranged a few students from Kohima Science College and some people from Jotsoma village to take us around the village and act as interpreters.

This was our first learning-by-doing: we learnt that anthropological fieldwork involves not only lengthy and first-hand observation of social life in the field site but it also (consciously or unconsciously) equips us to deal with uncertainty. Further, and relatedly, we learnt to develop sensitivity and appreciation for "other cultures" (whereby, inevitably one sees similarities in addition to differences) and develop skills in data collection using genealogy, interviews, etc. Fieldwork is also an act of social and personal development, personal learning and thinking skills such as independent enquiry, critical thinking, decision making and teamworking.

By participating in the daily life of the people, the fieldworker builds up a progressively deeper understanding of what the social reality is. For many fieldworkers, and especially for me, field experiences gained in Nagaland and later on in various places in Assam and north-eastern region throughout my career as an anthropologist, has not only been professionally enriching but also personally transformative.

After completing Masters with a First class from University of Delhi and specializing in Social Anthropology, I joined the Ph.D. programme under the supervision of Professor J.S. Bhandari who was interested in issues of identity in north-east India and who conducted his doctoral work among the Misings (a Scheduled Tribe community) of Assam. I opted to study the

Deori community of Assam and identity formation. At this stage, I was awarded the Junior Research Fellowship from the University Grants Commission, which included financial support to conduct fieldwork in Narayanpur village located in what was Lakhimpur district at that time. The Deoris are a Scheduled Tribe (plains) community from whose society is usually thought to have four subdivisions: Dibongiya, Tengaponia, Patorgoyia and Borgoyia. Amongst them, only the Dibongiyas have retained their dialect. They are largely concentrated in the north bank of the Brahmaputra River, distributed in Lakhimpur, Sonitpur, Dhemaji and in the Majuli islands. Historical and scholarly works define Deoris as a subsection of the Chutia community of Assam and also as a part of the larger Ahom community. This narrative was unacceptable to the Deoris of Narayanpur area. Given this view by the community in Narayanpur, I was keen that my research should take another look at the origin of the Deoris and their affiliation and relation with the Chutias and the Ahoms at large. Unfortunately, I could not complete this work due to logistical reasons. I could, however, write two publications from this research work.

In the August of 1988, I was appointed as a Lecturer in Gauhati University. I was honoured to share this professional space with some of the big names in anthropology of the north-east: B.M. Das, A.C. Bhagabati, T.C. Sharma, Priya Bala Das, D.N. Majumdar, Renuka Das to name a few. During this phase, I could gain valuable experiences through seminars, classes and discussions with my colleagues. Also due to the professional networks of B.M. Das and A.C. Bhagabati, we could interact with numerous scholars of repute from within the country and abroad who visited our department and delivered lectures.

It was here in Gauhati University, as a young Lecturer, I decided to re-start my Ph.D., this time, registering under Professor A.C. Bhagabati. My work was related to urban enterprises of street food vending in the city of Guwahati. The Ph.D. thesis "Street Food Vending in Urban Guwahati: An Anthropological Appraisal" traced the emergence of street foods in the urban precincts of Guwahati city in Assam. This doctoral work, completed in 1998, to my mind is perhaps the first of its kind in India, though work on the informal street vendors have been conducted across the world. My study highlighted how eating of prepared foods on the streets began to be socially accepted breaking barriers of caste restrictions linked to cooked food. Street foods which are popular edibles sold in almost every country of the world; encompassing anything sold on the streets that can be eaten without further processing. History says that eating of ready-to-eat cooked food on the streets has been in practise since the dawn of civilization. Today more than 2.3 billion people across the world consume street foods on a daily basis. Thus, this study revealed many aspects related to food, including concepts of cooking and eating and also that a large section of people, not necessarily the "poor" depended on such foods. In fact, such foods have become an indispensable part of urban life.

I understood street food vendors as a "community" in anthropological sense. Their economic and sociocultural contribution along with their plight, problems and journeys provided scope for much activism on my part to support their cause for legitimacy and recognition in urban planning and policy making. So, linking myself with local NGOs like the Society for Social Transformation and Environmental Protection (SSTEP) and the National Alliance of Street Vendors, India (NASVI), I attempted to create awareness among vendors and other stakeholders in the city. Through these collaborations and activities, I could clearly see how anthropology has contributed, and can contribute, to social policy research, practise and advocacy in a number of different ways.

Though anthropologists have generally had less influence than experts from other discipline such as economists in influencing policy, there are a number of ways in which we have made our opinions known. For example, anthropologists, by documenting the conditions of the peoples we study, or by taking up the role as their advocates, have shown how good academic research can have relevance for the society. Confined to the ivory towers of knowledge, gathering dust in the shelves of the library, a research study can have little value, in my opinion. Given these moorings, in my professional life, I have often tried to generate an applied angle to most of my work. It has been my earnest endeavour to utilize my theoretical readings and field experiences and put them to good work. In 2009, I had the opportunity to participate in a government scheme called Upgradation of Quality of Street Foods, sponsored by the Ministry of Food Processing Industries, GOI and the Guwahati Municipal Corporation (GMC). This scheme proposed a number of benefits to the street vendors along with improving hygiene, creating vending zones, licensing, etc. In this context, I undertook a Knowledge, Attitudes and Practices (KAP) study to help GMC understand needs of street food vendors so that the scheme could be effectively implemented. A Detailed Project Report was also submitted to GMC.

Since the 1970s, across the globe, the opportunities for anthropologists to work as short-term consultants for governmental and non-governmental agencies have expanded rapidly. This was true of north-east India as well. In 2005, I worked as part of an expert team to evaluate an externally-funded development project funded by the International Fund for Agricultural Development (IFAD) in the states of Manipur, Meghalaya and Assam. This external evaluation mission had five experts, each being a specialist having domain knowledge on agriculture, livelihoods, upland cultivation techniques, project implementation and gender and community development. To evaluate the progress of the project, we undertook extensive field visits to some of the most remote areas of the region. These visits have given me a rich experience of the life of the people. I also gained valuable insight on how anthropology can support project implementation with special reference to role and participation of women in such projects. Participation of anthropologists or sociologists in such projects were made mandatory in recognition of the unique inputs of such social scientists being invaluable specially to understand unexpected consequences, gendered impact and how projects interacted with existing social dynamics of an area. The use and application of anthropological theory, traditional anthropological approaches to fieldwork and the capacity for providing an emic perspective have given anthropologists the sensitivity to understand people at the grassroots.

Similarly, I was invited to advice the Institutional Capacity Development Consultancy team of The Guwahati Water Supply Project funded by Japan International Cooperation Agency (JICA) as a Social Development Expert on just and equitable distribution of drinking water in the slum areas of the Guwahati city. These experiences have broadened my horizon of anthropology and was even more convinced to apply academic knowledge to real life situations. Another challenging work that I undertook was to design Tribal Safeguard Plans for development projects in Tripura and Sikkim for a World Bank funded rural development project and in Meghalaya for an education related project for youth. The safeguard plans would ensure that the proposed development projects do not adversely affect the livelihoods and culture of the indigenous tribals.

These experiences that I gained had its benefits of a larger experience that supplemented in teaching and guiding research scholars at the Gauhati University. At our department, we have a Ph.D. programme in all three branches of anthropology. My field of research interest has been centered on issues relating to food and nutrition, health and health seeking behaviour, informal street vendors and culture. So far, I have had the good fortune to work with ten candidates who have successfully received their Ph.D. degrees under my supervision and eight more are in the various stages of completion. In addition, one student also completed her post- doctoral work under my supervision.

In 2014, I became the Head of Department at Gauhati university and in the three-year tenure, I was able to organize two national seminars and a regional workshop. In addition, my department was awarded UGC Special Assistance Programme-DRS-I in 2016 and for two years I coordinated the programme which had two thrust areas of Tangible and Intangible Cultural Heritage and Population Ageing and Growth and studied the Tiwa and Karbi populations in Kamrup, Morigaon and Karbi Anglong districts of Assam.

Looking back now to the summer of 1978 when I decided to pursue anthropology in Cotton College, I remember a sense of excitement at the prospect of studying this subject. Now, after many decades working as an anthropologist, I am glad to report that research in anthropology—and indeed there is so much vibrant work in the discipline these days—still fills me with the same excitement and interest.

My Books

2017: Sarit K. Chaudhuri & Mini Bhattacharyya Thakur (eds.) *Cultural Heritage of Assam*. New Delhi: Indira Gandhi Rashtriya Manav Sangrahalaya, Bhopal & Gyan Publishing House.

2022: *Street Food Vending in Urban Assam: An Anthropological Appraisal*. New Delhi: Gyan Publishing House.

33

Autobiography

Mithun Sikdar

Nothing disturbs a person than to remember his own life experiences and to share it in an open forum in the form of an autobiography. But when it comes out of an invitation from one of the famous anthropologists of India it becomes a part of yearning. The yearning erupted out of the invitation received from Professor P.C. Joshi on 8 February 2022 and that too when the name of Professor V.K. Srivastava was attached to it. My endeavour won't be an academic one; rather I shall be carrying out my duty targeting the aspirants of anthropology who may think anthropology as a subject doesn't have many prospects. Frankly speaking, Anthropology not only gave me subsistence but also the ability to think about every aspect of life very minutely.

Early life, Education, Family, Taking Anthropology as a Subject

I was born on 1 November 1979 at my maternal grandfather's house situated in a small town Bilashipara under Dhubri District, Assam. My mother Late Ratna Sikdar was a homemaker whereas my father late Uma Prasad Sikdar was a civil servant and was working as Assistant Superintendent under the National Sample Survey Organisation. My maternal grandfather Late Haridas

Bhowmik was the Headmaster in a local school and was well recognized in the town for generously defraying his entire post-retirement gratuity amount to establish a girls' school in the town. My maternal grandmother Late Usha Rani Bhowmik hailed from the famous Bose family of Kolkata. She was the niece of Dr Prafulla Chandra Ghosh, the first Chief Minister of West Bengal and one of the earliest doctorate holders in Chemistry from the University of Calcutta. My paternal grandfather Late Priyanath Sikdar hailed from the Pabna district of present-day Bangladesh and worked as a tax inspector under Khan Bahadur Abdul Latif during the British period and was posted in Mankachar, Assam where he got settled after the Indo-Bangladesh partition. My paternal grandmother Late Suprava Sikdar was a homemaker and was a very pious lady. In 1978, my father got his posting in Dibrugarh where I shared almost my initial thirty years. I got my first six years of schooling from Sister Nivedita School, an English medium School in Dibrugarh. With constant support from my parents, I used to stand first in the entire class. After six years of schooling, I was shifted to a vernacular Bengali medium school named Dibrugarh Bengali High School where I had to struggle a lot to cope with the new medium of instruction. My performance graph used to shudder in the new atmosphere but I could come out with First Division in the class tenth exam. I was gifted with mathematical skills from my parents and could secure a very high percentage in the tenth exam. I got admitted to Kanoi College, Dibrugarh in the science stream but never had the opportunity to study anthropology until my bachelor's degree. It was Professor Arun Dutta, Department of Physics, Kanoi College who suggested me to take anthropology at my graduation. It was Professor D.K. Limbu from Kanoi College (now at NEHU) who was instrumental in developing my interest in anthropology. In 2008 I married an anthropologist turned teacher Mrs Ivy Sikdar and we are blessed with one girl child Miss Rudrani Sikdar. My only younger brother Sri Soumen Sikdar has achieved success as Administrative Officer under the Life Insurance Corporation of India.

Doctoral Work, Teachers, Fieldwork, and Early Career

I completed my graduation taking honours in anthropology but I had to leave anthropology to get early employment through a professional course. I cracked the All India Management Aptitude test and got selected for several good management institutes across India. But I had to come back leaving everything in-between due to the sudden demise of my father. I had no other alternative but to look for a job in Dibrugarh itself to take care of my mother and younger brother. I started to do different trifling jobs along with taking up home tutorials. But my love for academics triggered me to take up further studies and here I got full support from my mother. After a year gap, I got admitted to Masters in anthropology from Dibrugarh University. I have seen my father as a great fieldworker as he was attached to the field operation division under NSSO and as such I found fieldwork tradition in anthropology very much captivating. I have been very fond of reading since my childhood and whenever I used to get pocket money from my parents it was ever laid out to books only. This practice has never let me down and helped me in every aspect of life. I was taught by the most fascinating teachers in my Master's degree. They were Professor Ramendra Kumar Kar, Professor Farida Ahmed Das, Professor Indira Barua, Professor Sarthak Sengupta, Professor Nitul Kumar Gogoi, Professor Deepanjana Dutta Das, Professor Dwipen Bezbaruah (now at Guwahati University) and Dr Hari Chandra Mahanta. It was a great learning experience from each of my teachers as they specialized in different sub-fields of anthropology. I continue to enjoy the guidance from all of my teachers as I was selected as a Fellow under SAP(DRS) project immediately after my postgraduation. At SAP-DRS project I worked on the project "Hemoglobinopathies in North-east India". It allowed me to work on the molecular genetics of abnormal Hemoglobin E in different population groups of north-east India. Further, I enrolled myself with Professor Farida Ahmed Das to work on the bio-social determinants of growth and nutritional status of Mishing children, one of the largest tribal populations of Assam. My doctoral thesis intended to understand the impact of perennial floods and their associated socio-economic factors on the nutritional status of Mishing children. I got the centrally administered Doctorate Fellowship from ICSSR to complete my Ph.D. thesis. Both projects allowed me to understand different aspects of anthropological analysis both at a molecular anthropological level as well as classical anthropological level. At that time two eminent anthropologists from India, Professor Surinder Nath from University of Delhi and Professor Tulika Sen from the University of Calcutta were the Subject Experts for the DRS, SAP Project. As such I got the opportunity to interact with these two eminent personalities quite often. During my doctorate work, I was blessed to have a mentor like Professor Farida Ahmed Das who was more like my parent than my guide. It was the time when I enjoyed the formative phase of my anthropology career.

Seminal Contribution to Anthropology, Important Papers and Books

In the initial phase of my career, I started writing up anthropology news in the local newspapers, the first one came out in Assam Tribune way back in 2006 on the scope of Molecular Anthropology in north-east India. My first research article was published in the Bulletin of the Department of Anthropology, Dibrugarh University in 2006 on the physical growth progression of the adult Bengali population of Dibrugarh. It was the outcome of my M.Sc. final year dissertation. It was followed by several articles in different national and international journals. To name a few, the traditional phytotherapy among the Nath community of Assam, the matrilineal marriage system among the Garo population of Assam, and many more. As SAP-DRS Fellow at Dibrugarh University, I was involved in the project on Hemoglobinopathies in north-east India with special reference to selective advantage where I was able to screen the abnormal hemoglobin in different populations of north-east India.

The year 2009 was celebrated as the Darwin Centenary year. As a student of anthropology, I wanted to give tribute to Darwin. His notable contribution was on natural selection and there was no other alternative for me but to think about anthropological input on natural selection. I came out with a new formula where I could deduce the force of natural selection acting on different population groups. I sent the formula to be evaluated in the *Journal Human Biology* published from USA. To my utter surprise, they accepted the formula after a review of six months. I tried to validate the formula on the Mishing tribal population of north-east India where I was doing my Ph.D. and the results were interesting. Immediately I sent a drafted paper for contesting the Young Scientist Award in the Indian Science Congress Association in 2009. After initial screening and presentation, I was selected as a Young Scientist Awardee. Later the paper was published in *Anthropologischer Anziger*, Germany. I had the opportunity to work among different population groups in India. In north-east India, I worked among different tribal as well as caste populations like the Sonowal Kacharis, Mishings, Morans, Apatanis, Garos, Mundas, tea garden communities, Tai-Khamti, and Tai-Khamiyang. There was a possibility for extensive research on the abnormal hemoglobin in north-east India. I tried to veer the attention of the academia on this issue in the form of a review article that got published in the journal *Anthropological Review* published from Poland.

While posted in Western Regional Centre at Udaipur, I was fortunate to work and contribute significantly towards understanding the genetic landscape of western India, particularly on the Saharia, the only PVTG of Rajasthan, and the Siddis, a PVTG from Gujarat of African origin. I had the chance to work among other population groups of western India like Garasia, Mathur, Dubla, Meena, Gadia Lohar, etc. where I could find the diverse sociocultural and biological characteristics working towards their adaptation. I was able to identify the dynamics of the interaction of different molecular biological markers like GSTM1 and GSTT1 towards understanding the dynamics of susceptibility to cancer in different population groups of western India which was published in the *Journal of Genetics*, one of the oldest journals of genetics.

It was with the mentorship of then Director Professor K.K. Mishra that Anthropological Survey of India started the project on Biocultural Diversity, Environment, and Sustainable Development. It was the restudy of the Indian villages studied earlier by the renowned anthropologists. I was fortunate to study the village studied by Professor A.M. Shah, i.e. Radhvanaj in Gujarat. I was also able to study the village called Nana Sanja studied by the Census of India in 1961 under the village survey monograph. During the same period, two other national projects were running simultaneously. One is type-2 diabetes in western India and DNA polymorphism in the contemporary human population, the reports of the same have been submitted to the government archives.

In 2015, Sanskriti, the North Eastern Institute of Culture and Religion, Guwahati conferred me with Professor B.M. Das award for which I delivered a memorial lecture. The same year the Department of Anthropology, at University of Delhi invited me for a talk at the national seminar on Anthropology of Cardiometabolic Adversities where I delivered a lecture on ethical issues for the research on cardiometabolic adversities: an anthropological perspective. In 2023, I received the young researcher award in World Anthropology Congress at Bhubaneswar.

There was a vast array of techniques available to define the socio-economic status of a particular population while conducting socio-economic surveys in health research. To minimize the variations, I tried to update Prasad's socio-economic classification for conducting health surveys which got published in Biolife, USA. In the meantime, I published a lot of papers arising out from my Ph.D. thesis which focuses on long-term environmental adaptations in terms of the human physical growth process.

Besides, I am working as the Associate Editor of the *Journal of Anthropological Survey of India* and *Plos One*. I am also working as the Editorial Broad member of *Annals of Anthropological Research and Reviews* published from Sidho-Kanho-Birsha University. I have two books to my credit. The first one appeared as an edited volume in 2015 with the contribution of more than twenty scholars across the globe. The foreword was written by none other than the famous pediatrician and then editor of the journal *Anthropologischer Anziger* Professor Michele Hermannusen. I was fortunate to be a part of the project "DNA Polymorphism among contemporary human population". Under this project we could complete the entire mitochondrial as well as Y-DNA sequence from seventy-five population groups across India. The full volume of the entire exercise was published in 2021 as a book through Springer.

Professor Vinay Kumar Srivastava had a great role in shaping my career further in the Anthropological Survey of India. His way of perceiving things gave a new stimulus to contribute in different ranges under the anthropological domain. I have contributed recently an article regarding my discernment of the different philosophies of Mahatma Gandhi which was published in *Oriental Anthropologist*. I was working with the project on epigenetics of human disease and migration. I am the Principal Coordinator of the national project undertaken by the Anthropological Survey of India on Gut microbiome genomic diversity among PVTGs of India. Apart from putting effort into contributing in research articles, I used to contribute to anthropology blogs on different online platforms.

Administrative and Institution Building

I joined the Anthropological Survey of India as an Assistant Anthropologist (Physical). It was not surprising for me to shoulder a number of administrative responsibilities for being joined as a Gazetted Officer. Immediately after joining I was given the charge of drawing and disbursing officer which allowed me to explore new financial responsibilities. I was also given the charge of chairman (purchase committee) and Officer-in-Charge, CPWD. Through these assignments, I was able to start the International Guest House at Western Regional Centre, Udaipur. As a chairman of the book selection committee at Udaipur Centre, I could add several new journals and books to the library section. It gave me immense pleasure to become a member of the committee that was responsible for organizing the annual Shilpagram Utsab at Udaipur. Several artifacts were being added to the Zonal Anthropological Museum, Western Regional Centre under my chairmanship and the most important was the inclusion of an age-old bullock cart used by the Gadia Lohar community of Udaipur. I became a part of the formative phase of the development of the DNA laboratory at Western Regional Centre, Udaipur. As an in-charge of the Physical Anthropology Section and DNA laboratory section, I was able to start the DNA banking at Udaipur Centre. Till I left Udaipur to join Mysore Centre, the DNA laboratory of Udaipur Centre was recognized as a repository of more than 2000 DNA samples from different population groups of western India. I was able to initiate health camp activities at Udaipur through which it was possible to detect different genetic diseases in different tribal populations of the Western Region. We could identify the presence of abnormal hemoglobin in different population groups of western India.

Southern Regional Centre, Mysore has given me the opportunity to explore more administrative duties. I was able to draw the attention of different academic institutions in Mysore to visit our Zonal Anthropological Museum through different outreach activities. As the Head of Office of Southern Regional Centre, I was instrumental in upgrading the Physical Anthropology Laboratory with an additional number of instruments including a bioimpedance analyser. I am acting as a member of the Research Advisory Committee at KIRTADS under the Government of Kerala (Kerala Institute for Research Training and Development Studies of Scheduled Caste and Scheduled Tribes). While working as an in-charge of Zonal Anthropology Museum at Mysore, I developed a visual documentation on the Sacred Grooves of Kodagu. A number of new avenues in terms of physical anthropology have been established and I was part of the committee for the upgradation of DNA laboratories up to the whole genome sequencing level at the Anthropological Survey of India.

Contribution Beyond Anthropology, Notable Students

Beyond my anthropological assignments, I have been attached to the legal wing of the Anthropological Survey of India in the Southern Regional Centre and could win a number of court cases in favour of the Anthropological Survey of India. I could gain compliments from Professor Srivastava the then Director of Anthropological Survey of India towards handling difficult cases. While serving the Western Regional Centre, Udaipur I was attached to different cultural wings which allowed me to interact with local cultures. In Mysore also I am attached to different organizations like Clean Mysuru Foundation that organizes cleanliness drives in Mysore and Kalpa Kshetra, a literary group from Mysore. There are a number of students from different colleges and universities who could complete M.Sc. dissertation under me. Now, most of them are established in different sectors. One of my students could get a scholarship for higher education in America. Another student got a scholarship to take training in Auxology from Germany. One of my students got the 56th rank in all Indian Administrative Service and is now posted in Gujarat. Some of them are established teachers and some are working in different administrative services. One of the students who was pursuing a Masters in Anthropology from distance mode under IGNOU could get an Indian second rank in UGC NET examination.

International Collaborations

The practice of reading books has given me enough opportunity to know the people across the world. It allowed me to know what are the current trends of research and who are the pioneer in their work. The advent of the Internet had added new impetus to interact with people more openly. I took the opportunity in every aspect and collaborated with a number of people in academic exchange. I was fortunate enough to collaborate with Professor Michael Hermannusen from the University of Keil and Professor Barry Bogin from Loughborough University in different dimensions of academic exchanges. I contributed one chapter for Professor

Hermannusen in his famous book on *Auxology*, whereas both of them contributed their write-up for my book on *Human Growth*. In 2014, the International Society for the Study of Human Growth and Clinical Auxology had invited me to deliver a lecture at the Department of Pediatrics, University Medical Center, Maribor and I could attend the same with the help of ICMR International Young Scientist travel fellowship. In 2019, in collaboration with the Ministry of Defense, Government of USA and Ministry of Culture, Government of India, I was fortunate to attend the training programme on Forensic Identification of Human remains. I could interact with a number of scientists working there which gave me another opportunity to identify human remains in plane crashes during the Second World War. I am fortunate to have collaboration with a number of scholars from foreign universities for academic exchanges. Presently I am working in collaboration with the University of Chicago and Birbal Sahni Institute of Palaeobotany to decipher the peopling of Southern India. With the help of the Director, Professor Vinay Kumar Srivastava, I was able to revive the International School of Anthropology at Southern Regional Centre, Mysore where several international talk series had been organized under the aegis of international collaboration.

Current Activities

In fourteen years of experience, the Anthropological Survey of India has given me enough opportunity to explore my capabilities. Officiating as a Superintending Anthropologist (Physical) and taking up the responsibility as Head of Office at Anthropological Survey of India, Southern Regional Centre, Mysore has given me the opportunity to explore new administrative and academic avenues. To sum up, it helped me to connect University departments with government set up in entire southern India. Apart from that I am actively engaged with different academic organizations across the world like the International Society for the Study of Human Growth and Clinical Auxology; the Indian Society of Human Genetics, the United Indian Anthropology Forum, etc. Besides, I am working as a referee in several reputed journals like *Anthropologischer Anziger* (Germany), *World Journal of Pediatrics* (China), *Anthropological Review* (Poland), *Current Science* (India), etc. I have been nominated as external examiner as well as paper setter for different Master's programme as well as Ph.D. programme in Mohanlal Sukhadiya University, IGNOU, Sidho-Kanho-Birsha University, Jahangir Medical College under University of Pune and Centre for Cellular and Molecular Biology. I was engaged in the prestigious project on ethnographic documentation of denotified, nomadic, and seminomadic communities of India that was conceived by none other than Professor Vinay Kumar Srivastava. Currently, I am engaged with the project on Gut Microbial Genomic Diversity among the PVTGs of India as Principal Investigator under Anthropological Survey of India.

Last but not least, I want to convey to the upcoming generation of anthropologists that no subject in the world comes with easy employment availability. If someone works with his or her full dedication and sincerity along with the blessings from their parents and teachers, one day or another the other success will come their way. Luck also works in their way, but it is only hard work that will remain with you if someone wants to maintain the success rate throughout his or her life.

34

Autobiography

Nilakantha Panigrahi

Early Life, Education, Family, and Taking Anthropology as a Subject

Born in a rural village named Budhaisuni, Polasara of Ganjam district of Odisha on 10 May 1962 to the parents Late Sashikala Panigrahi and Late Parakhita Panigrahi. At the age of 18 years, my father left the village and went to Rairangpur of Mayurbhanj, Odisha, which is one of the tribal dominated fully scheduled area districts of Odisha. He joined in Works Department of the state government on temporary basis and became permanent subsequently. My primary education started in the village Chatsali (private non-formal centre) and later on in government primary school and subsequently shifted to Rairangpur where I got my school education and college education with Honours in Political Science and Anthropology as pass subject both at Intermediate and Graduation level. Dr Sisir Kumar Kanungo, Dr Sapan Kumar Das and Dr Pritilata Parija were my teachers in the Department of Anthropology of the Rairangpur college laid my foundation in anthropology. I joined Sambalpur University for higher study with a hope that the department having Masters in Anthropology and Sociology will help me to appear UPSC examination in future. On completion of the Masters in 1984, I carried out my M.Phil. degree in the same department. Financial constraints of the family motivated me to join with Late Professor Jagannath Pathy, Professor of Sociology, South Gujarat University, Surat, in his Carrier Research Project awarded by ICSSR, New Delhi. While working in the project for one year I had the opportunity to carry out fieldwork in ten villages representing ten different tribes distributed in ten scheduled area districts of Odisha. That in fact motivated me to take anthropology as my career. I got married in 1994 and having a daughter.

Doctoral Work, Teachers, Fieldwork and Early Career

Anthropologists normally do rural studies targeting tribal and caste communities, with little exceptions. I was assigned by the department to carry out my M.Phil. dissertation research work in 1986 on inter-ethnic adjustment issues of the Gujaratis living in Sambalpur town. As a part of my Ph.D. work, I covered both Cuttack and Sambalpur town and studied the inter-ethnic issues faced by the Odiyas and the Gujaratis and ethnicity maintained by the Gujaratis at destination. It focused more on the ethnic formation of the Gujaratis, their migration from historical perspective and how occupation and ethnic criteria influences the Gujaratis to maintain their ethnic boundaries at various levels. I have also completed my Bachelor of Law Degree from Lala Lajpat Rai Law College of Sambalpur (morning programme), and PG Diploma in Human Resources Management from IGNOU (correspondence mode), New Delhi, which helped me immensely while performing different roles in development sector, research institutes and academics.

Before I was awarded with my Ph.D. degree, I joined as the "Socio-Economist" in an external aided bi-lateral development project of Danish International Development Agency of Denmark (DANIDA) which was working with the Government of Odisha in the coastal districts with headquarter at Bhubaneswar. The project was meant to take into account various anthropo-sociological dimensions in the promotion of safe drinking water through deep bore well, their maintenance, health and sanitation activities related to water, where I continued up to August 1993. In the project I had the opportunity to work with Civil and Mechanical Engineers, Geo-Hydrologists, Chemists and other social scientists in few C.D. Blocks of Cuttack, Puri and Balasore districts (undivided) of Odisha. The project was implemented in the government department of Urban Development, which later renamed as Rural Water Supply and Sanitation (RWSS) of the Government of Odisha. Working few years in coastal Odisha, an idea came to my mind that work experiences in coastal Odisha may not help much in my future days to act as an anthropologist. By the time I had a daughter of three months and I was living with kith and kins at Bhubaneswar. After March 1993 I was unemployed for couple of months when I got an opportunity to work in a World Bank assisted IEC evaluation in few tribal dominated districts of Jharkhand. The project was supported to one NGO DIPS Communication and implemented by one psychologist-cum-communication specialist in the field of development. I had the opportunity to carry out the evaluation of ICDS activities in May-June 1993 in few tribal dominated districts of Santhal Pragana region of Jharkhand.

Fortunately, another bi-lateral development project of DANIDA came in Koraput district of Odhisha for the development of the animal husbandry resources of the tribal people. The project was popularly known as the Integrated Livestock Development Project (ILDP) in Koraput district. A top competition took place for the post of Monitoring Specialist where I had to face the interview along with my seniors of the old project and finally, I was selected as the Monitoring Specialist of ILDP in a monthly package of less than 50 per cent remuneration compared to the previous development project. Leaving behind my family at Bhubneswar and the attraction of staying in a capital city, I left to Koraput a distantly located tribal dominated district infected with Naxalism and joined the project in June 1993 which was about to start. Here I had to work in 100 villages of four C.D. Blocks of Koraput district with Veterinary Doctors, Agriculture Engineers, young Social Scientists and Soil Conservationists. The project operation was highly dominated by the veterinary components and outlooks and many times I had to face a lot of challenges while implementing the project activities.

Seminal Contribution to Anthropology, Important Papers, Books

I have completed twenty-six research projects carried out in different tribal dominated and coastal regions of Odisha and Chhattisgarh. These research projects are funded by different international agencies like: The World Bank, The Ford Foundation, Overseas Development Institute, London; Danish Assisted Revised National Tuberculosis Control Programmes, Bhubaneswar; national funding agencies like ICSSR, New Delhi; different Ministries of the Government of India and the Government of Odisha; autonomous bodies like Odisha Information Commission, Lal Bahadur Shastri Institute of Management, Shastri Sadan, R.K. Puram, New Delhi; Council for Social Development, New Delhi, NALCO, India; National Labour Institute, New Delhi; General Administration Department, Government of Orissa; Committee of Governor, Government of India, etc. The research projects carried out by me cover various thematic areas like tribal livelihood: land, NTFPs, water; tribal health issues and health infrastructure, tendu leaf, displacement, rehabilitation and resettlement, preparation of socio-economic rehabilitation plans, disaster management, tribal development policies, constitutional provisions for tribal development, evaluations and impact assessments of MGNREGS, Mid-Day-Meal, Right to Information Act, Forest Right Act, Millennium Development Goals, National Child Labour Projects, Special micro projects for the PVTGs. The funding received from different agencies for all these research projects tunes to the extent of Rs. 1,04.00 lakh.

Three students have been awarded their Ph.D. degrees under my guidance on various tribal issues like health issues of the Santals, livelihood issues of the Bhuiyan women of Odisha, and sociocultural identity issues of the Sabar women of West Bengal. Nine students are continuing their doctoral research works under my guidance on various issues like: Problems of Widows, Indigenous System of Village Management, Changing Livelihood Resources among the Baiga Tribe, Socio-Economic Dimensions of Health of Pando Tribe, Forest Ecology, State Intervention and Cultural Responses: A Study among the Choukhutia Bhunjia Tribe, and Ethnicity among the rehabilitated Refugee Bengalis of Chhattisgarh.

My publication of research articles in different journals started in the year 1990 first in the *Journal of Indian Anthropologist.* A total of forty-three research articles have been published by me in different national and international journals of social sciences. A few of the journals includes *Tribal Studies: A Journal of COATS; South Asian Anthropologist; The Oriental Anthropologists; Orissa Economic Journal (OEJ); Indian Journal of Anthropological Survey; BIODIVERSITY WATCH: International Journal on Biodiversity Issues; Humanities Circle: An International Journal of Central University of Kerala; Asian Journal of International Law; Journal of the Indian Anthropological Society; Jo. of Adivasi; Man and Life; Man in India; Lal Bahadur Shastri Journal of Management and Research; MARGIN; Indian Journal of Human Rights and the Law; The Eastern Anthropologists; Indian Journal of Social Development; Journal of Review of Development and Change; Social Change; Man and Development; Madhya Pradesh Journal of Social Sciences,* etc. I have also published a total of forty-two research articles as book chapters edited by different authors.

I have delivered twenty-five special lectures/invited talks in refresher courses and orientation programmes being organized by the HRDCs of Utkal University, Bhubaneswar; Sambalpur University, Burla; Ptd Ravishankar Shukla University, Raipur; NIT Rourkela, Central University of Hyderabad, Hyderabad; and different Colleges/ Research Institutes, NGOs and INGOs. These presentations include various thematic areas like tribal development policies and programmes, tribal culture and ethnicity, research methodology, fieldwork and fieldwork traditions, Social Science Research in India, bio-cultural perspective of tribal health, etc. I have contributed research papers in different national and international seminar/ conferences/symposium/workshops organized by different universities, research institutes, NGOs, INGOs and Colleges. I have learned skills and special skills by attending different trainings/ workshops being organized by different training institutes, Government of Odisha, Government of Himachal Pradesh, Xavier Institute of Management, Danish International Development Agency and many national and international training institutes.

Administrative and Institution Building

Presently I am working as Professor, Department of Anthropology and Tribal Development, Guru Ghasidas Viswavidyalaya (GGV), A Central University, Koni, Bilaspur, Chhattisgarh since September 2016. I am engaged in teaching at undergraduate, postgraduate programme and doctoral research programme and in carrying out research projects and evaluation studies. I am also performing administrative responsibilities as the Head of the Department of Anthropology and Tribal Development since July 2016 additionally.

I have worked as the Coordinator, Centre for Endangered Languages, Guru Ghasidas Vishwavidyalaya, from 2017 till August 2023. This was a special Centre of UGC as a part of the initiative of the nine central universities of India who were engaged in the protection and preservation of the endangered languages of India. At the Centre for Endangered languages I manage to run PG Diploma and Certificate courses on "Computation Linguistic", undertook endangered language survey of Turi language in Chhattisgarh, prepared technical language dictionary both for the common people and the technical dictionary, mapping of the material culture of the Turi community, pictorial book on Turi language for primary level students and mapping of endangered languages of Chhattisgarh, organized national and international seminars and conferences which were some of the objectives of this centre.

Contribution beyond Anthropology

I have completed ten consultancy assignments funded by International Development Entrepreneurship—India, New Delhi; MISERIOR, German; Practical Action, Sri Lanka; Centre for Youth and Social Development (CYSD), Bhubaneswar,; TROCCAIRE, Ireland; Sir Ratan Tata Trust (SRTT) and ISEC, Bangalore under Visiting Fellowship programme; Indian Institute of Public Administration (IIPA), New Delhi, under Chronic Poverty Research Center; Danida assisted Revised National Tuberculosis Control Programme, Bhubaneswar, and International Water Management Institute (IWMI) and Sir Ratan Tata Trust. Such consultancy assignments were basically covered in the State of Odisha, West Bengal and Uttar Pradesh. The major thematic areas of such consultancies include to study the impact of small irrigation technologies; livelihood issues and integrating the poor with the Market System; utilization of water in Odisha; Ethnic and Communal Harmony in Kandhamal district Odisha; status of Millennium Development Goal in Odisha (MDG), Poverty and Hunger in Odisha, Role of Indigenous Institutions in Tribal Livelihood: An Empirical Study in a Tribal district of Odisha, Tribal Movements and Livelihood: Recent Developments in Odisha, Health Systems Research on Reaching the Unreached- Strategies to increase RNTCP coverage in remote Tribal Areas, Water based Livelihood enhancement effort for Tribals: A case of the impact of Treadle Pumps of International Development Enterprises (IDE's) in Koraput District of Odisha.

As anthropologists I am also involved with different civil society organizations represented by NGOs and INGOs. In Odisha my contribution to the issues of indigenous development in the field of agriculture, community organization and popularizing the FRA in Odisha among the tribal communities of Malkangiri and Kandhamal districts of Odisha are noteworthy.

My Books

2000: *The Trading Community of India: An Anthropological Study of Ethnicity*. Rawat Publications, (First Author, with Prof. P. Panda).

2005: *State, NGO and Disaster Management*. Rawat Publications, (co-Author, with Prof. K.C. Samal, Dr S. Meher and S. Mohanty).

2014: *Tribal Livelihood in Changing Perspective*. SSDN Publishers, New Delhi.

2017: *Tribals and The Indian Constitution: Functioning of Fifth Schedule in the State of Orissa*. Rawat Publications, New Delhi, 2006 (co-Author, with Prof. N.K. Behura).

2019: *Tribal Economy, Culture and Society in India*. Concept Publishing Company Pvt. Ltd., New Delhi.

35

More than a Thousand Miles

Many Steps in My Anthropological Journey

K.R. Rama Mohan

This brief article is about my engagement with anthropology as a teacher, researcher and a consultant for two decades and the various academic assignments in different parts of the world. Myriad experiences gained through anthropological understanding over the years is also presented in this article. Looking back at my academic journey in anthropology, all these years of my life illustrate a meaningful growth and development as an individual, teacher, researcher, colleague and a student—a purposeful journey which led me to this current position. Now, I believe that, I possess some degree of academic confidence to present my trajectory of academic interests and pursuits and few professional achievements in my well-rounded academic profile.

Introduction

It was a choice that I started my anthropological academic journey right from the undergraduate level. I was certain about my career path during my early stages. I come from a family where my parents were teachers with Ph.D. in Education and Social Work that had influenced my familiarity with the discipline of anthropology. After my Masters in Anthropology, I did another Masters in Psychology, since it was also very dear to my heart. My teaching career began at the age of 23 as a temporary faculty, while I was doing my Ph.D. in Anthropology at Andhra University. I have taught undergraduate students in psychology for more than five years.

Soon after completing my Ph.D. in Anthropology, the core anthropology teaching began when I joined Pondicherry University as a Guest Faculty in the year 2000. It was then a newly-established department. I taught Masters programme courses on Introduction to Anthropology, Indian Society, Fieldwork Methods and Techniques and Development Anthropology. Being a faculty in core anthropology, I shifted my earlier teaching methods from Psychology by quoting/giving everyday cultural experiences in the classroom. Pondicherry (Now, Puducherry) being a French colony for many years, is a mosaic of cultural diversity with Indo-French families, institutes and spiritual organizations. My regular interactions with "French Institute", where European Resident scholars had projects on Tamil culture, enriched my understanding about caste, family, religion and French Diaspora in Tamil Nadu and Pondicherry. During my teaching tenure at Department of Anthropology, I brushed up my understanding of theoretical concepts and methodological techniques in anthropology. I did not do any active research or publish any work in this period, but those years at the university gave me enough confidence and strength in teaching anthropology for Masters and Doctoral students.

During in the year 2002, coincidently, I accepted an assignment as the "Education Consultant" for about three months to a project called "STEP" (Sustainable Tribal Empowerment Project) funded by CARE International, exclusively for the tribal communities of Visakhapatnam district of Andhra Pradesh. Having a Ph.D. in educational process of tribal children in the tribal areas of Visakhapatnam, I was the right choice for the CARE International authorities to assign me as an Educational Consultant for the long-term project. The task was initially to identify the educational needs and problems associated and possible alternatives that can be implemented. Familiarity with schools, administrators, and community members in these tribal areas made my job easy and enjoyable and was also intellectually stimulating. It was also nostalgic when revisiting my field villages and respondents when I was working for my Ph.D. degree. Constructive inputs were given by me in the early draft preparation and operational issues for this project. Prior commitment, passion for teaching and learning at the university made me go back to the university, as this project experience lasted only for three months.

Stepping in a Cultural Mosaic of Southeast Asia: Teaching in Singapore

I had to leave Pondicherry University to take up a teaching position in Sociology for London School of Economics (University of London) in Singapore. I felt this teaching position in a prestigious, world-class university was a privilege and challenging, as I have to teach for international students. I was assigned to teach sociology for undergraduate students pursing B.Sc. in Sociology. This was demanding for me, as I had to reread many classical sociological theories to present myself authentically before the students who come from many countries. At this point of time, I was much fascinated by Anthony Giddens "Structuration Theory", from the modern sociological theory. Incidentally, he was also the Director of London School of Economics. I took lot of care with regard to the concepts while I was delivering lectures due to the fact that all lectures were video recorded for the benefit of students who could not attend the classes.

During my stay in Singapore my research interests grew around the Indian Diaspora, particularly Tamil communities, traditional ethnic communities like Chinese, Malay, and Indonesians who had settled in Singapore. A "potpouri" of multi ethnic communities, this Island country has opened up my deeper understanding around international migration issues, including my own, identity, linguistic diversity, varieties of food, music, religious faiths, social relations among ethnic communities in the Island State, etc. Carrying an anthropological lens and an understanding the cultural aspects, I was in perfect harmony with my Chinese, Eurasian, British and Australian colleagues at the university.

Before moving to stay in an individual house, I was a paying guest with a Singaporean-Chinese family; from here I picked up the nuances of Chinese culture, food and few functional Mandarin sentences. I reckon it was a like a "participation observation" in a Singaporean Chinese family. This has further equipped me empirically to teach exclusively on "family" as a part of the syllabus. Stella Quah's book on *Family in Singapore: Sociological Perspectives* was my every day reading. While teaching different theoretical perspectives on changing dimensions on family, I made most of the comparisons on "Joint Family" system in India, its sociological significance and its slow decline. Students much appreciated the comparative aspects of family system in Asian/Indian context.

At a personal level, I was involved in a small research project undertook by a psychology faculty member from Nanyang Technological University on mathematical learning among the children belonging to different ethnic communities. On the weekends data was collected from school-going children on their mathematical learning process. Interacting with parents, children and teachers was informative and enriched deeper understanding of cultural ways of acquiring particular mathematical skills. Hectic teaching load and lack of time did not allow me to do concentrated research in this country, except gaining a lot of knowledge about different ethnic communities, their histories and ethos. This was an everlasting wonderful experience for me as sociology faculty with an anthropology degree.

Vacation breaks and the virtue of nearby border countries allowed me to travel in the neighbouring countries like Malaysia and Indonesia. My interest was to observe and learn about the culture of these multiethnic groups in these countries. Most of the students in the class also coming from these communities further enhanced my interest. These casual trips in the rural and urban areas provided me some broader knowledge of students' sociocultural backgrounds enabling me to relate to them while teaching social institutions. Hectic teaching schedule did not allow me to publish much, except a joint paper published about developmental aspects among Tribes of Visakhapatnam during this period. I chose to leave this teaching assignment in Singapore keeping in mind my academic and research interests which were not conducive in this environment.

Shifting Towards Greener Pastures: Teaching in North-East Africa

I believe most of the anthropologists' wish to embark on journeys in different ethnographic terrains in their academic pursuits. Perhaps, this was an urge in me too, that made me accept the position of Associate Professor in the School of Social Sciences at University of Asmara in the State of Eritrea. I had lots of hope to study communities in this country, to have a cross-cultural comparison of these groups for research publications. There was no Anthropology Department; it was a combined teaching of Psychology and Anthropology to the undergraduate students in this setting. It was evident that most of the macro social structures dictate the educational process right from elementary to higher education in this country. It was an autocratic country, and still is, with no individual freedom and human rights. Except a lucrative salary and a higher academic position in my career, there was no opportunity to conduct any kind of research. One must take administrative approval and adhere to strict protocols to carry out any kind of research in their communities which is publishable; I decided not to, since it was a highly cumbersome process to venture into actual research. "Observer as a Participant" was only tool that I could employ to understand the historical and cultural profile of the multiethnic groups here. Interaction with colleagues, neighbours, occasional visits to rural areas equipped me to know more about the social fabric of this nation.

The only satisfying contribution during my academic stint in the university here was being a Member of Drafting Committee for a Project on "Status of Girls Education", I have appraised the concerned authorities to give "Cultural Orientation" to foreign teachers who come to teach school children in different parts of the country. At that time there was huge recruitment of Indian and Pakistani teachers for the elementary to higher secondary schools in the state. I was amazed at how teachers who had no clue about the country and its culture can teach from Day One in a completely different and alien sociocultural setting.

George Spindler's *Cultural Therapy* was very handy for me to suggest to the Board Members that there was nothing wrong in recruiting teachers form other countries due to a dearth of indigenous manpower that is trained. However, foreign teachers must be properly sensitized and given basic orientation about the cultural aspects of children who belong to different ethnic communities before they take up actual teaching and entering into the classrooms. Even teaching core science subjects need some background information about children's learning styles. Being an anthropologist, this is as much as I could offer to them. I was informed later, when I left this job, that there was some programme for the newly-recruited foreign teachers for the schools in the state. I was glad to know of the initiative they have taken based on my suggestions.

Coming Home: Teaching in My Alma Mater

In the year 2008, when I had to go back to Africa after my vacation, I stopped myself. There was a vacancy for Anthropology Faculty position in the newly-established "Centre for Study of Social Exclusion and Inclusive Policy" by the UGC at Andhra University, Visakhapatnam. I thought this was a better choice here than compromising for the teaching assignment in Africa.

Upon taking up this position at Andhra University, my immediate priority was to study academically the inequalities, marginalization process and vulnerability within the framework of

"Developmental Index" among the communities particularly in the North Coastal Andhra Pradesh. I chose to engage myself with the Scheduled Tribes once again along with the nearby marine fishing communities in Visakhapatnam region. In this process, I have published research papers on caste based social exclusion of Dalit communities and marginalization process among the Scheduled Tribes and Marine fishing communities of Visakhapatnam district. These two socio-economic groups remained my choice of academic interest for more than six years at this Centre in Andhra University. Simultaneously, the ICSSR has sanctioned me a Project on "Exclusionary Mechanisms of Psychologically Challenged Children and Adults with Psychiatric Disorders". This research project gave me opportunity to contribute inclusionary mechanisms in educational needs of the children with psychological impairments and vocational prospects for the adults with psychiatric issues.

In this period, the Department of Anthropology at Brigham Young University, USA started "Abroad Study India Programme" in Visakhapatnam in 2008 and I was the immediate choice to be the Local Supervisor for a semester-long programme, by the virtue of the Programme Director, Professor Charles Nuckolls, with whom I worked as a Research Assistant when I was a doctoral student for his study on Fishing communities in Visakapatnam. Being an Anthropology faculty, I took classes on Telugu Society and Culture and subsequently supervised their research projects every semester. In this process, I had initiated an "MoU" between Andhra University and Brigham Young University, USA to start a Course on "Telugu Society and Culture" for the Study Abroad Programme with more academic vigour. This was a success! Every year two batches of students started taking this course at my Centre. In this process, I received an offer to be a "Visiting Faculty" at the Departments of Anthropology and Sociology, Brigham Young University in the year 2011. Since then, I regularly visit these departments to deliver lectures and interact with students of Anthropology Department.

Along with my Ph.D. supervisor, I received another Major Research Project from UGC to study the problems associated with construction of medium range Dams and Reservoirs in Tribal areas of Andhra Pradesh. This was in tune with the objectives of social exclusion process experienced by the tribal communities who are displaced due to State Sponsored Developmental Projects. The research project recommendations were sent to the appropriate agencies for suitable alternatives for the welfare of the displaced tribal families in those regions.

An important research project was undertaken by me to study the reasons for Migration of Scheduled Tribes from their native habitats to Visakhapatnam urban areas. Using Guha and Gadgil's "Ecological Refugees" as a framework, along with other institutional factors, I have successfully completed a detailed study on the problems of livelihoods of Scheduled Tribes and reasons for migration. The same report with suitable recommendations was submitted to the concerned authorities for further action.

Aside from teaching and research activities at the university, I was instrumental in networking with local NGOs and similar bodies to hold national seminars, workshops, sensitization programmes on health, education, human rights and other developmental issues for the socially disadvantaged communities in the Visakhapatnam region. At Andhra University, being the parent university for my Bachelors and Ph.D. degree, things were accomplished due to familiar and long-standing relations. Though satisfying in all aspects as an anthropologist, contributed my knowledge and skills for the CSSEIP, at Andhra University, it was like a "building with no staircase" with little scope for advancement and growth in my career. I signed off on a good note and a feeling that I have internationalized this centre with my efforts.

Calling of the Himalayas: Anthropology Department at Sikkim University

Sikkim University at Gangtok, Sikkim is a newly-established university starting with few departments, and now has grown with more departments with the efforts of successful vice-chancellors. It was Professor T.B. Subba who was very much instrumental in starting Anthropology Department at Sikkim University in the year 2013 with two Guest Faculties. In the year 2014, I joined as an Associate Professor along with three other colleagues. Within a week of appointment, I was made Head of the Department to my surprise. Upon taking the prestigious responsibility for holding the First Anthropology Department in Sikkim, my immediate task was to strengthen the department with the help of my colleagues.

With no adequate infrastructure and operating from a compact temporary building, efforts were put into establishing a Physical Anthropology Laboratory to offer a specialization. Ably supported by my colleagues and by the higher authorities at the university, today we boast of a full-fledged Physical Anthropology Laboratory, which is no way inferior to any other established laboratories in the Anthropology Departments in Indian universities. As it started with Masters Programmes initially, another task was to start research programmes leading to M.Phil. and Ph.D. degrees. Coallating course work syllabus and getting necessary approvals from the concerned academic statutory bodies took time and the Department has started the M.Phil. and Ph.D. programmes in the year 2015. Apart my teaching activities, I was a Consultant and Resource Person for the newly-established "Tribal Research Institute" by the Government of Sikkim. I took up initiatives and supervised research projects funded by TRI on the ethnographic profile of the Scheduled Tribes of Sikkim. There were three more research projects I coordinated on the Evaluation of Developmental Projects in the State of Sikkim. I have been giving constructive anthropological inputs for the newly-formed "Primitive Tribal Welfare Board", Government of Sikkim, which looks after welfare of Lepchas of Sikkim. New terminology of "Particularly Vulnerable Tribal Groups" is yet to be formally declared in place of "PTWB". Research documentation was carried out on "Sacred Spaces", ethno-medicinal aspects of Lepchas under my supervision.

I had an opportunity to prepare a course material on "Ecological Anthropology" consisting of twenty-two modules for the e-PG Patasala funded by the UGC-MHRD in the year 2016. I have delivered lectures for more than fifty-five topics in e-PG Patasala video content. This is truly a satisfying experience as an anthropology teacher where I could reach many students all over India and abroad. I received due appreciation from those who have watched my lectures. I was well recognized when I used to go to seminars and workshops in other universities. Students and research scholars greeted me with a sense of gratitude. Truly Rewarding!

Being a local supervisor at Department of Anthropology, Sikkim University for the Ph.D. scholars and researchers from University of Alabama, USA, University of St. Andrews, Scotland and University of Vienna, all these years have empowered me with more understanding of the Sikkim Himalayan communities. I have invited and organized regular lectures from Faculty Members and Researchers from universities all the over the world with the help of my colleagues at the department in an effort to enhance the visibility of the department and to build potential linkages with these scholars for future prospects. Interacting with my students provided invaluable learning and opportunities to do research in Sikkim. During these years research papers were published by me jointly with my research scholars in reputed journals on the issues of Ethnic Identities, Ritual Specialists, Developmental aspects focusing on the communities in Sikkim.

Envisioning a full-fledged anthropology department with the three specializations, viz. social-cultural, physical and prehistoric archaeology, I proposed an ethnographic museum-cum-archaeology laboratory within a small space we have. We were successful in establishing a small, yet significant museum, now a place to showcase our curated material culture of different ethnic communities of Sikkim and north-east India.

In all the invited lectures as a Resource Person in Refresher courses in Research Methodology organized by the UGC Human Resource Development Centres in universities, my favourite topic is

"Ethnographic Method: Theory and Practice". I relished delivering lectures on this significant and unique topic, where anthropologists take pride quoting their research/field experiences during their academic pursuits.

The first Ph.D. and M.Phil. degrees in Anthropology in the State of Sikkim under my supervision is a milestone for the Department of Anthropology. Using "Auto Ethnography" as a main strategy, I have guided my research scholar to investigate and "Rediscover" her own community from an anthropological perspective for her Ph.D. Thesis. As a Dean, School of Human Sciences, an additional responsibility I was entrusted with, I facilitated useful workshops on Research Methodology and Visual Anthropology for the benefit of research scholars of the Sikkim University.

Conclusions

With my limited contributions to the field of anthropology in India, here and now, I stand behind the shadows of giants in the field of anthropology in India, who have taken the discipline of anthropology to the farthest heights in India and the rest of world. Having the essential knowledge and skills in which I was trained from all my teachers, I am more a student than a teacher of anthropology, and I shall remain ever so grateful to the discipline that has given me more than what I could ask for.

36

My Autobiographical Journey in Anthropology

Rajesh K. Gautam

Early life, Education, Family, taking Anthropology as a Subject

I was born on 2 October 1970 in a remote village known as Deogaon of district Mandla, Madhya Pradesh, India from the late mother Gulaba Devi. My late father, Shri Ramadhar was a Forest Guard and mother was housewife. My early life and education were very tough. Being eldest son, I had to support the mother for her routine work of household as well as of agricultural fields and take care of cattle also. In rural India, cow and oxen are common part of the family. It is a symbol of prosperity. More prosperous peasants may have larger herd of such pet including buffaloes too. Even unproductive cow and buffalo are given equal attention and care. It requires lot of labour to cater to even a small herd.

I grew up with extreme poverty, severe illnesses, scarcities and struggles. Caste hierarchy, untouchability, caste endogamy, joint and extended family, kinship, and feudal caste structure are some of the inherent characteristics of Indian villages in which I grew up. Still such conditions are common in Indian villages. My primary and middle school education was completed from the village school, where I born. Years of my early education were completed without school building in the shadow of an *amla* tree (*Phyllanthus emblica*) planted in the school premises.

For high school I was admitted to the Government Jagannath Higher Secondary Excellence School, Mandla (MP). Later on in 1992, I completed Bachelor of Science (B.Sc.) from Government Rani Durgavati PG College, Mandla (MP). I did postgraduation from Dr Harisingh Gour Vishwavidyalaya, Sagar (MP). I was awarded degree of Ph.D. on the thesis "Population Characteristics of Middle and High Altitude Kinnaura of District Kinnaur, Himachal Pradesh" from the University of Delhi (India) in 2006. In 2016, I was awarded prestigious Raman Post-Doctoral fellowship to pursue Post-Doctorate from Montclair State University, NJ, USA. My journey from a remote village of central India to USA was full of thrills, challenges, uncertainties and struggles.

Turn to Anthropology

The term anthropology was completely unknown to me until the early years of graduation. Initially I was interested to be a medical doctor, but the cost of MBBS degree was not affordable to my family, hence; I opted to be graduated in bio-science (chemistry, botany and zoology). As I was eldest among four brothers and one sister, the cost of my graduation could not be affordable to my family; hence I opted to earn and learn. And, any how I continued till graduation. Then I tempted to civil services but, there is lot of uncertainties in it; as well as, it was at least three-four year long project. Hence, I tried other examinations like—bank PO (Probationary Officer), later on I pursued M.A. in English. And for completing the degree reached Dr Harisingh Gour University, where I found the Department of Anthropology. The course on human genetics in anthropology tempted me to do M.Sc. in anthropology; and I completed the degree in 1998. This was a great shift. Along with Masters in Anthropology, I qualified UGC-NET in 1997, which was essential to be teacher in the University.

Doctoral Work, Teacherings, Fieldwork and Early Career

I found the discipline anthropology very fascinating. And even it was beyond my imagination. During masters, I got opportunity to conduct the fieldwork among the tribes of Andaman and Nicobar Islands. The whole trip was full of thrills and adventures, which further strengthen my interest in the discipline.

When, I travelled by a passenger cargo ship MV Nancowry from Chennai to Port Blair in 1998. I felt elevated remembering the journey of HMS Beagle by Charles Darwin. When, I studied the tribes of Andaman and Nicobar, my interest in the discipline was further strengthened. I found myself in the line of Bronislaw Casper Malinowski.

In the year 2001, I joined the Department of Anthropology, University of Delhi and got an opportunity to work with Professor Gautam Kumar Kshatriya in his ICMR (Indian Council of Medical Research) funded project on the tribes of Himalayan, Coastal and Desert region. I was part of a team of three young anthropologists. I did not had any experience of Himalayan, coastal or desert region. After a tough training of two-three months under the guidance of Professor Gautam Kumar Kshatriya, Professor Anup Kapoor and Satwanti Kapoor; the team reached to Rekong Peo, district headquarter of Kinnaur by a long bus journey of 24 hours.

The district Kinnaur is a scheduled area and its residents are known as Kinnaura. They are also known for the practise of polyandry. I decided to pursue doctorate on them and later on in 2006, I submitted a thesis on "Population Characteristics of Middle and High Altitude Kinnaura of District Kinnaur, HP, India".

Seminal Contribution to Anthropology, Important Papers and Books

In my career of twenty years, there are more than 130 publications including seven books, 90+ research papers and 20+ book chapters to my credit. I also contributed to sixteen modules of e-pg-Pathshala. I am the only faculty from my department who is recognized by AD Scientific Index 2021 as a world scientist. I am recognized as one of the ten scientists from my university. Probably I am the only anthropologist from India who is trained in mathematical modelling. I, along with collaborators from USA evolved allometric scaling of body weight to height for Asian population. The work was published in reputed journal of *nature* series of journals known as *Nutrition & Diabetes*. My work on polyandry is highly recognized and published by *Indian Journal of Physical Anthropology and Human Genetics*. I also published a good number of papers on human nutrition, obesity, growth and development. My work on menarche, menopause and reproductive life span is cited by many researchers.

Natural selection is one of the core areas of physical anthropology. I have given a new dimension to the study of natural selection among the Indian population. There is paradigm shift in the role of fertility and mortality in the natural selection and the findings are highly recognized by different scholars. The World Anthropology Congress 2023 recognized my contribution in the discipline and felicitated me on 13 August 2023.

Administrative and Institution Building

In spite being dedicated to academia; I also contributed to the efficient management of the campus, as I served highly prestigious positions, viz. Chairman Council of Wardens, Chairman of Board of Studies, Head of the Department, Deputy Coordinator (Remedial Coaching Center), Proctor, etc.

As a Chairman Council of Warden, I am looking at the management and administration of boys and girls hostels of the campus. The university has four boys' hostels of a total of 1,000 capacity of residents. Similarly, there are three girls' hostels with the capacity of 650. These hostels are headed by eleven wardens and ~200 employees of different cadres. At the same time, I am also serving as the Head of the Department where there were ~500 undergraduate and fifty postgraduate + Ph.D. students.

As a Deputy Coordinator of the Remedial Coaching Centre I am catering to 1,000 students of deprived section to provide them remedial coaching. As a Chairman of Board of Studies my responsibility is to upgrade and update the course curricula of different programme. The credit of introduction of a new course (paper) entitled: Computer Application and Bio-statistical Methods in Ph.D. programme goes to me only.

Contribution Beyond Anthropology, Notable Students

I am widely recognized for inculcating scientific temperament among the students as well as beyond university premises among general public. Often, I am part of public conventions and advocate eradicating superstitions. Alike other parts of the world, in India too, there are many societal problems and unscientific way of life and thinking. Many learned professors and scientist also practise ridiculous traditions, which are useless as well as causing harm to themselves and the society and environment, but they are compelled to practise such thing for the sake of traditions, religion, etc. This happen because of lack of scientific temperament among them and there is need to inculcate it among every sphere of people, whether they are scientist or peasants, urban or rural, elite or common, rich or poor. I am trying to inculcate scientific temperament among the students, co-workers as well as masses through various means like public convention, popular writings, webinars, etc.

International Collaborations

I am among few of the anthropologist of the country who has international collaborations with the scientist of USA and Europe. I have been actively engaged with Global Initiative of Academic Network (GIAN), a scheme of Government of India, under which I successfully organized following two courses:

S. No.	Country	Name of Faculty and University	Title of Course (and Duration)
	Poland	Grażyna Liczbińska Institute of Anthropology Faculty of Biology Adam Mickiewicz University in Poznan, Poland	Obesity and Longevity: New Paradigm of Population Transition (13-18 November 2017)
	USA	Dr Neeraj Vedwan Montclair State University, New Jersey, USA	Environmentalism: A cross-cultural perspective on its emergence and evolution in US and India (22-27 April 2019)

In 2016, I was awarded Raman Post Doctoral Fellowship by the Government of India. I completed post-doctoral research from Montclair State University, NJ, USA in 2017. During my post-doctoral research, I also served as an International Visiting Professor and taught a course ANTH 101SP 2017 entitled; Introductory Physical Anthropology; to the undergraduates of Montclair State University, New Jersey, USA. Simultaneously, I also collaborated with other faculty of the university, i.e., Feliciano School of Business. Inspite of Montclair State University, I collaborated with the faculty and students of US military academy, West Point, New York.

In 2018, I was invited by the University of Oxford (England) to deliver a talk in an International Conference held at Queens College of the Oxford University. During this visit I also made collaboration with the faculty of Loughborough University of Leicestershire, England. I am working on different projects with different scholars of reputed institutions of different parts of the globe. The outcome of these collaborative projects is being resulted into a number of publications in high impact factored journals.

Current Activities

I am actively engaged in teaching and research. I am serving as Head of the Department of Anthropology at Dr Harisingh Gour University, Sagar (MP). Seven students are pursuing Ph.D. under my guidance. Along with teaching, I am also working on different projects with various scholars of different institute of India, USA and Europe. With the collaboration of faculty of Institute of Anthropology, Adam Mickiewicz University of Poland, we are working on various bio-social dimension of onset of menarche among different human population. With the faculty of Montclair State University, we are working on systematic review and meta-analysis of health believe model and COVID-vaccination, theory of planned behaviour, etc.

At the end, I can summarize that I have a good exposure of working among the tribes of Andaman and Nicobar Islands to the tribes of central India, Gujarat and Himalayas. Beyond India I also visited England and USA. In USA, I also visited Amish. In Florida (USA) I interacted with a polyamorous group of youngsters.

I think, I am a highly admired teacher, prolific researcher and a disciplined administrator. As a team leader I am a guide, friend, philosopher and facilitator. I always try to provide opportunity to my students and co-workers to blossom in full capacity.

My Books

2006: A.N. Sharma, R.K. Gautam and A.K. Gharami (eds.). *Indigenous Health Care and Ethnomedicine.* New Delhi: Sarup and Sons.

2010: G.K. Kshatriya, R.K. Gautam and A.K. Kapoor (eds.). *Population Characteristics of Desert Ecology: Demographic Indicators in a Disadvantaged District of Rajasthan*, India. Germany: VDM Verlag Dr Muller GmbH & Co.

2010: R.K. Gautam, G.K. Kshatriya and A. Kapoor, *Population Ecology and Family Planning*. New Delhi: Serial Publications.

2011: *Baigas: The Hunter Gatherers of Central India*. New Delhi: Readworthy Publications.

2012: D.K. Adak, R.K. Gautam, J. Nanada, and P. Bharati. *People Health and Nutrition.* New Delhi: Mittal Publications.

2016: R.K. Gautam and P.K. Patra (eds.). *Human Growth and Nutrition: A Biocultural Synthesis*. New Delhi: Kalpaz Publications.

2019: R.K. Gautam, J. Jariya, S. Biswas and P. Bharati, (eds.). *Health and Nutritional Status of Indigenous Populations.* New Delhi: B.R. Publishing Corporation.

37

On My becoming an Anthropologist

Kh. Narendra Singh

I was born in a village called Sonai Shelu near Silchar at Cachar district of Assam (India) on 1 December 1966. My initial schooling of was started in a Bengali medium Lower Primary School in my village and thereafter I completed of my matriculation from Gobinda Nagar Shiv Bari High School in 1982, and in the year 1988 completed B.Sc. degree with Anthropology, Botany, and Zoology from Gurucharan College, Silchar (Assam). In the same year, I went to Pune University for higher studies. I had a great passion for the subject of anthropology from my school days as I was curious to study about the culture and civilization of different communities.

I obtained my Master's and Doctoral degree in Anthropology from Savitri Bai Phule Pune University (formerly University of Pune) Pune in 1991 and 1997, respectively. My Ph.D. topic was "Assessment of Nutritional Status of Warli Children" under the guidance of Late Dr Vijay S. Kukarni. I also got generous supervision during my entire Ph.D. fieldwork from Professor R.K. Mutatkar of Anthropology Department, University of Pune and I spent several weeks together with Professor Mutatkar in the tribal villages of Peth taluka (Maharashtra) and participated in the various socio-economic and cultural events. After staying in the community for several months, I was able to pick up the local language and that helped me to complete my fieldwork data collection.

My special areas of interest are Anthropology of Health, Tribal Development Studies, Nutrition and Health Communication and Ethno-medical Studies. I had the opportunity to work in various national and international level health survey projects for long time from 1998 to 2010 in the following, viz. District Level Household Survey on Reproductive and Child Health (DLHS-RCH), National Family Health Survey (NFHS), Revised National Tuberculosis Control Programme (RNTCP), Global Adult Tobacco Survey (GATS) under the Ministry of Health and Family Welfare, Government of India.

After completion of Ph.D. degree, I got my first job as a Research Officer in the year 1998 in a national level health project at International Institute for Population Sciences, Mumbai. In the next year, I met Dr Binod C. Agrawal, Director, TALEEM Research Foundation, Ahmedabad and got opportunity to work with him in various research projects in health and communication. I also had the opportunity to serve as Faculty and Coordinator in the Department of Architecture, Zee Himgiri University, Dehradun during 2006-09. In the year 2010, I joined Assam University, Silchar as Founder Faculty, Reader and Head of Anthropology Department at the Diphu Campus of Assam University located at Diphu in Karbi Anglong district of Assam. I was promoted to the post of professor in 2016 and continued my position as head of the department, which I had held since 2010.

I have authored some edited volumes and published articles/ research papers in international journals of repute. Some of my publications are: Maternal Health and Child Mortality Condition, Vision and Challenges; Tribal Life in north-east India, Ethno-cultural Practices and Reproductive Health Issues, Tribal Culture, Health and Development: A Study of North-East India, Contesting Gender History, Politics and Identity. I attended at the IBSSS The Global Symposium on Social Sciences, held at Okinawa, Japan in 21-23 November 2013 and presented a paper on "People and Culture of north-east India: An Anthropological Study".

I have organized various national and international conferences as Head of Anthropology Department as Organising Secretary and Coordinator, on various topics, viz. (i) Maternal and Child Health in India: Issues and Challenge, (ii) "Emerging Frontiers of Anthropology". Indian Anthropology Congress: 2016, (iii) Contesting *Self* and *Other* Identities of Caste, Tribe, Gender and Beyond (Jointly with History dept.) and (iv) Culture, Health and Development: The Situation among the tribes of north-east India. I am also the reviewer and joint editors of several international journals. I have also guided dozens of research scholars for Ph.D. degree.

Since joining in the Department of Anthropology, I have been engaged in administrative activities of Assam University, Diphu Campus in various capacities, viz. In Charge Pro Vice-Chancellor, In Charge of Administration, In Charge of Examinations, In Charge of IQAC and Deputy Dean, Student's Welfare. I was also the Chairman of Board of Postgraduate Studies, Board of Undergraduate Studies and Research Advisory Committee of Anthropology Department as well as Member various committees of the universities, viz. School Board, Board of Research Studies and Academic Council of Assam University.

Currently, I am working as the Head of the Anthropology Department and since the beginning of the Department in 2010, I continue to serve as Head of the Department till today (2023). Besides academic teaching I am also engaged in various community development activities.

My Books

2015: Co-edited with Binod C. Agarwal. *Tribal Culture, Health and Development: A Study of North-East India*. New Delhi: Concept Publishing Company (Pvt.) Ltd.

2016: Co-edited with Vulli Dhanaraju. *Contesting Gender History, Politics and Identity*. New Delhi: Dominant Publishers and Distributors Pvt. Ltd.

2017: Co-edited with Sarit K. Chaudhuri. *Tribal Life in north-east India: Ethno-cultural Practices and Reproductive Health Issues*. New Delhi: Gyan Publishing House.

2022: Co-edited with Nitish Mondal. *Maternal Health and Child Mortality Condition: Vision and Challenges*. New Delhi: Concept Publishing Company (Pvt.) Ltd.

38

My Adventures into Anthropology

Bela Kothari

My interest in anthropology arose out of a conversation with my grandfather late Dr D.S. Kothari. At that time, I must have been in my early college years. Once I asked him, if he thought it was really correct not to walk along a road which had just been crossed by a cat. His answer surprised me.

> "As a scientist—a physicist, I would say that there is no scientific evidence or rationale in such a belief. It is just a nice little cat which is perhaps crossing our road for fun or by chance. But at the same time, I won't mind following this practise in presence of your grandmother just to please her. She really believes in this and would rebuke you if she saw you violating the cat-custom. Man is a social animal evolving over thousands of years and there is no harm in following such harmless traditions. Science does not profess that there is nothing beyond science."

Of course, when I questioned him further on many such funny traditions in our family he finally said, "Why don't you study these social aspects of man and then try to weed out those traditions which actually harm others—man, animals or even plants." That's how I gradually drifted into anthropology, the study of man in relation to his cultural ways over thousands of years of human development. This article is a recollection of some of the studies undertaken by me and the people who have left an afterimage in my mind and shaped the anthropology practiced by me.

The method of anthropology differs from the methods of other science disciplines because of what it studies—subjects not objects as the natural sciences. The laboratories of our physics or chemistry departments are rooms fitted with equipment and machines of all sorts; whereas, the real lab of anthropology is our society at large—the people young and old, men and women we come across every day. The two central ideas crucial to the practise of anthropology are worth mentioning here. Anthropology is a vibrant discipline, in the sense that cultures, people and their surroundings shape the anthropology being practised by an individual. The social interactions made by an anthropologist during the fieldwork invariably change the "self" of the anthropologist thereby changing his or her research interests and writings. Second, anthropology is the science of humans. So, the best instruments for researching in this field are drawn from human qualities: the ability to develop rapport with the subjects, sensitivity to observe and extract meaning from the complex network of human relations and keep an open mind and record things that one may not expect or approve.

The first anthropological fieldwork done by me was an interesting study on Jain *sadhvi*s. Having been born into a *Jain* family, I was intrigued by the severe austerity, self-denial and idealism practiced by Jain *sadhu*s and *sadhvi*s. The type of life lived by them is practiced by very few religious practitioners in the world. As different from any other so-called God-men and God-women who accumulate great material wealth and even socio-political power, the Jain *sadhu*s and *sadhvi*s are a universal example of practicing simple living and high thinking. In a world where materialism and leisure some lifestyle grips everyone, it was difficult to imagine what inspired young women in particular to choose this difficult path. Was it some god sent inspiration or an escape from some personal problem or some other reason? Intrigued by these questions, a study was undertaken to explore the background and change in the lifestyle of the *sadhvis* in the context of the process of learning and unlearning involved in the making of a Jain *sadhvi*. After I had almost written the conclusion some senior colleagues asked me to rethink on the whole matter. This brought an important aspect of anthropological research. The *sadhvis* properly accepted in the *Jain* order of monks now followed a very strict and sacred way of life. Their dress, food, social interactions were all strictly regulated and austere and apparently accepting it voluntarily.

Was it therefore necessary to explore and expose now their pre-*sadhvi* life? For them that had all erased from their life now. This was full-encompassing phase II of their life. Phase I was supposed to be gone out of reckoning. Research does not mean invading the privacy of the individuals. In this context research on Jain *sadhvis* was indeed very tricky. A compatibility was needed between the honesty of the research subject and the honesty of the researcher. Because of these considerations I was very hesitant in sharing my findings with others and publishing them as well. I did not want to trespass on the privacy of these honoured religious ascetics. But in a broad way some relevant findings were as follows: The girls outnumbered boys in the very religious family of these *sadhvis*. Girl education was rather neglected and training into the practise of the religion began at an early age as girls accompanied their mothers quite regularly to the places of worship. They mostly belonged to small trading families with adverse economic condition. After adopting the *sadhvi* life, these women had accommodated quite well to the new way of life in the physical sense but the process of acquiring the religious attitude of mind was slow. The monastic life seemed to provide a secure, safe and moral alternative to those religiously inclined women who were caught in the adverse circumstances of insecurity and deprivation.

What took me later to a different study was an interesting sentence written by the well-known anthropologist Margaret Mead:

"Every human society is faced with not one population problem but two; and how to beget and rear enough children and how not to beget and rear too many." Initially, the first part of the sentence just remained unrealized to me as I thought that the problem related to population was only of population explosion. With time, I came across a few people around me who were struggling with the distress and stigma of childlessness. It really surprised me that we in India were so much concerned with overpopulation and population control that no attention was being paid to the problem of infertility which Margaret Mead had foreseen. More so, that the blame for infertility was exclusively and mercilessly put on women whereas biologically 50 per cent of the problem could be with males as well. This inspired me to undertake a study on infertility from a social viewpoint. A research project across six districts of rural Rajasthan was undertaken. Interviews were conducted with medical experts working in the region, traditional healers and infertile couples. A total of 124 infertile couples were studied in which on medical examination 73 had male related infertility and 51 had women related infertility.

Infertility is an age-old problem, biologically we can say that it is as old as the human race. The story of *Mahabharata* also contains many references to infertility and reproductive problems. This study brought out that infertility is not an isolated problem. Anthropology and medical science will have to work together to be of any practical use. At least in the field of population control and infertility management, there is a need to adopt a binocular vision, anthropology-sociology and medicine examining together the one reality of people's reproduction to bring any useful change in society. For example, an observation on infertile women who became pregnant after some treatment was interesting. Such women were asked to throw away their iron pills being provided by the government for anaemia so prevalent in our country. The mother-in-law insisted on throwing away the iron pills because of the belief that these black pills will give a black colour to the baby. Anthropologically, it is difficult to say how or when such customs have arisen but they need to be scientifically examined and countered.

Another study undertaken by me was a rather unusual one on menstruation, its unusual aspect being the enquiry into the attitude of men in the family. This aspect has generally been ignored. The study brought out the fact that men in general took no interest as regards the knowledge about materials used by women during the menstrual period. Even when they came to know about something new through the television or some magazine, they did not pass-on the information to female members in their family, not even their wives. Years later, in 2018 the film under the title *Padman* featured this very relevant issue warranting desirable public attention. This was indeed a satisfying moment for me, more so because the idea of undertaking a study on this taboo issue was not quite welcome. *Padman* is a film on the life of an individual who had devised a machine to produce low cost, hygienic and effective sanitary napkins for use by women during their menstrual periods. Actually, this is a real problem in our country because poverty forces the young girls and women to use all sorts of odd things during this period. This includes anything from dirty worn out clothes to sand and grass sandwiched between layers of cloth. A terrible problem associated with this is the disposal of these blood-stained articles. *Padman*, therefore, obviously made a very noble effort to provide an easy access to cheap and hygienic sanitary napkin for women. The two studies show that men in the family should share the biological and social responsibility in these reproductive matters. When a couple in the family is childless it is very difficult to convince to the mother that something could be wrong with her son also apart from her daughter-in-law. Because of this, women often fight unnecessarily, continue to be ostracized and the husbands just take no responsibility.

One unique feature of anthropological research I found was that a researcher also grows and develops with time and our social perceptions may also undergo some modification. What the anthropologist saw at age 30 may appear somewhat different at his or her age 60. I learnt this particularly from my contact with Professor Yogesh Atal, an eminent social scientist. During my interaction with him as a short-term consultant in the High Powered Committee on Gurjars' demands appointed by the Government of Rajasthan, Professor Atal entrusted me with the responsibility of exploring the core cultural features in the entire documentation which substantiated the Gurjars demand for the "Scheduled Tribe" status. A total of 14,625 representations and a couple of photo albums were received along with affidavits and other materials. It was surprising to note that barring a few the representations were submitted by two communities: Gurjars favouring the demand and Meenas refuting their demand. Out of the total representations, 10,724 were submitted by Gurjars in favour of their claim. These representations were made by individuals, groups of people, institutions and organizations. A significant observation from these documents was that most of these claims were associated with women in the form of traditional jewellery, costumes, rituals and folklore. They claimed that Gurjar women were not exposed to urban life, they were shy and kept their faces veiled, practised polyandry, child marriages were prevalent and Gurjar women acted as wet mothers for princely families. The photographs provided proof of the little exposure and lesser access to technology particularly at the level of women. However, the photographs provided evidence of the fact that the women were very good handicraftswomen and innovative while fulfilling their day-to-day necessities. These women may not be aware of and using modern gadgets but their technological skills could not be underestimated. A significant question that cropped up from this entire exercise was: the differential access to modern technology has often been co-related with the status of women as subordinate. This discrepancy later formed the basis of a research project entitled "Women as Users and Producers of Technology in Their Gender Roles", and resulted in a doctoral thesis to explore how women in rural areas conceptualize technology and what factors discourage them from participating in the patriarchal "cult" of technology?

The research was conducted in two villages of district Karauli located in the eastern part of Rajasthan. Although the villages selected were located closeby, yet they were quite different on the availability of basic amenities including lack of electrification in one of them. The word nearest in meaning to "technology" in colloquial terms was *saadhan* (literally "a means"). In a very helpless tone the women summarized their life as *dhandha, kanda, gobar, pani, yeh hi hai meri kahani* meaning thereby that cattle, fuel, cow dung and water was all around which her life revolved. Many examples of novelty or innovation in the tools or in their use by women were found which can be categorized as *jugaad* in the absence of full-fledged technology. These clever tricks by women were intended for a pragmatic solution with the available resources often referred to as "quick fix solution". Simple and limited did they appear but these surely, were examples of human ingenuity providing solutions for their daily problems. An example of the use of worn out clothes in the study area would justify this. Women were making use of these clothes to produce a variety of goods like mattress (*gudari*), ring for holding pots (*edoni* or *chumda*), basket for keeping *chapattis* (*chaboli*), a *cheeka* for hanging pots from the roof, rope and balls for kids besides using it for cleaning purpose. A latent advantage of this was also that the quantity of waste produced by these women to be thrown out of the house was almost negligible. In other words, we can say, their carbon footprint on the planet is minimal.

This study brought out that women should not be ignored as "worthless" particularly in matters related to technological know-how. There is a necessity of somehow bringing simple technological advances into the homes of women submerged in age-old traditions of their daily work life. Social anthropologists and the technical innovators have to join hands to solve the common problems of the common people.

Now when I look back, all the studies undertaken by me can be woven together by a common underlying thread that is women. The very aspects in all these studies include religion, health and technology, quite diverse in terms of their interconnectedness. Was this a deliberate effort to study women or just a coincidence? The answer lies in that a true social scientist should be honestly receptive to what she/he observes and put away his/her own views on things, his/her likes and dislikes. Some instrument-based research is however a part of anthropology also—biological anthropology in which the evolution of the human race is examined from the perspective of the community's social life.

Some more interesting areas are being examined anthropologically which tend to show how expansive and exciting is the research in anthropology today. For example, the study of changes in life pattern over generations through detailed and careful examination of diaries and account book (*bahi khaata*) kept by some families. On the other hand, attention is also being paid to the study of reproductive health of men from childhood to old age.

My limited teaching and research experience says that anthropology can play an effective role in building scientific temperament in society. The thought process of the layperson seems to be prejudiced and replete with biases affecting day-to-day functioning of the people be it in the form of superstitions linked with eclipses, or a man marrying multiple times in the hope of a son or evil eye behind the cause of a child's ill health. I have realized that our anthropological research should not be limited to academic journals for our own professional purposes but must be made available in simple terms to the common people through popular media. This may require the use of regional languages also. But ultimately the future of man must be enriched to some extent by the study of his past. Anthropological research would continue to fascinate and guide the further adventures of our race.

39

Anthropology and Beyond

Encounters of a Different Kind

Seetha Kakkoth

My foray into the realm of anthropology began on a wintry morning in the late 1980s. We, a group of students, had embarked on a journey as part of a nature club headed by Professor John C. Jacob, an eminent naturalist-cum-zoologist. Our morning stroll through the hills of Kodencherry in Kozhikode district of Kerala opened up a whole new world of humankind. It was a tiny tribal hamlet and a girl sitting alone in a small leafy hut which aroused my curiosity and perhaps to be my first encounter with a different cultural practise other than mine. My queries took my gaze to a world which hitherto was unknown to me. The professor later told me that customs and rituals around the world shared a broad canvas under the banner of a subject called "Anthropology".

I graduated in zoology but somewhere deep down my encounters had left an indelible mark which was why in the course of my admissions for a master's in zoology, a newspaper advertisement of a Master's in Anthropology caught my eye. Anthropology in all its hues and colours of the story of humankind proved irresistible in my quest for knowledge. I was thrown open to a whole lot of readings mostly basic which the library did have and then there was no looking back. Basic works on anthropology (available in our department at that time) such as Beals and Hoijer; Haviland, Keesing; fieldwork and emic perspective of Malinowski; Torres Straits expedition; classic works of Radcliffe-Brown, Raymond Firth, Evans-Pritchard, W.H.R. Rivers, Margaret Mead, Ruth Benedict, Marjorie Shostak, Peter Gardner, James Woodburn and Brian Morris opened an ocean of knowledge on various cultures around the world. Apart from these, one month fieldwork, among the Adiyan tribe of Wayanad, as part of M.A. programme gave me an opportunity to understand the wonderful way of life of the Adiyan and other tribes in Wayanad. This remarkable experience made me to choose tribal area as the realm of my research work and pursue to do my doctoral research in the same area.

Doing doctoral research (with a Doctoral Research Fellowship from the Ministry of Tribal Affairs, New Delhi) at Kerala Institute for Research, Training and Development Studies of Scheduled Castes and Scheduled Tribes (KIRTADS), one of the Tribal Research Institutes of India, under the guidance Dr N. Viswananthan Nair, the then Director of KIRTADS; and later beginning my career as Research Officer (Anthropology) at the same institute had provided me plenty of opportunities to travel across the state to understand the length and breadth of rural and tribal life in Kerala.

My doctoral research was among the Aranadan, Pathinaicken and Kattupaniyan tribes of Nilambur forests of Malappuram district in Kerala. All the three tribal communities are still numerically small and their survival mechanism in the changing environment was the focus of my study. Of these communities, Aranadan having a population size below 300, face survival threat are resettled into the government built houses located in the fringes of forests, whereas Pathinaicken and Kattupaniyan live inside the forests. The unwritten law of keeping the boundaries between the communities, resource intake within one's own territory, concern for environment, sharing resources/food within the members of the hamlet were indeed a remarkable know-how for me.

Needless to say that undertaking fieldwork inside the Nilambur forest was an unforgettable experience for me. I was born in a patriarchal family where women and girl children enjoyed limited freedom with prescribed do's and don'ts. They were seldom allowed to travel alone and even if they go out, they were supposed to reach home before dusk. Hailing from such a background, living and roaming inside the Nilambur forests with Aranadan, Cholanaicken, Pathinaicken and Kattupaniyan, sleeping on rocks with the Mathi, Cheera and Ayya by enjoying the beauty of star filled sky; collecting tubers and honey; fishing; dining together and walking inside the evergreen forest during rain were treasured experience for me. The remarkable characteristics that I noticed in the tribal communities during my fieldwork are: sharing and caring; autonomy of children, care given to aged and concern for their environment. During night time children used to sit around their parents or elderly in the hamlet and listen to their talk, songs and stories. This is a kind of reminiscence of my childhood. Care given to the elderly was also similar to the family in a rural village where I was born and brought up. But, the egalitarian nature of tribal life, freedom enjoyed by children, their skill in learning things and tribal philosophy of life were totally new to me. Living as a member of tribal communities, made me to think that I should unlearn many things that I learned from my culture and re-learn a lot from the life of these amazing people. However, I had been observing the changing pattern of life among them and long years of my association with the elderly made me to look deep into their aging experience for my post-doctoral work.

Indeed, doing Post-Doctoral Research at Asia Research Centre, London School of Economics and Political Science (LSE), England under Sir Ratan Tata Fellowship (2007-08) was a turning point in my life. Though leaving my family, especially three-year old daughter was painful; the unconditional support of my husband and family helped me to pursue my assignment at LSE. When I reached London on a freezing morning of October 2007, I also experienced the "culture shock" we anthropologists usually speak about. I was away from my kith and kin, landed in an alien continent, alien people, alien culture, alien food and alien weather. It was Professor Ruth Kattumuri, the then Co-Director of Asia Research Centre helped me to get into the academic life of LSE. She has guided me in my work by giving me timely advice to meet the anthropologists in various universities and colleges in and around London to discuss my research work.

During my stay at LSE, I visited various universities, institutions and libraries in and around London. I could visit Cambridge University, Oxford University, School of Oriental and African Studies (SOAS), Goldsmiths College, University College of London (UCL), Royal Anthropological Institute and British Library among other institutions. I had the wonderful opportunity to engage in very fruitful discussions with eminent anthropologists like Professor James Woodburn, Professor Chris Fuller, Professor Jonathan Parry, Professor Jerome Lewis, and Professor Brian Morris, whose writings I have come across in the course of my research work. I was moved by the genuine interest shown in my project by Professor Brian Morris. I met him at Goldsmith College to discuss my research work. As he had worked among Malai Pandaram, another hunter-gatherer tribe of Kerala, he showed keen interest in my studies. During my stay at LSE, I met him many a time and once he came to LSE exclusively to discuss my work and gave me his published books for my reference. Likewise, James Woodburn has also given a bundle of copies of his work and insisted that when I go back to India, I should keep all these material in my hand bags only and never put them in baggage, as there is chance to miss luggage while travelling. During my stay at LSE, I used to discuss my paper with both Brian and Woodburn and was lucky enough to get James Woodburn and Brian Morris as Chair and Discussant respectively for my Ratan Tata Seminar at LSE in April 2008. Association with these anthropologists helped me immensely in strengthening methodological skills and conceptual clarity both in my research works and writings.

After the successful completion of my post-doctoral research work at LSE, I got opportunities to attend international workshops/

conferences at Max Planck Institute for Anthropology, Germany (2008), Moscow University, Russia (2009), Liverpool University (2013), Cambridge University (2016), Universite Saints, Malaysia (2018) and UiT, The Arctic University of Norway (Tromsø) (2023). These conferences provided a space for bringing some of the anthropological works of Kerala at international platforms. I also got an opportunity to meet Professor Peter Gardiner (a doyen in the field of hunter-gatherer studies) in Liverpool in 2013. Since then, he has been guiding me in my academic writings. When I placed an idea of publishing a book compiling a few articles of mine, he happily agreed to write a foreword for my proposed book and did it.

Like Professor Peter Gardiner and Professor Ruth Kattumuri, the role of Professor Vineetha Menon (Department of Anthropology, Kannur University, Thalassery Campus, Kannur District) was instrumental in my academic life. Working with Professor Vineetha Menon, especially for UCG-SAP project has helped me to sharpen my skill in fieldwork. During her period in the department, she has taken a key role in conducting Kannur University Lecture series by bringing eminent anthropologist from various universities in India. The lectures delivered by Professor Vinay Kumar Srivastava, Professor P.C. Joshi, Professor Ventaka Rao, Professor Hussain Khan, Professor Subhadra Channa and Professor Susan Viswanathan had provided interactive space for the budding anthropologists in the department. My close association with Professor Vineetha Menon continued even after I moved away from the department to take up a new position at Indira Gandhi National Open University (IGNOU) Regional Centre at Cochin, Kerala as Assistant Regional Director. Though the working atmosphere of IGNOU was of academic administrative in nature, I continued to pursue my interest in anthropology by activating Masters Degree programme in Anthropology (MAAN) at one of the study centres of the Cochin Regional Centre and enrolling myself as an Academic Counsellor of the programme.

My passion for the subject led me to leave the job at IGNOU and join back to Kannur University in December 2015 as Assistant Professor at the Department of Rural and Tribal Sociology, Kannur University, Mananthavady Campus, Wayanad district. The department is located in tribal area and offers M.A. programme in Tribal and Rural Studies. As part of popularizing the subject, the department offers an elective course called "Cultural Anthropology" at National Institute of Fashion Technology (NIFT), Mangattuparamba, Kannur district. Myself and my colleague, P. Hareendran are the co-ordinators of this course and we conduct this course in each semester (every six months). Offering this elective course has created more rooms for the subject.

In addition to this, the department has undertaken projects in collaboration with Anthropological Survey of India (AnSI), Kolkata and Institute for Social and Economic Change (ISEC), Bangalore. "Safeguarding Endangered Mother Tongue: Preparation of Dictionary for Kattunayakan Tribe of Nilambur" is the ongoing project of the department, financially supported by Kannur University. The aim of this project is to prepare a pronunciation enabled tri-lingual dictionary for the Kattunayakan tribe of Nilambur forests and to provide the same to Ashram School (where Kattunayakan children are enrolled) for helping the teachers to offer primary education to the children in their own language.

Apart from these, the department runs an international Project on "Tribal Education Methodology (TEM): Sustainable Education through Heritage" in collaboration with University of Lincoln, United Kingdom (UK). The aim of the project is to develop a curriculum for tribal youth in Wayanad to prevent the school dropout, which is an ongoing issue in tribal education.

My anthropological encounters have been stimulating intellectually but beyond that it has also thrown up a window to an amazing world of shared experiences. A very interesting anecdote which left an indelible mark is what I would like to share and sum up this journey of mine in the domain of anthropology. As part of a Child Rights and You (CRY) project on Ashram school drop outs of Nilambur forests, in the course of my field trip I had ventured deep into the forest with two children to accompany me. Out of the blue we stopped in our tracks as we had sighted an elephant at a distance. I was dumbfounded and unable to move. My little companions asked me to stay cool and the next few seconds were truly a revelation. One of the boys put his finger into his mouth and pointed in the direction of the elephant. In a few seconds he said there was no cause for alarm and we moved silently ahead and reached our destination safely. His magic finger was like a magic wand which kept the elephant away. When I asked him about it he equipped "pointing my wet finger in the direction of the elephant made my finger cool". He could gauge the wind was blowing from the side of the elephant because of which it (the elephant) couldn't smell our presence. He was certain that the elephant wouldn't attack us. Amazing indigenous wisdom indeed! Such invaluable indigenous knowledge and skill are treasures that are yet to be unearthed and incorporated in the knowledge domain of anthropology.

My Books

2021: *Lost Lullabies of South India: Tale of Vanishing Indigenous People of Nilambur Valley*. New Delhi: Mittal Publications.

2022: Chitra, S. Nair and Seetha Kakkoth (eds.). *Revealing Social Vulnerability: People, Places and Resilience.* New Delhi: Mittal Publications.

40

Making of a Medical Anthropologist

An Auto-Ethnography

Ravinder Singh

I use auto-ethnography and narratives of lived experiences during my early years in learning anthropology (1982-85) at university then I continue to elaborate on higher academic pursuits in University of Delhi (1986 to 1996). In brief in this auto-ethnography and narratives I have discussed how I had become the student of anthropology and give a brief of my experiences in anthropology fieldwork, academic reading of books, influenced much, with my written notes and from my diary. Then it further mentions about self-reformation and reflection during the entire period of learning the anthropology during graduation and postgraduation.

Learning anthropology in early stages at the age of 17 years, when one is just out of the school and joins the core of the university education imposes seldom problem to learner. For example, in University of Delhi where teaching of anthropology falls in the Faculty of Science and its admission is directly under the control of latter and only senior secondary school examination with science are eligible. In Delhi science students normally pass senior secondary examination with: physics, chemistry, mathematics, biology or mechanical/engineering drawing and a language, preferably English. Anthropology is not the wide choice of the students at the undergraduate level of the teaching in the university.

I am discussing in following text what had prompted me to study the discipline and *how* I choose and circumstances constraint me to remain in and how at every stage of its learning *affected* my life; the way you think, look others, etc...? Finally, it expresses—how did I make my place in where I am now, present engagement in medical anthropology in neuropsychiatric tertiary care institute.

This trajectory emphasized *how* and *when* I had chosen the Anthropology Honours after my senior secondary schooling in Delhi. The following explains that how I opted for Anthropology honours. Was it painful destiny? Was it emotionally disturbing when I began to learn anthropology? How did I feel on coming out after three years of undergraduate learning in anthropology? It had altogether made me a different person on learning very different, anthropology, at an early age. Further what motivated me to remain in anthropology and how did I finally ended up in my recent engagement in teaching and practising the medical anthropology, in a neuropsychiatric hospital and future challenges for the discipline at the workplace? This is very interesting trajectory, reflects how the learning of the various anthropologies affect you in your daily life, does its learning improve you or give you different perspectives to see the people around you or away you? Do you feel that you have become more concern or sensitive to the people whom you are associated or working in the field or dealing in your engagements? Further how does it affect your personal or interpersonal family relations in the life. I began with these questions examined in the trajectory of my own engagements in past to present during one decade.

I recall that I went for admission to University of Delhi with my father, who had been acquainted to University of Delhi area, as he used to live when he was student of printing technology, in Kingsway Camp with his teacher during 1958-59. We reached university. My father was constraint to leave me alone, on the Probyn Road, in front of Law Faculty in University of Delhi. As I moved towards the Science Faculty, I saw a small bilingual sign board showing "Manav Vigyan/ANTHROPOLOGY", on that fine day of July 1982; this day "turned" or rather that "moment turned" my entire life when did I see it; it was lateral side of Department of Anthropology and the "same sign board" had been seen there at same place after 28 years when I began to write on this.

My senses had lost in these two words "Manav Vigyan/ Anthropology". As young student of seventeen I remained under its influence in my deep thoughts while I was moving towards Science Faculty housed in Old Barrack. I made my mind to study it as it appeared more similar to human biology and will definitely help me in studying the medicine during July 1982. In those days I was aspirant for pre-medical test in Delhi, as usual in those days and still it continues even today. I reached the Faculty of Sciences in University of Delhi. It was housed in old barracks. I began to walk in the corridor while waiting. I inquired a lady, Section Officer, dealing with admission of B.Sc. (Hons.) Anthropology. I had decided to seek admission in B.Sc. (Hons.) Anthropology after reading that sign board while going towards science faculty. I told lady officer about my decision to study Anthropology Honours, and then she became very furious, seemingly as if I had said something which I should not. She saw me from "top to bottom" as I was wearing *kurta* and *pyjama* with slipper and one *khadi* bag on left shoulder containing important papers. I was very different in my dress as compared to the contemporary students of my age. She calmly asked me about my interest and I told the "same", then again, my answer annoyed her more. For few minutes, I could not imagine what went wrong! Then she again questioned me who told you to opt for Anthropology Hons.? Then I plainly replied me, myself. Then she was little disturbed and suggested me—you can take admission in other honours: physics, chemistry, botany, zoology and mathematics as you are eligible. But why you wish to take up Anthropology Hons.? I could not reply satisfactorily. Finally, she asked me to "wait" and "think" and come after the lunch what you want to study. I waited eagerly. As soon as lunch was over, I went again to her room and she was disturbed again on seeing me. She consulted some of her colleagues sitting nearby. They suggested her something positively and finally she gave me the admission slip and advised me to go to Hans Raj College (HRC), famous college of time in the university and still it is even today for Sciences Hons. I was very happy and rushed towards the college but I reached late at 4.00 p.m. and college office told me to come with certificates and fee next day in morning. Next day I went to HRC took admission in the Anthropology Honours and happily returned home and influencing friends as I got admission in North Campus, University of Delhi, then very prestigious to get admission.

Few days later I went to the Delhi Public Library, Patel Nagar to return some books. Meanwhile I looked around while gazing for the books on the anthropology. I saw one and picked "first book" on "anthropology" titled *Anthropology Made Easy* by John Lewis and I glanced through its first few pages. I could see only the harpoons, skeletons, cave pictures, text...more text...only text! I was completely confused and began about "to fell" in hysteric state beside the bookrack as I could not understand a single word and it was in a "different language" for which we were "neither trained nor taught" in school. Then I felt where I have entered in higher academics. Now I felt and realized well that "why" that lady officer had asked me several times "who told you to opt this stream" i.e. Anthropology Honours?

I was just cursing myself "why" I had ignored her suggestions. From July 1982 to November 1982, I neither "read" a single word in any of the book on anthropology nor did I try to do so, except taking the classroom notes. But I enjoyed its practical classes as it involved the drawing of the long and small human bones, seems more closer to as studying the medicine, during the first year. I used to read *Grays' Anatomy*, a bible for the students of medicine, for osteology and osteometry. I used to listen carefully in the class of physical anthropology—primatology as well as primates' behaviour.

But on other side, theory classes of my teachers, particularly of Professor J.D. Mehra, teaching society and culture, were above my head. He used to teach us social anthropology—society, social structure and function, caste, village structure, etc. This I could not understood well what it is? Why it is being taught to us? Though I had been the student of pure sciences—physics, chemistry, biology, and higher mathematics in my senior secondary level examination and this all making more disturb and uncomfortable in learning anthropology. But somehow, I could understand the physical anthropology chiefly concerned primatology and paleontology as were more similar to biological sciences. In the practical classes, I was interested as I could understand what I am learning. But on other part, chiefly concerned cultural aspects of society were above my head, I was in state of depression and had decided to leave Anthropology Honours.

In the depressed state, I went back to my school for re-admission in 12th Class in October 1982 as I wished to repeat the Senior Secondary School examination in order to better prepare the medical entrance in forthcoming year. I met my class teachers and expressed my desire but Principal who refused straight to readmit me as CBSE had declared as successful. But rather they advised me to appear as private student in next year CBSE examination. I was discussing it all in the office of the Principal, Shri Pyare Kishen Chaddha. Other science subjects' teachers also joined our discussion, but its outcome was not in my favour. Rather a teacher of History and English, Shri Raj Kumar Kakkar, PGT (English) who used to teach us English, told me about anthropology as it is very good. But I was not in state of its affirmative listening. Rather in the disappointed state I left my school where I spent seven years, 1975-82. I decided to go to CBSE office near ITO next day. Here I spent one day in filling the form and again it has to be signed by the School Principal. Then I could visualize similar situation of rejection by my School Principal last attended. Then I decided to let it off and continued in Anthropology Honours after discussion with my father who rather suggested to continue with Anthropology Hons.

Alas! I could not leave it. I remained there till November 1982 in the depressive phase. One fine day, one of my teachers, Professor P.K. Seth (PKS), used to teach primatology and paleontology practical in the class of physical anthropology, said to some of my classmates that they all will go to the field on primate's behaviour. I was little hesitant as I thought this field visit might be a kind of the picnic for the fun and of course with girls! It was not easy for me to be with the girls in the picnic. Never! Unfortunately, there were only six students, two boys and four girls, in the entire class of Anthropology Hons in the university. I did not deposit the money for the field visit. Then Professor Seth called me in his room and convinced me to join field trip.

I decided to go Dehradun as per instruction of Dr P.K. Seth, our field teacher for primate's behaviour. We were five students in the whole university. I requested my father for Rs. 200 INR and my younger brother helped me in packing-warm clothes, bedding, etc. We reached ISBT early in the morning at Dehradun Bus Stand. I left along with others—Dr P.K. Seth and class mates by bus to Dehradun. In my life I went outside Delhi alone for such a different task—fieldwork. We stopped at Forest Guest House, Mohad range, in Rajaji Sanctuary before Dehradun. Here there were no light in the night. In day hours we travelled in dense forest to follow the Rhesus Monkey, *Macaca malatta*, it is common monkey nearby areas. We began to do fieldwork with our senior Ph.D. research scholars, working on the primate's behaviours. In the evening we enjoyed a lot. Eating and signing together. We also travelled to Mussoorie, Lal Tibba several other places where we all enjoyed the snow. Often, we conducted the observation on "black mouth, long tailed languor". We stayed here for two weeks. This was a virgin experience in my life, changed my life, my thought pattern about the discipline, its impact remained as fresh as of even today. While returning to Delhi, I had made my mind to study it further more about primatology and its behaviours. Here "I could learn more about the girls and their behaviour"—to care other as they had cooked for me, the vegetarian foods too during this fieldwork.

I remained here since 1982 November. After returning from fieldwork, I spent late evening in Central Reference Library (CRL) to work on my field report on Primates Behaviour and I submitted in January 1983 as the draft of Field Report to Dr Seth and he examined it and expressed his satisfaction. This fieldwork of two week had transformed my "inner self". In Delhi, I never went out alone, moreover never with "girls", it was unique experience—"to look, to write and then study same in the books". My teacher and other research scholars were very affectionate during the field. This fieldwork has not only transformed my perspective to look life in surrounding and understand better the people around. Further it also helped me to understand my parental family, kinship structure, marriage, etc.

I was promoted to second year in 1983. I learned pre-historic archaeology or Indian prehistory. My teacher, Dr D.K. Bhattacharya (usually popular among students as DKB) used to encourage a lot, as I was only boy among five students in the university. I went on fieldwork in pre-historic archaeology in Dindori tehsil near district Mandla during late November 1983. Mandla is most primitive tribal district in Madhya Pradesh of central India. Here I was influenced by this fieldwork—assessing the cultural evolution through the artefacts reflecting the cognitive development of the prehistoric man might have evolved in India. I realized here how do you do fieldwork and do write the report based on different theme particularly in pre-history.

Then in third year of my graduation I went to Udaipur in 1984 where I studied the Gamaties and Dangi, two agricultural communities of Udaipur. I was working on the dermatoglyphics, somatometric characters and their economic system of the village people in these two communities. By this time, I was exposed to the village life in the anthropological ways. These fieldworks taught me: how "to meet" the "Other" people and conduct the anthropological fieldwork. Meanwhile I was learning the new things in anthropology: religion and magic, rituals, family, kinship, marriage, primitive laws and rules and regulations governing the simple societies and primitive societies. I was fascinated by anthropological literatures whether physical or social, as its reading reveal the society and its structures. It influenced me much and I was the most benefitted as I could care my younger brothers and parents in the better way. I was learning in the class but outside the class on the road it was anthropology in my eyes penetrating the people.

In late November 1984, V.K. Srivastava (VKS) joined as lecture in social anthropology in the department. He taught Tribe and Peasantry to our Class in November 1984. He took our extra classes on "Tribe and Peasantry" during December 1984 to February 1985. He used to take our Class of 3 to 5 students since 9.30 a.m. to 6.30 p.m. in evening with little break. This was his only class I had a chance to have. But his guidance and checking/reading my Draft Third Year Dissertation in Anthropology continued further till my final year's exam in May 1985.

I took admission in M.Sc. Anthropology programme in July 1986 in University of Delhi. I found most of the syllabus was similar to what I had studied during graduation. While I was making notes for the M.Sc. Programme, one day I was watching television then *Karamchand Jasoos,* a detective serial of Pankaj Kapoor, which was being telecast during the 1984-85. I saw one episode—in which kidney transplantation was shown and recipients of the kidney died few days after the kidney transplant. It was found that how "mismatching of HLA antigens" converted into matching with the donor. It was transplanted which finally killed the recipient. HLA complex was one of the sections in serology papers and I was interested in this paper because of its relevance in transplantation sciences, but its utilities in illuminating the molecular variations in understanding the social structure of the people. It is what had I was fascinated me to be with everyday phenomenon in the anthropological ways.

Learning Anthropology (1982-88): Self-Reformation and Reflection

During my doctoral research I set for myself higher goals more focused in anthropology to know more about the family, caste, village structure, marriage, sex, etc. such accounts can be read in the books. Further I decided to learn the human variations: molecular variation among the human beings and hence I opted physical anthropology and other three optional for laboratory-oriented papers such as human cyto-genetics, biochemical genetics and serology. My aim to study these aspects about the man was to acquire the more molecular variation within the body and how do two people vary on one side and other side I wanted to have first-hand knowledge about prevailing variations in social institution in simple and socially complex societies. In this sense I observed anthropology as ever moving, always "in action", a discipline always in action—its engagements always been changing and so often it is difficult to define. For example, "how lived experiences" of one contribute to understanding the people around you *or* at the work which you do in the family or how does it is related to status and role within family? I try to enumerate the rituals being observed in the family which later on resulted into "Dissociative Disorder" and also illuminate the child caring and development in the family in this difficult time.

My learning in anthropology during 1982 to 1996 which had been multifaceted mainly concerned to daily life within family or at the workplace. I focused on anthropology earlier in birth defects as research fellow of ICMR, child growth and development as UGC research fellow for research degree programmes in Anthropology Department of University of Delhi, and then as officer for child care, social policy and legislation in government, and finally I made my place to understand better mental health issues and their teaching, training, treatment in present working place, neuropsychiatry Institute, a tertiary care facility.

My Books

2012: Ravinder Singh and Ajita Rani, *Handedness and Gender*. Lambert Academic Publishing.

2017: Ravinder Singh and Ajita Rani. *Human Behaviour*. Chennai: Notion Press.

41

I am Learning Aanthropology Regularly

A Brief "*Atmakatha*"

Somenath Bhattacharjee

I was brought up in the family of teachers and under very strict discipline. During the school education, I was deeply attracted in the subjects of human biology, Indian history and geography. After my honours degree, only due to the kind advice of my teacher, I had taken admission in anthropology as my postgraduation subject. In the University of North Bengal, I was one of the first batch student in anthropology during the session 2002 to 2004. Honestly to be accepted, it has changed my view about society, with a new vision of life. Fortunately, I feel blessed to be a teacher of anthropology today and trying my best to dedicate myself in the teaching and research of anthropology.

Early life, Education, Family, Taking Anthropology as a Subject

To begin with, honestly speaking, I was born in a very disciplined and culturally value-oriented Bengali Brahmin family. Teaching profession is our long ancestral tradition. My great grandfather was a prime teacher of Sanskrit and mathematics in the traditional rural *pathsala*. My grandfather dedicated his life in the service of our Nation, being an Army man. In my life, each and every discipline had been affectionately transmitted by him. On the other hand, the parental family of my mother is directly related with legendary Bengali novelist Tara Shankar Bandyopadhyay. By sitting on the lap of my both grandfathers, for the first time, I came to know about the great ethnic and cultural diversity of India, the beauty of rural Bengal, it's rich heritage of education, art, music and culture. My father (Lt. Shri Tapan Kumar Bhattacharjee) was a teacher of chemistry and my uncle (Shri Tushar Kanti Bhattacharjee) is still a teacher of English. Further, one of the maternal uncle of my mother, was a Professor of Chemistry (Dr Amalendu Bandyopadhyay) in Jadavpur University and one of my own maternal uncle Professor Uttam Bandyopadhyay was a Professor of Statistics in University of Calcutta. I was born and brought up in Cooch Behar. In our school, there were two (Honourable) President award winning teachers. Actually, from the school I became deeply attached to Indian history, geography and human biology. My profound attraction in human biology attracted me to select zoology honours in my degree level in one of oldest college of West Bengal (A.B.N. Seal College, established in 1888 under the Cooch Behar Kingdom). However, I have found really no interest in invertebrates or vertebrates. However, I got tremendously attracted in human genetics, human evolution, physiology and secured good score in those papers. At this point of life, my respected teacher of Honours course, Dr Niloy Roy suggested me that in my Master degree, I must take anthropology, after the completion of my degree in the year 2002.

Doctoral Work, Teachers, Fieldwork and Early Career

In my academic life, the year 2002 was a big turning point. Under the University of North Bengal, I took admission in M.Sc. Anthropology, being the 1st batch student, in the year 2002. Our founder Head of the Department was Professor Seikh Rahim Mondal, a sky-high personality but with heart full of affection for the students and there were two other founder teachers Professor Samar Kumar Biswas and Professor Subir Biswas. The classes on Anthropological Theories and Research Methodologies, taken by

Professor S.R. Mondal Sir is still living in my mind, due to his excellent skill of teaching and unparallel analysis, with plentiful of quick and surrounding examples. Honestly speaking, only due to Professor S.R. Mondal Sir, I became deeply attracted to Social-Cultural Anthropology. On the other hand, from Professor Samar Kr Biswas Sir, I have learnt how to do a rigorous and systematic fieldwork. In the first year, he took us for fieldwork on the Rabha Tribal group and taught us the skills to do a good anthropological fieldwork. During that time, as visiting faculties Professor Buddhadeb Chaudhuri Sir, used to take our classes on Medical Anthropology and Human Rights, Professor Arup Ratan Bandyopadhyay Sir took our classes on Human genetics, Professor Subho Roy Sir took our classes on Human Genetics. All of those classes attracted me very much and will always live in my memory. After the completion of my M.Sc. (first class first) in 2004, and NET (June 2005, December 2005, June 2006), I selected my doctoral research on the occupational health issues and co-related human rights aspects, among the stone crushing occupational group of Balasan riverbed under the supervision of Professor Buddhadeb Chaudhuri and Professor Samar Kr Biswas. The concerned people were all belonged to the Rajbanshi Scheduled Caste group. They were settled agriculturist and were dwelling in Bangladesh. During 1971, due to severe political unrest in Bangladesh, followed by communal riots, they were forced to get displaced and became roofless and almost resourceless. They got resettled in the Balasan riverbed and got involved in the stone based occupation. Gradually, they had lost their identity of a caste group, totally left their caste based traditional occupation of agriculture and became known as an occupational group to the rest of the society. However, their economic condition was still poor. Their fundamental rights of safe occupational environment, safe drinking water, adequate sanitation were grossly violated. Moreover, several occupational injuries, diseases had created a miserable livelihood condition for them. By birth, a child could see acute poverty, hunger, misery and severe struggle in livelihood. Related to my Ph.D. through my long fieldwork and by getting deeply attached with them, I had seen very clearly what actually poverty means and what actually the crisis of survival means to a large section of marginal people of our nation. Meanwhile, I must mention that, during this time, in different seminars and conferences, I was fortunate to listen the spell-bounding academic excellence of very respected Professor Vinay Kumar and Professor P.C. Joshi. Such lectures had helped me a lot to shape up my data analysis with theoretical interpretation, methodological specification, from many new dimensions. On July 2010, I was selected for the post of Assistant Professor, in Anthropology of Assam University-Diphu campus.

Seminal Contribution to Anthropology, Important Papers, Books

Starting from my Ph.D. research tenure till date, my major publications are mainly divided into two categories, that is during the Ph.D. tenure and during my teaching-research period. The paper, "Misery of Displacement: A Study of the Rajbansis of Tarijot Colony" had discussed about the struggle for survival and different types of occupational health hazards among the Rajbanshi stone crushers. The issues of displacement and its consequent human rights violations in the lives of the Rajbanshi stone crushers had been discussed in the paper, "Displaced People and Their Issues of Human Rights". In the contemporary era of globalization, the crisis on the Tribal folk culture had been discussed in the paper, "Folk Culture in Front of Serious Challenge: A Case Study on the Tribes of North Bengal".

After my joining in the Diphu Campus, in 2010, I worked on the ethnography, material culture, indigenous knowledge of the Karbi, Dimasa, Bodo, Mishing Tribal groups of Assam. The UGC funded research project on the importance of indigenous knowledge in preservation of local ecological resources, as well as supervising one awarded Ph.D. thesis on the ethno-ecology of the Karbis and one awarded M.Phil. dissertation on the material culture of the Karbis, had opened up my scope to collect detail ethnography on the Karbis. In this regard, the paper, "Sacred Groves in Karbi Anglong: An Anthropological Observation" had focused on the significance of sacred grooves, in the Animistic religious practises of the Karbis. Importance of oracles and magico-religious healing, to redress a number of ailments among the Karbis was analysed in the paper, "Healing Through Oracles: A Study on the Lodeps' of Karbi Tribal Group in Assam". Two very significant practises in the Assamese society have been comparatively discussed in the paper, "Satra Tradition and Bihu: Interraction Between Great and Little Tradition in The Assamese Society".

Through the ICSSR-NERC funded research project, on the Socio-Cultural Perspectives of Goalpariya Folk Songs, and supervising one awarded Ph.D. thesis on the Hajongs of Bodoland and one awarded M.Phil. dissertation on the material culture of the Bodos, detail ethnographic study has been done on them. ICMR funded research project, on the importance of local ecological resources related to the reproductive mother-child health of the Karbis and supervising one awarded Ph.D. thesis on the concept of health, disease and treatment among the Karbis, revealed the significance of locally available floral and faunal resources as a source of traditional medicine among the Karbis. It has been discussed in the paper, "Indigenous Knowledge of Health Care System among the Karbi Tribal Group of Assam".

ICSSR-IMPRESS funded research project on the significance of traditional medicine, among the selected Tribal groups of Assam, has revealed the significance of ethno-medicinal practises, behind the successful reproductive-mother child health cases.

Administrative and Institution Building

Being the first and founder faculty of Anthropology Department in Assam University Diphu Campus, always my core focus is to create the affection among the students over anthropology. In most of the cases our students are from different other subjects. From the very beginning, I am assigned with the responsibility of Departmental IQAC, Career counselling, Examination coordinator. Karbi Angolng comes under 6th Schedule area in Assam and Diphu is the district headquarter. Most of our students are from different local tribal groups, with their diversified dialect and cultural practises. Unfortunately, all most among them, have never heard about anthropology at all in their academic levels. Always I have taken it as blessing in disguise. I have introduced anthropology, as a source of fresh air to them, by citing examples from their own material culture, family, marriage, kinship system, rituals, economy, traditional political organization and several cultural practices as they execute in their day-to-day life. Our students have always found the subject a very familiar one, because I have always tried to teach them the critical theories and courses with handful of their own familial examples, which are related to them since their childhood. As a member of Research Advisory Committee of several other departments like Life Sciences, History, Geography, Political Science, Commerce and tried to disseminate the knowledge of Anthropology in different other fields too. Being the co-ordinator of IQAC and career counselling, I focused on to develop the skill of critical thinking and logical interpretation of facts among my students. In Diphu, I tried to develop anthropology, as a subject with the people, by the people and for the people only. I have concentrated to teach anthropology, as a subject, which can widen up the vision of the students, beyond the textual level to the contextual level; the students have learned the subject to apply its knowledge, for the well-being of the grass root level of marginal people, to gain the confidence of the people within their own culture as well as of different cultures. The passed out students are gradually getting involved in the Anthropological Survey of India, Tribal Research Institute, Directorate of Census operations. Under the department of folk music, traditional handicraft, ethno-medicinal practices of Karbi Anglong Autonomous Council are getting well placed due to their empirical field experience and academic degree of anthropology. In 2016, I had proposed the university administration for a model village adoption programme through certain interdisciplinary approach. It is on a gradual progress in step wise phases, where Anthropology Department is playing a vital role in social awareness programme, preservation of different traditional knowledge and practises, protection of folk cultural heritage. It is to be mentioned here that, the local ethnic groups are very rich in their traditional agriculture, handicraft and weaving. I had personally approached, with a model proposal, to different rural banks and corporate banks of Diphu, to explore their possibilities in promoting such rich traditional occupational avenues under public-private partnership or corporate social responsibilities. Assam Gramin bank under their functional procedure has initiated a number of significant steps in this regard. Keeping in view of the rich material cultural diversity among the different ethnic groups of entire north-east India in general and Assam as well as Karbi Anglong in particular, a number of material cultural implements have been collected through fieldwork by myself and students, in different period. I am trying to open up an ethnographic museum in the department as well. Meanwhile, in different period of time, I have done a number of digital recordings on the folk cultural, religious, traditional healing practises of the Karbis, Dimasas, Bodos. A small digital archive has been prepared in the department to permanently preserve such practises.

Contribution Beyond Anthropology, Notable Students

Although being a teacher, it is very difficult to differentiate among the students, still I must specially mention the name of two of my Ph.D. awarded scholars, Dr Bamonkiri Rongpi (working as a teacher of anthropology in a junior college at present) and Dr Nijora Sharma (working as a in the Directorate of Census Operations, Assam and one M.Phil. awarded scholar Ms. Franky Bodo (working as a teacher of anthropology in a junior college at present). Along with their profession, on a regular basis they are doing a number of works silently, to help the marginal and oppressed section of people. Particularly during the pandemic crisis, periodical lockdown and economic scarcity of the grass root level of people, we had taken some initiative to arrange minimum groceries for a section of people. Moreover, the students of marginal families, who were not getting familiar with the digital education, I had taken an initiative with our passed out students, for their door to door academic guidance without any economic burden to them. Moreover, we are still providing totally free of cost academic materials supports for the very marginal students. Mainly we are arranging the funds from our own selves only and from the relatives, friends who are supporting our heartfelt efforts. Personally, I have taken the responsibility of education for two children, who belong to very marginal families. This is under the initiative of our Shri Ramkrishna Ashram in Kolkata.

International Collaborations

My first academic visit in abroad was in 2013, to participate in the IUAES World Congress, held in the University of Manchester. Further, in 2015 I had visited in the Thamassat University, to participate in the IUAES Inter Congress. In 2017, appropriate co-operation had been extended to the BBC news channel, to make a documentary on the tigers in different forest areas of Assam, to explore the man-animal association, in the contemporary period of environmental degradation and ecological, climatic changes. A constructive development has taken place with the Department of Anthropology, University of Ottawa, Canada for joint collaborative researches, by keeping in view about biological and cultural diversity of Southeast Asia. Similarly, with the Asia institute in the University of Melbourne, a constructive academic planning is going on for the collaborative researches and student, research scholar exchange programme. Certain developments are going on in the process of application in Wenner-Gren Foundation, for "Global Initiatives Grants" as well as to organize international conferences and workshops to develop and train the young budding students of anthropology. Similar approaches are also getting explored through Ford Foundation also. Keeping in view, on the crisis over human rights issues, in the Southeast Asian countries, joint collaborative research programmes have been communicated to the Asian

Resource Foundation very recently. After the major three waves of COVID-19 pandemic, possibilities are getting explored for post-doctoral research programmes, from Fullbright programmes, ICSSR International Collaboration grants mainly. Very recently, through digital platform, interactive sessions are getting framed with the doctoral students of anthropology in Ottawa University, Canada. Some joint supervising research works are getting matured with the scholars of anthropology, studying in the University of Peloponnese, Greece. It can be admitted that due to pandemics for more than two years, the earlier taken initiatives are getting accelerated to the best possible ways.

Current/Post-Retirement Activities

Since July 2010 up to 14 May 2023, I was working as an Assistant Professor, in the Department of Anthropology, Assam University Diphu campus. In this region, a larger section of people is economically very marginal and a huge section of students are the first generation in their families, who are attached with the college and university level of education. It is never possible for them to afford their education in the universities located in urban metros. Although I was the only faculty of Social-Cultural Anthropology here, but keeping in view of the local circumstances, I tried my level best to teach the students in diversified papers related to this specialization, so that they can get the confidence to get succeed in different national level examinations, competitions and job sectors. Along with that, I motivated the students to do in-depth researches related to the social problems or any other problems, which is persisting in this region and to find out its solution anthropologically, as desired by the local people. I strongly feel that, for the society the need of the hour is to get culturally tolerant human resource, who can gain the confidence of the grass root level of people. Recently, on 15 May I have joined as Professor of Anthropology in Nagaland University. It is a new challenge for me to develop an Anthropology Department in a geographically challenging area. Gradually I am getting settled in the new working environment and exploring the new areas of field. Meanwhile, my participation in the World Anthropology Congress 2023 in KISS Bhubaneswar, has widened up many inter-disciplinary and trans-disciplinary research approaches to me under the post COVID-19 period. I am really fortunate to receive the award of "Promising Anthropologist".

Anthropology is such a subject, which can develop and configure many hidden qualities among the youths and can make them a creative human resource in the process of nation building. This is a continuous and rigorous process, which can be done through active participation of the students, their family members and the entire society, in an integrated manner. Being a small part of this big venture, I am steadily working on it.

Concluding Remarks

I am blessed that, I am a student of such a subject, which has been developed and flourished by uncountable globally famous stalwarts, both from India and abroad. I am a student of anthropology and always trying to learn this subject, in my day-to-day livelihood only. I am trying to be a good teacher of anthropology, who can build up an affection about the subject among the students, as well as to do some significant research contribution in our subject, with the prime focus on nation building from the Indian perspective.

Index